INDIA'S ECONOMIC REFORMS
AND DEVELOPMENT

Dr Manmohan Singh

INDIA'S
ECONOMIC REFORMS
AND DEVELOPMENT
Essays for Manmohan Singh

Editors

Isher Judge Ahluwalia
I.M.D. Little

OXFORD
UNIVERSITY PRESS

OXFORD
UNIVERSITY PRESS

YMCA Library Building, Jai Singh Road, New Delhi 110001

Oxford University Press is a department of the University of Oxford. It
furthers the University's objective of excellence in research,
scholarship, and education by publishing worldwide in

Oxford   New York

Athens   Auckland   Bangkok   Bogota   Buenos Aires   Calcutta
Cape Town   Chennai   Dar es Salaam   Delhi   Florence   Hong Kong
Istanbul   Karachi   Kuala Lumpur   Madrid   Melbourne   Mexico City
Mumbai   Nairobi   Paris   Sao Paolo   Singapore   Taipei
Tokyo   Toronto   Warsaw
with associated companies in   Berlin   Ibadan

Oxford is a registered trade mark of Oxford University Press
in the UK and in certain other countries

Published in India
By Oxford University Press, New Delhi

© Oxford University Press 1998
The moral rights of the author have been asserted
Database right Oxford University Press (maker)
First published in Oxford India Paperbacks, 1999
Third impression 2000

ISBN 019 564988 5

Typeset by Rastrixi, New Delhi 110 070.
Printed in India at Pauls Press, New Delhi 110 020
Published by Manzar Khan, Oxford University Press
YMCA Library Building, Jai Singh Road, New Delhi 110 001

Contents

Contributors

Isher Judge AHLUWALIA
  Research Professor, Centre for Policy Research, New Delhi

Montek Singh AHLUWALIA
  Finance Secretary, Ministry of Finance, Government of India, New Delhi

Amaresh BAGCHI
  Emeritus Pofessor, National Institute of Public Finance and Policy, New Delhi

Jagdish BHAGWATI
  Arthur Lehman Professor of Economics and Professor of Political Science, Columbia University, New York

Raja J. CHELLIAH
  Chairman, National Institute of Public Finance and Policy, New Delhi, and Chairman, Madras School of Economics, Chennai

Lord Meghnad DESAI
  Professor, London School of Economics, London

Ashok GULATI
  Chief Economist, Agriculture and Rural Development, National Council for Applied Economic Research, New Delhi

Vijay JOSHI
  Fellow, Merton College and Reader in Economics, Oxford University, Oxford

Deepak LAL
  James S. Coleman Professor of International Development Studies, University of California, Los Angeles

I.M.D. LITTLE
  Emeritus Fellow of Nuffield College, Oxford University, Oxford

V.A. Pai Panandiker
Director and Professor, Centre for Policy Research, New Delhi

Kirit S. Parikh
Director and Vice-Chancellor, Indira Gandhi Institute of Development Research, Mumbai

C. Rangarajan
Governor, Andhra Pradesh. Formerly Governor, Reserve Bank of India, Mumbai

Ajit Singh
Professor, Faculty of Economics and Politics, Cambridge University, Cambridge

Amartya Sen
Lamont University Professor, and Professor of Economics and Philosophy, Harvard University. From January 1998, Master Trinity College, Cambridge University, Cambridge

T.N. Srinivasan
Director, Economic Growth Center, and Samuel. C. Park, Jr. Professor of Economics, and Chairman, Department of Economics, Yale University, New Haven, Connecticut

Suresh. D. Tendulkar
Professor, Delhi School of Economics, Delhi

Introduction

Isher Judge Ahluwalia and I.M.D. Little

It was only fitting that when Manmohan Singh came to the helm of economic policy-making in India as Finance Minister in 1991 at a time of deep economic crisis, he was finally able to implement what his early research findings had told him was the right thing to do. Four decades earlier, in his PhD thesis, young Manmohan had set out to examine the role that foreign trade could play in India's quest for self-reliance. His was an empirical enquiry in pursuit of well-defined, policy-oriented questions. His findings reinforced his instinct about the potential benefits of export orientation for the Indian economy. However, India's policy-makers had put India on a different growth path, and though Manmohan Singh became a part of the economic policy establishment in 1971, considerable time was to pass before policy changes in that direction could be made.

Manmohan Singh has clearly been the economist's economist in the government. He is the only person to have held every important position in the economic/civil service hierarchy in India including Secretary, Economic Affairs in the Ministry of Finance; Governor, Reserve Bank of India; Deputy Chairman, Planning Commission, and then Finance Minister. In his long career in government, Manmohan Singh is widely known to have been a voice of sanity, good sense and moderation through a period when Indian planners and policy-makers followed policies of import substitution and public sector domination which today do not command the enthusiasm they once did.

It is difficult to identify the contribution of individual policy makers functioning as civil servants. For example, it is never possible to say what bad decisions are averted, or which good policy measures are initiated at the instance of an individual. In fact, it is a civil servant's 'dharma' to advise an elected government freely and at the same time defend the policies that finally emerge.

Manmohan Singh has been known for his mild-mannered but firm approach in pushing good ideas while trying to carry others along and avoiding confrontation. Although he was, during the 1970s, very much a part of the policy establishment which created a highly regulated and heavily protected policy regime, he was always an advocate of practical measures and never a votary of ideological posturing. When the opportunity came, he seized it to bring about not only macroeconomic stabilization but also long overdue reforms significantly reducing domestic regulation and, more significantly, opening the Indian economy to foreign trade and investment to help the process of efficient industrialization.

Manmohan Singh's first big challenge in government came when a sharp acceleration in the international price of oil in 1973 exacerbated the problem of inflation at home. In a poor society where majority of the population lived at the margin of survival, inflation rates of over 20 per cent were clearly unacceptable. Indira Gandhi's government was determined to control inflation and it fell to Manmohan Singh to design the severe anti-inflationary package that was put into effect in July 1974. This included, for the first time, measures to directly restrict disposable incomes. The policy began to have an impact after September 1974. By March 1975, the price level had declined by 5.7 per cent over September 1974. The success of the package established Manmohan's reputation both domestically and internationally.

An equally significant though less visible contribution to policy by Manmohan Singh was the imparting of a certain degree of flexibility to exchange rate management in the Indian economy. In the Ministry of Finance in the second half of the 1970s and more particularly in the Reserve Bank during 1982–5, he was instrumental in ensuring that the exchange rate of the rupee was managed so as to depreciate in real terms without inviting adverse comment. The steady increase in the real effective exchange rate which had begun in 1979 was arrested in 1984. Thereafter the rate began to decline, thereby improving the competitiveness of Indian exports.

It is well known that as Member–Secretary of the Planning Commission, Manmohan Singh effectively shifted the focus of the Sixth Plan to efficient import substitution and improvement in productivity. The Plan prepared the ground for the gradual dismantling of the system of domestic regulation during the 1980s.

However, though easier access to imports and simplification of trade policies and procedures was part of the effort to improve efficiency in the use of resources, the inward orientation of the Indian economy remained pretty much intact. The attempts to offset the anti-export bias of the inward-oriented regime by offering budgetary subsidies clearly failed to bring about the desired result of improving efficiency and export competitiveness.

Manmohan Singh represented India with distinction at international meetings on monetary cooperation and development assistance. He was an active member of the Committee of Deputies which assisted the ministerial level Committee of Twenty and was set up to recommend reform measures for the Bretton Woods System. His modest and unassuming ways as well as his evident wisdom and vast experience won India many friends and supporters in international fora. When the South Commission was set up in the mid-1980s, to explore the issues facing the developing world, Manmohan Singh was Julius Nyerere's choice for the position of Secretary General.

It was fortuitous (and for the believers in destiny, pre-ordained) that Manmohan Singh thus spent three years between 1987 and 1990 in Geneva, spelling out issues facing the South in an increasingly interdependent world. His extensive tours to different parts of the developing world and detailed review of the policy measures which were successful in delivering better standards of living for the people of these economies, especially in Southeast Asia and East Asia, made a very deep impression on him.

In June 1991 Manmohan Singh was invited by Prime Minister Narasimha Rao to be finance minister. He took over the reins of office during the worst ever crisis for the Indian economy, and that too in a minority government. Few finance ministers have come to the job with the international reputation that Manmohan Singh enjoyed as an economic administrator, and this reputation was now put to a tough test.

Many doubted whether the government would last for a reasonable period, let alone its full five-year term. The knowledge of the bitter medicine that he would have to administer could not have strengthened Manmohan's own perception of the government's longevity. Severe macroeconomic imbalances and cumulative problems resulting from the poor productivity performance in the economy had created a situation where growth had collapsed, inflation was rising and foreign exchange reserves had dwindled to a level barely enough to meet India's normal import needs for ten days. Despite India's impeccable record of external debt management, there was a loss of confidence in her ability to meet her international repayment obligations. The challenge of restoring macroeconomic balance also had to be combined with the long overdue task of removing those policy-induced distortions that had serious adverse effect on productivity. Only then could India be put on the path of sustained growth with low inflation which alone could provide a lasting solution to India's poverty problem.

Manmohan Singh set about the task with the zeal of a reformer. Wide ranging tax reforms were fitted into a scheme of fiscal stabilization, and there was some action on the expenditure front as well. Containment of defence expenditures, cuts in fertilizer subsidies and slow and systematic efforts to reduce the interest burden on the budget were some of the more significant achievements. Thus, a process of fiscal reforms was initiated by a new finance minister who also had to undertake the political task of convincing the Parliament, and more important, the people of India, that his policies were the right policies for the Indian economy. In the years that followed he was to succeed beyond the expectations of many, although much still remained to be done when he left. It is a moot point that the very success of the new policies in the early years weakened the resolve to carry the reforms further as the sense of crisis in the balance of payments abated and foreign exchange reserves rose from less than $1 billion in June 1991 to over $10 billion in June 1993.

Manmohan Singh's historic contribution to Indian economic policy-making in 1991 was to initiate a decisive break away from the strongly inward-oriented trade policy regime in India, thereby providing an environment for efficient industrialization and better export performance. Recognizing the importance of international competitiveness in an increasingly interdependent world, he struck at the root cause of India's high-cost low-quality industrial structure which had brought about a steady long-term decline in India's share of world exports from 2 per cent in 1950 to 0.5 per cent in 1990. Import licensing was done away with for most goods except consumer goods, while import duty rates were cut so that by 1996 the import-weighted tariff had declined to 27 per cent from its pre-reform level of 87 per cent in 1991. The cash subsidy to exports was abolished, while the exchange rate was devalued by about 20 per cent at the very outset. It was a bold beginning. Foreign investment policy was also drastically transformed so as to actively seek foreign investment, particularly in infrastructure sectors. While intellectuals and policy-makers continue to debate on the anomalies in the tariff structure, the need to delicense consumer goods imports, and the desirability of foreign investment in consumer goods, there is no denying that the focus of the debate has shifted, from whether to open the Indian economy to how best to pace the process of opening up.

The initial response to the opening up in the form of faster growth, better export performance and greater self-reliance (larger financing of imports through export earnings) has certainly helped the reformers to argue for faster liberalization, but the constraint from infrastructural bottlenecks and resistance from vested interests (established industry, organized labour and the bureaucracy) is creating new concerns. Indeed, infrastructure is an area which was neglected in the early phase of reforms. More generally, public sector reforms were not high on the policy agenda. Similarly, only a beginning was made in the area of financial sector reforms. Action was much slower than was needed but faster than many had expected. However, industrial policy reforms which had begun in the 1980s were pushed further to provide larger scope for the private sector to participate in the growth process. Manmohan Singh's reforms have also been criticized for paying inadequate attention to human resource development. It was partly in response to such criticism that after the first year of cutbacks of plan expenditures on health, education and rural development, he tried in subsequent years to restore these cuts. However, the problems facing these sectors were the result of long neglect of policy and could not simply be handled by increased public expenditures.

The most durable achievement of Manmohan Singh's economic reform process has been the changing of the political mindset in the country. Today the Congress Party is no longer in power, but a 13-party coalition government at the Centre is speaking the language of reform. What is more, the states are becoming active partners in the reform process. Of course, there are populist distractions in the course of the journey, but the bold beginning made in 1991 and the economy's very favourable response to it holds out the promise of further progress. Manmohan Singh can look at these developments with some satisfaction.

This volume was conceived to honour Manmohan Singh on his sixty-fifth birthday. The contributors to a festschrift must have some special relationship to the honorand. This by itself may not be sufficient to avoid the contributions seeming like a random collection of essays. In this case, most of the contributors have been in some way associated with the reforms initiated by Manmohan Singh, and this greatly helped us to plan a cohesive volume. In so doing we were gently dirigiste in trying to get contributions that could be grouped under four main headings: 'Development Strategy', 'Transition to an Open Economy', 'Poverty and Reform', and 'Reform and Federalism'. We seem to have been fairly successful.

The first part 'Development Strategy' is the least closely linked to the reforms, and is consequently somewhat less focused than the others. Bhagwati, Desai and Sen are concerned mainly with the past strategy of development for the real economy, though their analyses clearly have lessons, sometimes explicit, for the future. Rangarajan's essay, is mainly about monetary policy, and is more explicitly forward-looking.

Bhagwati considers that Indian thinking on development in the 1950s was eminently sound. The main objective was poverty reduction through employment, though the social sectors were not neglected. Growth which must therefore be labour-intensive was instrumental. He berates those who have attacked Manmohan's reforms as neglecting poverty alleviation. According to Bhagwati the reforms represent a return towards the strategy of the 1950s which emphasized poverty reduction. The role of the government was then mainly indicative. Investment in infrastructure and sound macropolicies were expected to inspire confidence in private investors to raise the level of investment. Development began to fail in the 1960s, and the primary reason for this was the choice of an import-substitution strategy rather than export promotion. High-cost state production and intervention followed. This strategy implies that demand is limited by agricultural growth, and therefore very high growth rates are impossible. The alternative export-oriented strategy is exemplified by the East Asian economies. Bhagwati emphasizes that trade can jack up the growth rate indefinitely via increased imports of relatively cheap but productive equipment.

A literate labour force further enhances the productivity of such equipment, and the spread of the benefits of growth.

What are the priorities for reform now that the Indian economy is much more open? Bhagwati puts his finger on privatization, and the reform of labour laws needed for labour-demanding growth. He also thinks that NGOs must be coopted for wise expenditure in social sectors.

Desai's essay chimes in well with Bhagwati's. He thinks that a Vakil–Brahmananda model, which would have led to greater emphasis on employment and agriculture, might have been better than the Mahalanobis model with its emphasis on self-sufficiency in capital goods and its neglect of agriculture. Greater production of consumer goods would have permitted higher employment and exports to pay for the import of capital goods needed for the consumer good industries. Thanks to Manmohan Singh, India now has a second chance to follow a better path of development.

Sen makes a careful sympathetic examination of Manmohan Singh's 1964 book.[1] Manmohan accepted in broad outline Nurkse's thesis of sluggish demand for the exports of developing countries and hence the need for balanced growth. Yet he went on to argue that foreign trade had an important role to play. In particular, export promotion was needed to finance the required imports even with a relatively balanced growth. Sen draws attention to the qualified and defensive way in which Manmohan argued the need to promote exports, and attributes this to the climate of opinion at the time when one risked being classed as a reactionary outcast if one emphasized the benefits of trade (see also Bhagwati's and Desai's essays). Above all, Manmohan's painstaking empirical work showed that the cause of India's sluggish exports lay mainly with India's own policies and not with the slow growth of a developed country demand. India's export performance and the causes of export pessimism are also examined in Srinivasan's paper in Part II.

Sen salutes Manmohan as being wiser than he, who wrote about Indian development as that of a closed economy (with neither import substitution nor export promotion). Sen then admits the superiority of the East Asian model, but emphasizes that the full

---

[1] Manmohan Singh, *India's Export Trends and the Prospects for Self Contained Growth* (OUP, Clarendon Press, 1964).

benefits of export orientation will not be realized, and that wide-spread participation will not occur, unless the workforce is literate, which is very far from being the case in India. He suggests that the Indian reforms have paid little attention to this, or to land reform and 'female empowerment'.

India's export trends certainly began to lift the veil of export pessimism from our eyes. But Manmohan Singh did not then see exports as a means of using India's resources, especially labour, to the best advantage, but rather, as Sen notes, as a means of financing the imports required for growth. The emphasis was thus simply on growth, and not on the labour-intensive growth he was to emphasize in the 1990s. There was, we believe, a further development in this thinking about the benefits of trade between 1964 and 1990. Manmohan Singh's later budgets also did a good deal to increase expenditure on education, which Sen must approve.

Rangarajan is primarily concerned with an issue that is relevant to any economy at any time. His essay is thus less closely related to particular Indian reforms of the 1990s. But it is highly relevant to future Indian policy. He gives us a brilliant exposition on the state of our knowledge about the neutrality or non-neutrality of money, that is on the trade off, if any, between changes in the quantity of money and real output or growth in the short- as well as long-run. This is a much debated issue, and the debate may never end.

Rangarajan is clear that monetary policy can affect output in the short run. But if there is some influence in the short run, it must also surely extend to the longer run. One cannot believe that there is some long-run trend set in supply side stone that is impervious to short-run changes. This would imply that instability of output had no effect on growth, which is contrary both to common sense and empirical findings. However, it may be that a money-led boost to output while having some slight effect on long-run growth has a greater effect on inflation. Indeed this is what Rangarajan finds. In the long run, any significant influence exerted is probably through the inflation tax. Some effects of inflation may well be beneficial, provided that inflation is kept at a low level — the level itself depends on the circumstances of each country. Rangarajan argues that in India inflation should not exceed 6 per cent per annum. Vijay Joshi and Ian Little too are in agreement. In *India's Economic Reforms*, they argue that 5 per cent is a prudent rate of inflation to aim at.[2]

In the second part, 'Transition to an Open Economy', all five contributors examine reforms at the sectoral level. These also happen to be areas where reforms have not gone far, or have had somewhat disappointing results.

Montek Ahluwalia examines India's experience in infrastructure development in the first five years of reforms and attempts to draw lessons from this experience for the future. He argues that the Eighth Plan strategy for infrastructure development was dominantly a public sector strategy with only a supplemental role envisaged for the private sector. In practice, however, public sector investment fell considerably short of plan targets in all infrastructure sectors except telecommunications. Lack of resources with the public sector was one of the key constraints on expanding public investment. But there are also serious operational weaknesses in the public sector organizations dealing with infrastructure which exacerbate the scarcity of resources and reduce the effectiveness of the use of available resources. Except for the power sector, the strategy for inducting private investment in infrastructure was implemented only relatively recently and it is too early to assess its success. In the case of power, progress has been painfully slow, reflecting inadequate preparatory work to deal with the serious problems which arise when private sector projects are sought to be phased into a highly regulated infrastructure sector. However, Ahluwalia argues that a great deal of learning has taken place on how to deal with problems of regulatory interface and risk mitigation which should help future projects, although availability of finance, especially domestic debt, is likely to be a critical constraint.

Ahluwalia further argues that India was able to achieve an acceleration in growth in response to the reforms despite inadequate expansion in the capacity of infrastructure because of the slack in the system. But this has now been used up, and growth in the future will require massive expansion in the capacity. The government will have to ensure a substantial increase in public investment even if it decides to make maximum use of private

---

[2] Vijay Joshi and I.M.D. Little, *India's Economic Reforms 1991–2001* (Delhi: OUP, 1996).

investment potential. Expansion in public sector investment in infrastructure will depend critically upon the ability to raise resources through rational user charges and improved operational efficiency of public sector agencies. Attracting private investment will require a much more pro-active approach on the part of the government to create the pre-conditions needed for financing private infrastructure projects.

Ashok Gulati tells us in his paper how limited the progress towards the opening up of the agricultural sector to trade has been. Cereals, the largest segment, remain virtually insulated from world markets. Some progress in permitting trade in other sectors has been made, but it is patchy. In Gulati's words, 'In the case of cash crops, the approach seems to be to allow imports if there is net deficit and allow exports if there is comfortable surplus'. Trade is still taking place as a 'residual' between domestic demand and supply rather than as a policy instrument to integrate domestic agriculture with world agriculture, and so to optimize the use of resources. He goes on to point out that there are large differences between the relative costs of different crops and their world prices, leading to large potential gains from trade. He dismisses the argument that trade would undermine food security by pointing out that it was the drive for self-sufficiency in edible oils that resulted in the need to import wheat in 1992–3. Despite the failure to liberalize agricultural trade, Gulati finds that there has been some improvement in the agricultural terms of trade, though the response from agriculture has been inadequate. He suggests that it is important to remove various bottlenecks in production to get full mileage from freeing trade. He singles out the need for institutional reform, and public investment in canal irrigation, which should be financed by cutting input subsidies.

Vijay Joshi addresses the serious problem of the public sector deficit, progress towards the reduction of which has been barely perceptible since 1991–2. He argues convincingly that a long-run growth rate of 6 per cent per annum requires fiscal prudence and a large reduction in the deficit of the non-financial public sector (NFPS). With existing levels of deficit the use of monetary policy to keep inflation in check results in high interest rates which threaten output and growth. Joshi calculates that a reduction in the primary deficit equal to 3 per cent of GDP is needed. But taking interest into account it would still leave an approximately

7 per cent deficit of the NFPS, which would require interest rates too high for a desirable level of private investment to be sustainable. The interest burden of the public sector can be adequately reduced only by extensive privatization (which he advocates, as do Bhagwati and Srinivasan in their contributions). The reduction in the primary deficit must be achieved mainly by cuts in current expenditure. There should be little expectation of increased revenues, say 1 per cent of GDP, since desirable rises in direct taxation should be largely offset by desirable reductions in indirect taxation. Joshi then vehemently opposes those who have argued that current expenditures are mainly pre-committed and therefore irreducible. According to him very large savings, of upto 4 per cent of GDP, could be achieved by reducing hidden subsidies (which amount to about 7 per cent of GDP). Explicit subsidies could also be reduced. None of these accrue significantly to the poor. If to these some savings on government wages and salaries are added and one reaches a total saving of much more than the deficit reduction required. This is all for the good, for increased government saving is required to finance a rise in public investment in agriculture and infrastructure.

Apart from the deficit problem, which is mainly a problem of the government's current expenditure on the wrong things, Joshi has interesting comments on redundancy (closely related to privatization), on agricultural trade (related to the reduction of subsidies), on the size of the balance of payments deficit and the financing of infrastructural investment, on devolution and fiscal incentives of the states, and finally on the idea of an independent central bank (he prefers a constitutional limit to central government borrowing).

Ajit Singh reports that financial liberalization has permitted Indian corporations to raise very large amounts of capital through share issues in India, to which foreign institutional investors have recently been able to subscribe. They have also been permitted to raise funds abroad. The scale of this external financing has been very surprising because in the industrialized countries corporations tend to use the stock market only as a last resort, and have relied predominantly on their own savings. For various reasons, one might expect such self-reliance to be even more true of developing countries. This, however, is far from being the case as in the 1980s, in a sample of ten developing countries, only Pakistan used equity finance to a lesser extent than India. In the 1990s India may have been catching up in this respect. But Ajit Singh does not find any evidence of benefit for the economy from the growth of stock market activity in the 1980s.

However, the main message of his paper is a warning against encouraging or even allowing a market in corporate governance. Drawing on his own research and that of others, he claims that takeovers, and the threat thereof, are an extremely expensive and sometimes perverse way of keeping managers on their toes. He commends the success of Germany and Japan that have had no open market in corporate control. He calls for a serious discussion on the desirability of such a market in India, and one cannot disagree with that.

In the final essay in this section, Srinivasan, like Sen, opens with a brief review of our honorand's 1964 book. Like Sen, he emphasizes the climate of 'development' opinion at the time, which minimized the role of trade. Manmohan's contribution was to insist that trade remained important, and to counter the export pessimism of the time by showing that India's dismal export performance could be better explained by her own policies rather than by the slow growth of world demand. Manmohan's own gloomy conclusion about the adequacy of future Indian exports was fully justified. Indian exports continued to lose their share of world trade at least until the 1990s.

Srinivasan then reviews recent theory and econometric debates about the value of openness to international trade and investment. He refutes the theory that opening up trade can have only a 'level' and not a growth effect. While there may be econometric problems with some of the large number of exercises which show a very favourable effect of openness on growth, the weight of the evidence is overwhelming. Srinivasan concludes that 'the empirical evidence from a number of studies points to a strong and significant effect of openness to trade on growth performance'.

The growth performance of Indian exports since 1986 has been impressive compared with the earlier record. 'Nevertheless, even this performance pales in comparison with what India's competitors have achieved in the same period, indicating India's competitive disadvantage in a broad sense'. It was to be expected that low-wage cost countries would gain as the Far Eastern countries moved out of labour-intensive activities. The figures that

Srinivasan presents for eight labour-intensive manufactures are deeply depressing. Since 1980, China not India, has occupied most of the room vacated by Korea, Taiwan and Hong Kong. Why so? India fails on quality, timeliness and reliability of supply. This points to the well-known infrastructural deficiencies, especially ports. Srinivasan writes, 'Unless the political differences within the coalition government are resolved and a consensus is built towards tackling the issues of privatization and the related labour reforms head on, infrastructural problems will not be resolved'.

But China's success is partly due to multinationals using it as an export base for world markets (other Asian countries have also, of course, benefited in this way). India's absorption of foreign direct investment has been a small fraction of that of China. Foreign investors continue to be put off by Indian bureaucratic practices which survive their theoretical elimination, and tariffs on capital goods are still high. We would add Indian labour laws, the reservation of production for small-scale units, and continuation of quantitative restrictions on consumer goods imports as other factors inhibiting labour-intensive exports.

The essays in the third part are concerned with 'Poverty and Reform'. There is very general agreement that the poor must share the benefits of growth, and even enjoy a disproportionate share for some time, if that is possible without significantly reducing the growth rate. It can be claimed that this was always the objective of Indian planning (at least it was so in the beginning of the era of planning, as Bhagwati has stressed). But while plenty of lip service was paid to this principle, the actual measures taken and the laws passed tended to have the opposite effect. This implies that the removal of poverty requires reform.

There is a tendency to attack reform as being hostile to poverty. This shows ignorance or prejudice. Reform is or should be designed not only to be good for growth, but also to be good for labour-intensive growth, and increasing the demand for relatively unskilled labour is the only way to reduce the massive widespread poverty that still pervades India today.

Deepak Lal stresses that there is no conflict between growth and poverty alleviation. He distinguishes three types of poverty (i) mass structural poverty, (ii) destitution, and (iii) conjunctural poverty. In a large multi-country study which he directed with Hla Myint it was found that there was a clear positive effect of per capita income growth on mass poverty redressal in all countries studied (which did not include India) for 1950–85. He claims that if India could achieve the spectacular growth rates of East Asia, mass structural poverty could be eliminated within a generation. Destitution arises when people are unable to work, and do not find adequate support from families. Destitutes are a highly heterogeneous group. Conjunctural poverty arises when people suffer a temporary loss of income either because of drought, political failures, or economic shock. Both destitution and conjunctural poverty require transfers for their relief.

The two most important questions that arise with transfers are first whether they should be universal or targeted, and secondly whether they should be public or private. Most, though not all, public transfers in the rich industrialized countries are universal, that is they are available to everyone, even though some prefer not to use them. This is the essence of the welfare state. But the fiscal strain has become too great, and most OECD countries are trying to reduce their assumed obligations. Deepak Lal points out that in the developing world, in the countries which created welfare states (he cites Uruguay, Costa Rica, Sri Lanka and Jamaica) growth was retarded, and welfare commitments became unsustainable. It is evident that India should be extremely cautious about extending universal benefits which usually end up benefiting the middle classes most, and that targeting should be resorted to whenever possible, as has been suggested for the PDS (see Parikh's essay).

Turning to the second question, one needs to distinguish public subsidization from public provision. Public provision is often inefficient and private provision may be subsidized instead. Food stamps are an outstanding example. They would permit the provision of subsidized food without the extremely inefficient and corrupt Food Corporation of India and could be used as a vehicle for targeting. Similar possibilities are open in education and health care. Indeed, with respect to these, Lal says, 'Even if there is a case for public financing there is none for public production'.

Like Bhagwati, Lal considers that NGOs should be involved, and makes an extremely radical suggestion. Lastly, like Joshi, he considers that severance payments are an important issue, and has interesting suggestions concerning their design. Moreover, he stresses the crucial importance of reforming the labour market.

Parikh writes on 'food security'. He identifies this concept with the prevention of hunger, and the prevention of hunger is little different from the abolition of poverty. He makes the same distinction as Deepak Lal between persistent (or mass structural) and transient (conjunctural) poverty, together with destitution.

The solution to persistent poverty is growth. But here Parikh stresses that one of the main causes of persistent poverty is that the demand for labour has not kept pace with the growth of its supply. So the growth must be sufficiently labour-demanding. Parikh echoes Sen that much more must be spent on education to make the work force more employable. But it is no use making labour employable, if there is not enough demand.

Parikh then examines the PDS and public employment schemes such as the EGS. He considers their potential for alleviating both persistent and transient employment (at least until such time as persistent poverty and hunger is a thing of the past). The PDS is virtually useless as an instrument for poverty alleviation. Even if it were targeted so that only the poor got the cheap food (and this would in fact be impossible to achieve), the cost in terms of both grain and money would be prohibitive. Employment guarantee schemes are far more effective. Together with relief for the destitute who cannot benefit, Parikh estimates that 'it should be feasible to pursue a vigorous policy to provide food security to all through the EGS provided there is sufficient grain available in the country to pursue such a policy'. Adequate supplies can be assured by a combination of trade and public buffer stocks. Parikh then introduces an elaborate model to estimate the optimum provision of stocks of wheat and rice. This depends most sensitively on the costs of stocking by the Food Corporation of India (FCI). Even if determined reform of the FCI halved stocking costs, the optimum maximum levels of stocks are quite small, 6.5 million tonnes for rice and 1.5 million tonnes for wheat. Liberalization of trade in cereals is essential for food security.

In his paper Tendulkar writes that the worldwide evidence of the importance of growth for poverty relief means that it can be taken for granted that the Indian reform movement that had begun in 1990–91 will alleviate poverty once India is settled into a growth path higher than that of the earlier years. But there have been widespread attacks on the reform movement as being hostile to the poor. Tendulkar agrees that during the transition period, before the benefits of higher growth materialize, a number of factors could have negative impact on the poor.

Tendulkar divides what he calls 'reform related' policies into: (1) stabilization, (2) opening up to world markets, and (3) deregulation of domestic markets. The latter two are commonly called structural reforms. Of these, stabilization may hurt the poor as it involves fiscal retrenchment, which in turn reduces demand in general, but may also include a cut in expenditure on the social sectors. The structural reforms could also cause unemployment or a fall in real wages, or both, in the short term.

Tendulkar expected reform-related policies to have a greater impact on the urban sector, since almost all the reforms were focused on industry: indeed there has been virtually no reform in agricultural trade, either domestic or foreign. Also public expenditure is more closely related to the urban economy. The impact on the rural sector could be indirect and delayed. These expectations have not borne out. In 1992 when the stabilization measures hit hardest there was a small rise in urban poverty, but rural poverty rose almost catastrophically by around 30 per cent. By 1993–4 the level of urban poverty fell by nearly 20 per cent, while rural poverty was reduced to about the 1990–91 level (all the above comparisons are made with 1990–91 level).

The obvious explanation is that the rise and fall in the level of rural poverty had very little to do with any structural reform, and not even much to do with the stabilization measures. Previous work has shown that changes in rural poverty are dominated by agricultural production. A fall in production hits the poor in two ways, by reducing the demand for labour and by raising the price of cereals. There was a fall in foodgrain production in 1991–2. The devaluation which was part of the stabilization package must have contributed to the rise in the price of foodgrains which caused a fall in real rural wages in 1991–2. But the government's procurement and issue prices seem to have been raised more than was necessary. Also there was reduction in employment under the Jawahar Rozgar Yojana, and no drought relief works were carried out. The fact that rural poverty did not improve by 1993–4 over 1990–91 is attributed by Tendulkar partly to the mismanagement of public intervention in the market for foodgrains with immoderate rises in procurement and issue prices, and increases in public stocks. Despite the recovery in output, the availability of cereals was actually 2 per cent lower in 1993–4 than in 1990–91, and 6–7 per cent lower per head.

Tendulkar has dealt at length with rural poverty changes since 1990–91 but has little to say about urban poverty. He attributes the unexpectedly smaller rise in urban poverty in 1992 to the devaluation offsetting tariff reductions; and otherwise to the slowness or lack of reform and the rigidities in the labour market. But he says nothing about the large fall in urban poverty since 1992. One is left to wonder whether deregulation might not have something to do with it, even though there has been no reform in the labour market. Admittedly, Tendulkar was unable to separate stabilization measures from structural reforms. Stabilization was forced, but structural reforms were not. Those who have attacked the reforms confused the two. The advocates of reform looked at structural reforms as a means of reducing poverty, whereas stabilization was a much needed condition for sustained growth.

The fourth and final part deals with reforms and Centre–State relations. Until Manmohan Singh initiated reforms, the centre tried to control the patterns of production, investment and growth in considerable detail. This implies the reservation of economic power in the centre with little room for independent manoeuvre by the states. Derestriction and the change in economic philosophy more generally should allow the state governments to acquire greater responsibility and independence, and to show greater initiative than in the past. The resources available to the states, and their source is thus intimately related to the programme of reform that began in 1990–91.

As in any federation the assignment of taxes to the different levels of government is crucial. Bagchi discusses this in considerable detail. According to him there are four problem areas. First there is a sharp imbalance between taxing powers and spending responsibilities necessitating large transfers from the centre to the states. This is normal in federations and creates serious problems only if the transfers are made in such a way as to erode the fiscal discipline of the recipients. Secondly, the tax bases assigned to the centre and the states overlap, and are split. Thirdly, the states try to shift the incidence of indirect taxes to other states (tax exporting), and they compete for investment in giving tax concessions (tax competition): the safeguards against these practices are inadequate. Lastly, there are constitutional limitations which severely weaken the tax base:

the centre cannot tax agricultural incomes, and there are also difficulties with the taxation of services. A detailed discussion of the severity of these problems that seriously reduce the efficiency of production and exchange leads Bagchi to observe that 'all in all, the tax scene in India is chaotic'.

Indirect taxation is probably the worst offender against economic efficiency. Central excises and state sales taxes overlap, and their effective incidence defies economic logic. And India is not even a common market, for internal trade is taxed. As Bagchi writes, 'it would appear that the approach towards a rational structure of indirect taxation in the country lies in installing a system of destination type VAT to replace all taxes on domestic production and trade with a comprehensive base covering both goods and services'. How best to achieve this, and how to secure the cooperation of the states in arriving at a good solution is another very difficult problem. Bagchi is not very optimistic, and his concluding remark bears repetition: 'A pre-requisite for any move for fundamental reform in an area so sensitive as Centre–State division of tax powers is public recognition of the need for radical change. That in turn calls for a national debate. It is a pity that when rethinking on tax assignment is going on even in well- established federal democracies like Canada and USA, in India the debate has not even begun.'

Chelliah, the Chairman of the Tax Reform Committee, whose report has guided the extensive reforms in central taxation that have been enacted, covers some of the same ground as Bagchi in his paper, but concentrates more on the division of responsibilities of the centre and states and the financial transfers from the centre to states. He notes that the states were in a situation of near-subjugation under central planning and the operation of Article 356 of the Constitution. The decline of central planning has resulted in a resurgence of regional aspirations. These could largely be satisfied by a reduction in the activity of the centre in the fields which are concurrent under the Constitution. The centre should lay down broad outlines, and leave operations to the states; residual powers should also lie with the states. But the centre must retain sufficient powers to ensure that India is a nation and not a mere confederation of states. Apart from defence and foreign affairs, it must be responsible for maintaining macroeconomic stability, and a common market (not yet existing), and for guarding the constitutional rights of citizens, and mitigating interstate inequalities.

Chelliah's discussion of tax and expenditure assignment conforms closely with that of Bagchi. He most strongly condemns the central sales tax and tax exporting proclivities of the states, together denying the benefits of a common market. But he offers no precise plan as to how these defects can be remedied. He discusses more fully tax devolution and the modes of grant-giving by the centre.

The gap-filling tendencies of the Finance Commissions, whereby increases in a state's expenditure are partly financed by others, must be curbed. Some percentage of the pooled tax revenue of the centre should devolve (it seems that the government has now accepted this), and this percentage should remain fixed for 15–20 years. The statewise distribution should be mainly on a population basis. Grants are given by the Planning Commission for revenue plan expenditure, and by the Finance Commission for non-plan revenue expenditure. The plan and non-plan distinction should be ended, and all grants should flow through the Finance Commission: these like the distribution of devolved tax revenue should be on some basis unrelated to expenditure, such as fiscal incapacity. Planning Commission assistance should be only through loans for capital expenditure.

These reforms would greatly encourage fiscal discipline in the states. But they could hardly be enacted without the centre imposing fiscal discipline on itself. Chelliah welcomes the phasing out of ad hoc treasury bills. There should be only limited predetermined support from the RBI. Market borrowing should be shared on an agreed basis with the states. Much more consultation between the centre and the states is needed. The centre must try to promote cooperative federalism, and the states should abjure policies inconsistent with a common market while recognizing that the centre needs a surplus in order to help the weaker states. Chelliah ends with eight points that certainly add up to an important plan for reform in Centre–State relations.

In the final paper of the volume Panandiker reviews the great diversity of Indian polity and how it is changing. The two most significant changes would seem to be (1) the transfer of power under democracy from a western educated urban middle class to a regionally educated rural and agricultural class, in particular to the scheduled castes (SCs) and other backward castes (OBCs), and (2) the demand for more power for the states. The latter is partly the consequence of the former, but also the result of deregulation and the decline of central planning, as has also been remarked by other contributors in this volume.

The transfer of power does not seem to bode well for the future of the reforms for Panandiker tells us that the new power elite has no understanding of macroeconomic management. It is not concerned with industrialization and development, but rather with maximizing non-plan expenditure 'often on a highly bloated bureaucracy'. It is ironic although predictable that it is strong in the very poor states such as UP and Bihar where growth per head has been stagnant and even negative.

The states are very diverse in many dimensions. First, of course, there is size. Ten states out of 25 have over 80 per cent of the total population, and five states have over half. Four of these five are among the poorest. This is of obvious relevance when some of the most urgent reforms in India depend upon interstate agreement. The ability of states to agree may depend on their diversity in other respect, income per head and poverty, the degree of industrialization, and religion and demography. These all vary greatly. Punjab's income per head is three times that of Bihar. In 1987–8 only 7 per cent of the population of the Punjab was below the poverty line against 45 per cent of Orissa. Industry and Mining constituted over 30 per cent of the state GDP in Maharashtra against 20 per cent in UP and 18 per cent in Rajasthan. But the wealthier states tend to question the centre's efforts to favour the poorer and weaker states.

The divergences extend to demographic trends as well. The birth rate is 15 per thousand in Goa and 36 in UP. Death rate and infant mortality rates also vary largely. There is ethnic and religious fertility competition, which blunts the influence of the family planning programme.

Panandiker believes that for the next fifteen years political economy will be greatly influenced by the OBCs and SCs. But in the long run the rapidly growing middle class will be the most formidable influence. There is danger clearly implicit in these movements, and in the divergences already apparent.

The essays in this festschrift make it clear that Manmohan Singh's tenure as finance minister was an event of critical importance in India's economic history. But it is still unclear whether the reforms he initiated will lead on to a radical transformation of the economic system, one which most if not all of the contributors believe is required if extreme poverty in India is ever to be eliminated.

I

India's
Development Strategy

1

The Design of Indian Development

*Jagdish Bhagwati**

Manmohan Singh's 65th birthday, and the 50th anniversary of India's Independence, are an appropriate occasion for reflecting on where we have been and where we should be headed. For me, this is also a special moment. Manmohan Singh followed me just a year later to St. John's College, Cambridge, and then for a postgraduate stint at Nuffield College, Oxford. I have thus had the privilege of over four decades of friendship with him, and as an additional dividend, this Festschrift is being edited by our common and uncommonly gifted teacher, Ian Little, and by my accomplished student, Isher Ahluwalia: they form a splendid editorial team.

More than all this, however, this Festschrift celebrates a truly great man. After over a generation, nearly three decades, lost to a policy framework that handicapped our explicit objective of assuring minimum incomes to the country's numerous destitute and poor, Manmohan Singh was given the opportunity by Prime Minister Rao in 1991 to reverse India's course. He seized it, and has succeeded. That is glory indeed.

His success must be explained by several factors, not all within his control, but his own determination, never disguised (contrary to the absurd suggestion in the recent India Survey in *The Economist* of 'surreptitiousness' about the reforms initiated

* This essay has been prepared for the festschrift for the former Finance Minister, Dr Manmohan Singh, organized by Ian Little and Isher Ahluwalia. Inevitably, I have drawn heavily on my recent writings, especially the K.R. Narayanan Oration that I gave last year at the Australian National University.

in 1991), surely played a role. So did the fact that he was so clearly a man of supreme integrity, and wholly without guile or hypocrisy, that he stood out among the politicians as one whose actions, even when causing pain, were actuated simply by the pursuit of social good and hence were to be applauded more often than resented.

And when economists wedded to the old ways criticized him for sacrificing 'social opportunity' and poverty amelioration to economic reforms, the criticisms sounded hollow not merely because they were wrongheaded (as I argue below) but partly because it was ironic to see well-heeled economists criticizing in this fashion the utterly simple and almost spartan Finance Minister who was obviously far closer to the poor.[1] Indeed, the huge success that he enjoyed in the country was a reflection of this Gandhian simplicity and his clear empathy for the Indian masses as he sought to guide the economy towards a reformed regime.

So, the failures afflicting India's earlier policy framework, and hence by implication the rationale underlying the reforms that he initiated, and the architecture of what India's developmental strategy should have been and should be, are the themes that I now wish to analyse as my tribute to Manmohan Singh.

I. INDIAN ECONOMIC PERFORMANCE: THREE PHASES

In the 1950s and early 1960s, India's developmental efforts were attracting attention worldwide, and the attention and interest were equally from economists. To understand this, and also to put the subsequent disenchantment into perspective, let me explain why what we were doing in India through the 1950s was sensible *and* worthy of the huge interest everywhere.

I.1 Phase I, India in the 1950s: On Track

At her Independence in 1947, India was already a country with a fair degree of industrialization under her belt. Textiles and steel were among the many industries that had come up exclusively

---

[1] Many of my non-Indian economist friends who have visited India confess to astonishment that in India, virtually alone among the world's developing nations, there still are trained economists who doubt and even oppose, as against leading, reforms.

from market forces and with domestic investment, under a colonial government that certainly had not seen itself as a developmental agency and had therefore virtually abstained from 'infant industry' protection or promotion. India also enjoyed the presence of an active entrepreneurial class and a modest but definite integration in to the world economy. The country was also endowed with a first rate civil service and administrative structure, world class leaders, and a democratic form of government.

But the poverty was immense, with corresponding standards of living appalling for many, the literacy levels were abysmal even as the higher levels of education were impressive, and the challenge to the new government was clearly huge.

The *key strategy* that defined the resulting developmental effort was the decision to target efforts at accelerating the growth rate. Given the immensity of the poverty, the potential of simple re-distribution was considered to be both negligible in its immediate impact and of little sustained value. The central anti-poverty strat-egy had therefore to be the creation of increasing numbers of jobs that would draw ever more of the underemployed and unemployed into gainful employment that would yield them both greater in-comes and higher standards of living. Accelerated growth was thus regarded as an *instrumental* variable; a policy outcome that would in turn reduce poverty, which constituted the true objective of our efforts.

I have often reminded the critics of Indian strategy, who attack it from the perspective of poverty which is juxtaposed against growth, that it is incorrect to think that the Indian planners got it wrong by going for growth rather than attacking poverty: they confuse means with ends. In fact, the phrase 'minimum income' and the aim of providing it to India's poor were very much part of the lexicon and at the heart of our thinking and analysis when I worked in the Indian Planning Commission in the early 1960s. The basic ideas even predated us, as T.N. Srinivasan has often written in a rude reminder to those who have discovered the poverty issue only belatedly.

Equally, the populist notion that pushing growth to kill poverty is a passive and conservative '*trickle-down*' strategy is wholly obtuse. In the Indian context, it was an active and radical, what I have called '*pull-up*' strategy. Nor were we unmindful that added policy instru-ments were necessary to ensure that the growth process would indeed extend to all groups. For instance, just as the United States has a 'structural' inner-city problem, we have (among others) a 'tribal' problem: each underprivileged group fails to have equal and ready access to the mainstream economy. Nor were social expenditures relegated to oblivion. The First Five Year Plan itself had addressed this matter, and the Planning Commission had at the time a distinguished social worker, Mrs Durgabhai Deshmukh, as a Member who formidably minded her portfolio on the social questions.

Those intimately involved in India's plans fully understood, contrary to many recent assertions, the need for land reforms, for attention to the possibility of undue concentration of economic power and growth in inequality. These 'social' tasks, which of course also can redound to economic advantage, were attended to and endlessly debated in the ensuing years, with reports commissioned (such as the Mahalanobis Committee report on income distribution in 1962) and policies continually devised and revised to achieve these social outcomes. Even as spending and social engineering to advance education and public health were also among our concerns, we understood that such spending could not be expanded or even sustained unless a growing economy produced in the first place the added revenues to finance these and other expenditures.

To those who use the cliché of 'development with a human face' to decry efficiency, growth, and the economic reforms, I respond: 'Yes, indeed. But remember that the face cannot exist by itself, except as a mask in a museum, but must be joined to the body; and if the body is emaciated, the face must wither no matter how much we seek to humanize and pretty it up'.

So, we return to growth as the centerpiece of the Indian strategy for assaulting poverty and providing minimum incomes to the poor, and we must remember that it was the government's task to accelerate economic growth. I believe that we could say, in a stylized way but with plausibility, that the central conception underlying India's growth-accelerating strategy was the devising of a planning framework that would produce the enhanced investment rates. Thus, the objective was to jolt the economy up into a higher investment mode that would generate, say a 5 per cent growth rate as against the conventional lower investment equilibrium with a 2 to 2.5 per cent growth rate.

The planning framework then rested on two legs.[2] *First*, it sought to make the escalated growth credible to private investors so that they would proceed to invest on an enhanced basis in a self-fulfilling prophecy. *Second*, it aimed at generating the added savings to finance the investments so induced.

The Five Year Plans framework was an important aspect of this two-pronged policy. Simply by demonstrating that the government was committed to a higher growth rate, it assured potential investors that demand would grow at higher rates and the risk of investment would be correspondingly reduced. Besides, at the core of the Plan, there was commitment to substantial governmental spending, mostly on infrastructure, that added yet greater credibility to the high growth scenario in what was otherwise an 'indicative' Plan in terms of its investment profile. Moreover, the commitment to use fiscal policy to raise public savings to levels necessary to finance the projected growth of investment was also a credibility-enhancing factor to bring about the enhanced investment.

The bulk of the 1950s can then be called the favourable Phase I of Indian developmental effort; and it broadly coincides, in approach, to much of the East Asian experience where, however, the Five Year Plans framework was not utilized: the governmental intervention, as described, led to an investment boom and hence to enhanced growth. I may indeed, re-characterize what happened, in more familiar technical terms, by reference to the Rosenstein–Rodan argument that has now been formalized by Vishny and Shleifer as a case of multiple equilibria. In his classic 1943 *Economic Journal* article, which is arguably the most beautiful piece of creative writing on development, Rosenstein–Rodan was basically arguing that, for developing countries stuck in a Nash equilibrium with low levels of investment, there existed a superior cooperative equilibrium with higher levels of investment and growth.

The Indian planners, in formulating the First Five Year Plan (1951–6), were essentially exploiting this insight. This was an indicative Plan, without the straitjacket of controls and targeted allocations that would presumably reflect the contours of the superior equilibrium. Indeed, it is absurd to imagine that anyone, either in India or in East Asia, could have worked out such a

[2] I refer only to the 'economic' framework. A third leg was, of course, the provision of social opportunity through land reforms and social programmes and expenditures on health and education, in particular.

Rosentein–Rodan–Vishny–Shleifer equilibrium even if there had been complete information to do so! What did happen instead was that, as I have already suggested, the large component of *public* spending on infrastructure which was built into these indicative programmes made the government's *commitment* to kicking the system up into some bastardized version of the Rosentein–Rodan–Vishny–Shleifer equilibrium quite *credible* to the private sector, triggering the self-fulfilling *private* sector investment response that lifted the economy into higher investment and growth rates.

I.2   Phase II, What Went Wrong: Derailment after the 1950s

What went wrong with India can be characterized by contrasting India with East Asia once we go beyond the 1950s. Indeed, by understanding better why East Asia went ahead to build greater success in the post-1950s helps us to understand why India went ahead to decline instead in her economic performance: hence, I will for the present, focus on East Asia's success and its causes.

Let me begin by observing that, in my judgment, the critical difference was that India turned to the IS (import substitution) strategy, East Asia to the EP (export promotion) strategy.

(i) The Inducement to Invest

A central implication is that India, during this Phase II, handicapped the private *inducement to invest*, while East Asia wound up enhancing it.

India turned inwards, starting with a balance of payment crisis in 1956–7 that precipitated the imposition of exchange controls which then became endemic to the regime, reflecting the currency overvaluation that implies the effective pursuit of an IS strategy. Again, the explicit pursuit of an IS strategy was also desired, reflecting the economic logic of elasticity pessimism that characterized the thinking of India's planners.

The result was that the inducement to invest in the economy was constrained by the growth of demand from the agricultural sector, reflecting in turn the growth of that sector. But agriculture has grown almost nowhere by more than 4 per cent per anum over a sustained period of over a decade, so that increment at the margin in India's private investment rate was badly constrained by the fact that it was cut off from the elastic world markets and forced to depend on inevitably sluggish domestic agricultural expansion. Thus, it became customary for Indian economists (such as Professor Sukhamoy Chakarvarty and K.N. Raj) to talk about 'balanced growth' and about the problem of raising the investment rate which, by the mid-1980s, was still in the range of 19–20 per cent.

By contrast, the East Asian investment rate began its take-off to phenomenal levels because East Asia turned to the EP strategy. The elimination of the 'bias against exports', and indeed a net (if mild) excess of the effective exchange rate for exports over the effective exchange rate for imports (signifying the relative profitability of the foreign over the home market), ensured that the world markets were profitable to aim for, guaranteeing in turn that the inducement to invest was no longer constrained by the growth of the domestic market as in the IS strategy. Private domestic savings were either raised to match the increased private investment by policy deliberately encouraging them or by the sheer prospect of higher returns.

(ii) Importing New-vintage Equipment

The flip side of the process was, of course, the generation of substantial export earnings that enabled the growing investment to be implemented by imports of equipment embodying technical change.

Now, if the Social Marginal Product (SMP) of this equipment exceeded the cost of its importation, there would be a 'surplus' that would accrue as an income gain to East Asia and would also, as I argue below, boost the growth rate. For this argument to hold, however, the international cost of the newer-vintage equipment must not reflect fully its SMP for East Asia. In a competitive international market for equipment, therefore, I must assume that East Asia was a small player whose higher SMP did not pull up the world price to reflect the higher SMP, i.e. that East Asia could, even without 'piracy' and 'theft' of intellectual property (which was widespread in the region until the new WTO regime), get embodied technology at bargain prices. This seems a reasonable assumption to make, especially when we see that the world prices of the last-but-one vintage equipment fall drastically due to rapid obsolescence in the climate of quick product innovation: for example, an economy in 1970, such as Soviet Russia's, which was confined to using its own 1930s-vintage technology in equipment would *not* lose to East Asia which could use a heuristically 20 times more productive 1960s technology if East Asia had to pay a 20 times greater price for it. The surplus arises because East Asia pays, say, only a 5 times greater price in world markets for equipment that is 20 times more productive in East Asia.

But there may also be another reservation about this argument's effect on the growth rate, as distinct from its effect on income. It is fair to say that, thanks to the focus on the steady state in Solow-type models, it has now become fashionable to assert that gains from trade, like any allocative efficiency gains, amount to one-time gains, not affecting the growth rate. This is however wrong-headed as a general assertion. Thus, consider the simple Harrod–Domar corn producing–corn growth model with labour a slack variable. If allocative efficiency regarding land use (say, from one inefficient farm to another efficient farm) leads to a greater return to the total amount of ('invested') corn being planted, the marginal capital output ratio will fall, *ceteris paribus*, and lead to a permanently higher growth-rate. Similarly, it takes no sweat for a first rate theorist to construct models where trade in capital goods leads to higher growth rates, without building in externalities, etc. and relying exclusively on the fact that they can be imported more cheaply than constructed under autarky.

Thus, T.N. Srinivasan has extended the Mahalanobis-type putty–clay model to include trade and demonstrated precisely this.[3] Thus, he assumes (in place of just one capital and one consumer good in the autarkic version) that there are two of each class of goods, with the marginal product of capital constant in each sector as in the Harrod–Domar model. The social utility function and the function that transforms the output of the two investment goods into aggregate investment are Cobb–Douglas. There is no intersectoral (i.e. between the consumer goods and the capital goods sectors), as against intra-sectoral (i.e. between the two goods in each sector), mobility of capital: this is the clay assumption.

Assuming that all four goods are produced under autarky, that

[3] See his 'Comment on "Two Strategies for Economic Development: Using Ideals and Producing Ideas", by Romer', *Proceedings of the World Bank Annual Conference on Development Economics 1992*, World Bank, Washington, D.C., 1993.

free trade is undertaken at fixed terms of trade, and that the share of investment going to augmenting capacity in each of the two sectors is fixed exogenously, Srinivasan then demonstrates plausibly that free trade in consumer goods (but with autarky continuing in investment goods) will raise welfare relative to autarky but not affect the growth rate of income or utility. On the other hand, freeing trade in investment goods will have a positive effect on transitional as well as on long-run (steady state) growth, and also a beneficial welfare effect relative to autarky. The vulgar belief that trade gains cannot affect the growth rate is thus easily disposed of.

However, how does one reconcile the 'surplus' argument with the findings that TFP growth has been a negligible factor in East Asia? So, is my story plausible but not borne out by the facts, as is often the case with our most interesting theories? I think not.

Thus, consider precisely the case where the imported equipment is 20 times more productive in Period 2 than in Period 1, but its price in only 5 times as high. If the valuation of this equipment is at domestic (producer) opportunity cost, as it should be, then it will indeed be priced 20 times higher than the older-vintage equipment of Period 1, so the measure of capital contribution at the level of the industry will rise commensurately and I presume that the estimated TFP growth in the industry will be zero: in that case, my thesis about the surplus is totally compatible with measured TFP emerging as negligible. But, of course, if the equipment is priced at its international cost, then I presume that TFP growth will pick up three-fourths of the gain that accrues from the 'surplus' of SMP over the international cost. My guess then is that, in East Asia, the former was the case. This might have been, not because the accountants were smart and valued Period 2 equipment at domestic opportunity cost, but because I guess that much of the imported equipment may have gone through importing trading firms that collected the three-fourth premium rather than the producing firms.

(iii) Literacy and Education

The role of literacy and education comes in precisely at the stage of the second step in my story above. For, the productivity or SMP of the imported equipment would be greater with a workforce that was literate and would be further enhanced if many had even secondary education. Thus, with Social Marginal Product rising with literacy and education, yet greater surplus would arise for any given international cost of newer-vintage equipment.

Of course, as these economies grew more rapidly, the demand for secondary and higher education in turn would rise and a virtuous circle would follow: primary education would enhance the growth that EP strategy brought whereas the enhanced growth would demand and lead to a more educated workforce. I see therefore primary education and literacy as playing an enhancing, rather than an initiating, role in the EP strategy-led East Asian drama.

Thus, to conclude this line of argument, my explanation of East Asia's success, and by contrast that of India's failure, combines in its own way three major elements, in that order: (i) the enhanced inducement to invest due to the EP strategy; (ii) the benefit from the surplus of domestic SMP over international cost of imported newer-vintage capital equipment; and (iii) the raising of this SMP by the presence of a literate workforce. India failed to embrace the outward-oriented EP strategy, and so failed to profit from the first two of the growth-enhancing factors outlined above. At the same time, India also failed to pursue the expansion of literacy so that the illiteracy rate by 1990 for Indians aged 15 was still almost as high as 60 per cent!

(iv) Direct Foreign Investment

If the main plot is this, the story has doubtless many subplots. I will touch on just one of them, especially as the analysis dates back to the early 1970s and to the NBER project which I had the pleasure of codirecting with Anne Krueger.

In my synthesis volume[4] for the NBER Project findings, I noted that among the advantages of the EP strategy, which the Project had found beneficial, you had to count the fact that trade barriers-jumping DFI in the IS countries was likely to be limited for these countries by the size of the domestic market by which it was motivated — there are shades here of the inducement-to-invest argument, but only in the faintest strokes. Secondly, such DFI as was attracted in the IS countries was also likely to be less productive because it would be going into economic regimes characterized by significant trade distortions that could even generate

---

[4] Bhagwati, 1978, op. cit.

negative value added at socially relevant world prices — a possibility that was discussed by me (based on an extension to the DFI issue of the contribution by Harry Johnson to the theory of immiserizing growth in tarrif-distorted economies)[5] and then nailed down in well-known articles into a certainty under certain conditions by Hirofumi Uzawa and by Richard Brecher and Carlos Diaz Alejandro independently.

I should mention that both these (thoroughly plausible in terms of their economic rationale) hypotheses have been examined, with some success, in cross-country regressions by a former student of mine, V.N. Balasubramanyam, Lancaster University and his co-authors.[6] So, this element of explanation may also be added to the explanation of East Asia's superior performance relative to that of the IS strategy-plagued countries such as India.

(v) Overall Inefficiency of Investments

Indeed, the inefficiency of the limited investment that did occur is the other side of India's miseries in the post-1950s Phase II. As India turned inward, the absence of competition and its salutary effects on efficiency were also lost. This loss was further compounded as the original, promotional apparatus established in the Ministry of Industry (the DGTD) instead transformed itself swiftly into a restrictive agency. The government turned from indicative planning to becoming a mechanism for masterminding, with the aid of a stifling and indeed Kafkaesque *licensing system*, the production, investment, and import decisions in the economy to a degree unimaginable to anyone outside the regime. I am reminded that eventually, when in the early 1990s just prior to the beginning of the reforms in earnest in 1991 under what we might call Phase III, *The Economist* ran a long piece on India, describing

[5] See Jagdish Bhagwati, 'The Theory of Immiserizing Growth: Further Applications', in Michael Connolly and Alexander Swoboda (eds), *International Trade and Money*, Toronto University Press: Toronto, 1973.

[6] See, in particular, V.N. Balasubramanyam and M.A. Salisu, 'EP, IS and Direct Foreign Investment in LDCs', in A. Koekkoek and L.B.M. Mennes (eds), *International Trade and Global Development: Essays in Honour of Jagdish Bhagwati*, Routledge: London, 1991, for the former hypothesis; and V.N. Balasubramanyam, M.A. Salisu and David Sapsford, 'Foreign Direct Investment and Growth in EP and IS Countries', *Economic Journal*, Jan. 1996, for an indirect test of the latter hypothesis (explaining growth as the dependent variable).

and denouncing its policies, a visiting Russian economist, Maxim
Boycko, who then went on to play a major part in the Russian
privatization programme of Anatoly Chubais, told me: 'that article
could well have been describing the Soviet Union'. We had clearly
reproduced beautifully the disadvantages of communism, without
any of its benefits!

In addition, the early policy adopted in the 1950s itself, under
which a growing share of the country's investments would occur
in the public sector, spawned inefficient *public sector enterprises*
whose losses would make a significant contribution to a macro
crisis in the 1980s. In addition, they crippled the efficiency of the
private sector too, since the public sector enterprises supplied, or
rather failed to adequately and efficiently supply, infrastructure
inputs such as electricity and transportation over which they were
granted monopoly of production.

(vi) Conclusion

If I were to summarize briefly the period of three decades between
the end of the 1950s and of the 1980s, I would reach the following
sobering conclusion:
We had started out in the 1950s with:

- high growth rates
- openness to trade and investment
- a promotional state
- social expenditure awareness
- confidence that poverty would be seriously dented by growth
- macro stability
- optimism; and hence
- admiration of the world

But we ended the 1980s with:

- low growth rates[7]
- closure to trade and investment
- a licence-obsessed, restrictive state
- inability to sustain social expenditures

---

[7] The 1980s had higher than the 'Hindu growth rate' of 3.00 to 3.5 per
cent during the preceding two decades but, as has been discussed by many,
it was based on excessive internal spending and both internal and external
borrowing, and hence was clearly unsustainable. It in fact led directly to the
huge external crisis that forced the reforms of Phase III.

- loss of confidence in the efficacy of growth in reducing poverty[8]
- macro instability, indeed crisis
- pessimism; and therefore
- marginalization of India in world affairs.

I.3 Phase III, Why did the Reforms Happen? The Sources

The full story of why the reforms finally began to happen in 1991, under the minority government of Prime Minister Rao, awaits research: we are still too close to it. But I have some candidates that have a bearing on my speculation as to the prospects of India not reversing the existing reforms and of her continuing to undertake further reforms.

First, 1991 saw India perilously close to declaring bankruptcy as the reserves shrank rapidly towards nothing. A full-blown macroeconomic crisis, developing steadily as the internal budget deficit got out of hand and reliance on external borrowing became unprecedented, was finally at hand. As many have observed for South America, a macroeconomic crisis, where you rush for the lifeline that the Bretton Woods institutions provide, clears your head as well as the prospect of a hanging. It would appear that India, during what I have called Phase II here, had finally come to a turning point where it was more readily manifest than ever that her economic policies could not be allowed to continue unchanged. And so the changes, attempted sporadically in the past, would finally begin in earnest.

However, no Bretton Woods support would have been forthcoming without a dose of conditionality pointing in the same direction. The spread of reforms worldwide, before India was getting to them, meant that the IMF–World Bank conditionality could no longer be plausibly dismissed as ideological; it had been legitimated as a sensible prescription that only reflected what we had all learned in three decades of experience.

---

[8] A number of anti-growth schools of thought developed, including several who argued that, in reality, growth would hurt the poor. I have dissected and rejected their arguments in several writings, chiefly, the Vikram Sarabhai Lecture on 'Poverty and Public Policy', reprinted in the fifth volume of my essays, edited by Douglas Irwin and published by MIT Press, Cambridge Mass., 1991; paperback edition, 1996.

But I suspect that it also reflected a realization by the Prime Minister and his chosen Finance Minister Manmohan Singh, who would spearhead the reforms, that *they* had here an opportunity to make history by putting the economy finally on to a path that many in India now yearned for and which, by all evidence, was bound to work. An India which had played a major role in world affairs in the 1950s was now a marginal player on that very stage, a reflection of her having shot herself in the foot. The most apt historical parallel is with Gorbachev contemplating the decline of the Soviet Union and opting for *perestroika*: the English Sovietologist Archie Brown has recently recorded in his fascinating book on *The Gorbachev Factor* how Gorbachev and Scheverdnadze had discussed that things simply could not go on as they had in the Soviet Union, and that they had to seize the moment.[9]

I should also add that India's élite, including the bureaucracy, also came to realize that there was a growing dissonance between India's traditional claim to respect and attention, and her shrinking ability to command them as her economic policies and failure became more widely known and a subject of derision. As I have remarked earlier, in my 1992 Radhakrishnan Lectures at Oxford, the worst psychological state to be in is to have a superiority complex and an inferior status.

II. THE REFORMS TO DATE AND PROSPECTS

The reforms that have been initiated are many; and they have continued to arrive in many little moves almost continually. But much of importance remains to be done, as T.N. Srinivasan and I argued pointedly in a report that we prepared at Manmohan Singh's request in 1993 and as Vijay Joshi and Ian Little have recently argued brilliantly, and with the unfinished agenda laid out fully, in their 1996 book. Should we condemn the reformers for hastening only slowly?

To some extent, changing India's uniquely damaging policy framework, nourished for over three decades, is a task akin to cleaning up after a typhoon: the task is enormous and cannot be done all at once. It is also hard to double guess politicians beyond

[9] I am indebted to Padma Desai for this observation.

a point when, while they move in the right direction, they claim that they must be allowed to traverse the political minefields in a democracy as *they*, and not we *technocrats*, see fit as far as speed and strategy are concerned. The last time when technocratic full-speed-ahead advice to a reforming government backfired badly was when shock therapy for macro stabilization was prescribed for Russia, with a backlash that gave Russia much political turmoil and little economic progress while returning Jeffrey Sachs unceremoniously to begin a life again at Harvard. I am reminded of his famous line: 'You cannot cross a chasm in two leaps', to which Padma Desai, now the Gladys and Roland Harriman Professor of Comparative Economic Systems at Columbia, replied: 'You cannot cross it in one leap either unless you are Indiana Jones; so you drop a bridge instead'.

Yet governments can indeed be too slow for their own, and their societies', good. My judgement is that the initial speed and scope of reforms in India were just about right. India took very definite and substantial steps towards freeing the economy. By now, the industrial licensing system has been virtually dismantled, current account convertibility is virtually in place, and the astringent attitude to direct foreign investment (DFI) that had led to an incredibly low annual inflow of equity capital of just about US $100 m annually by 1990, has been reversed both in rhetoric and in policy actions.

The early harvest is not yet sumptuous, however, for these reforms need to be further deepened. The current account convertibility still goes hand in hand with wholly muddled thinking that permits nearly all consumer goods to be still subjected to strict import controls on the silly ground that we 'do not need such imports'! The DFI policy, while better, is still far from what is necessary to attract substantial inflows. The Enron affair, where a contract signed with this corporation was reopened with a change in the state government and became a cause célèbre, and the repeatedly reported withdrawals of major firms such as Siemens from the scene and the continuing failure to attract much enhanced inflows of DFI strongly underline the fact that much needs to be done, and fairly quickly, if India is to move effectively into its outward orientation mode nearly a quarter century after the East Asian NIE countries did and about a decade after the other ASEAN NECs have done.

There is some room for optimism since I believe that these dramatic instances will, given India's open democratic system and the undoubted enthusiasm amongst the public for speeding up the reforms, lead to enough pressure from below to weed out the remaining inefficiencies. The greater difficulties lie, however, in the speed at which important residual reforms can-be carried out, now that the Rao government has been replaced by a weak coalition government. The two areas where reforms are necessary and critical, if the outward orientation is to produce growth rates of 9–10 per cent rather than of 6 per cent and if we are to truly reproduce the East Asian miracle (rather than a pale and anaemic copy thereof) a quarter century behind schedule, are (i) the public sector which cries out to be privatized now (but where the ability to deal with the entrenched unions is a major obstacle) and (ii) the ability of firms to extract greater efficiency from the labour force, including the application of changed laws that permit workers to be laid off as necessary, though with appropriate safeguards. In neither area can we confidently expect this coalition government, which has two Communist cabinet members with trade union backgrounds, to bite the bullet. True, the communists in Bengal have shown flexibility in going out to get DFI and talked the talk of 'capitalist roaders'. But what you do when the rules are set by the Centre which you have little part in, so that you must compete for resources in the market place at the state level, is entirely different from what you would do if you are at the Centre making the rules.

On the other hand, one may derive optimism from the fact that the new Finance Minister, Mr Chidambaram, is as committed to reforms as Manmohan Singh; indeed, the two had joined hands in the Rao government as the leading reformers of their time. And the budget he presented this year was a clever one that managed to restore, through tax cuts, a sense of momentum that effectively disguised, for the time being, the lack of progress on the critical aspects of pending reforms.

These pending reforms include not just the issues such as privatization and the removal of labour market inflexibilities which will ensure that growth creates more jobs and revenues to support direct expenditures on social issues, exactly as we contemplated from the earliest period of our systematic thinking at the start of this half century. As Manmohan Singh is aware, and as I argued in my 1992 Radhakrishnan Lectures when highlighting our abysmal overall failure on literacy, we need now to focus clearly on the lessons that can be learnt and translated into promising policy experiments to advance the social agenda. In doing this, I have little doubt that we will have to work with NGOs, using our growing civil society institutions in a shared partnership with government to find and implement the solutions that have largely eluded us.[10]

Thus, the developmental agenda that I see for India as it builds on Manmohan Singh's monumental achievements must reflect the following principles:

- efficiency and growth must be enhanced by the unfinished economic reforms;
- this would amount to a successful implementation of the 'indirect' anti-poverty, 'pull-up' strategy that relieves poverty by providing gainful employment;
- it would also generate resources that must then be increasingly used to sustain, even enhance, the social expenditures, thus supporting the 'direct' anti-poverty strategy;
- social engineering to enhance returns from these expenditures, just as economic liberalization will enhance returns from investments, must be considered an important national priority (while recognizing, that it is a lot harder to agree on what to do here than with economic reforms where we do know what needs to be done);
- the task of this social engineering will inevitably involve a shared partnership with NGOs wherever they operate: the NGOs have the commitment and the micro-knowledge, and governments have the resources, so that the developmental effort rests on the two legs of the 'indirect', or pull-up growth strategy and the 'direct' social expenditure and social-engineering strategy, while resting the latter in turn on two other legs: governmental resources in symbiotic partnership with NGO activity.

[10] This was a theme of the 12th Vikram Sarabhai Memorial Lecture that I gave in 1987 and has been reprinted as Ch. 25 in my fifth volume of collected essays, edited by Douglas Irwin, *Political Economy and International Economics.* MIT Press, Cambridge, Mass., 1991; paperback edition in 1996. Here I also, distinguished for the first time between the 'direct' and the 'indirect' strategies to attack poverty whereas, until then, it was customary among many to treat growth as if it had little to do with poverty amelioration.

2

Development Perspectives: Was there an Alternative to Mahalanobis?

Meghnad Desai[*]

I. Introduction

Without any doubt, Manmohan Singh's finest and most durable contribution was to be the architect and the implementer of the New Economic Policy of 1991, which marked a major and irreversible shift from political/administrative to a market based ethos in Indian economic policy-making. By the wave of a magic wand, as it were, the planners of the previous week became the liberalizers on Monday morning. Unlike Poland, Czechoslovakia, and Russia, where reform brought a complete change of personnel — Balcerowicz, Klaus, and Gaidar for instance — Indian economic policy was turned around by an insider. Not all the insiders agreed about this change by any means. Differences were there and persist, but, Manmohan was not an outsider like Balcerowicz bent on destroying the old system. It was all done in a very Indian fashion, by compromise and consensus rather than conflict and confrontation.

In this essay in his honour, I want to focus on an alternative model of development that was on offer but was not adopted. From the time of the famous blueprint by Mahalanobis submitted to Nehru as a framework for planning, Indian economic theory and policy have been directed away from the market. The academic

* I am grateful to Joanne Hay of the LSE for help in obtaining the sources used for this contribution. I continue to use the older name Bombay rather than Mumbai because that was the name then.

backbone for this revolution was provided by Calcutta. The ISI, Presidency College, the University of Calcutta, and later the Delhi School of Economics, were the recruiting fields for the economists who shaped the framework that Manmohan began to dismantle/ transform in 1991. There was, however, an alternative model of growth that was presented as such by the Bombay economists C.N. Vakil and P.R. Brahmanand. It is thus an alterative that I wish to examine.

II. THE MAHALANOBIS MODEL

The Mahalanobis model is well known. It focused on the need to achieve self-sufficiency in the production of capital goods as the first priority with a view to enhancing the output of consumer goods at a later stage. In the original paper Mahalanobis presented a two and a four sector model with technical coefficients and a growth path. Questions of resource availability, inflation, and employment were neglected. There was some revision in this by the time the Mahalanobis framework became the Second Five Year Plan. The added element was a role accorded to cottage and village industries that were expected to resolve the dual problem of providing employment and economic goods.

Criticisms of the Mahalanobis model and the Draft Plan Frame, for example by the Panel of Economists covered by the Planning Commission were rejected. The framework set Indian economic planning on its set path for the next thirty-five years. This was despite the fact that soon after its launch, the Plan ran into a resource constraint and had to be pruned in 1958. Inflation, especially of foodgrain price, hit the economy in the late 1950s. The Plan's neglect of agriculture (inherited from the Mahalanobis model) became a major problem and remained so through the 1960s. Only the happy accident of the Green Revolution, a combination of Western technology, plus generous price incentives to India's largest private sector (agriculture), removed the foodgrains constraint in the 1970s.

But the policy of priority for the machine goods sector (Dept I in Marxist economics terminology), of restrictions on production by the mechanized consumer goods industries, of self-sufficiency and no imports of foreign equity capital remained. In the 1980s there was a policy of foreign borrowing but on debt rather than equity account. The money so borrowed did not yield high enough returns to be able to make the debt servicing affordable. The economy hit the rocks in 1991.

Through the thirty-five years 1956–91, employment growth has remained sluggish and output growth, despite the pick up in the 1980s, has been low by international standards. Low output and employment growth have led to a persistence of poverty in India while countries such as Indonesia and Malaysia, to say nothing of the Asian Tigers, have done better. Could India have done better?

III. THE BOMBAY ALTERNATIVE

Right from the outset, the two Bombay economists C.N. Vakil and P.R. Brahmanand criticized the Second Plan and offered an alternative. Their model was not as elegant and rigorous as the Mahalanobis one. Their book, *Planning for an Expanding Economy: Accumulation, Employment and Technical Progress in Underdeveloped Countries* (*PFE* hereafter), offered an account of the recent developments in the Indian economy (Part I), a detailed examination of the projections and assumptions of the second Plan (Part II), and the Alternative (Part III).

The book purported to base its alternative on a different theoretical basis more suited to the conditions of an underdeveloped economy. The more general theoretical critique is not my concern here though it may have detracted from the book's immediate message. There was also no attempt made to present a set of targets or sectoral investment allocations. The emphasis was on putting together an alternative vision of how the Indian economy worked and how it could be made to grow faster.

The basic idea was that the Indian economy was characterized by disguised unemployment that was different in character from that in classical or Keynesian theories which was more suited for developed countries. The disguised unemployed had to be maintained even though at a fraction of the real wage of the productive worker. This feeding of the disguised unemployed represented a pool of saving. The task was to transfer these disguised unemployed to more productive work in the investment sector.

Ideas of surplus labour had suddenly come into vogue in the early 1950s. Nurkse had written his book on this topic in 1953 and Lewis' classic article was published in 1954. [The Bombay authors quote Nurkse but do not cite Lewis]. Lewis's model however, assumed that in moving surplus labour from agriculture to industry, there would be no problem of wage goods as in some sense these migrants will carry their 'lunch packets' with them. [Nurkse, 1953; Lewis, 1954].

The Bombay model starts by assuming that while productive workers get paid a wage, w, the disguised unemployed get only a fraction, say, λw. The surplus in the wage goods sector (food producing agriculture) is thus effectively reduced by the number of the disguised unemployed time λw. But if these people are to be redeployed to other activities and be productively employed, the missing fraction $(1 - \lambda)$ of the wage has to be found. For each unit of wage good produced, the number of disguised unemployed who are transferable is obviously $(1 - \lambda)^{-1}$.

If we allow for higher consumption on the farms, this multiplier has to be modified. It is not obvious of course that consumption will rise if the farms were organized on capitalist lines and the employed workers were already receiving their marginal product. (This is the implicit assumption in the Table 'The Impact of Disguised Unemployment on PFE', p. 205.) If the farms are organized according to Chayanov principles, there will be no difference between the consumption of the productive workers and the disguised unemployed. But assume that the wage of stay-on-farm workers goes up by a proportion μ of the prevailing wage, and that c is their marginal propensity to consume, then the multiplier is:

$$M = [(1 - \lambda) + \mu c]^{-1} \qquad (1)$$

Clearly, it is the difference $(\lambda - \mu c)$ which is crucial to the size of the multiplier (a similar formula is given in PFE, p. 263, but assuming $\mu = \lambda$).

The authors were not hopeful of extra wage goods output. They rely instead on a forced savings argument. This has echoes of the debate in the Soviet Union in the 1920s concerning Preobrazhensky's ideas. The authors do not estimate the likely size of forced savings, but they deploy the wage goods multiplier further in the argument by saying that if projects are chosen with a high output investment ratio as well as a low ratio of wage costs to output, rapid accumulation can be achieved. They call the combination of the output–investment ratio and the profit–output ratio, the investment net revenue ratio. Call this r. Then

If we multiply the investment net revenue ratio by the value of the consumption multiplier, we get the value of the *accumulation coefficient*. Accumulation increases at the rate given by the value of the *accumulation coefficient*. If the investment net revenue ratio is 10 per cent, and the value of the consumption multiplier is 2, accumulation will grow at the rate of 20 per cent. [PFE, p. 242.]

The idea here is that the labour released from agriculture will be engaged in simple investment schemes where, without additional need for equipment, employment will turn into output. The analysis is not transparent here. A 'marginal capital–labour ratio' (dk/dl) equal to unity is needed somewhere in the argument to link up the wage goods/consumption multiplier that translates investment into profits. If we assume, Cambridge fashion, that all profits are invested we get:

$$\Delta K = (\pi/Y)\ (Y/I)\ (dK/dL)\ M\Delta s \qquad (2)$$

Here Δs is the forced savings. $M(= dL/dQ)$ is the multiplier. The first term on the r.h.s. is the profit–output ratio and the second the output–investment ratio, together forming the investment–net revenue ratio. Thus $M\Delta s$ number of workers released from agriculture at the unit marginal capital–labour ratio translates into investment I, which then works up to π. Of course (dK/dL), is not so much 'marginal capital–labour ratio' as the productivity of labour in terms of capital goods that constitute investment. Each worker fully fed constitutes equivalently one unit of investment.

Details apart, the basic idea of *PFE* is that unemployment in India was not due to shortage of capital, in the form of machine goods, but due to the shortage of wage goods. If low capital intensity, high yield projects were to be selected, employment, output, and accumulation could be expanded from the bottom up as it were. Full employment was not impossible.

IV. Some Political Economy

The contrast between the two approaches could not be greater. The Mahalanobis framework draft had neglected employment and the issue of inflation arising from shortages of consumer goods.

It was, after all, a version of the Feldman model with priority for Dept I. As against this, the Vakil–Brahmanand plan was the equivalent of the Bukharin NEP strategy.[1] To counter criticism from all quarters, the Second Five Year Plan document deviated from the Mahalanobis framework, but only by sweeping the problem under the carpet. It was said that the cottage and village industry sectors would be responsible for supplying the non-agricultural wage goods. Since these were labour intensive, i.e. low productivity, by a miracle the problem of employment was also thereby solved. This assertion does not bear serious examination and subsequent development showed its hollowness (Desai, 1992).

The mid-1950s were heady days when Nehru persuaded the Congress Party to accept the 'Socialist Pattern of Society' as its aim. There was also the growing friendship with the Soviet Union. Things Soviet were in fashion. In any battle between a machine goods oriented Feldman–Stalin Plan against a consumer goods oriented Bukharin Plan, victory was guaranteed for the former. Bombay lost. The opposition between Bombay and Calcutta was not so much Plan versus Market but about an employment versus an accumulation strategy. The Second Plan wanted rapid industrialization via the machine sector to achieve self-sufficient growth as soon as possible. Alternative strategies were suspect because they envisaged an open economy, dependent on indefinite imports of capital goods.

V. A COUNTER-FACTUAL QUESTION

Their model was not as fully worked as Mahalanobis's. But once having demonstrated that surplus labour could be mobilized as an investible resource by providing it with additional wage goods, the Bombay authors had done their work. It would have been possible, given the will, for the Planning Commission to have utilized this insight. It would have meant investing more in agriculture to increase the supply of food-grains rather than rely on forced savings. It would have meant redeploying surplus labour in rural infrastructural schemes and some small agro–industrial enterprises. In the industrial sector, it would have meant expanding the

---

[1] For a simple analytical presentation of the Feldman model with Dept I priority and the Bukharin alternative with Dept II priority, see Desai (1979), Ch. 16.

manufactured consumer goods sector but with an eye on exports as well as for home consumption. It would have meant postponing or giving low priority to the machine goods industry.

Could India have tried the Vakil–Brahmananda path? This is an interesting counter-factual question of Indian economic history. It meant opting for employment and output growth but also a continued reliance on imports of capital goods.

A possible constraint could have been foreign exchange, but this would hardly have been peculiar to this strategy. The Second Five Year Plan ran into this constraint by 1958. Sterling balances were exhausted and foreign aid became necessary. Could the same have happened to the Bombay strategy? Perhaps not, and that for the following reasons. On the one hand, the capital goods to be imported were for consumer goods' industries, postponing the build-up of these industries. This capital would have been quicker yielding than was the case in the Mahalanobis model. On the other hand, there were export possibilities open in the Bombay strategy. This would have relaxed the foreign exchange constraint. Highly capital intensive, excess capacity creating investment would certainly have been avoided and, indeed, India could have received foreign investments. Thus output and employment growth could have been faster than was actually the case.

All this is conjecture. In the 1950s, India wanted self-sufficiency, no foreign investments, and rapid industrialization. It was steel mills rather than textile factories that were taken to be the proud symbols of growth. It was the urban intelligentsia who had these visions, and they were in power. They not only rejected laissez-faire which in any event had little support in India, but also dismissed all alternative development paths as not being socialist enough. [I recall how, in the debate about the size of the Third Five Year Plan during the late 1950s, we thought of anyone advocating a higher share for agriculture as more or less right wing, an agent of the US, etc. Naïve perhaps, but very much the fashion of the day.]

VI. Conclusion

The price of self-sufficiency was paid for in terms of relatively low growth of per capita income and of employment. In the 1950s perhaps this policy choice could be attributed to prevailing economic theory and the ideology of left nationalism. But India had another opportunity during the 1970s when many countries switched from an import substitution to an export promotion strategy. But even then India refused to switch. More foreign borrowing was pursued in the 1980s, but without a change in the economic structure and incentives. This policy led to the foreign debt crisis of 1991 since the foreign exchange had been borrowed as debt rather than equity and was frittered away in low yield projects (Desai, 1993). Thus, after having avoided the strategy in the 1950s, or even in the 1970s when the Asian Tigers began exploring export-oriented growth, India has finally come face to face with the alternative strategy. This time the result will be growth of output and employment, and the improvement of living standards and reduction of poverty rather than self-sufficiency in Dept I. It is to Manmohan Singh's credit that India has a second chance.

REFERENCES

Desai, M. (1979): *Marxian Economics* (Oxford: Blackwell).
—— (1992): 'Is There Life after Mahalanobis? The Political Economy of India's New Economic Policy', *The Indian Economic Review*, Special Number in Memory of Sukhamoy Chakravarty, pp. 155–64.
—— (1993): 'Capitalism, Socialism and India's Economic Development', EXIM Bank Lecture.
Lewis, W.A. (1954): 'Economic Development with Unlimited Supplies of Labour', Manchester School, vol. 2, May, pp. 139–91.
Nurkse, R. (1953): *Problems of Capital Formation in Underdeveloped Countries* (Oxford: Blackwell).
Vakil, C.N. and P.R. Brahmanand (1956): *Planning for an Expanding Economy* (Bombay: Vora & Co).

3

Development, Inflation, and Monetary Policy

*C. Rangarajan**

In his professional life, the major concern of Dr Manmohan Singh had been with the issues connected with economic growth and development. However, anyone dealing with the problems of growth in developing economies cannot ignore the problem of inflation at one time or another. Dr Manmohan Singh in fact had a major role to play in evolving a package of measures for controlling inflation in early 1970s when the inflation rate had crossed the level of 20 per cent in two successive years. However, Dr Manmohan Singh's thoughts on price stability and the conduct of monetary policy began to crystallize only after he took over as the Governor of Reserve Bank of India in 1982. These found fuller expression when as Finance Minister, he had to grapple with the problems of stability in the wake of the crisis that erupted in 1991. One of his first tasks after becoming Governor was to appoint a Committee to Review the Working of the Monetary System under the Chairmanship of the distinguished economist Prof Sukhamoy Chakravarty. It was Dr Manmohan Singh who drew attention to the fact that inflation hit hard the poor as they possessed no hedges against inflation. That was why he at one time described inflation control as the best anti-poverty programme. As Finance Minister, he made it clear that the major objective of monetary policy should be the control of inflation. He called it the Central Bank's *dharma*. He felt that the greatest contribution to growth that monetary policy could make was to ensure a reasonable degree of price stability. He was

* The author is grateful to M.S. Mohanty for his generous assistance in the preparation of this contribution.

never apologetic about the policies that were pursued in 1995–6 to bring down the inflation rate after it had crossed the double digit level in the previous two years.

Dr Manmohan Singh's contribution to India's growth process are varied and many. The stance of economic policy underwent a fundamental change in 1991 and the results of this change are now before everyone to see. We are today comfortable with the idea of achieving a growth rate of 7.0 per cent and above when hardly a decade ago a growth rate of 5.5 per cent to 6.0 per cent was considered to be the best we could realize. This paper addresses one aspect of India's economic policy which of late has received the increasing attention of Dr Manmohan Singh, namely price stability and its implications for the conduct of monetary policy.

Regulation of money supply in order to secure the maintenance of internal and external value of the national currency has been the principal concern of central banks. Even as central banks the world over have been engaged in managing this crucial task, the objectives and conduct of monetary policy have in recent years come under intense public discussion and scrutiny. At the very base of the debate is the question: what should constitute the objectives of monetary policy? Should price stability be the sole objective or should the central bank seek to achieve some combination of growth and price stability. The question, in essence, presupposes a possible trade-off between price stability and growth, if not in the long run, at least in the short run. The belief that the development process involves a choice between faster growth and low inflation was entrenched in the experiences of developed countries in the 1940s and 1950s which seemed to vindicate the Keynesian strategy of demand-led growth, under the strong assumptions of wage–price rigidity and 'money illusion'. However, the persistence of high inflation and low growth in the 1970s brought about a profound change in the approach to economic policy, and the policy focus in the developed economies tilted towards maintenance of price stability with the aid of monetary policy.

A similar trend is also discernible in developing economies. Much of the early literature on development economics focused on real factors such as savings, investment, and technology, as main-springs of growth. Very little attention was paid to the financial system as a contributory factor to economic growth. Indeed, many writers felt that inflation was endemic in the process of economic growth and was accordingly treated more as a consequence of structural imbalance than as a monetary phenomenon. However, with accumulated evidence, it became clear that any process of economic growth in which monetary expansion was disregarded led to inflationary pressures with a consequent adverse impact on economic growth.

The turnaround in thinking on the macroeconomic policy issues concerning development strategies is based on pragmatic considerations of what is achievable and how best this can be achieved using various policy instruments. With regard to inflation control and development strategy, three facts stand out as clear guideposts of recent thinking. First, the experience of a prolonged period of 'stagflation' in both developed and developing economies in the 1970s raised doubts about the efficacy of the policy to promote growth through monetary expansion and in the process the sustainability of the economic system. The hardening of interest rates and wage rates in the face of monetary expansion clearly demonstrated the growing role of inflation expectations in the economic system and the breakdown of the inverse relation between growth and price stability, raising a fundamental question regarding the role of money in the process of economic growth. Second, there has been a growing realization that the long run growth constraints in economies are largely an outcome of the structural rigidities in the economic system that distort incentives and price signals and promote inefficiency. Third, with most countries clearly preferring to pursue structural reforms to promote efficiency and competitiveness in their economies, the hidden costs of inflation and their distortionary impact on growth have attracted greater attention. The commitment to maintain low inflation essentially implies making the future less uncertain for investors and creating a policy environment that builds confidence in the economy and its credibility.

As a consequence, several industrial countries in recent years have shown a clear preference for maintenance of price stability and moving into an inflation rate of no more than 3 per cent per anum. In these countries, there has been a distinct recognition of what monetary policy can and cannot do, and how multiple objectives can at times lead to counter-productive results. Yet the controversy is far from over. This is more so in the case of developing countries that have opted to pursue policies which more often than not has meant shifting goals between growth and inflation control.

The rest of this contribution is organized in three sections. Section I discusses the role of money in the development process and draws a few theoretical perspectives on the growth–inflation relationship. Section II presents some empirical evidence on the impact of inflation on growth in the cross-country and Indian context. Section III deals with the stance of monetary policy in India.

I. MONEY AND THE DEVELOPMENT PROCESS: THEORETICAL PERSPECTIVES

Much of the monetary policy debate today centres around the age old theoretical controversy about what money can do to promote economic activity, and whether it has any role at all in achieving high economic growth. In the literature, the role of money in the development process has been discussed in two important contexts, i.e. the stabilization of economic activity and promotion of growth. On both these aspects, theoretical perspectives differ widely across various schools of thought.

Historically, it is the stabilization objective of monetary policy that generated heated controversies in the industrially developed economies, where sustaining full-employment output had been a major concern of macroeconomic policy. The precise nature of this debate relates to whether money can be considered neutral in relation to real economic variables, familiarly known as the 'money neutrality' proposition. In contrast, in the context of promoting economic growth, money is often viewed as an essential requirement in generating resources to enable saving-constrained economies to achieve higher levels of domestic investment.

I.1 The Money Neutrality Proposition

Hardly any branch of economic literature is as divided as that concerning the money neutrality proposition. The central question is: how does money influence real variables such as employment and output? Or, do real variables remain invariant to monetary fluctuations in the economy? Answering this question would require an understanding of the process of economic growth itself and the forces that bring about equilibrium in the real economy. Most growth theories are non-monetary in nature. They assume growth to depend on such real factors as capital accumulation, population, technology, and innovation. In the long run it is technology and innovation that have a special role in sustaining growth in an economy. Clearly, in this construct, money has no role in either initiating or sustaining the growth process.

Despite the money neutrality assumption in growth theories, economic research and public policy have scarcely supported this proposition as true. Indeed, as Blanchard (1990) observes in his opening remark in his survey paper on money and output:

Much of research on economic fluctuations has focused on the effects of nominal money on output. This is not because money is the major source of movements in output; it is not. Rather it is because economic theory does not lead us to expect such effects. Indeed, it holds that, with flexible prices money should be approximately neutral, with changes in nominal money being reflected in nominal prices rather than in output.

The perception of money neutrality changed substantially in the twentieth century as a consequence of the influential writings of Wicksell (1907), Irving Fisher (1920), Keynes (1936), Haberler (1952) and Tobin (1965). The reasoning that money is non-neutral and could have significant influences on real variables received support from two angles: first, it was recognized that the financial system in general and money supply in particular caused sustained, and at times accentuated, business cycles; and second, money supply had an influence on interest rates which in turn had an impact on capital accumulation. Fisher's account of the behaviour of the US economy and the substantial connection between the cyclical variations in money supply and real economic activity laid the base for discretionary monetary policy to moderate business fluctuations. The key assumption in Fisher's analysis was the slow adjustment of interest rates to monetary changes, which allowed profits and investment to rise or fall in accordance with monetary expansion or contraction. Furthermore, an explicit recognition by Wicksell that monetary impulses cause the market interest rate to fluctuate around the 'natural' interest rate due to a significant presence of 'money illusion' became an important factor in the stabilization attempts in various countries. However, the link with money was found to hold good only in the short run.

This was because of the inherent slow adjustment of wages and interest rate to their long-run values. While this provided the logic behind non-neutrality of money in the short run, the classical and neoclassical economists assumed that in the long run, with full adjustment of wages and interest rates, money was neutral in relation to real variables. As a logical corollary, therefore, the classical policy discussion centred around rules rather than discretionary policy. The rule based monetary policy saw its zenith during the days of gold standard which accepted the 'law of one price' as a standard objective. This, in effect, implied strict observance of rules in the growth of money supply.

Anchoring monetary growth to supply of gold prevented governments from attempting to achieve real growth or other objectives by creating inflation. The remarkable feature of this strict rule-based policy was the prevalence of virtual price stability in all the major industrial countries for a very long period up to the Second World War, apart of course from the occasional war period outbursts in inflation. Price data collected by the British historians Sir Henry Phelps-Brown and Sheila Hopkins indicated that between 1711 and 1931 the price level in Britain rose by only 30 per cent (Bootle, 1997). However, faith in the gold standard and the rigid rules governing money supply changed drastically as economic conditions changed, first the great depression and later the post-Second World War boom. As Roger Bootle observed (1997) in his recent research on the history of inflation in major countries, ' . . . the discipline afforded by the Gold Standard was not imposed but self-imposed, because of a set of beliefs about the way the economy worked. And in the end, it was a change in that set of beliefs that killed it.'

I.2   The Keynesian Revolution:
The Trade-off Between Growth and Price Stability

The neutrality proposition central to the classical and neoclassical view on money and output underwent a change in the Keynesian analysis. This change had three important effects on public policy discussion during the period between the 1950s and 1960s. First, Keynesians accepted the classical proposition that employment is dependent on real wages, but with an added assumption that nominal wages are more rigid than prices that are themselves assumed to be sticky. A logical consequence of this assumption is that an increase in money supply will lead to an increase in the price level and decrease in real wages, and bring about an improvement in real economic activity over the underemployment level. This significantly introduced non-neutrality of money and gave rise to an apparent trade-off between price stability and growth. Second, although classical and neoclassical economists also assumed slow adjustment of wages and prices to monetary impulses, implying short-run non-neutrality of money, this was largely viewed as a temporary departure from the equilibrium position, which is determined by long-run forces unrelated to money. While Keynesian analysis was entirely focused on short-run consequences, the neutrality view was abandoned as a guide to public policy since the long run was conceived of as a succession of short runs. The Phillips curve, depicting the inverse relationship between unemployment and wage inflation, provided the empirical basis for the non-neutrality proposition of the Keynesian school. Third, the Keynesian revolution also brought about a directional change in the thinking on monetary policy. Emphasis shifted from a rule-based policy of monetary growth to the discretionary policy initiatives by the central banks to offset specific events causing business fluctuations. The liquidity preference hypothesis implied that monetary policy can affect interest rates and influence investment decisions, except when the economy fell into a 'liquidity trap'. This is a special case of money-neutrality in the Keynesian literature, which also led to the ascendancy of fiscal policy in the demand management of the economy through changes in the tax and expenditure policies in the government budget.

The validity of Keynesian economics came under severe criticism by the 1970s, when inflation rates in all the major countries touched their historical highs, and unemployment rates increased to very high levels, and remained stubborn for a prolonged period of time. In the US the average rate of increase in the consumer price index reached 7.1 per cent in the 1970s and 5.6 per cent in the 1980s, in comparison to 2.8 per cent in the 1960s and 2.1 per cent in the 1950s. In the UK the average inflation rate touched 12.6 per cent in the 1970s and stayed around 7 to 9 per cent in France and Canada. This became a sufficient reason for a counter-revolution in the thinking on the conduct of monetary policy. As noted by Burnner and Meltzer (1993), Keynesian analysis came under attack in three stages. First, the view that sustained high money growth relative to output is a sufficient condition to cause inflation, and that discretionary monetary policy accentuated cyclical expansions and contractions as money growth tended to vary pro-cyclically during some business fluctuations, began to take root. Strong evidence in favour of this contention was produced by Friedman and Schwartz (1963) in their survey of monetary history in the US.

In the second stage of attack, the discussion was focused on the Phillips curve that had earlier provided basic empirical support for the Keynesian contention that there existed a permanent trade-off between unemployment and inflation. The Phillips curve analysis was found not only to be severely flawed theoretically, but also less evident empirically in the subsequent period (Friedman, 1968 and 1970 and Phelps, 1967).

The third stage of criticism of Keynesian analysis began with the rational expectations revolution that revived interest in the money-neutrality proposition and provided a new direction to monetary policy formulation. Individuals form their expectation on the basis of rational judgement in a forward looking framework, which means that, apart from random events, people's expectation about the future fully reflect the actual events. An implication of this theory is that since expected events are the same as actual events, discretionary policies are ineffective in influencing real economic variables — a powerful idea that theoretically strengthened the money-neutrality proposition, even if it did not make it entirely convincing. The rational expectation hypothesis implies strict adherence to monetary policy rules, since anticipated monetary changes will lead to proportionate changes in nominal variables without affecting real economic activity.

While economists such as Friedman, Phelps, and Lucas have challenged the basic microeconomic underpinning of the wage–price mechanism that leads to the possibility of a trade-off between price stability and growth, the theoretical debate is far from settled. There is however a general recognition of the position that while anticipated inflation does not affect real economic activity, unanticipated monetary shocks can have positive effects on output. However, given the long run flexibility of the labour market and financial market to changes in prices, monetary shocks may have an output effect only in the short run. In other words, in the long run, repeated monetary shocks to bring about a sustained improvement in growth will lead to ever-accelerating levels of inflation. There is, therefore, a general consensus that sustained money supply growth in the long run will show up on prices rather than on any meaningful improvement in output.

Much of the discussion on the trade-off between employment and inflation has centred around the effect on output and demand of changes in real wages arising from inflation. However, in the context of developing economies which have a large unutilized potential of real resources,.but inadequate financial systems and external financing constraints, the impact of monetary policy on output may be seen not only through the wage–price mechanism, but also through credit availability. The demand for credit from the banking system reflects the gap between the potential investments of firms and the availability of internal funds to meet such financing needs. Monetary policy can therefore, affect the potential output by influencing the credit demand through the interest rate route as well as by meeting a part of such demand by expanding credit. The credit channel of monetary policy transmission is believed to be of a special significance for growth, when monetary policy changes create balance sheet effects for firms, such as net cash flow or asset price impacts (Bernanke and Gertler, 1995). While there is no doubt that credit forms an important input in the production system, the question of supply of such credit through money creation raises the issue of the sustainability of such financing from the point of view of its implications for inflation.

I.3 Developing Country Case — The Inflation Tax Argument

In the developing country context, the trade-off debate generally centres on the fiscal arguments relating to inflation. The narrow base of conventional taxes, and the difficulty in accessing the tax base in these countries, often give rise to·a need to explore alternative ways of mobilizing revenue to finance public sector developmental projects. This generally takes the form of an inflation tax, which is a tax imposed by inflation on currency and other non-interest earning money holdings of people. It may be noted that, in terms of distortionary costs to the economy, conventional taxes are a much more efficient way of mobilizing revenue than the inflation tax, since the welfare costs are higher in the latter case than the former. The revenue yields of the inflation tax depends on the nature of the demand for real money balances and its sensitivity to changes in the price level. High inflation rates strengthen people's motives to economize on cash balances, and encourage them to switch over to other forms of financial and physical assets. As the inflation rate increases, while revenue from a given stock of real money balance is higher, there is an adverse effect on revenue that stems from the shrinkage in the base of the inflation tax itself. While theoretically the effect of inflation tax on revenue is ambiguous, the analysis leads to a general inference that the higher the elasticity of real money demand to inflation the lower is the potential additional revenue from an increase in the inflation rate.

I.4 Costs of Inflation

Inflating the economy on a continuous basis for a hoped for additional gain in output provides only a partial view of 'trade-off'. It is also important to evaluate the economic and social costs of inflation, which constitute yet another crucial aspect of 'trade-off' (Fischer, 1994). Inflation affects virtually every aspect of economic life, although the degree with which such effects are felt depends on the severity of inflation itself and the availability of inflation protection measures. The trade-off argument considered only the wage cost aspect of production decisions. A relevant question however is: what other factors influence production decisions and how does inflation influence productivity growth? These questions address the long-run impacts of inflation on growth and not the short run trade-off implied by the Philips curve. It is instructive to list here a few adverse consequences of inflation on production decisions (Huizinga, 1993 and Jarrett and Selody, 1982). First, high rates of inflation create uncertainty about future inflation and adversely affect production decisions. This is a major source of distortion in the allocation of resources in the economy. Second, inflation reduces the information content of price signals and distorts relative price signals through which resources are allocated among different industries. Third, inflation uncertainty encourages substitution of nominal assets into real assets, and may shorten the optimal contract length. Firms are discouraged from undertaking long run contracts, which increases contracting costs and adversely affects investment prospects. Fourth, increased inflation uncertainty is observed to be associated with accumulation of unproductive inventories and build up of buffer stocks by firms. Finally, in the presence of non-neutral tax laws, inflation adversely affects after-tax profits, which acts as a disincentive for capital accumulation in the economy.

A significant cost of inflation in the context of developing countries relates to the adverse implications of inflation uncertainty on the financial system and the growth of domestic savings. Increased inflation uncertainty is associated with high inflation risk premia in the financial markets, overshooting of real interest rates, and increased chances of systemic risk for the financial system. A stable price environment is particularly important in the early stages of financial liberalization, for keeping the interest rate risks under control which might dampen further liberalization efforts. It is also important to evaluate the cost and benefit of price stability from the viewpoint of incentives for domestic savings. Although, the theoretical and empirical literature is inconclusive about the direction of impact of inflation on savings, intuitively there is a significant negative impact in the presence of uncertainty about future changes in the price level. An uncertain price environment encourages savers to move away from financial assets that are inadequately protected from inflation to real assets and other forms of hedging which have a dampening impact on financial intermediation in the economy.

There is also a fiscal cost of inflation, which must be weighed against the revenue motives behind the inflation tax. Inflation affects fiscal balance in several ways. It adversely affects fiscal deficit when elasticity of expenditure to inflation is higher than that of revenue. A more significant impact of inflation arises from its effect on interest rates and the dynamic sustainability of a fiscal situation. High rates of inflation signal the weak resolve to control inflation and imply higher expected inflation in future. This gives rise to downward rigidity in nominal interest and leads to a high debt service burden on the budget, thus reducing the manoeuverability of fiscal management.

Apart from these economic costs, inflation has much wider social implications in developing economies, like India on account of its adverse impact on the real income of the poor, who are largely unprotected from price rise. The adverse distributional implications of even a moderate inflation is significantly high in India in comparison to the output gains of inflation. This underscores the importance of the social dividends of a low and stable price environment, which have a far greater ramification than the perceived growth benefits of inflation.

II. INFLATION AND GROWTH: EMPIRICAL EVIDENCE

Empirical evidence in the cross-country framework generally supports the contention that a high and volatile inflationary environment adversely affects capital accumulation and productivity growth and brings down the growth potential in the economy. What is of significance is that the adverse impact of inflation on growth tends to rise at a non-linear rate with the increasing rates of inflation.

Experiences of inflation and growth performance in recent times, both in the case of developed and developing countries, suggest that a steady improvement in the economic condition in many of these countries was accompanied by significant achievement in the area of price stability. Most, if not all, developed countries in the 1990s so far have moved over to an inflation rate range of two to four per cent, while their economic growth has shown progressive recovery to around three per cent from the recessionary conditions that prevailed during the 1980s and the early part of 1990s. It needs to be recognized, however, that the growth potential in developed economies is limited and their pursuit of price stability is largely driven by the objectives of stabilizing output around potential level and of the compulsions of the open economy, particularly in maintaining and improving the external competitiveness of their economies. A comparison of inflation and growth performance of developing countries in the 1990s so far indicates that by and large the countries which grew at a faster rate during this period are those that kept a tight control on inflation (Table 3.1). For example, the six fastest growing countries in this decade so far, namely China, Thailand, Malaysia, Singapore, Korea, and Indonesia showed a mean growth rate of 8.4 per cent during the period 1990–4 with a mean inflation rate of about 6.0 per cent. Among these, the consistently high performing economies such as Malaysia, Singapore and Thailand,

TABLE 3.1
INFLATION AND REAL GDP GROWTH IN SELECTED COUNTRIES

	Real GDP growth			Inflation rate		
	Average 1970–9	Average 1980–9	Average 1990–4	Average 1970–9	Average 1980–9	Average 1990–4
Developing Countries						
China	7.6	9.4	10.2	1.8	13.7	9.2
Ghana	1.8	2.2	3.5	38.8	13.6	23.1
Kenya	6.6	4.3	1.8	10.9	12.7	27.9
India	3.6	6.0	6.1	8.6	12.6	10.5
Chile	2.2	3.3	6.4	174.5	12.4	17.5
Pakistan	3.7	6.6	4.7	11.8	12.1	8.8
Mexico	6.5	2.0	3.0	14.7	12.0	16.3
Israel	17.1	3.2	5.8	32.5	10.7	14.3
Korea	9.4	8.1	7.6	15.2	8.3	7.0
Indonesia	7.8	5.8	6.9	16.9	8.2	8.9
Mauritius	6.3	6.2	3.1	11.0	8.2	8.6
Fiji	5.9	2.1	1.3	10.6	8.1	5.1
Jordan	4.4	3.6	6.1	10.8	8.2	7.3
Malaysia	8.1	5.8	8.6	5.5	8.2	3.8
Singapore	9.5	7.3	8.3	5.9	8.3	2.9
Thailand	7.4	7.3	8.9	8.0	8.4	4.9
Developed Countries						
Spain	4.3	2.3	0.1	14.39	10.25	5.6
USA	3.2	2.6	2.3	7.09	5.55	3.6
Netherlands	3.4	2.1	1.9	7.08	2.86	2.8
Norway	4.6	2.5	3.5	8.38	8.35	2.7
France	3.7	2.4	1.1	8.9	7.38	2.6
Sweden	2.5	2.3	–0.3	8.56	7.93	5.8
Australia	3.8	3.2	2.7	9.84	8.41	3.0
Austria	4.0	2.2	2.0	6.1	3.83	3.4
Denmark	2.5	1.9	1.8	9.29	6.71	2.1
UK	2.4	2.4	0.8	12.63	7.44	4.6
Germany	3.1	1.9	2.6	4.88	2.91	3.5
Newzealand	2.3	2.3	1.3	11.46	11.86	2.5
Canada	4.7	3.1	1.0	7.38	6.51	2.8
Ireland	4.5	3.5	4.7	12.75	9.33	2.7

showed inflation rates comparable to those of developed economies while their growth rate ranged from 8 to 9 per cent. These casual observations point to the fact that a reduction in inflation rate to the range of 5 to 6 per cent would not imply adverse consequences on growth; rather it could eventually help accelerate it in the medium to long run period.

Empirical research on inflation and growth linkage in the cross-country framework, though not conclusive, leads to a general finding that inflation adversely affects growth in the long run and that this impact is stronger beyond a threshold inflation rate. Fischer's (1993, 1994) study of inflation and growth performance of a large number of countries based on panel regression reports that 'The evidence points strongly to a predominantly negative longterm relationship between growth and inflation'. The estimates presented by Fischer show that a ten percentage point increase in inflation rate results in 0.4 per cent decline in output growth per annum, and 0.18 per cent decline in productivity growth. Furthermore, using spline regression and excluding some cases of extreme inflation, Fisher argues that the negative effects of inflation on growth are higher at high rather than low rates of inflation. The contention that high inflation rates have adverse effects on growth is also vindicated by some other recent studies. For example, Bruno (1995), based on a World Bank study, shows that while relatively moderate inflation may not imply immediate adverse effects on output, but eventually this may lead to higher inflation and lower growth. This study, as well as Fischer's paper, raises an important question whether there could be a significant structural break in the relation between inflation and growth beyond which adverse effects of inflation on growth tends to dominate the positive effects. The estimates presented by Sarel (1996) show that this threshold inflation rate is close to 8 per cent, beyond which adverse effects of inflation on output tend to rise.

Most studies that examined the cross-country linkage between inflation and growth suffer from an important limitation in that these do not differentiate the country specific characteristics which could be an important source of heterogeneity, blurring the underlying relation between inflation and growth. Furthermore, empirical regressions on inflation and growth need to be interpreted with caution due to the problem of endogeniety inherent in the relationship between these two variables. An adverse supply shock, while it affects growth, is also likely to increase inflation. Barro (1995) while correcting for these limitations, reinforces the results of earlier studies that inflation is negatively associated with growth. His estimates like Fisher's suggest that an increase in the inflation rate of 10 percentage points in each year during the period 1960–90 on the average resulted in a decrease in per capita real GDP growth by 0.2–0.3 percentage points per annum and a decline in the investment ratio to GDP by 0.4 to 0.6 percentage points. He shows that over a long time period of 30 years, a 10 percentage point permanent increase in the inflation rate, is estimated to bring down the level of real GDP by 4 to 7 per cent. In sum, the international evidence on the relationship between inflation and growth largely suggests that inflation beyond a threshold rate has significant adverse implications for growth, and this makes a clear case for price stability to promote growth. But what the appropriate inflation threshold is, beyond which costs tend to exceed benefits, needs to be estimated for each country separately. Nevertheless, people worry about even moderate inflation levels because, if not held in check, a little inflation can lead to higher inflation and eventually affect growth.

II.1 Evidence in the Indian Context

By the standards of some of the high inflation Latin American countries, inflation in India, as measured by the wholesale price index (average basis) has remained fairly low. This is evident from the fact that during the period 1950–1 to 1989–90, the average rate of increase in the WPI was at 6.3 per cent per annum. During 1990–1 to 1995–6 the average inflation rate increased to 10.7 per cent due to two high inflation years in this period, i.e. 1991–2 and 1994–5. The trends in inflation over the past two decades show that during the 1970s and the 1980s the average inflation rate remained at about 8 to 9 per cent per anum.

Table 3.2 presents data on both the annual and three-year moving average trends in real GDP growth, inflation and money supply growth in India from 1970–1 to 1995–6. The table suggests that while there has been a large year-to-year variation in all the three variables, whenever there was a large increase in the money supply, or a supply shock that affected output, the inflation rate generally accelerated in that year or in the following few years.

TABLE 3.2
MONEY SUPPLY, INFLATION AND GROWTH:
1970–1 TO 1995–6

(Per cent)

Year	Growth rates			Moving average (3–year)		
	Real GDP	Inflation (WPI)	Money supply	Real GDP growth	Inflation (WPI)	Money supply growth
1970–1	5.01	5.50	13.39	4.18	4.97	13.67
1971–2	1.01	5.60	15.20	1.90	7.05	15.63
1972–3	−0.31	10.04	18.30	1.75	11.95	16.97
1973–4	4.55	20.21	17.40	1.80	18.49	15.53
1974–5	1.16	25.21	10.90	4.90	14.78	14.43
1975–6	9.00	−1.09	15.00	3.80	8.73	16.50
1976–7	1.25	2.08	23.60	5.91	2.09	19.00
1977–8	7.47	5.29	18.40	4.74	2.46	21.30
1978–9	5.50	0.00	21.90	2.59	7.46	19.33
1979–80	−5.20	17.10	17.70	2.49	11.77	19.23
1980–1	7.17	18.22	18.10	2.69	14.87	16.10
1981–2	6.10	9.29	12.50	5.46	10.80	15.73
1982–3	3.10	4.90	16.60	5.79	7.24	15.77
1983–4	8.18	7.53	18.20	5.04	6.30	17.93
1984–5	3.84	6.47	19.00	5.37	6.17	17.73
1985–6	4.08	4.50	16.00	4.07	5.57	17.87
1986–7	4.28	5.74	18.60	4.23	6.15	16.87
1987–8	4.32	8.21	16.00	6.42	7.11	17.47
1988–9	10.65	7.38	17.80	7.29	7.68	17.73
1989–90	6.89	7.46	19.40	7.64	8.39	17.43
1990–1	5.37	10.32	15.10	4.35	10.50	17.93
1991–2	0.80	13.73	19.30	3.76	11.35	16.70
1992–3	5.10	10.00	15.70	3.63	10.69	18.10
1993–4	5.00	8.35	19.30	5.77	9.75	17.50
1994–5	7.20	10.90	17.50	6.43	9.02	16.67
1995–6	7.10	7.80	13.20			
Correlation between inflation and growth		−0.33			−0.50	

The moving average trends in inflation, growth and money supply show that while a steady trend in money supply growth maintained the pressure on prices, there was, at the same time, some degree of negative association between inflation and growth as shown by the correlation coefficient.[1]

II.2 Money, Output, and Prices in India

There is a general consensus in India that money affects both the level of prices and output. In the context of an open economy, monetary policy has a wider ramification because of its impact on the exchange rate, current account deficit, and capital inflow. Any framework to analyse the transmission channels of monetary policy should therefore focus on the intermediate variables, such as the interest rate, credit, and exchange rate, and the simultaneous process through which these variables influence prices and output.

The framework of the monetary transmission mechanism in the Indian context needs also to be analysed in relation to the institutional arrangement through which the fiscal deficit of the government is financed, and its impact on the monetary situation. The fiscal deficit affects money supply by the direct central bank financing of the resource gap during a year, as also through the dynamic evolution of inflation, deficit, and money supply in the

---

[1] The price equation can be modelled as an inverted money demand function, on the assumption of the unitary elasticity of prices with regard to broad money (M_3) in the long run. The empirical version of the price equation for the sample period 1972–3 to 1990–1 is

$$\ln P = 2.963 - 0.481 \ln YR + 0.271 \ln M3$$
$$(2.509)\ (2.196) \qquad (3.653)$$
$$+ 0.739 \ln P(-1) + 0.147\ DUM\ 74$$
$$(7.678) \qquad\qquad (5.555)$$
$$+ 0.069\ DUM\ 80$$
$$(2.085),$$
$$R^{-2} = 0.995,\ \text{h} = -1.56,\ SEE = 0.03,$$

where P is price level, YR is real income at factor cost, $M3$ is broad money aggregate, and DUM 74 and DUM 80 are the two dummies for inflation outliers representing oil price shocks. The short-run elasticities of price with regard to money supply works out to 0.271, while the long-run elasticity is close to unity (1.04). The implicit income elasticity of money demand is placed at 1.77.

subsequent years. Inflation affects fiscal deficit by both widening the primary deficit and the interest payment. This dynamic nexus between deficit and inflation is of particular concern in the Indian context in the absence of a formal ceiling on the extent to which fiscal deficit can be monetized during a year — a position that prevailed until recently.

In India, the output effect of money supply, stems from three major sources, namely through the aggregate demand effect and through the impact on the quantum and cost of credit. Although the management of aggregate demand falls, more appropriately, within the purview of fiscal policy, it is believed that a countercyclical monetary policy can play a useful role in sustaining the demand impulses in the economy, and thus bring about a short-run adjustment of output to the full capacity level. This is only a short-run benefit since changes in money supply will soon bring about a price change and reduce the real demand over a period of time.

Since the process of money creation is a process of credit creation, there is also a direct impact of money on output (Rangarajan and Arif, 1990) through the availability of credit. The third source of impact, through which monetary policy is considered to be more effective in influencing output, arises from the effect of money supply on interest rates. A change in monetary policy, by way of a decline in the reserve requirement of banks or open market purchases, is expected to influence the short-run interest rate in the economy, and through the term structure the entire range of long-run interest rates. To what extent this would translate into a reduction in interest rates would depend on the increase in inflation and inflation expectations.

The monetary transmission mechanism outlined above needs to be empirically tested to determine the implications of a monetary shock on inflation and output. In this context, a recent macroeconometric model of the Indian economy by Rangarajan and Mohanty (1996) for the period 1970-1 to 1990-1 provides some useful insights. The model features the monetary transmission mechanism outlined above in the open economy context. The model was simulated for a policy experiment that involved a 10 per cent sustained increase in real public investment in the non-agricultural sector financed by an increase in net RBI credit to government. The quantitative impact of this policy change on the major endogenous variables are summarized below.

TABLE 3.3
IMPACT OF A SUSTAINED 10 PER CENT
INCREASE IN REAL PUBLIC INVESTMENT IN
NON-AGRICULTURAL SECTOR FINANCED BY MONEY CREATION

Endogenous variables	RMSPE for dynamic simulation	Annual average percentage deviation over reference simulation		
		Impact (first year)	Short run (first two years)	Long run (15 years)
Public sector fiscal deficit	8.8	18.8	19.5	32.2
Money supply	4.1	5.8	9.0	27.3
Price level	4.0	1.2	2.3	16.9
Real capital stock in nonagricultural sector	1.0	0.8	1.4	4.5
Real income	2.0	0.7	1.0	2.7
Exports of goods and services (constant US$)	4.9	−0.3	−0.5	0.2
Real imports of goods and services	4.8	3.8	5.2	12.8
Current account deficit as percentage of GDP	42.1	0.2	0.6	0.3

RMSPE – Root Mean Square Percentage Error

The simulation results show that the 'trade-off' between price stability and growth is sharper in the long run than in the short run. A sustained 10 per cent increase in real public investment in the non-agriculture sector increases money supply by 5.8 per cent over the base run in the immediate period in which the shock occurs. The price level rises by 1.2 per cent in the first year, and output grows by 0.7 per cent. In the short run while prices rise by 2.3 per cent on an average over the base run, output rises by about 1 per cent per annum. In the long run, the dynamic inter-action between deficit, money supply and inflation results in an acceleration of the price rise to 16.9 per cent and the additional output gain slows down considerably to average 2.7 per cent. This implies that in the long run a sustained improvement in the growth scenario through monetary financing of deficit could involve a severe trade-off in terms of inflation — every 1 per cent additional output growth implies a rise of nearly 6 to 6.5 per cent in the price level in the long run. There is also an adverse external implication of this financing policy as it leads to a deterioration in the current account deficit in the balance of payments, largely through the import leakage. What this policy scenario implies is that a high and disproportionate growth in money supply, whatever may be its origin, will in the long run, worsen both the internal and external balance in the economy. This needs to be weighed against the 'trade-off' that it may have in terms of output gain.

III. Stance of Monetary Policy in India

The broad concerns of monetary policy in India have been, (1) to regulate monetary growth so as to maintain a reasonable degree of price stability, and (2) to ensure adequate expansion in credit to assist economic growth. The objective of price stability has assumed additional significance in the context of the current phase of macroeconomic reforms and the critical need to maintain the internal and external stability in the economy. This does not however mean that the growth objective has become less important for monetary policy. Creating a stable price environment that would reduce uncertainty and improve efficiency of resource use is itself regarded as important in achieving a faster rate of economic growth.

The monetary policy in the post 1991 reform period has undergone a noticeable transformation both in terms of the institutional setting in which monetary policy operates and the instruments used to exercise control. The most important changes in institutional arrangements have occurred in the area of improving the degree of monetary control in the economy, through reforms such as the phased abolition of the system of ad hoc treasury bills that results in automatic monetization of the budget deficit, promotion of a market for government securities, easing of external policy constraints on banks, such as high cash reserve and statutory liquidity ratios and deregulation of interest rates in the economy. These institutional changes have been accompanied by a distinct shift from direct quantitative controls to indirect monetary controls. The reliance on open market operations and the gradual reduction of governmental pre-emption of resources have enhanced the efficacy with which monetary policy is able to pursue its ultimate objective.

In recent years, a new debate has arisen in several developed countries on the appropriate intermediate target for the conduct of monetary policy. While many countries have abandoned 'monetary targeting' as the appropriate intermediate target, countries such as the US, the UK, New Zealand, Canada and some others, have shifted their policy focus to either interest rate targeting or direct inflation targeting, because of the failure of monetary aggregates to predict inflation due to structural breaks in the money demand function. Instances of instability in the demand for money in India have been also cited by a few studies. The overwhelming empirical evidence in the Indian context, however, points in the direction of the stability of money demand (Parikh, 1994 and Arif, 1996).

The appropriateness of monetary aggregates as an intermediate target in India can be justified on several grounds. First, since the money demand function for India has remained reasonably stable and continues to predict price movements with reasonable accuracy, at least over the medium term, there is as yet no compelling reason in the Indian context to abandon monetary targeting. Secondly, a money stock target is relatively well understood by the public at large. Moreover, with a money supply target, the stance of monetary policy is unambiguously defined and gives a clear signal to market participants, which helps the formation of market expectations.

This is not to say that monetary authorities should confine their attention to just one aggregate. Undoubtedly, a range of aggregates including total credit should be continuously monitored. Several monetary authorities have adopted a 'menu' or 'checklist' approach, but the larger the checklist, the less useful it is as guide to policy.

III.1 Acceptable Inflation

The conflict between the short run output benefits of inflation and the several indirect costs of inflation is at the heart of the policy dilemma in selecting a target rate of inflation for any economy. It has been argued in the Indian context that curtailing growth in money supply might adversely affect output, because money, apart from being relevant as a means of influencing aggregate demand, also plays a crucial role as an input for the productive sectors in the economy in the form of credit. As the empirical evidence presented in the previous section revealed, this is a visible benefit only when inflation remains at a moderate level and there is a policy commitment to maintain reasonable price stability in the economy. In such a situation the costs of inflation are minimal and non-distorting.

The ongoing macroeconomic reform process has underlined the importance of maintaining price stability in the economy in the context of the significant degree of openness achieved in the Indian economy, both in terms of external orientation and liberalization of the domestic financial sector. Interest rate flexibility requires that there is a reasonable degree of price stability to dampen adverse inflation expectations. There is also considerable concern now to align domestic prices with those of our export competitors to ensure a competitive exchange rate in the economy. Maintenance of fiscal sustainability is also conditional on price stability because of the dynamic implications of inflation for the interest rate and the future debt-servicing burden on the budget.

It is well recognized that adverse implications of inflation are higher at high rates of inflation, while a moderate rate of inflation could be manageable without implying severe costs. One important caveat in interpreting the threshold of the inflation rate beyond which costs exceed benefit is the provision of inflation protection measures available in various economies, which tend to a degree to attenuate the adverse social implications. Countries with moderate inflation rate but inadequate social safety net measures may show a higher degree of sensitivity to inflation than those with low inflation.

The recent shift of focus of economic policy the world over to maintenance of price stability has, however, not gone without protest from some critics. For example, Prof. Paul Krugman (1996) writes

... the belief that absolute price stability is a huge blessing, that it brings large benefits with few if any costs, rests not on evidence but on faith. The evidence actually points the other way: the benefits of price stability are elusive, the costs of getting there are large, and zero inflation may not be a good thing even in the long run.

The observations of Prof. Krugman, as they stand, are not directed against price stability as an objective but are aimed against a policy that seeks 'absolute' price stability and attempts to bring down the inflation rate from around 2 per cent to almost zero. This is evident from what he himself advocates ' . . . adopt as a long run target fairly low but not zero inflation, say 3–4 per cent. This is high enough to accommodate most of the real wage cuts that markets impose, while the costs of the inflation itself will still be very small.' Interestingly, in India, the Chakravarty Committee (1985) treated an inflation rate of 4 per cent as 'the acceptable rise in prices' purported to facilitate 'changes in relative prices necessary to attract resources to growth sectors'.

It is therefore necessary to have an appropriate fix on the acceptable level of inflation in the Indian context. The objective of the policy should be to keep the inflation rate at around 6 per cent. This itself is much higher than that which the industrial countries are aiming at and therefore will have some implications for the exchange rate of the rupee. Monetary growth should be so moderated that, while meeting the objective of growth, it does not push the inflation rate beyond 6 per cent.

REFERENCES

Arif, R.R. (1996): 'Money Demand Stability: Myth or Reality — An Econometric Analysis', Development Research Group Study No. 13, Reserve Bank of India.

Barro, Robert J. (1995): 'Inflation and Economic Growth', *Bank of England Quarterly Bulletin*, vol. 35 (2) (May).

Bernanke, Ben S. and Mark Gertler (1995): 'Inside the Black Box: The Credit Channel of Monetary Policy Transmissions', *Journal of Economic Perspectives*, vol. 9 (4), pp. 27–48.

Blanchard, O.J. (1990): 'Why Money Affects Output?', in B.M. Friedman and F.H. Hahn (eds), *Handbook of Monetary Economics* (New York: North Holland), vol. 2..

Bootle, Roger (1997): 'The Death of Inflation', *World Economic Affairs* (winter), pp. 11–15.

Bruno, Michael (1995): 'Does Inflation Really Lower Growth?', *Finance and Development*, September, pp. 35–8.

Burnner, Karl and Allan M. Meltzer (1993): *Money and the Economy: Issues in Monetary Analysis* (Cambridge: Cambridge University Press).

Fisher, Irving (1920): *The Purchasing Power of Money* (New York: Macmillan).

Fischer, Stanley (1993): 'The Role of Macroeconomic Factors in Growth', *Journal of Monetary Economics*, 32, pp. 485–511.

—— (1994): 'Modern Central Banking', in Forrest Capie, Charles Goodhart, Stanley Fischer and Nobert Schnadt (eds), *The Future of Central Banking, The Tercentenary Symposium of the Bank of England* (Cambridge: Cambridge University Press), pp. 262–308.

Friedman, Milton (1968): 'The Role of Monetary Policy', *American Economic Review*, vol. LVII, no. 1 (March), pp. 1–17.

—— (1975): 'Unemployment versus Inflation? An Evaluation of the Phillips Curve', *Occasional Paper* 44 (London: The Institute of Economic Affairs).

Friedman, Milton and A.J. Schwartz (1963): *A Monetary History of the United States, 1867–1960* (New Jersey: Princeton University Press).

Haberler, Gottfried (1952): *Prosperity and Depression* (3rd edn) (New York: United Nations).

Hossain, Akhtar and Anis Chowdhury (1996): *Monetary and Financial Policies in Development Countries* (London: Routledge).

Huizinga, John (1993): 'Inflation Uncertainty, Relative Price Uncertainty, and Investment in U.S. Manufacturing', *Journal of Money, Credit and Banking*, vol. 25, no. 3 (August), pp. 521–49.

Jarrett, J. Peter and Jack G. Selody (1982): 'The Productivity-Inflation Nexus in Canada 1963–1979', *The Review of Economics and Statistics*, vol. LXIV, no. 3 (August), pp. 361–7.

Keynes, J.M. (1936): *The General Theory of Employment, Interest and Money* (London: Macmillan).

Krugman, Paul (1996): 'Stable Prices and Fast Growth: Just Say No', *Economist*, 31 August, pp. 15–18.

Parikh, A. (1994): 'An Approach to Monetary Targeting in India', Development Research Group Study No. 9, Reserve Bank of India.

Phelps, Edmund S. (1967): 'Phillips Curves, Expectation of Inflation and Optimal Unemployment Over Time', *Economica*, 34, (August), pp. 254–81.

Rangarajan, C. (1988): 'Issues in Monetary Management', Presidential Address, Indian Economic Association, Calcutta.

—— (1996): 'Some Issues in Monetary Policy', Administrative Staff College Foundation Lecture, Hyderabad.

Rangarajan, C. (1996): 'Monetary Policy and Price Stability', Address at the Second Conference of the Econometric Society's Regional Chapter for India and South Asia, New Delhi, *Reserve Bank of India Bulletin*, January 1992.

Rangarajan, C. and R.R. Arif (1990): 'Money, Output and Prices: A Macro Econometric Model', *Economic and Political Weekly*, 21 April, pp. 837–52.

Rangarajan, C. and M.S. Mohanty (1996): 'Fiscal Deficit and External Imbalance — A Macro Econometric Model', Working Paper, Reserve Bank of India.

Reserve Bank of India (1985): 'Report of the Committee to Review the Working of the Monetary System' (Chakravarty Committee).

Sarel, Michael (1996): 'Nonlinear Effects of Inflation on Economic Growth', *IMF Staff Papers*, vol. 43, no. 1 (March), pp. 199–215.

Tobin, James (1965): 'Money and Economic Growth', *Econometrica*, vol. 33, no. 4, pp. 671–84.

Wicksell, Knut (1907): 'The Influence of the Rate of Interest on Prices', *Economic Journal*, June, pp. 213–19.

4

Theory and Practice of Development

Amartya Sen

I. INTRODUCTION

John Major, I am told, was the only boy ever to run away from a circus to become an accountant. Manmohan Singh is not the only professor to run away from a university to take charge of governance, but he has certainly been the most successful one to do so. After leaving Delhi University, Manmohan became a leading civil servant with quiet efficiency, and followed this up by becoming a statesman ushering in courageous and innovative reforms. He has achieved feats that few academics can dream of accomplishing.

It is interesting to contemplate the transformation that Manmohan went through in moving from one position to the next. I have had the privilege of seeing Manmohan in different roles: first as a fellow student (a totally brilliant one), then as an international civil servant, then as a wonderful colleague at Delhi University, then as senior civil servant, followed by the period when he was running the international South Commission, and finally as a statesman, including his time as the most innovative Finance Minister in the history of modern India. There are many transmutations here and, in terms of Manmohan's own life, it is not obvious to me that the move from the academic universe to the world of practice was the biggest jump. Indeed, the metamorphosis of an efficient but extremely quiet civil servant into a determined and vocal — and in some ways, stubborn — Finance Minister was probably the biggest leap.

I am delighted to have this opportunity of writing in the

Festschrift for someone I have had the privilege of knowing closely and whose intellect and dedication I have always admired. Our areas of specialization are not the same (I try not to write on international trade and usually succeed), but there is such a thing as an 'outsider's view' which may be of some interest (it tends, alas, to be of greater interest to the outsiders themselves than to insiders). This is perhaps an occasion also to consider a few aspects of the very general issue of the interrelation between academic theorizing and practical policy-making, in the context of honouring someone who has moved easily between the two and who has distinguished himself remarkably in both fields. Indeed, some interesting questions came up when I revisited, in the present context, Manmohan Singh's (1964) classic study. That will be my point of departure.

II. Shifting Roles and Changing Times

Surprise has sometimes been expressed at the fact that Manmohan Singh, as Finance Minister, could reject and denounce so firmly the economic policies that he himself had helped to implement, as a pre-eminent and leading civil servant. It is as if Achilles were suddenly to tell his comrades, lying in wait around Troy: 'Friends, let us quit wasting time and lives (and stop playing with that wooden horse). I will now lead you home to do something useful, like industry or agriculture'. There is, of course, no mystery here. As a civil servant in a democracy, Manmohan could not but follow the policies of the elected government. As a Finance Minister he could make his own policies.

To see whether there is a break in Manmohan's own thinking, we have to compare his *academic* writings with the policy reforms that he initiated. That comparison indicates that there is nothing here to give the 'contradiction school' much comfort. On the contrary, mild and non-combative as Manmohan's academic style always is, his support for greater openness in trade and for a less controlled·economy was clearly articulated in his earlier writings. Indeed, in the remarkable book on India's exports, referred to earlier, published nearly two decades before Manmohan introduced his liberalizing reforms, his principal conclusions included an affirmation of 'the function of international trade' as something of great 'importance for most underdeveloped countries in their quest for higher rates of economic growth'. We also find him insisting that the 'ability to utilize the above-mentioned benefits of trade is crucially dependent on its export capacity' (Singh, 1964: 4–5).

To be sure, Manmohan's defence of trade and export orientation does not take the form of a shrieking proclamation (dismissing contrary arguments on sight). Qualifications abound throughout the entire exercise, even though the final conclusion is firm and unequivocal. Also, the basic conclusions are not developed out of high theory, invoking a general argument from gains from trade or comparative costs. It is a contingent defence, based on detailed empirical reasoning.

I shall presently try to make a few remarks on the nature of Manmohan's arguments, but before that I want to consider the form in which the arguments are presented, which has, I think, some interest of its own. The presentation of the pro-export argument is remarkably defensive. It is clear how much the entire subject was dominated in the 1960s by presumptions — and arguments — against taking the merits of free trade for granted.[1]

From this point of view it is quite instructive to see the references that Manmohan gave to theoretical arguments, and the authors who were seen as being in the forefront of the critique of free trade. When 'the free-trade argument' is explicitly considered in the book (this happens in the context of examining 'regional trade'), the two authors that are cited as sceptical of free trade are Harry Johnson and Ian Little, who would probably not be seen today as being the fiercest opponents of free trade. Harry Johnson appears once in the book, as the author of the demonstration that 'even after a series of retaliations had occurred one country might conceivably be still better off in a tariff-ridden world than in a free-trade world'.[2] Ian Little also makes one appearance:

The argument that free trade maximizes world welfare assumes that all the usual Paretian conditions of optimum production and exchange are satisfied in all countries, and in addition, as Dr. Little has pointed out in his *Critique of Welfare Economics*, that the distribution of income

[1] On this and related issues, see Anne Krueger's (1997), Presidential Address to the American Economic Association.

[2] Singh (1964), p. 275. The reference is to Johnson (1953–4), pp. 142–53.

among different countries is a matter of indifference.[3] [Singh, 1964: 274.]

After qualifying the defence of free trade by taking note of these contrary arguments of Little and Johnson, Manmohan asserts, modestly enough, his basic sympathy for the free trade position:

All these objections are so well-known as hardly to require any elaboration. Nevertheless the free-trade doctrine has often provided a powerful intellectual basis for trade-liberalization policies on a regional basis. [Singh, 1964: 275.]

At the applied level, the opponent that Manmohan wrestles with most is Ragnar Nurkse. This concerns Nurkse's reasoning as to why 'there are important factors at work, emanating from industrial countries, which are preventing a fast-enough growth of the export demand for the products of underdeveloped countries' (Singh, 1964: 1). Manmohan notes the cogency of Nurkse's position:

Therefore international trade cannot now be an effective 'engine of economic growth'; and in the strategy of growth, underdeveloped countries have of necessity to lay emphasis on 'balanced growth' — a coordinated development of local industries in accordance with the growth and structure of domestic demand.

But Manmohan goes on to argue: 'The acceptance in broad outline of the Nurkse thesis does not imply that the foreign trade sector has no important role to play in the process of economic development'. Manmohan points in particular to the 'increase in import requirements' that 'the initiation of the process of "balanced growth" à la Nurkse' would entail. Indeed, this need to meet import requirements becomes a crucial factor in Manmohan's argument for the importance of export promotion (on which more presently).

The intellectual climate in the early 1960s was such that any defence of export orientation had to be embarked upon with much hesitation — and a partial concession to contrary arguments — before presenting a qualified affirmation. Interestingly, Nurkse himself qualifies his export pessimism by acknowledging

---

[3] The reference is to Little's *Critique of Welfare Economics* (Little, 1957). The other appearance of Little in the book is in being warmly thanked in the 'Acknowledgements'.

but disputing the likelihood of *even worse* outcomes through trade. In this context, he considers the argument for concentrating on domestic markets to escape 'immiserizing growth', as Jagdish Bhagwati called it:

Output expansion for home markets is of interest in the present setting as an escape from Immiserizing Growth. This concept, as already mentioned, envisages growth in the factor stock as leading to impoverishment through bad effects on the terms of trade produced by output expansion for export in the face of unfavorable external demand conditions. [Nurkse, 1959: 58.]

The reference is, of course, to Jagdish Bhagwati's elegant writings on 'immiserizing growth' (Bhagwati, 1958a, 1958b). Nurkse is not entirely persuaded that these fears of adverse trade conditions are fully justified:

As a theoretical scarecrow it undoubtedly has its uses, but it need not be accepted as an inevitable necessity in a spirit of economic determinism. . . . It is perhaps only natural that a concept which implicitly denies capacity for transformation should point a way to impoverishment rather than development. [Nurkse, 1959: 58–9.]

But there is enough of a damper in Nurkse's own suspicions about export markets for Manmohan to have to further qualify Nurkse's already qualified fears about overreliance on them.

How should we view these 'sights and sounds' of the 1960s? I shall return to this question, but before that I want to consider Manmohan's own low key but reasoned and firm insistence on the importance of export orientation.

III. EMPIRICAL ARGUMENTS AND EXPORT ORIENTATION

Manmohan Singh's defence of export-orientation is deeply empirical in content. While criticisms of free trade get some airing and a qualified but firm rejection, the case for export promotion is not constructed here through a generic defence of gains from trade. Ricardo does make one appearance in defence of 'mutually profitable international trade', but this happens in a very specific context, providing ammunition for Singh's chastizement of the protectionism of 'developed countries' (p. 277, fn 10). The positive case for export promotion, especially in the context of India, is linked by Manmohan to rather more immediate considerations.

As was mentioned earlier, Manmohan pays special attention to the 'increase in import requirements' in raising the rate of growth, and the argument that this cannot be easily met by anything other than export promotion.

To sum up, whatever the development strategy, the function of international trade as a supplier of 'material means, indispensable for development' is likely to retain its importance for most underdeveloped countries in their quest for higher rates of economic growth. . . . Imports, however, have to be paid for either by current export earnings, or by withdrawal from reserves of foreign exchange, or by a fresh capital inflow. The withdrawal from reserves is not an unlimited process, and in India's case seems to have been carried too far already. Capital inflows (and other outright grants) ultimately lead to higher service charges and repayment obligations. In the long run, therefore, the import capacity of an economy and its ability to utilize the above-mentioned benefits of international trade is crucially dependent on its export capacity. [Singh, 1964: 3–5.]

This sets out what needs to be done, but rapid increase in exports would be impossible if the export pessimism prevailing at that time were well-grounded. Much of the rest of the book, with its very careful and painstaking empirical arguments, proceeds to demonstrate that it was not so well-grounded after all. Along with this demonstration comes the thesis, which would be very relevant later on for Manmohan Singh the Finance Minister, that 'the stagnation of export earnings was partly a consequence of faulty Indian economic policies'.

Manmohan pays attention to S.J. Patel's (1959) influential critique of India's export prospects and his thesis that 'India's stagnant export earnings have to be explained in terms of stagnant world demand for Indian exports'. Peter Bauer (1961) and Anne Krueger (1961) are cited as differing from Patel, and placing the responsibility of export stagnation on domestic policies. While these critical arguments are welcomed by Manmohan, they are seen as being rather general — more effective in finding fault with Patel's reasoning than in establishing the real prospects of export promotion for India.[4] Manmohan wanted to rebut the

---

[4] Anne Krueger was very aware of the empirical conditionalities. As Manmohan Singh himself notes, 'Dr Krueger herself admits that it is merely an alternative hypothesis which requires to be tested' (Singh, 1964: 14; Krueger, 1961: 440; see also Krueger, 1997). Peter Bauer's own reasoning has also

pessimistic view with detailed empirical work, combined with a critique of the Indian economic policies that were responsible for export stagnation. The book did just that.

IV. Empirical Conditionalities

I have tried to indicate why it is possible to see a clear and unbroken line of reasoning from Manmohan Singh's academic writings to the policies he chose to initiate and implement. But why, we might ask, did he rely so much on empirical details rather than on invoking the general and ubiquitous merits of free trade, arising from comparative costs or economies of scale (as it is now quite normal to do)? Part of the answer lies undoubtedly in Manmohan's greater involvement with the palpable need to have to pay for the imports, which the process of economic growth would require, than with the more abstract certainty of gains from trade through comparative costs or increasing returns. But we have to consider also the fact that the nature and definiteness of these gains were being vigorously qualified at that time (as has already been discussed) by theorists who were by no means 'anti-free trade' in any general sense.

The climate of opinion has shifted since then, and now we find a more sanguine and less qualified defence of free trade as the standard position; it is the message of the time. While these grand generalizations are sometimes seen as following directly from pure theory, there is more than that in the story. In the early 1960s Japan was about the only consistent example of fast economic growth, using export promotion, from a state of underdevelopment. And even Japan's growth rate (for the long stretch up to that point) was relatively moderate by the standards of what would soon become quite common, especially in east Asia. Japan's own industrialization also involved a long history of import restriction and an extensive role for governmental leadership and intervention. The empirical picture then had not sorted itself out as clearly as it has by now. Soon, however, one country after another would make extensive use of export orientation — often following a period of import substitution — with great success: Japan herself,

been consistently empirical (see also Bauer, 1971, 1991). Manmohan Singh's significant departure related to his careful scrutiny specifically of *Indian* trade experiences.

South Korea, Taiwan, China, Thailand, and so on (not to mention the city states of Singapore and Hong Kong).

It is in the nature of 'pure theory' that various different possibilities can be foreseen, and which one of them will turn out to be the most relevant cannot be determined on grounds of theory alone. Doubts about what trade can do must, therefore, be raised and considered. Harry Johnson was right to establish the theoretical possibility that 'even after a series of retaliations had occurred one country might conceivably be still better off in a tariff-ridden world than in a free-trade world'. Ian Little was right to worry about the effects of trade on distributional inequality. Jagdish Bhagwati was right to discuss the possibility of immiserizing growth.

On the other hand, the things that *could* under some circumstances occur might not, in the event, occur. It may emerge that some of the possibilities 'in theory' may be so uncommon that policy initiatives should not sensibly be restrained by them. This would not change the fact that these are indeed 'possibilities', but their relevance to practical decision-making may be, over time, severely undermined. This is one way the climate has shifted.[5] However, even if, in hindsight, it looks as if one particular scenario, among various possible ones, is the 'natural' result to which pure theory pointed, the confidence that the 'natural' result is this particular one (and not one of the other cases which may by now be seen as 'way out') is really parasitic on the *empirical* lessons. It is partly from *observing* the world, rather than from purely analytical reasoning, that we tend to guess what theoretical possibilities can be sensibly taken as being 'way out'. What appears, in the context of application, as 'results' of pure theory are often nothing of the sort, but understandings generated by an irreducible mixture of theory and empirical observation.

If this is accepted, then Manmohan's extreme concentration on the empirical picture — and relative neglect of pure theory — can be better understood. It would not be good enough simply to assert that in pure theory we could, quite possibly, expand exports easily enough through, say, a change in relative prices, and that this need not make inequality much worse. We have to recognize that in

---

[5] That these empirical experiences have been crucial in influencing our understanding of the process of development has been well shown by Peter Bauer (1971, 1991) and Ian Little (1982).

theory there can be other possibilities too, including quite unattractive ones. Manmohan's concentration, thus, was on trying to show, with empirical investigation, that some fears (in particular those related to 'export fatalism') are actually not empirically well-founded. If Manmohan's approach was not one of pure theory, there was an excellent reason for that.

How astute was Manmohan's rejection of what he called 'export fatalism'? It was clearly of greater insight than many assumptions that were the norm at the time Manmohan was writing. For example, Manmohan's track, in *challenging* the inescapability of stagnant export earnings, was a lot wiser than mine, in trying to work out the *implications* of such stagnation, if true (see Sen and Raj, 1961). My joint paper with K.N. Raj (contrary to a frequently repeated interpretation) said *nothing* whatsoever about the case for import substitution (which did not figure in the model), but it did confine the analysis of growth to alternative feasible paths given export stagnation (and no import substitution).

Effectively, the Raj–Sen paper continued the tradition of pursuing growth theory in the context of a 'closed' economy (with a window half-open and firmly *stuck* right there). Since much of growth theory has been developed with the assumption of *completely closed* economies, we need not, I suppose, apologize for doing what we did. However, Manmohan's debunking of the assumption of export stagnation (published three years later) eliminates the *context* of the paper, and what little merit it may have rests on seeing it as an exercise in growth theory and intersectoral relations (on which see Atkinson, 1969 and Cooper, 1983). While I must not fall for the implicit self-flattery of thinking that someone who saw something I could not see must be unbelievably perceptive, I have to acknowledge Manmohan's superior wisdom. The point, however, is not so much what Manmohan Singh did 'see', but what he could definitively establish with impeccable empirical reasoning. The art of shooting oneself in the foot, as practised in the export–import policies of the Government of India, was laid bare by Manmohan's careful empirical studies.

V. Answers and Questions

If the preceding argument is correct, then our basic theories and presumptions about what can or cannot be done are typically dependent on our empirical readings (even if the theories may superficially appear to be free standing). Theories not only contribute to the making of practical policies, they also draw on the results of practical policies. The mutual interdependence is important in Manmohan's own work, both as a statesman and as an academic researcher (as I have tried to show).

So far I have not expressed any disagreement with Manmohan's economic policies, but sought to understand and explain the intellectual background of his work and the rationale behind the research he has done. I have, however, criticized Indian official policies elsewhere, including policies from the period when Manmohan was Finance Minister. In particular Jean Drèze and I have argued, in our joint book (Drèze and Sen, 1995), that the success of liberalization and closer integration with the world economy may be severely impaired by India's backwardness in basic education, elementary health care, gender inequality and limitations of land reforms.[6] While Manmohan Singh did initiate the correction of governmental *over-activity* in some fields, the need to correct governmental *under-activity* in other areas has not really been addressed. How do these qualifications relate to what I have just been discussing?

If the 'strategy' behind India's economic reforms and liberalization draws not only on 'theory' (such as comparative costs, economies of scale, and so on), but also crucially on the empirical observation of successful experiences of export-oriented growth in other countries, particularly in east and south-east Asia, then the question has to be asked whether the relevant conditions — both social and economic — are really similar. The fact that high growth rates can be achieved via this route has been brought out by the experiences of a great many countries across the world. But the conviction that this can be done with considerable equity is based largely on observations in a relatively few countries — mostly in east and south-east Asia.

These countries all share some conditions that are particularly favourable to widespread participation of the population in economic change. The relevant features include high rates of literacy, a fair degree of female empowerment, and quite radical land

---

[6] See also the companion volume of edited essays (Drèze and Sen, 1996), with papers by V.K. Ramachandran, Haris Gazdar, Sunil Sengupta, Mamta Murthi, and Anne-Catherine Guio, in addition to those by Drèze and myself.

reforms. Can we expect in India results similar to those that the more socially egalitarian countries have achieved, given that half the Indian population (and two-thirds of the women) are still illiterate, that female empowerment is very little achieved in most parts of India, that credit is very hard to secure by the rural poor, and that land reforms remain only partially and unevenly executed? Should we not have expected more in. the direction of breaking the terrible neglect of these concerns, on which the basic capabilities of the Indian masses depend? Were the reforms much too conservative in keeping intact governmental under-activity in social infrastructure, while trying to cure governmental over-activity in trade and manufacturing industries?

I end this essay with these uncomfortable questions because· they are, I believe, important for the direction of Indian public policy right now, especially for policies aimed at the basic 'social' areas. This critique, in so far as it is appropriate, has a methodological similarity with Manmohan's own approach: it comes not from pure theory, but from empirical observations in attempting to discriminate between different theoretical possibilities. Manmohan has stood solidly for critical scrutiny of the empirical picture, rather than a large reliance on theory, and it would be in the tradition of his research to point out that the relevant empirical picture includes — in the context of the east and south-east Asian success stories — not just an orientation towards exports but also widespread public efforts in basic education, public health care, female independence, land reforms, and other components of social infrastructure.

In general, much of what we take to be 'development theory' is far from pure; it is highly qualified and deeply contingent on empirical understanding. It is in the light of this methodological interdependence between theory and practice that we have to appreciate the remarkable insights and achievements of Manmohan Singh. The critical questions I have raised towards the end of this paper have a common basis — a shared ground — with the admiration I have for what Manmohan Singh has done for the country and for economics.

REFERENCES

Atkinson, A.B. (1969): 'Import Strategy and Growth under Conditions of Stagnant Export Earnings', *Oxford Economic Papers*, 21.

Bauer, Peter (1961): 'Import Capacity and Economic Development', *Economic Journal*, 71; rpt in Bauer (1991).

—— (1971): *Dissent on Development* (London: Weidenfeld & Nicolson).

—— (1991): *The Development Frontier: Essays in Applied Economics* (Cambridge, MA: Harvard University Press).

Bhagwati, Jagdish (1958a): 'Immiserizing Growth: A Geometrical Note', *Review of Economic Studies*, 25.

—— (1958b): 'International Trade and Economic Expansion', *American Economic Review*, 48.

Cooper, Charles (1983): 'Extensions of the Raj–Sen Model of Economic Growth', *Oxford Economic Papers*, 35.

Drèze, Jean and Amartya Sen (1995): *India: Economic Development and Social Opportunity* (Delhi: Oxford University Press).

—— (eds) (1996): *Indian Development: Regional Perspectives* (Delhi: Oxford University Press).

Johnson, Harry (1953–4): 'Optimum Tariffs and Retaliation', *Review of Economic Studies*, 21.

Krueger, Anne (1961): 'Export Prospects and Economic Growth: India — A Comment', *Economic Journal*, 71.

—— (1997): 'Trade Policy and Economic Development: How We Learn?', *American Economic Review*, 87.

Little, Ian (1957): *Critique of Welfare Economics*, 2nd edition (Oxford: Clarendon Press).

—— (1982): *Economic Development: Theory, Policy and International Relations* (New York: Basic Books).

Nurkse, Ragnar (1959): *Patterns of Trade and Development* (Stockholm: Almqvist & Wiksell, 1959).

Patel, S.J. (1959): 'Export Prospects and Economic Growth — India', *Economic Journal*, 69.

Raj, K.N. and Amartya Sen (1961): 'Alternative Patterns of Growth under Conditions of Stagnant Export Earnings', *Oxford Economic Papers*, 13.

Singh, Manmohan (1964): *India's Export Trends and the Prospects for Self-sustained Growth* (Oxford: Clarendon Press).

II

Transition to an
Open Economy

5

Infrastructure Development in India's Reforms

Montek S. Ahluwalia

It is a privilege to contribute to this volume honouring Dr Manmohan Singh. I first met Dr Singh in 1970, when I was a very young staff member of the World Bank and it was at his encouragement that I later left the World Bank to join the Ministry of Finance as Economic Advisor. Many years and two other assignments later I returned to the Finance Ministry in 1991, a few months after Dr Manmohan Singh became Finance Minister and thus had an inside view of economic reforms which were to become inseparably linked with his name. It is a manifestation of this linkage that when my good friend Swaminathan Anklesaria Aiyyar, then Editor of the *Economic Times*, coined the term 'Manmohanomics' to describe the economic rationale of the new policies, it quickly gained currency, as if plain vanilla 'economics' had been irretrievably appropriated by the other side!

The five years during Dr Manmohan Singh's stewardship of the Finance Ministry saw a remarkable change in the mind-set of those interested in economic policy. The reforms, which were initially seen as an unpleasant though necessary package to stabilize the economy, began to be perceived as the only way of raising India's hitherto modest growth performance to the 'high growth — poverty reducing' combination enjoyed by many East Asian countries. Although it is too early to pronounce success the early results are certainly promising. After a swift recovery from the 1991 crisis, economic growth accelerated to an average of 7 per cent per year in the three years ending in 1996–7, taking the average for the Eighth Plan period, 1992–3 to 1996–7, to 6.5 per cent which is significantly better than 5.6 per cent in the 1980s. India's relatively closed economy has been made much more open to trade and foreign investment, with none of the negative effects feared by critics, and with every expectation of reaping efficiency gains in future.

These successes notwithstanding, there are also some deficiencies which could limit the effectiveness of the reform package. One such deficiency relates to infrastructure development. Acceleration of growth to East Asian levels of 8 per cent will generate a massive demand for infrastructure services, such as electric power, roads, ports, railways and telecommunications. Since these services are all non-tradable, the additional demand arising from faster economic growth has to be met by expanding domestic supply in each of these sectors.[1] Furthermore, since growth will in future occur in a more open trading environment, with strong pressures to improve competitiveness, the quality of infrastructure services will also have to improve significantly. Indian industry will not only need adequate power supply, but also high quality power, free of interruptions and voltage fluctuations. Similar upgradation of quality is relevant for other infrastructure services also. The economic reforms must therefore be accompanied by a strategy for infrastructure development which can meet the increased demand for infrastructure services both in terms of quantity and quality.

Does India's reform programme have such a strategy for infrastructure development? This paper analyses the approach to infrastructure development adopted in the reform programme and evaluates performance in individual sectors. Some lessons are drawn for the future from the experience thus far.

---

[1] The term infrastructure is used more loosely in Indian official literature and often includes tradable items such as steel, cement, fertilizers and petroleum products. However 'important' they may be, they are all importable and therefore cannot be a physical constraint on the expansion of the economy in the same sense as non-tradables. Of course, the dependence on imports may pose foreign exchange problems and this has to be viewed as part of the strategy for managing the balance of payments. The expansion of domestic supply of these items in that context has to be justified as part of an optimal production response to balance of payments problems, taking account of other possibilities of expanding production of exports and other import substitutes.

I. STRATEGY FOR INFRASTRUCTURE DEVELOPMENT

Infrastructure problems were not the central focus of policy when the reforms began in mid-1991. The agenda for reforms in the early years was understandably dominated by crisis management and the need for domestic and external stabilization. The primary focus therefore was on reducing the fiscal deficit to restore macroeconomic stability and introducing a package of efficiency-oriented reforms aimed at deregulating the domestic economy, reforming trade and exchange rate policies and liberalizing foreign investment policy. Besides, infrastructure was not a significant constraint on short-term economic performance at the start of the reform programme because there was slack in the system with considerable scope for expanding supplies of infrastructure services in the short run through better utilization of existing capacity.

The first articulation of a strategy for infrastructure development as part of the reform programme is to be found in the Eighth Five Year Plan which was published at the end of 1992. Contrary to the impression conveyed by many critics that the reforms relied excessively and unrealistically upon private investment for development of infrastructure, the strategy outlined in the Plan, as the quotation below makes clear, envisaged a continuance of public sector dominance, with the private sector playing only a supplemental role.

Since the scale of construction in these areas is very large and these are of direct and immediate benefit to large sections of the society, the public sector will continue to play a dominant role in the area and will have the ultimate responsibility of meeting the demands. However if private initiative comes forward to participate in creating such infrastructure like power plants, roads, bridges, social housing, and industrial estates on reasonable terms and with full protection of peoples interest such initiatives must be positively encouraged.

Eighth Five Year Plan Vol. I, para 1.4.26.

The Plan did break from past tradition by recognizing a possible role for the private sector in building infrastructure — the Seventh Plan for example had made no mention at all of private investment in infrastructure — but the scale envisaged for private-sector activity was limited. This conventional approach reflects the institutional arrangements then prevailing, with infrastructure services being supplied almost exclusively by the public sector.

Electric power generation included some independent private
utilities supplying power to Ahmedabad, Mumbai and Calcutta,
but over 95 per cent of generation and distribution of electricity
for sale (i.e. excluding captive power generation by some large
industrial units) was in the Central or State public sector. Roads,
ports, railways and telecommunications were exclusive public sector areas.

The cautious approach of the Eighth Plan contrasts with the
rethinking taking place elsewhere in the world questioning the
traditional acceptance of the public sector as the natural supplier
of infrastructure services and shifting towards a positive preference
for private sector suppliers wherever possible. This shift has been
triggered by several factors. One is the general disillusionment
with public sector performance, which has created a perception
that public sector operations are inherently inefficient and com-
paratively insensitive to consumer concerns. On this view, the
public sector is a natural supplier of infrastructure services only
where the service involved is of a basic nature, with relatively low
expectations of quality and a low ability to pay. As expectations of
quality increase, with corresponding willingness to pay for better
services, it is appropriate to shift to private sector suppliers. Privatization has also been driven by technological developments in
some sectors which make it possible to introduce private sector
suppliers where it was infeasible earlier. The development of
cellular and wireless telephony, for example, makes it possible to
have more than one competing supplier for local telephone services whereas earlier, economies of scale prevented introduction
of a competitor operating an overlapping wire-telephone network.
Even if full competition in all parts of the system is not feasible,
it is possible to 'unbundle' the system and introduce competition
in some segments. In the power sector for example, electricity
distribution may have to be organized on the basis of a single
supplier for each area because of the expense of creating an overlapping distribution network, but there can be competition in the
generation of electricity with independent power producers selling
electricity to the distribution system on the basis of suitable long-
term contracts combined with spot sales.[2] Another major factor

---

[2] Advances in electronic metering in billing made it possible in the U.K.
for electricity distributing companies to optimize purchase of electricity from

triggering the shift to privatization is the tremendous growth in capital markets and innovative means of finance which makes it possible to finance large infrastructure projects despite the long payback periods involved.

The economic rationale for private investment in infrastructure has to be grounded in the expectation that private sector suppliers, operating within a competitive framework, will reduce costs to the economy and thus promote efficiency. It is important to distinguish here between costs to the economy and costs to the consumer. Public sector supply of infrastructure services may appear cheaper for the consumer because the service is often provided at highly subsidized rates or, as in the case of roads, even free of charge. However, low user charges in these cases are less a reflection of economic efficiency than of hidden subsidies, usually in the form of tolerance of large losses. Consumers pay for these subsidies either directly in the form of higher taxes or indirectly in the form of other government expenditure foregone, but these costs are not always recognized. In any case continuation of low-cost, public sector supplies is not an option because our ability to bear the hidden subsidies involved is now severely limited. Increasingly therefore infrastructure services, especially of the higher quality variety, will have to be provided on the basis of full cost coverage, whether through the public sector or the private sector. Consumers consequently have a direct interest in ensuring economic efficiency and if private sector operations are more efficient, it is logical to devise infrastructure strategies which encourage private investment in infrastructure.

There was little discussion of these issues in the Eighth Plan document, and certainly not enough recognition of the positive need to introduce private-sector suppliers in order to achieve greater efficiency or improve the quality of service. Telecommunications is perhaps the only sector where the Plan came close to recognizing this aspect of privatization.

Without a bold initiative for allowing private enterprise in areas hitherto kept as a preserve of the public sector it is apprehended that the long term objective of improving telecom services in the country

---

competing suppliers quoting rates for electricity, depending upon availability in different parts of the system, which vary within the same day.

to international standards and to match even the level obtained in the more progressive developing countries will not be achieved.

Eighth Five Year Plan Vol. II, para 10.8.2.

For the other sectors, private investment was viewed essentially as a supplement to the public sector effort, to be welcomed primarily because the task before the public sector was so huge and resources so scarce that any additional contribution would help.

II. An Overview of Performance

Despite the dominant role accorded to the public sector in the Eighth Plan period for infrastructure development, the actual experience was one of public sector investment falling short of targets in most sectors. Table 5.1 compares the targets for public sector plan expenditure (which may be treated as a surrogate for public investment) with actual expenditure for each of the five infrastructure sectors for the Seventh and Eighth Plan periods. Plan expenditure on the five infrastructure sectors taken together in the Eighth Plan was 14.4 per cent lower than the target. By comparison, the shortfall for these sectors in the Seventh Plan was only 3.6 per cent. It is worth noting that the shortfall in infrastructure expenditure in the Eighth Plan was greater than the shortfall in Plan expenditure on all sectors. The shortfall was especially large in power generation (22 per cent) and ports (57 per cent) with marginal to modest shortfalls in railways (6.7 per cent) and roads (6.5 per cent). Telecommunications alone present a different picture with expenditure exceeding the plan target. The superior performance of telecommunications is particularly remarkable since this is a sector where the target for the Eighth Plan represented a larger growth over the Seventh Plan than for any other infrastructure sector.

Measuring plan performance in terms of shortfalls in expenditure from plan targets suffers from obvious limitations. It tends to understate the severity of the infrastructure problem particularly when expenditure targets may have been inadequate to begin with. Besides, expenditure may not always lead to commensurate additions to capacity on account of poor project management. It is more useful to look at performance in terms of physical expansion in capacity and we turn to this aspect later in this paper.

As the Plan progressed, the resource constraints on expanding public investment became more apparent and this brought home

Table 5.1
Plan Expenditure

	Seventh Plan 1985–6 to 1989–90 (Rs crore at 1984–5 prices)			Eighth Plan 1992–3 to 1996–7 (Rs crore at 1991–2 prices)		
	Target (1)	Achievement (2)	(2) as % of (1)	Target (3)	Achievement (4)	(4) as % of (3)
Power	34,274	31,615	92.0	79,589	61,675	77.5
Telecommunications	7,135	6,296	88.0	25,137	25,829	103.0
Railways	12,334	13,524	110.0	27,202	25,911	95.3
Roads	5,200	5,191	100.0	13,210	12,349	93.5
Ports	1,105	1,287	116.0	3,557	1,502	42.2
Sub-Total	60,048	57,913	96.4	1,48,695	1,27,266	85.6
Total Plan Expenditure	1,80,000	1,80,655	100.4	4,34,100	3,96,863	91.4
Infrastructure as % of Plan	33	32		34.3	32.1	

NOTE: Seventh and Eighth Plan targets are as given in the respective Plan documents at 1984–5 prices and 1991–2 prices respectively. Amounts shown under Achievements are calculated from the annual expenditure levels in current prices during the Plan period deflated by the Wholesale Price Index to the relevant base year for each Plan. The conversion factor (to convert expenditure in 1984–5 prices to 1991–2 prices) is 1.72.

the urgency of stimulating private investment in infrastructure. Policy announcements to attract private investment in various sectors were made in a phased manner. The earliest was for private investment in power, followed by telecommunications, and then ports and roads. In the following sections of the paper we examine the performance of each of these sectors in the Eighth Plan period, focusing on the constraints on expanding public investment in each sector, and the success achieved in promoting private investment. While there are some commonalities, there are also interesting differences across sectors, and important lessons to be learnt from these differences.

III. Power: Constraints and Challenges

Shortage of power was perceived to be a critical constraint at the start of the Eighth Plan period which began with an average energy shortage of 8 per cent and a peaking shortage of 19 per cent. The demand for power was expected to grow much more rapidly than the economy and this clearly required a substantial expansion in capacity. There is no doubt that performance in expanding capacity has been very disappointing. The Plan began with a base level of capacity of 76,000 MW and the requirement for new generating capacity to be added during the Plan period was initially estimated at 40,000 MW. This was subsequently scaled down to 30,538 MW. Even this reduced target could not be achieved. As shown in Table 5.2, the actual addition to capacity during the Plan period was only 16,423 MW, or a little over half the target. This was significantly lower than the 21,402 MW of additional capacity added in the Seventh Plan period.

Public sector generating capacity consists of plants owned by the State Electricity Boards (states sector) and plants owned by central public sector undertakings such as the National Thermal Power Corporation and the National Hydroelectric Power Corporation (central sector). The states sector accounts for about 70 per cent of total capacity while the central sector accounts for 25 per cent. The share of the private sector is 5 per cent. The largest shortfall in the Eighth Plan was in the states sector which achieved only 46 per cent of the target for new capacity creation. Private sector capacity addition at 50 per cent of the target was also much below expectation.

TABLE 5.2
ADDITIONS TO CAPACITY IN THE POWER SECTOR

	Seventh Plan		Eighth Plan	
	Target	Achievement	Target	Achievement
I. Generating capacity (MW)				
Central sector	9320	9528	12858	8157
State sector	12925	11873	14870	6835
Private sector	–	–	2810	1430
Total	22245	21401	30538	16423
II. Transmission (Circuit Km)				
a] 400 KV				
Central	9600	11237	5066	4896*
State	3406	2558	4295	3461
Total	13006	13795	9361**	8357
b] 220 KV				
Central	2495	2650	1575	1280*
State	12735	10946	11435	11670
Total	15230	13626	13010**	12950

*   For the year 1996–7 the achievement is based on capacity added upto Oct. '97 only.
**   The target for 400 KV lines was originally fixed at 21600 circuit kms and for 200 KV lines at 32,500 circuit kms, consistent with the generating capacity target of 30,538 MW. However, these targets were revised downward year by year in line with actual growth of generation capacity.

III.1 Problems Facing Public Sector Power

The poor performance of the public sector in expanding capacity is largely a reflection of the deteriorating financial health of the State Electricity Boards (SEBs). Although the SEBs are expected to generate a rate of return of 3 per cent after allowing for depreciation, their operations have actually shown large and growing losses, even after taking credit for the subsidy they receive from the state governments (see Table 5.3). The rate of return (after subsidy) is negative and has deteriorated from –6.6 per cent in 1992–3 to –13.7 per cent in 1996–7. Lack of resources with the SEBs in an environment in which the state government budgets are unable to make up the shortfall through budgetary support has naturally slowed down capacity expansion in the States sector and even affected maintenance and renovation of existing plants creating a vicious circle of deteriorating performance. Financial problems affecting SEBs have naturally spilled over to the central sector in the form of nonpayment of dues to central sector power stations which supply power to SEBs.

TABLE 5.3
FINANCIAL CONDITION OF STATE ELECTRICITY BOARDS

	1992–3	1993–4	1994–5	1995–6	1996–7 *(estimated)*
1. Losses of SEBs (Rs in crore)					
i] Before subsidy	4560	5289	6642	7524	10,000
ii] After subsidy	2725	3007	3243	5408	7420
2. Rate of return on capital (%)					
i] Without subsidy	–12.7	–13.3	–14.4	–14.6	–17.9
ii] With subsidy	–7.6	–7.6	–7.0	–10.5	–13.7
3. Average Cost	1.28	1.44	1.58	1.73	1.86
4. Average realization (per kwh)	1.05	1.19	1.29	1.44	1.49
5. Transmission and distribution losses (%)(per kwh)	19.8	19.4	19.5	18.5	n.a.
6. Plant load factor of SEB thermal stations (%)	54.1	56.6	55.0	58.0	n.a.

A major reason for the poor financial performance is the pre-valence of very low electricity tariffs for certain categories of consumers. The average cost of power sold to consumers (including costs of both generation and distribution) in 1996–7 was

Rs 1.86 per kwh (Table 5.3). However, the tariff charged to domestic consumers (16 per cent of total sale) was only Rs 0.90 and the tariff charged to farmers (33 per cent of sales) was as low as Rs 0.21. Under charging of these consumers is offset to some extent by higher tariffs for industrial and commercial consumers (around Rs 2.30). However, despite this cross subsidization, the average realization from all consumers in 1996–7 was Rs 1.49, which covered only 80 per cent of the average cost. An increase in electricity tariffs for consumers, especially for agricultural consumers, is clearly essential to restore financial viability. A proposal for adopting a minimum agricultural tariff of 50 paise was accepted in the National Development Council in 1992 but was not implemented by the states. In fact since then some states have actually lowered agricultural tariffs.

Tariff increases in agriculture have to be accompanied by steps to improve the operational efficiency of SEBs. Better utilization of existing capacity is an obvious way of achieving higher operational efficiency. There has been some progress in this area, with the Plant Load Factor (PLF) of thermal generating stations run by the SEBs increasing from 54 per cent in 1992–3 to 58 per cent in 1995–6 (Table 5.3). However, this leaves a great deal of room for further improvement. The average PLF achieved in central sector power plants was 71 per cent, and many plants operate at PLF levels of 85 per cent. Part of the reason for low levels of PLF in the states sector is the poor resource position of most SEBs leading to neglect of maintenance and renovation of plants. However, managerial deficiencies are also important. Excessive political interference and frequent changes of top management has created a situation where managerial structures are weak and there is serious overmanning and very poor labour discipline. Of course, the situation varies from state to state, as reflected in the variation in PLF levels from 17 per cent in Bihar and 47 per cent in UP at one end of the spectrum, to over 75 per cent in Tamil Nadu and Andhra Pradesh at the other end. Clearly, efficiency levels at the lower end are unacceptably low.

Another area where operational efficiency can be increased is in transmission and distribution (T&D) losses. India's T&D losses were almost 20 per cent in 1992–3. While there has been a marginal improvement to 18.5 per cent in 1995–6, this is still too high. These losses should be below 10 per cent by international standards.

While part of the T&D loss is due to technical factors, such as sparse distribution of loads in rural areas and under- investment in distribution systems, a large part is due to plain theft of electricity, much of it with the connivance of the SEB staff. Improvements are certainly possible within the existing public sector framework, as indicated by variation across States with T&D losses ranging from 16 per cent in Maharashtra to over 20 per cent in Bihar and U.P. However, this is an area where privatization could have a major impact. Experimental efforts at privatizing distribution in some limited geographical areas have shown dramatic reductions in T&D losses, from 24 per cent to 9 per cent in one case.

III.2 Problems of Private Sector Power

While the public sector investment programme suffered because of the financial and managerial weaknesses of the SEBs, the effort to attract private investment in power ran into a number of un-anticipated difficulties. The policy for private investment in power was announced as early as March 1992. Private investors were offered a remunerative two part tariff with potentially attractive post-tax returns on equity linked to levels of capacity utilization.[3] The foreign investment policy was liberalized to allow 100 per cent foreign equity in the power sector. The policy also provided for automatic adjustment of the power tariff to reflect the impact of exchange rate changes on the return to foreign equity and on debt service payments.

The initial response to the new policy was enthusiastic, with 127 potential investors signing Memoranda of Understanding (MOU) with various SEBs to set up power plants amounting to 69,000 MW of capacity. While some of these MOUs were expected to fall by the wayside, there were many which involved serious and credible investors. Even these projects ran into a variety of hurdles which illustrate the diverse problems that arise when switching from public sector monopoly supply to private supply within a framework of regulation.

The earliest private sector power project, a 740 MW gas-based

[3] Under the 1992 policy, tariffs for independent power producers are fixed on the basis of a cost plus formula under which capital costs are fully recovered together with a 16 per cent return on equity at 68.5 per cent capacity utilization, with higher levels of return for increases in capacity utilization.

power plant at Dabhol in Maharashtra sponsored by the Enron Corporation, ran into public controversy on the issue of reasonableness of the tariff and the capital costs. Some of the public criticism was clearly ill-conceived and based on comparison of the Dabhol tariff with the average cost of generation of all plants in the public sector system, including old depreciated plants. The issue was politicized and the project was cancelled when a new government took over in Maharashtra following state level elections, but was subsequently re-negotiated with the same government with certain modifications. The renegotiated project was challenged in court by public interest groups alleging failure of diligence by the state government as well as environmental violations by the project. However, the project survived several legal challenges at different levels and is now under construction, with completion expected in 1998. The experience of the Dabhol project reveals the vulnerability of cost-based tariffs to public criticism on the grounds of cost padding.[4] Recognising this problem, the government has announced that in future, all private sector power projects will be awarded through competitive bidding on the basis of the electricity tariff to be paid to the producer.

A major constraint on financing private sector power projects is the perceived risk of non-payment for electricity. Since power projects are expected to sell their electricity to the SEB as the sole purchaser, the bankability of the project depends crucially upon the financial health of the SEB which, as pointed out earlier, does not inspire confidence in most cases. Thus, the very factor which is responsible for the inadequacy of public sector investment in power is also a major constraint on financing private sector investment. Many private investors therefore sought credit enhancement through government guarantees for the payment obligations of SEBs. State Governments were generally willing to provide guarantees, but lack of confidence in the creditworthiness of many State Governments led investors to seek sovereign counter-guarantees from the Central Government. In 1993, the Central Government agreed to extend counter-guarantees for

---

[4] It is interesting to note that although tariffs for public sector generating stations are also based on a cost plus formula, this issue became a matter of public concern only in the context of private sector projects. The level of due diligence and transparency demanded was clearly higher where the potential beneficiary of tariff fixation was a private sector company.

eight private sector power projects.[5] Though the decision to extend counter-guarantees was criticized as papering over the basic problem in order to provide comfort for private sector investors, it helped start the process of private investment in power in the initial stages. In the absence of sovereign guarantees, some private investors have sought credit enhancement through banking agreements whereby receipts of SEBs from designated bulk consumers are paid into escrow accounts earmarked for payment of dues of independent power producers. Several power projects are currently being financed on this basis. However, escrow arrangements are also a temporary solution as they only reduce the payment risk for the beneficiary project at the cost of enhancing the risk of non-payment by SEBs to other claimants.

Interruption in fuel supply arrangements is another major source of risk which needs to be tackled before private power projects can be financed. The Dabhol project relied on imported LNG and included construction of dedicated port facilities to handle LNG imports, thus assuring fuel supply as long as there is no disruption in world supplies.[6] However, management of fuel supply risk can pose serious problems for projects depending upon domestic fuel. The Visakhapatnam 1040 MW coal-based plant, for example, is linked to domestic coal supplied by Mahanadi Coalfields Ltd. (MCL), a public sector company. The power producer has sought a coal supply contract with penalty provisions such that shortfalls in coal supply below a tolerable limit would trigger compensation payments to the power producer equal to the loss of fixed capital charges which would have been payable if generation had not been affected by the shortfall. The public sector coal company was reluctant to enter into such an arrangement which involved heavy contingent liabilities and was entirely novel since coal supply agreements with public sector power

[5] Of these, two counterguarantees have been issued (Dabhol and GVK), one project (Spectrum) went ahead without waiting for a counterguarantee, one project (Ib Valley) is being renegotiated following a change in Government and counterguarantees for four projects (ST-CMS in Tamil Nadu, Cogentrix in Karnataka, Bhadravati in Maharashtra and Visakhapatnam in Andhra Pradesh) are at various stages of being processed.

[6] Since fuel prices are passed through into the tariff, variations in market prices of fuel do not affect the economics of the project as long as supplies are physically available in world markets.

plants did not involve such penalties.[7] In the end, the Government intervened to ensure that MCL would assume the full risk, and charge a suitable premium.[8] Similar problems have also arisen regarding the quality of the fuel supply agreement for gas-based projects, where the supplier is again a government company.

The difficulties enumerated above explain why the pace of induction of private investment in the power sector was slower than originally expected. Many of these problems were not anticipated when the policy was announced because the complexity of the arrangements needed to induct private sector suppliers into a regulated sector was underestimated. The problems were more acute in the larger projects, where the amounts at risk were larger and lenders, especially foreign lenders, demanded a higher degree of risk mitigation. It is not surprising therefore that the volume of private sector capacity actually created in the Eighth Plan was only 50 per cent of the target. However, behind this apparently poor performance, the positive feature is the great deal of learning has taken place in the process. Today there is a much greater appreciation of the preparatory work needed to create the preconditions for attracting private sector investment. Many power projects now in the pipeline have made significant progress. Eleven projects accounting for around 3400 MW have received all necessary clearances and have reached financial closure. Another thirty projects amounting to around 15000 MW are at various stages of the approval process prior to financial closure.

The key to financing these projects is the assurance that power producers will be paid for the power they produce. And, this in turn depends upon whether the State electricity systems can be

---

[7] It is a common phenomenon that contracts between public sector organizations are not characterized by tightly defined penalty provisions partly because it is felt that the risks are internal to the public sector as a whole and there is little point in imposing penalties on one segment to be paid to another. However, this approach is mistaken since the imposition of penalties is likely to stimulate a greater search for efficiency on the part of all participants. For a more detailed discussion see Ahluwalia (1997).

[8] The determination of an appropriate premium also presented problems in the absence of commercially reliable estimates of the probability of a breakdown in coal supply arrangements and the cost of efforts to reduce this probability through special action which can be justified by the premium charged.

made financially sound, which calls for fundamental reforms. The broad outline of what needs to be done has been spelt out in the Common Minimum National Action Plan for Power which was endorsed by a Conference of Chief Ministers in December 1996. Key features of the proposed reforms are

- Depoliticization of tariff fixation, with tariffs being fixed by independent State Electricity Regulatory Commissions so as to achieve a 3 per cent rate of return for SEBs.
- The principles of tariff fixation should ensure that no sector should pay less than 50 per cent of the cost of power. In the case of agriculture, the tariff should be raised immediately to 50 paise per kwh and to 50 per cent of average cost within 3 years.
- Tariffs fixed by the SERC will be mandatory and no government can lower the tariffs unless it provides a corresponding amount in the Budget to cover the loss.
- There should be a gradual programme of private participation in distribution, initially in one or two viable geographical areas covering both urban and rural populations.

Legislation to set up the Central Electricity Regulatory Commission and the State Electricity Regulation Commission has been introduced in Parliament. Some States have already begun the process of restructuring of the power sector. Orissa, for example, has replaced the monolithic SEB by separate corporations dealing with thermal and hydro generation, distribution and transmission. It is intended to introduce private participation gradually in each of these areas. Similar reform proposals are under consideration in Andhra Pradesh, Haryana, Rajasthan and Gujarat. Implementation of these changes could make a big difference to the power sector in these states in a relatively short time.

IV. Telecommunications: A Comparative Success Story

Although, India's telecommunications network is the fourteenth largest in the world, telephone density at 1.3 telephones per 100 persons is much lower than in other emerging market economies, e.g. 24.7 in Malaysia, 8.1 in Brazil, 4.7 in Thailand and 2.3 in China. There is clearly a great deal of catching up to be done.

Fortunately, this sector has shown considerable dynamism in recent years. As shown in Table 5.1, the Eighth Plan target for public sector expenditure in telecommunications showed a larger increase over the Seventh Plan level than for any of the other infrastructure sectors, and yet this target was actually exceeded. Almost the same picture emerges from Table 5.4 which shows capacity expansion in physical terms. The target for new direct exchange lines to be added in the Eighth Plan period was 7.5 million lines, more than a four-fold increase over the number of lines added in the Seventh Plan. Other Eighth Plan targets, such as for long distance switching capacity and transmission lines, were equally ambitious, and even these were for the most part actually exceeded.

TABLE 5.4
TELECOM SECTOR EXPANSION

Scheme	*Seventh Plan*		*Eighth Plan*	
	Target	*Actual*	*Target*	*Actual*
1. Local switching system				
i] Total switching capacity (million lines)	2.1	2.0	9.3	11.0
ii] Direct exchange lines (million lines)	1.6	1.7	7.5	8.72
2. Long distance switching capacity (TAX) (thousand lines)	131	55.8	700	762.3
3. Long distance transmission system				
i] Coaxial cable system (thousand kms)	8.6	6.0	3.0	3.6
ii] Microwave system (thousand kms)	11.3	10.5	20.0	16.8
iii] UHF system (thousand kms)	12.9	9.9	90.0	39.7
iv] Optical fibre system (thousand kms)	5.1	2.3	40.0	46.0

It is perhaps relevant to ask why the public sector was able to deliver in telecommunications when it could not do so in power.

An important reason is the financial viability of the system. Unlike the power sector, which is burdened by heavy commercial losses, the telecommunications sector has generated a substantial surplus for re-investment. This, in turn is because the tariff structure is financially viable. Although local call charges, especially for low volume users, are underpriced, the charges for long distance traffic are set at very remunerative levels from the point of view of the service provider. The public sector system has been able to exploit its monopoly position to overcharge this category because they are viewed as high income consumers, and populist pressures to keep charges low do not arise. The net result is that revenues per line are 45 per cent higher than expenditure per line, ensuring a healthy growth of internal resources which have helped to finance a substantial expansion in capacity in the public sector. This is in sharp contrast to the power sector where revenue realization per unit of power generated is only 80 per cent of the average cost and the system generates large annual losses.

Another important difference between the public sector tele-communications system and public sector power, which may have a bearing on relative performance, is that telecommunications is under the control of the central government whereas the power system is largely under state government control. For all the limita-tions of a public sector mode of operation, the central government has been able to ensure a higher degree of professionalization of management and managerial accountability, including steps to-wards corporatization and even partial privatization. International telecommunications traffic for example is handled by a public sec-tor corporation, Videsh Sanchar Nigam Limited (VSNL), and the telephone system in the two metro cities of Bombay and Delhi (which together account for 25 per cent of the total number of lines) is handled by another public sector corporation, Mahanagar Tele-phone Nigam Limited (MTNL). Both corporations are commer-cially successful organizations which have been partly privatized and are widely perceived as among the most attractive Indian stocks, not only in the domestic capital markets, but also among foreign investors investing in Indian equity.

Remunerative tariffs combined with a willingness to pay and rapid growth in demand creates ideal conditions for attracting private investment into this sector. An experimental first step was taken in 1993 when bids were invited from private investors to provide cellular telephone services in the four metro cities of Delhi, Mumbai, Calcutta and Chennai. Processing of the bids and issue of licenses was delayed because of legal challenges by unsuccessful bidders, but despite these delays, cellular services in the metro cities commenced operation in 1995. The total number of cellular subscribers in these cities is now estimated at 0.5 million and, while this is lower than the level initially forecast by investors, it is nevertheless sizable.

A comprehensive policy towards private investment in telecommunications was outlined as part of the National Telecommunications Policy announced in 1994. The public sector monopoly in basic telephone services was formally ended and private sector operators were allowed into the sector with foreign equity upto 49 per cent. The country was divided into 20 telecom circles and each circle was thrown open for private sector participation. Bids were invited in January 1995 for one private operator per circle for basic telephone services, in competition with the existing public sector supplier, and two competing private sector cellular operators.[9] Eight private companies were awarded letters of intent for introducing basic services in 12 circles and thirteen companies were awarded 33 letters of intent for introducing cellular services in 18 circles.

As in the power sector, several unexpected problems arose which delayed project implementation:

i]   Three investors having submitted the highest bids for the telecom licenses were awarded letters of intent but failed to pay the license fee. These investors challenged the government decision to invoke the bank guarantee for non-performance and their cases are currently in court.

ii]   There were complaints that the interconnection charges imposed on private operators by the Department of Telecommunications, which were expected to be based on the cost of interconnection, were actually fixed at much higher levels on the basis of average cost rather than marginal cost principles. The DOT subsequently reduced these interconnection charges to acceptable levels and this has helped to speed up implementation.

[9] Bidders were invited to bid in terms of license fees payable and certain criteria relating to the urban rural balance, use of indigenous equipment and proposed pace of expansion.

iii]   Private investors were concerned that they would be competing against the public sector system controlled by the Department of Telecommunications which would also exercise regulatory power over private investors giving rise to possible conflicts of interest. A consensus therefore emerged in favour of establishment of an independent regulatory authority which would assure private investors of even-handed treatment. An independent Telecommunications Regulatory Authority of India was established in 1996. Shortly thereafter, in a dispute between private investors and the Department of Telecommunications, the authority ruled in favour of the private investors, and this has led to a considerable gain in its credibility.

iv]   Banks and financial institutions were unwilling to finance telecom projects unless the license agreements provided for assignability of licenses at the option of the lender in the event of default on debt service. Initially, it was felt that it may not be legally permissible to build assignability in the manner required by lenders into the license agreement. However, this issue was finally resolved to the satisfaction of lenders in 1997.

v]   The restriction of foreign equity to 49 per cent created problems because some Indian companies were unable to raise their share of the equity to meet the heavy capital requirements of telecom projects, especially in view of the high license fees involved. The problem was ultimately solved by a conscious decision to allow foreign partners to take a minority stake in Indian investment companies in which the Indian partner had a majority, and then allowing such investment companies to contribute equity in the licensee company, treating this investment as Indian equity.

With the resolution of these problems several telecommunications projects are expected to be in operation in 1998. For all the difficulties and delays, the time lag between the announcement of the policy in 1994 and actual implementation is much shorter than in power, thus indicating the learning process that has taken place.

It is interesting to note that there are two features of telecommunications which distinguish it from power generation and make it easier to attract investment in this sector. The first is the absence of any adverse consumer reaction. This is primarily because, unlike the case in power, the tariffs in telecommunications are not cost-based but are independently fixed for both the public and the private sector. Private sector suppliers are therefore seen by consumers as providing a competing alternative to the existing public sector supplier. The second positive feature is that investors in telecommunications do not suffer from payment risk because private telecommunications service providers directly bill their customers and this is a sector with a high willingness and ability to pay. Telecommunications projects, however face greater market risks than power projects. Power projects have no market risk because a minimum off-take is normally assured under power purchase agreements, whereas telecommunications projects face a competitive market situation with some uncertainty about the size of the market. However, the prospects for growth of demand for telecommunications in the medium term are generally regarded as excellent, and the market risk is therefore acceptable.

V. Road Development: Prolonged Neglect

India's 2.9 million km road network is the third largest in the world, but the quality of the network is very poor. This is partly because road development in India has traditionally emphasized rural connectivity rather than investment in arterial highways. The national highways (34,000 km) and state highways (1,29,000 km), which together carry 40 per cent of the total traffic, make up only 6 per cent of the total network, the rest consisting of local and district roads. Of the national highways, there are no expressways, only 5 per cent are 4 lane, 80 per cent two lane and 15 per cent single lane. In the case of state highways, only 1.2 per cent are four lane, 22 per cent two lane and 76.8 per cent single lane. Large sections of the highways suffer from encroachments, lack of by-passes to avoid urban areas, and proliferation of inter-State tax barriers, all of which leads to serious problems of congestion. Commercial vehicles are able to run only 200–250 km per day instead of 600 km per day in developed countries.

The Eighth Plan was not able to provide any significant increase in the scale of public investment in roads. The Plan target for the road sector (see Table 5.1) was 3 per cent of the total Plan expenditure which was almost the same as 2.9 per cent in the

Seventh Plan. However actual expenditure in the Eighth Plan proved to be 7 per cent lower than the target. The picture appears worse when we compare achievements with targets in physical terms (Table 5.5). The Plan target of 604 km. for widening national highways from 2 lanes to 4 lanes was only half met and there was a significant shortfall of 21 per cent in the target for widening to 2 lanes.

TABLE 5.5
EXPANSION OF CAPACITY IN ROADS
(NATIONAL HIGHWAYS)

	Seventh Plan		Eighth Plan	
	Targets	Achievements	Targets	Achievements
1. Widening to 2 lanes (km)	1503	1636	1076	852
2. Widening to 4 lanes (km)	116	96	604	323
3. Strengthening weak 2 lane roads (km)	3351	4025	3331	3717
4. Bypass	11	12	14	11
5. Major bridges	70	56	3	54
6. Minor bridge including Railway overbridges	375	392	326	303

Unlike power and telecommunications, which generate resources from user charges, the roads sector in India relies almost exclusively on funds provided by the central budget for national highways and by the state budgets for state highways and other roads. There is no tradition of toll roads to generate revenues, even to cover maintenance costs.[10] Though the total volume of road user taxation in India (mainly taxes on fuels and vehicles) is 2.1 per cent of GDP and compares favourably with other countries, expenditure on roads as a percentage of road user taxes is only 48 per cent. In the absence of earmarking, there has been persistent underfunding of the roads sector, which in turn has

[10] Earmarking of road user taxes is limited to a small cess of 3.5 paise per litre on petrol which is paid into the Central Roads Fund to be spent on approved state road programmes.

led to spreading resources thinly across too many projects, and also accepting low construction standards for roads. A major casualty of these financial constraints is maintenance expenditure. It is estimated that expenditure on maintenance of the existing road network is only 60 per cent of the desired amount, thus contributing to the vicious circle of deterioration in existing assets.

Recognising the severe constraints on public sector investment in roads, it is logical for the government to try and attract private investment into the roads sector. However, there are several reasons why it may be more difficult in this sector than in power or telecommunications.

i] The established practice of not charging for the use of public roads creates consumer resistance to paying tolls. This may not be a problem where the toll road is an entirely new road, but it is difficult to envisage construction of new roads in heavily trafficked corridors. The land acquisition problems alone would be formidable. What is feasible in India is upgrading of existing roads, including conversion of existing 4 lane roads into expressways or upgrading 2 lane highways into four lane highways and introducing tolls on these upgraded segments. The government has amended the law to make it possible to introduce tolls in such situations but consumer resistance is likely to be strong. In practice, this will limit the tolls to relatively low levels, which will present its own problems.

ii] Since road development is often characterized by a high degree of externality, it may not be possible to recover all costs and ensure adequate returns through tolls alone. In such situations, private investment is only feasible if there is an explicit subsidy or some other way of internalizing the external benefits, e.g., by giving private investors land development rights in areas where potential commercial value is created by the road.

iii] Road projects face a high degree of market risk because of uncertainty about the likely volume of traffic, especially if new toll roads are operated along with untolled alternatives. This is especially so because road projects typically have a long pay back period and traffic projections therefore have to be made over a long period.

iv]   Since tolls are fixed in domestic currency, and at best likely
to be adjusted over time in line with domestic inflation, the
private foreign investor has to bear the risk of exchange rate
variations. Given the long payback period in roads and the
absence of long term hedging instrument, these projects will
require much larger proportion of domestic debt and a lower
proportion of foreign debt.

The government has attempted to deal with these problems in
the new policy on private investment in roads announced in 1997.
Private participation will be invited in selected road projects, including several smaller projects such as railway over-bridges, by-
passes, bridges etc. and larger projects such as construction of
expressways and 4 laning of existing two lane national highways.
Private investors will be invited to submit competitive bids for
implementing these projects on a BOT basis with a concession
period upto 30 years. Tolls chargeable will be fixed by the Government, keeping in mind the willingness to pay and these tolls rates
will be adjusted once in two years to reflect domestic inflation. The
criterion of public acceptability in fixing tolls could make the
project unviable, but since the government is bundling an existing
road into the project at no cost to the project, this should help the
project's financial viability. The policy allows investors the rights
for commercial development of highway related facilities such as
restaurants, motels and parking space in areas to be acquired by the
Government. Foreign equity upto 74 per cent is allowed automatically and higher percentages can be considered on application.

It is obviously too early to judge whether this effort to attract
private investment in roads will succeed. There are formidable
problems of risk mitigation and it is not clear whether the policy
of restricting tolls to modest levels will provide sufficiently remunerative returns. However, a number of projects have been approved.[11] A realistic assessment is that it will be possible to attract

----

[11] These include two bypass projects (Thane-Bhiwandi in Maharashtra and
Udaipur in Rajasthan). One railway over bridge (Chalthen in Gujarat) and six
bridges on NH5 in Andhra Pradesh. Offers have been received for five
bypasses (Coimbatore, Nellore, Hubli, Dharwad, Durg and Patalganga and
two bridges (Vivekananda and Narmada). Projects on offer include 4 laning
of ten segments of the existing national highways, covering a total 1300 km
and construction of 55 bridges and bypasses. Additional 4 laning projects
amounting to 2700 km are expected to be identified.

some private investment into the roads sector, but the contribution of the private sector over the next five years can be modest at best.

The bulk of road development will therefore have to be undertaken by the public sector. Since fiscal constraints are likely to continue in future, it is important to try and put the funding of road development on a more automatic and self-sustaining basis than has been the case hitherto. Two ideas are worth pursuing in this context:

i]   A cess on petrol and diesel earmarked to fund road development in both the central and state sectors. A cess of 50 paise on both petrol and diesel (which would increase diesel prices by 5 per cent and petrol prices by 2.5 per cent) would yield Rs 3000 crores per year for road development.

ii] Public sector projects for upgrading heavily trafficked sections of the national highway could be converted into separate toll roads which could then be privatized and the resources raised from the privatization could be used to construct new highways.

Some innovative steps are certainly needed if India's road network is to be significantly improved in the next five years.

VI. PORTS: MASSIVE REFORMS NEEDED

India's ports are a major handicap in her effort to accelerate growth and especially to achieve global competitiveness. At the start of the reforms, ports were entirely in the public sector with 11 major ports effectively controlled by the central government and 139 minor ports operating under the control of state governments. Total port capacity is inadequate, and the ports are characterized by obsolete technology, hopelessly restrictive labour practices and outdated customs clearance procedures, all of which contribute to long delays in clearing cargo and much higher costs compared with other Asian ports. Ship turnaround time has improved from almost 12 days in the Seventh Plan to an average of 8.5 days, but this compares with turnaround times as short as 8 hours achieved in Singapore! Delays in berthing of ships has meant that liner ships avoid major Indian ports, preferring to tranship cargo to India from Colombo or Dubai. This denies Indian exporters access to shipping services with guaranteed time of shipment. Moreover, container handling costs are much higher than in competitor countries. This is partly because of low handling efficiency — the number of twenty foot equivalent units (TEUs) handled per hour varies from 7 in Mumbai to 15 in Madras compared with 26 in Colombo and 32 in Singapore — and partly also because of higher payments of 'speed money'.

Inadequate investment is clearly a major cause of poor performance. Plan expenditure on ports in the Eighth Plan was projected to increase significantly but actual achievement was only 42 per cent of the target (Table 5.1). This is in sharp contrast to performance in the Seventh Plan when plan expenditure on ports actually exceeded the target. However, there were large shortfalls in physical targets in both the Seventh and the Eighth Plans as shown in Table 5.6. The shortfall in capacity creation has in part been offset by improvements in physical productivity. Although total capacity at the end of 1996–7 was only 187.71 million tonnes, the total tonnage actually handled by the ports in 1996–7 was 227.13 million tonnes, implying a utilization of 121 per cent of capacity. High utilization rates are sometimes presented as an index of efficiency, and in one sense they may be, but they also reflect congestion in the ports, which is the root cause of berthing delays and long turnaround times.

TABLE 5.6
ADDITIONS TO PORT CAPACITY
(MILLION TONNES)

	Seventh Plan		Eighth Plan	
	Target	Actual	Target	Actual
POL	16.5	8.0	21.50	11.50
Iron ore	–	–	–	–
Coal	2.2	1.0	16.50	1.0
Fertilizers	4.10	4.10	–	–
Containers	5.82	3.0	2.15	2.15
General carg	0.10	0.25	6.33	4.08
Total	28.72	16.35	46.48	18.73

*   As per midterm appraisal.

The failure of ports to expand capacity in line with Plan targets is much less attributable to lack of resources than in the case of roads. Unlike the road sector, ports generate substantial surpluses from their incomes from port charges and their investment programmes are also supported by multilateral funds routed through the Central Budget. The low pace of investment is largely due to deficiencies in organizational capacity, including especially lack of financial autonomy. Unlike public sector corporations, the ports until recently did not have financial powers to approve even modest levels of capital expenditure, and had to come to the Ministry of Surface Transport for such approvals.

What is needed in the ports sector is a radical overhaul of the present organizational structure under which the ports are managed by a Board of Trustees consisting of representatives of various interests such as customs, shipowners, shippers, the State Government, defence and labour, with a full time Chairman who is a generalist civil servant. In this system the port authority functions both as a commercial entity and a regulatory authority. An alternative institutional arrangement would be to repeal the Major Ports Trust Act and allow the major ports to be converted into autonomous corporations, functioning on a commercial basis, but subject to a separate statutory regulatory authority. The government has not adopted this approach thus far. Instead, steps have been taken to increase the financial powers delegated to the ports. The limit of capital expenditure which can be approved by the ports without seeking Ministry approval has been raised from Rs 5 crores earlier to Rs 50 crores for new assets and Rs 100 crores for replacement of existing assets. This enhancement will certainly help, but the case for radical restructuring deserves full consideration. Conversion of the ports into autonomous corporations, even if the corporations remain in the public sector, will go a long way towards developing a commercial culture for operating the port and undertaking long term planning. It will also help to focus attention on modernizing labour practices, without which it is difficult to envisage significant improvement in productivity.

As in other infrastructure sectors, a policy for private investment in ports was announced in 1997. Major ports will remain in the public sector, but it is proposed to encourage privatization of individual activities, such as (a) leasing out of existing assets of the port to private operators, (b) allowing construction and operation of new assets such as container terminals and cargo berths, and (c) allowing private investment in warehouses, dry docking and ship repair facilities. Private investment will be invited on the basis of competitive bidding for specified projects on a BOT basis. Tariffs to be charged will be fixed and revised by a newly constituted Tariff Authority for Major Ports. Foreign investment upto 51 per cent is automatically allowed with higher amounts allowed on application.

The first major private investment in ports is a two berth container terminal in Jawaharlal Nehru Port, Navi Mumbai which was awarded in 1997 on the basis of competitive bidding to an Australian-Malaysian consortium. The terminal involves an investment of about $200 million and will double the container capacity of the port. Several smaller projects have also been approved in various major ports including leasing of berths to shipping lines or bulk users, leasing of land for storage facilities, setting up dry docking and ship repair facilities and creation of jetties for handling oil imports. State governments have taken bolder steps for private sector development of minor ports. Maharashtra, Gujarat and Andhra Pradesh have offered entire ports for private sector development and the first such private port, at Pipavav in Gujarat State, was commissioned in 1997.

As in other infrastructure sectors the policy for private investment in ports is relatively recent and the results will be evident only in the Ninth Plan. However, international experience suggests that it is relatively easy to attract private investment into ports. There are attractive returns to be made and there is no payment risk and relatively little market risk. Foreign exchange risk need not present problems since port charges can be fixed in foreign exchange, though this is not being done as yet in India.

VII. Prospects for the Future

The conclusion which emerges from our review of infrastructure in the first five years of economic reforms is that there was inadequate expansion of capacity in all sectors except telecommunications. Public investment fell short of the target, and efforts to attract private investment were either stalled by unanticipated problems, as in the case of power, or were initiated too late in the period for results to be evident. Economic growth accelerated in response to reforms despite these problems, because there was some slack in the system that allowed growth to accelerate despite insufficient expansion in infrastructure capacity, but this process cannot continue indefinitely. We certainly cannot assume continuation of growth in future without a substantial increase in capacity in infrastructure sectors.

Recognizing the constraints on financing infrastructure needs in the medium term, Dr Manmohan Singh in 1994 appointed an Expert Group on Commercialisation of Infrastructure Projects (hereinafter referred to as the Expert Group) to examine these constraints and make recommendations for the future. The Expert Group made projections of the capacity expansion required in various infrastructure sectors over the ten year period 1996–7 to 2006–7 to support an acceleration of economic growth to 7.5 per cent by 2001–2 and 8.5 per cent by 2005–6. The Expert Group's projections imply substantially larger additions to capacity in the Ninth Plan period 1997–8 to 2001–2 than was actually achieved in the Eighth Plan. In power generation, the requirement of additional capacity ranges from 38,000 MW to 48,000 MW. Even the lower estimate is more than double the capacity added in the Eighth Plan (Table 5.2) and this is regarded as adequate only if several steps are taken to improve the efficiency of the existing system, including modernization and de-bottlenecking of existing plants, along with steps to improve management of demand through rational energy pricing and other measures.[12] Similarly, the report projects a requirement of 21.7 million telephone lines which is about three times the number of lines added in the Eighth Plan. In ports, where decongestion is urgently needed, the report projects a requirement of 154 million tonnes of additional cargo handling capacity, which is almost eight times the addition in the Eighth Plan. In the case of roads, the report envisages a similar expansion with 2,000 km of expressways and upgrading of 10,000 km of national highways in the Ninth Plan period.

The total investment required for all four sectors ranges from Rs 325,000 crores to Rs 394,000 crores (both at 1995–6 prices) depending upon whether the lower or higher estimate for power

[12] Apart from realistic electricity pricing giving the right signals to conserve energy use and invest in energy efficient systems, there is also considerable scope for smoothing peaks in demand through time of day energy pricing which helps the total requirement of capacity in generation.

capacity is adopted. There is no prospect of resources on this scale being available in the public sector. Sectoral investment allocations for the Ninth Plan have not yet been fixed but the total size of the public sector Plan has been fixed at Rs 875,000 crores in 1996–7 prices. The share of power, telecommunications, roads and ports in the Eighth Plan was 28 per cent in terms of the original expenditure targets and only 26 per cent in terms of actual expenditure. Even if their share in the Ninth Plan is 28 per cent, the total public sector resources available for these sectors will be only Rs 245,000 crores in 1996–7 prices. Converted to 1995–6 prices to make it comparable with the Expert Group estimates, this is only about Rs 230,000 crores, which is only 70 per cent of the lower estimate of total requirements for these sectors. Even this volume of public sector resources cannot be taken for granted since actual availability could fall short of the initial projection as happened in the Eighth Plan.

The strategy for infrastructure development in future will have to focus on two fronts. First, we must ensure that public investment takes place on a much larger scale than in the Eighth Plan period. This is necessary even if we want to maximize the involvement of the private sector simply because the scale of total investment needed in infrastructure is so large, and the public sector at present so dominant, that a large part of the expansion in capacity in the next five years has to come from the public sector. Second, private sector involvement in infrastructure must be much more actively pursued than was possible in the Eighth Plan. Private investment should not be viewed as playing only a supplementary role. It should be seen potentially as a major contributor to infrastructure expansion in future, with the additional merit that involvement of private sector suppliers would create a more competitive environment and thus contribute to overall efficiency.

The ability to increase public sector investment in infrastructure will depend critically upon the ability to mobilise resources for this purpose. In the past, public investment has been financed by a combination of direct support from the budget, internally generated surpluses and borrowings from the capital market. The prospects for expanded levels of budget support are not encouraging given the fiscal constraints affecting both the Centre and the States. The combined fiscal deficit of the Centre and the States together is around 8 per cent of GDP, which is among the highest of all developing countries. There are strong macroeconomic compulsions for reducing the deficit, which in turn limits the growth of budget expenditure. Given the pressure to increase expenditure in the social sectors and in poverty alleviation schemes, which have to rely solely on the budget, it is difficult to envisage a large increase in budget support for infrastructure. Resources for public investment in infrastructure therefore will have to come from improved financial performance of the relevant public sector agencies leading to larger internal surpluses available for investment. This depends crucially up on the ability to levy viable user charges. The experience with telecommunications in the Eighth Plan period demonstrates that, with viable user charges it is possible to finance substantial expansion of capacity in the public sector and this lesson could be profitably applied to sectors such as power, ports and the railways.[13] It is less applicable for road development which may have to remain heavily dependent upon budgetary support for some time to come, and it is therefore important to achieve automaticity in financing of this sector by the levy of a cess on diesel and petrol.

Lack of resources is not, however, the only problem limiting the ability of the public sector to expand capacity in infrastructure. There are also serious organizational weaknesses in various government agencies involved in these sectors, such as the State Electricity Boards, the Port Trusts and the Public Works Departments responsible for road construction. These weaknesses are reflected in poor levels of utilization of existing capacity and also in poor use of resources to expand capacity. Unless these weaknesses are addressed, a mere injection of additional resources into the existing system will not yield optimal results. A possible approach to institutional reform is to reorganize these agencies

13 The problems facing the railways in expanding capacity have not been discussed in detail in this paper. As with other sectors, the railways have seen a decline in budget support as a source of financing plan expenditure, forcing an increased reliance upon internal resource generation. The Indian Railway system is unique among publicly owned railway systems in that it makes a profit. However, the extent of internal resource generation is less than it should be because of underpricing of passenger fares which are cross-subsidised by overcharging freight. These are limits to such cross subsidization since high freight rates only lead to switching rail traffic to roads. Indian passenger fares are among the lowest in the world and it is increasing clear that unless the extent of subsidy in passenger fares is reduced it will not be possible to finance the modernization and expansion of the railway system which is urgently needed.

wherever possible on the lines of corporations rather than government departments. This would encourage development of a commercial culture with better financial planning and professionalization of management.

Turning to private investment, it must be recognized that it is not easy to attract private investment in infrastructure. Infrastructure sectors are highly regulated and involve complex and multi-level interface between the private investor and various government agencies. Therefore it is necessary to work actively to create the pre-conditions which are necessary to attract private investment. These include public acceptance of the need for private investment in infrastructure (which helps to reduce perceptions of political risk), a structure of tariffs which can assure remunerative returns for investors, clarity of government policy and transparency of procedures governing the interface between private investors and various public authorities to reduce uncertainty and finally, establishment of independent regulatory agencies charged with ensuring fair treatment for private investors. Fortunately, the policy environment in India has evolved precisely in these directions over the past few years, partly responding to the experience gained with the early private sector projects. The policy has also gained credibility as the first private sector projects are being seen to get underway in power, telecommunications and ports. Nevertheless, there is room for further improvement. The private investment policy in each infrastructure sector should be comprehensively reviewed and aligned as closely as possible with current best practice in countries which have been successful in attracting private investment in infrastructure.

Despite these positive developments, questions remain on whether private investment can really take place on a large scale. Even if the pre-conditions enumerated above are successfully established, the scale of private investment will be constrained by the availability of finance. There are several problems in this area. At a macroeconomic level, the availability of finance depends upon the flow of domestic savings, and the inflow of foreign savings and policies which expand these flows will increase resources available for private investment in general, and therefore also for investment in infrastructure. India's gross domestic savings rate is around 26 per cent of GDP and the current account deficit around 1.5 per cent. The Expert Group has projected an increase in the savings rate by a little over 2 percentage points over the next five years. The current account deficit, could also be increased to around 2.5 per cent of GDP without endangering the viability of the external payments position, especially if the higher deficit is financed largely by a corresponding increase in foreign investment and not external debt. These projections are not unrealistic and suggest that there could be a significant increase in total resource availability over the next five years. However focusing on aggregate flows ignores the special problems in financing infrastructure projects.

One set of special problems relates to risk mitigation. All projects face normal commercial risks but infrastructure projects are subject to higher risks because of their high capital intensity, high degree of regulatory control and relatively long payback period. Since these projects are typically financed on a non-recourse basis, lenders have no recourse to the sponsors of the project but only to the revenue stream of the project itself. The risks associated with the revenue stream are therefore carefully assessed, and financing is possible only if risks are acceptable. The usual approach to ensure the financeability of the project is to unbundle various types of risks and assign each risk to the agent best able to manage it, thus reducing the risk borne by the project to acceptable levels at some cost to the project.[14] This is essentially a technical problem of structuring projects to achieve suitable risk mitigation. Government agencies and financing institutions in India have gained considerable experience in this area while dealing with the first infrastructure projects. Clarity of government policy, the existence of credible and independent regulatory authorities and most important of all, a track record of successful implementation of

---

[14] The increase in cost to the project as a result of reassignment of risks is not necessarily an increase in cost to the economy or even to the users of the service since, in a public sector framework, the risk is borne by the project with attendant costs of disruptions in supply and losses. There is a tendency, among public sector organisations, to ignore problems of risk unbundling on the grounds that the risks are in any case borne by the public sector system as a whole. This shifting risk of fuel supply from a public sector power plant to a public sector coal company may seem pointless. However, this ignores the fact that pricing of risk mitigation and shifting risks to agents best able to manage them reduces the probability of adverse developments at least cost and thus increases total efficiency. For a detailed analysis of these issues see Ahluwalia (1997).

private sector projects, can help reduce risk perception very substantially.

Another set of problems relates to the availability of suitable types of finance. Infrastructure projects have long payback periods which implies a need for long term debt. They also typically generate revenues in domestic currency on the basis of tariffs which are usually fixed in the domestic currency and linked to domestic inflation. As a result, these projects cannot rely too heavily on external debt without exposing themselves excessively to foreign exchange risk. The financing of infrastructure projects therefore depends crucially upon the access to long term domestic debt.

The availability of long term domestic debt is therefore a critical constraint on the pace of private investment in infrastructure. Unfortunately, the domestic debt market is as yet at an early stage of development in India as in many developing countries. Several factors are involved in developing strong debt markets. A high rate of private savings is clearly one factor as is a sound macro-economic balance, reflected in modest fiscal deficits. High fiscal deficits distort domestic debt markets by putting strong upward pressure on interest rates, which in turn makes it difficult to develop deep and liquid markets for government debt. An important institutional requirement for a healthy domestic debt market is the existence of long term contractual savings organizations such as insurance companies and pension funds, which have a natural appetite for long term high quality debt. Reforms in the insurance sector are therefore crucial for the increase of private financing of infrastructure. This is an aspect of financial sector reform which is currently on the government's agenda and needs early implementation.

To summarize, infrastructure development is clearly a critical constraint and poses a special challenge to policy-makers in the years ahead. Fortunately, there is today a much wider recognition of the need to make radical departures in the way these sectors are organized and financed, and also in the role of the private sector in future expansion. The policy framework to make radical departures possible has taken time to evolve, and is not yet fully in place, but there has been very substantial movement in most areas. With continued effort on a broad front, there is a good chance that the Ninth Plan period will see a convincing turn around in infrastructure performance in both the public and the private sector. Unless this is achieved, the objectives of the reforms unleashed in 1991 cannot be realized.

REFERENCES

Montek S. Ahluwalia (1997): 'Financing Private Infrastructure: Lessons from India', in *Choices for Efficient Private Provision of Infrastructure in East Asia*, Harinder S. Kohli, Ashoka Mody and Michael Walton (eds), The World Bank, Washington, DC.

Expert Group on Commercialisation of Infrastructure Projects *The India Infrastructure Report: Policy Imperative for Growth and Welfare*, vols I, II & III.

Planning Commission, *Eighth Five Year Plan*, vols I & II.

6

Indian Agriculture in an Open Economy: Will it Prosper?

Ashok Gulati

> *We have to recognize that high protection for industry constituted a heavy implicit taxation of agriculture, leading to reduced resource generation in agriculture and the increasing diversion of the available surplus for industrial development.*
>
> [Manmohan Singh, 1995]

I. BACKDROP

Indian policy-making has suffered from a typical 'anti-agriculture' bias since 1956. Although there has not been any significant direct taxation of agriculture, yet it has proved to be a heavily 'taxed' sector. This is effected through the subtle instrument of trade policy, that always worked against it. High protection to industry, for far too long and well past the stage of infancy, and an over-valued exchange rate, inflicted heavy implicit taxation on agriculture. The relative incentive environment was tilted against agriculture. Agriculture had to bear the brunt of generating resources for the newly emerging industrial sector — the darling of development. The underlying assumption perhaps was that a rapidly growing manufacturing sector would siphon off labour from agriculture in due course. This would allow the agricultural sector too to modernize itself with a more favourable land–man ratio, and raise productivity in agriculture. But history proved it otherwise. Over four decades of development from 1951–91, while the share of agriculture in national GDP slid from 56 to 32 per cent, its share in the working population fell only marginally from 71 to 64 per cent. As a consequence, intersectoral inequalities increased, creating a chasm between rural–urban India. Rural India appears to have been betrayed, but kept alive with occasional injections of technology and subsidies.

The political economy of food compelled our policy-makers to periodically look back to agriculture, whenever the spectre of hunger loomed large or donors (under PL 480) twisted our arms. The first shot was given in mid-sixties. In January 1965, under the Prime Ministership of the late Lal Bahadur Shastri, the Agricultural Prices Commission and the Food Corporation of India were created to give high and effective price support to farmers. C. Subramaniam steered through the political debate on the import of 18,000 tonnes of HYV wheat seeds. With these dramatic changes, a negative price policy era (1951–65) turned into one of a positive price policy (Krishna and Raychaudhuri, 1980). Along with imports of new technology, it saw the ushering in of the green revolution in the late 1960s, but it was short lived.

After the world oil crisis of 1973–4, once again industry became the focal point of development planners. The green revolution started greying in the late 1970s, but the new rice seeds and positive price policy for rice gave it a new lease of life. Thereafter, since the 1980s, it is surviving on an increasing dosage of input subsidies, creating large price distortions, bankrupting the input supplying agencies, and placing an unsustainable financial burden on the exchequer.

The reforms of 1991, especially the trade policy reforms, perhaps for the first time, aimed at correcting the 'anti-agriculture' bias in trade policies. If the momentum of trade policy reforms is accelerated, and protection for industry is brought to the same level as that for agriculture, the reformers will accomplish a great deal more for the Indian peasant than several well wishers and development planners of the past. What Indian agriculture needs is a 'level playing field' with domestic industry, in an open economy environment. This would be a precondition, not necessarily a sufficient one, for a new paradigm of growth where agriculture triggers growth impulses in other sectors through its backward and forward linkages. Growth would be widely distributed to the countryside, where the soul of India resides.

Will the process of globalizing the Indian economy, initiated since 1991, include agriculture to any substantial degree? What will be the impact of this globalization on Indian agriculture? It is precisely these questions that I wish to explore in this contribution. Accordingly, after this brief backdrop, I first delineate in Section II the progress of the Indian economy in terms of opening up during the period 1991–6. It broadly covers industry and agriculture. Section III explores the likely implications of globalizing the economy for Indian agriculture, both as a sector, as also for major crops. Section IV presents some concerns arising from the globalization process, especially the issues of supply bottlenecks and food security. I also enunciate in this section a compressed policy package to overcome the critical constraints to enable agriculture to realize the potential gains from the process of globalization while minimizing its likely adverse effects, especially on the poor.

II. Towards an Open Economy, 1991–6

The process of opening up an economy involves replacing quantitative controls on imports and exports by 'tariffication', and then lowering the tariffs; removing biases in incentive structures to produce for exports or the home market, or between tradeables and non-tradeables, by allowing the exchange rate to be determined by market conditions; and removing restrictions on the flow of foreign capital in the various sectors. While the process of opening up the Indian economy started in the early 1980s, picked up some momentum in the late 1980s,[1] yet the real breakthrough came in 1991.

II.1 Opening up Trade and
Investment in the Manufacturing Sector

It started with adjustment of the exchange rate. The rupee was devalued by 22 per cent in July 1991. The Exim Scrip Scheme, introduced a sort of dual exchange rate by granting exporters freely tradeable import entitlements equivalent to 30 per cent of their export earnings. In February 1992, the Liberalized Exchange Rate Management System (LERMS) was introduced, resulting in partial convertibility of the rupee, allowing 60 per cent of the foreign exchange earnings to be converted at the market-determined

[1] This is especially in terms of allowing the rupee to depreciate in line with market conditions in the foreign exchange market.

exchange rate. In March 1993 the rupee was made convertible for most current account transactions. Invisibles were added to this list in August 1994, thus completing full convertibility of the rupee on current account. However, the capital account still remained controlled.

The Interim Report of the Tax Reforms Committee (GOI, 1991) suggested the future course of trade policy: the import weighted average level of tariffs (excluding countervailing duty) to be brought down from 87 per cent in 1989–90 to 45 per cent by 1995–6, and to 25 per cent by 1998–9 (GOI, 1991).[2] These recommendations saw the light of day through the EXIM Policy 1992–7 in varying degrees. Going by the targets of the TRC, progress in this direction has been much faster than expected. By 1995–6, the import weighted average tariff was just 27 per cent for all goods; 15 per cent for agricultural goods, 30 per cent for capital goods, 24 per cent for intermediate goods, and 39 per cent for consumer goods (see Roy in Kelkar and Rao, 1996: 232). But if we compare these achievements against the recommendations of the TRC's Final Report (GOI, 1992), there is still scope for further reduction in import duties on several products. Also, if we look at import weighted tariffs in countries like Mexico with 10 per cent tariff in 1990, Brazil with 14 per cent in 1993, Indonesia with 10 per cent in 1989–91, and Korea with 9 per cent in 1985–92, Indian tariff rates are still very high (Ahluwalia, 1996). Nevertheless, compared to its own past, the progress in tariff reductions has been reasonably impressive, except in consumer goods.

The process of opening up goes much beyond the magnitude of import duty rates. When the reforms began in July 1991, out of 5021 tariff lines (Harmonized System at 6 digits' code) about

---

[2] The Final Report of the Tax Reform Committee remarked, 'We now feel that the basic reform of the tariff structure could be completed by 1996–7 or latest by 1997–8. By that time the import weighted average rate of duties should have come down to around 25 per cent (excluding any zero rated commodities, but including consumer goods) . . . we are recommending that by 1997 or 1998 March end, the structure of ad-valorem rates of duties in place should be: 5, 10, 15, 20, 25, and 30. In addition, when non-essential consumer goods are allowed to be imported, there should be another "slot" for them, namely 50 per cent' (GOI, 1993: 5–6). Thus, the recommendations in the final report were bolder than in the interim report. Even by the targets of the final report, the progress in this direction has to date been quite satisfactory.

4000 (i.e. about 80 per cent) were under the import licensing regime. By December 1995, over 3000 tariff lines covering raw materials, intermediate and capital goods, were freed from import licensing requirements. Besides, 1487 tariff lines, whose imports are otherwise restricted, can be imported under freely tradable Special Import Licences being granted to export houses/trading houses/star trading houses and super star trading houses (GOI, 1996: Box 6.3, 110). This is a major initiative towards globalization of the economy.

The inflow of foreign capital has been liberalized. Automatic approval for FDI (equity participation) up to 74 per cent has been entrusted to the Reserve Bank of India (RBI). But despite the liberalized norms, and approvals worth over US$15 bn given during the period 1991–5, the actual inflows have been pitiably low at only about 23 per cent of approvals. This speaks of several hurdles ranging from red-tape to political uncertainty in the country. From that perspective it has been a poor show.

II.2 Opening up Agriculture

What have been the changes since 1991 which may be deemed to lead towards globalization of Indian agriculture? The Tax Reform Committee (GOI, 1993) had recommended that agricultural commodities should basically attract three rates of import duties. First, essential agricultural commodities like wheat and rice should be imported at zero per cent duty; secondly, commodities like oilseeds and pulses should attract 10 per cent duty; and thirdly, non-essential agricultural goods like almond and cashew nuts should be imported at 50 per cent import duty. All this transformation in import duties should be achieved by 1996–7 or latest by 1997–8.

Besides, India became a signatory to the Uruguay Round trade negotiations, including agriculture. Though the general direction of commitments under the UR was towards opening up agriculture in all the countries,[3] there was enough scope to negotiate a stand

---

[3] The signing of GATT on 15 April 1994 at Marrakesh, implied that physical controls on exports and imports of agricultural commodities would have to be replaced with tariffs, that tariffs have to be bound, and then gradually reduced — faster by the developed countries than by the developing countries like India. It also implied that the export subsidies on agricultural

that would slow down the process of opening up agriculture (see Ingco, 1995; Martin and Winters, 1995). India, for example, bound its tariffs for most agricultural products at very high levels: 150 per cent for meat and fish, 100 per cent for milk and cream, 150 per cent for yoghurt, 40 per cent for butter, butter oil, and cheese, 100 per cent for wheat, barley, rye, oats, and pulses. Most of the fruits and vegetables, and their preparations, are also bound at 100 per cent. Edible oils like soya, rapeseed, mustard, olive and colza are bound at 45 per cent, while all others including coconut and palm oils are bound at 300 per cent. Raw cotton and sugar are bound at 150 per cent, and raw tobacco at 100 per cent. All these tariff levels, if applied, would be prohibitive, and India can therefore effectively insulate its agriculture from world markets. The only exceptions are commodities like rice, maize, sorghum and millets, which have zero import duty. But this does not mean much as the imports of these commodities at present are canalized. The problem would arise on account of these commodities once the quantitative restrictions on their import are abolished.[4]

What then have been the changes in trade policies relating to major agricultural products since 1991, and do they indicate a movement towards globalization of Indian agriculture?

To respond to this question, we should look specifically at three levels of policy change. First, have the quantitative restrictions on imports and exports of agricultural products been removed? Second, have the exports and imports of these commodities been decanalized? And third, have the tariff levels been brought in line

---

commodities have to be reduced and also the domestic support as measured by Aggregate Measure of Support (AMS). Those countries that do not want to bind their tariffs at 'acceptable' levels will have to give minimum access to imports of agricultural commodities from other countries: 3 per cent of domestic consumption of that commodity to start with, going up to 5 per cent by 2001.

[4] In January 1997, GOI set up an expert committe to 'Assess the Impact of removal of Quantitative Restrictions on agricultual commodities *vis-à-vis* WTO requirements'. The initial deliberations of the Committee revealed that these zero tariff bindings for some commodities like rice, plums, fresh grapes, and dried skimmed milk were committed in 1947 (Geneva Protocol 1947). Some other commodities like maize, millet, spelt were bound at zero import duty in Torquay Protocol of 1951. Sorghum was bound at zero import duty in Geneva Protocol of 1962 (Dillon Round). India would like to open up this issue with WTO and ask for their upward revision once the BOP cover to India is withdrawn.

with those indicated in the Tax Reform Committee (GOI, 1993), i.e. at zero, 10, and 50 per cent for different categories of agricultural products? Viewed from these angles, the performance of trade policy since the 1991 reforms has been dismal.

The *grain sector*, which is the largest segment of Indian agriculture, remains largely controlled and insulated from global markets. Imports remain tightly regulated through canalization, with a notable exception of pulses that can be freely imported at 5 per cent import duty. Exports of common wheat and rice on private account were opened in late 1994, but brought back under controls in 1996.[5] Within the *oilseeds sector*, imports of oilseeds remained practically banned during 1991–6. Exports of hand-picked select (HPS) groundnut were allowed, and in 1995 even exports of rapeseed/mustard and sunflower seeds were permitted. Edible oils, however, saw some major changes towards opening up of import policies.[6] But exports of edible oils remained virtually banned. Exports of oilcakes remain open. *Cotton* imports have been decanalized at zero import duty in 1994, but exports remain restrictive through export quotas. *Sugar* has finally been freed from all import and export restrictions. Imports were decanalized at zero import duty in March 1994, with molasses following in March 1995 at 10 per cent import duty. Exports of sugar have only recently been truly freed.[7] Gur was always freely exportable.

---

[5] Some steps, which were taken to soften the degree of controls on exports of foodgrains during this period are recounted here. The minimum export price (MEP) for *basmati* rice was abolished in January 1994, and for common rice in October 1994. October 1994 also saw the lifting of a ban on the export of non-durum wheat. Export quotas were retained, but the ceilings were raised. As a result, India exported over 5 m.t. of rice and emerged as the second largest exporter in the world, but the drop in procurement of wheat by almost 4 m.t. in 1996–7 (April to March) over the previous year resulted in a reversion to export controls on wheat and wheat products. Import of wheat had to be resorted to on a canalized basis on government account, although wheat flour mills were allowed to import directly. Similarly, imports of rice or coarse cereals are also canalized.

[6] In March 1994, first palmolein imports were put under OGL at an import duty of 65 per cent. In February 1995, all other major edible oils were also put in the same basket with a drastic cut in import duty to 30 per cent, which was further lowered to 20 per cent in the Central Budget of 1996–7, with a notable exception of coconut that still remains a canalized item.

[7] In the 1991–2 reform package, exports of sugar were opened. But domestic pressure groups did not allow true decanalization of exports until

Amongst *other commodities* of Indian agriculture, jute remains free both in terms of imports and exports. Fruits and vegetables are largely free to be exported, with a notable exception of onions, but import tightly regulated. Similarly, tea and coffee remain free to be exported (although influenced by their Commodity Boards), but their imports remains practically banned. Similar treatment is meted out to spices. Natural rubber can be freely exported but imports are licenced. Tobacco is exportable with MEP, but imports are banned. Dairy products, especially, skimmed milk powder (SMP) and butter oil were opened for import in March 1995 at zero and 40 per cent import duties, respectively. Exports are decanalized but subject to export quotas.

TABLE 6.1
TARIFF STRUCTURE 1990–1 TO 1995–6

(percentage)

Year	Maximum tariff	Import weighted average tariff				
		Overall	Agl. goods	Capital goods	Inter-mediate goods	Consumer goods
1990–1	350	87	70	97	117	164
1991–2	150	n.a	n.a	n.a	n.a	n.a
1992–3	110	64	30	76	55	144
1993–4	85	47	25	49	42	94
1994–5	65	33	17	38	31	48
1995–6	50	27	15	30	24	39

n.a.   not available
SOURCE: Roy (1996).

Thus, *overall*, it appears that India has taken rapid strides towards globalizing the economy since the 1991 reforms, but the larger part of this remained restricted to the industrial sector. Agriculture experienced a lot of hiccups in trade liberalization, and

---

the beginning of 1997. Earlier they were being canalized through the STC, and later 'managed' by the Indian Sugar and General Industries Export and Import Corporation, a company floated by sugar mills, and supported by the government.

within agriculture the cereals group remained largely insulated from world markets. The reluctance to open up the cereals sector appears to stem from the issues relating to food security, which I shall take up in Section IV. In the case of cash crops, the approach seems to be to allow imports if there is a net deficit and allow exports if there is a comfortable surplus. Trade is still taking place as a 'residual' between domestic demand and supply rather than as a policy instrument to integrate domestic agriculture with world agriculture, and so to optimize the use of resources.

III. LIKELY IMPLICATIONS OF GLOBALIZATION

Theoretically, the process of globalization of the Indian economy would involve reduction of import duties on the highly protected manufacturing sector, and freeing agricultural exports, which are somewhat disprotected. This should inevitably lead to the terms of trade moving in favour of agriculture, and improvement in the relative incentive environment for agriculture. Other things remaining constant, it should invite higher private investments, spurring growth in agriculture. Enhanced agricultural incomes should then generate enough demand for industrial products through its backward and forward linkages. It would also stimulate and sustain off-farm activities in the rural areas. This, therefore, can spark-off an upward moving virtuous circle of development. Since the pivot of this development process would be the rural economy, growth could be widely diffused, reducing intersectoral and interpersonal inequalities. This could be a major gain in the long run as it would lay the foundation of a stable and sustainable secular growth process. Further, there is enough empirical evidence to show that growth in agriculture and off-farm activities in rural areas is the surest way of rapidly cutting down poverty. With all these potential gains from globalization, it is a matter of wonderment why the reformers have been so slow in this area.

There are thus likely to be large sectoral level implications from globalization of the economy, and within agriculture too there is likely to be quite substantial change. Different crops will react differently to this changing incentive environment, and so will different regions and different farmers. There will be losers and gainers, and a need to change cropping patterns to align well with the matrix of international prices of different crops. The gains would go to farmers and regions that are producing, or are quick to switch over to, crops that have greater comparative advantage in production, the comparative advantage being measured in an open economy framework of analysis.

III.1 At the Sectoral Level

In order to test the theoretical postulates spelt out above, we must look for empirical evidence from the experience of similar developing countries, and also from within India of the relationships amongst different variables. In this context, it is worth noting that Schiff and Valdes (1992) have empirically estimated the impact of government intervention on the growth of agriculture, and also on the overall growth of the economy of 18 developing countries.[8] Government intervention is measured in terms of various policies that make the domestic prices diverge from world prices, and also that leads to overvaluation of exchange rates. The protection accorded to industry and overvalued exchange rates constitute an 'indirect tax' on agriculture, while keeping domestic agricultural prices below world prices constitutes a 'direct tax'. In countries where the total 'implicit tax' (direct and indirect) was –46.2 per cent of the value of agricultural produce, the rate of agricultural growth was only 2.7 per cent per annum over the period 1960–85. In contrast, countries that taxed their agriculture lightly (–8.3 per cent), experienced growth in agriculture of 5.2 per cent per annum (Schiff and Valdes, 1992: 9). In other words, by taxing agriculture substantially, these developing countries constrained the growth of their agricultural sectors by as much as 90 per cent. This obviously had an impact on their overall growth of GDP. Extreme taxers (total taxation –51.6 per cent) had GDP growth of 3.3 per cent per annum for the period 1960–85, as against 5.1 per cent for representative taxers (taxation –36.4 per cent), 5.3 per cent

[8] The 18 developing countries are divided into four categories based on the rates of 'implicit taxation' on agriculture as a percentage of agricultural output. These are: (I) Extreme taxers (average tax 51.6 per cent): Cote d'Ivoire, Ghana, Zambia; (II) Representative taxers (average tax 36.4 per cent): Argentina, Colombia, Dominian Republic, Egypt, Morocco, Pakistan, the Philippines, Sri Lanka, Thailand, Turkey; (III). Mild taxers (average tax 15.8 per cent): Brazil, Chile, Malaysia; (IV) Protectors (average tax –10.4 per cent): Korea, Republic of Portugal. The average tax across the entire sample of 18 countries was 30.3 per cent.

for mild taxers (taxation –15.8 per cent), and 6.5 per cent for protectors (protection 10.4 per cent) (Ibid.: 11). India was not one of these 18 countries, but recent research on protection to manufacturing and agriculture (Gulati and Pursell, 1996) has revealed that India also belonged to the category of representative taxers in the mid-1980s. The manufacturing sector was protected by about 46 per cent while agriculture was being disprotected by about 20 per cent, leading to a large implicit 'discrimination' against agriculture. The aggregate measure of support (AMS) for Indian agriculture worked out at –22 per cent for the triennium ending (TE) 1988–9, –21 per cent for the TE 1992–3, and –17.6 per cent for the TE 1994–5 (Table 6.2). Even in the case of a state like Punjab, which is supposed to be receiving fairly substantial input subsidies, Bhalla and Singh (1996) have estimated the AMS to be as high as –28.7 per cent for the triennium ending 1992–3.

TABLE 6.2
PRODUCT SPECIFIC AND NON-PRODUCT
SPECIFIC AGGREGATE MEASURE OF SUPPORT (AMS)

(Rs bn)

Support type	TE 1988–9	TE 1992–3	TE 1994–5
Product specific AMS			
(a) Based on support prices	–242.25 (–27.74)	–427.89 (–26.33)	–483.31 (–23.09)
(b) Based on farm harvest prices	–151.03 (–17.29)	–295.21 (–18.17)	–295.93 (–14.14)
Non-product specific AMS	45.77 (5.24)	86.45 (5.32)	114.71 (5.48)
Total product specific and non-product specific AMS			
(a) Based on support prices	–196.48 (–22.50)	–341.44 (–21.01)	–368.59 (–17.61)
(b) Based on farm harvest prices	–105.26 (–12.05)	–208.76 (–12.85)	–181.22 (–8.66)

NOTE: Figures in parentheses are percentages to the total value of
            agricultural production (excluding forestry and fishery).
SOURCES: Gulati and Sharma (1995, 1997a).

In some years, such as 1989–90, it was as high as –63.25 per cent. For the entire 12 year period between 1981–2 to 1992–3, the average AMS for Punjab turns out to be –32.64 per cent of the value of agricultural production (Table 6.3). This is much higher than we have estimated at the all India level (but there are some differences in methodology in the two studies). Such AMS obviously had an adverse impact on the growth of Indian agriculture, which remained much below its potential.

It is noted that since the early 1980s, the Indian economy had been experiencing some form of liberalization, which was accelerated in 1991. What impact did this have on the terms of trade,

TABLE 6.3
TOTAL AGGREGATE MEASURE OF
SUPPORT (AMS) TO PUNJAB AGRICULTURE
ON THE BASIS OF THE OFFICIAL EXCHANGE RATE

(Rs millions)

Year	Product specific AMS	Non-product specific AMS	Total AMS (2+3)	Value of agriculture production	Total AMS as percentage of agricultural production (4/5) × 100
(1)	(2)	(3)	(4)	(5)	(6)
1981–2	–10015.6	352.1	–9663.5	28190.3	–34.28
1982–3	–6003.2	631.4	–5371.8	30597.8	–17.56
1983–4	–5955.9	1017.9	–4938.0	32413.5	–15.23
1984–5	–9275.6	2201.7	–7073.9	37728.7	–18.75
1985–6	–26377.0	2904.5	–23472.5	43860.0	–53.52
1986–7	–18174.6	1653.7	–16520.9	44655.9	–37.00
1987–8	–29175.9	2848.8	–26327.1	53646.0	–49.08
1988–9	–14334.6	4381.5	–9953.1	58567.2	–17.00
1989–90	–49224.6	5900.9	–43323.7	68499.0	–63.25
1990–1	–26900.7	4994.0	–21902.7	71365.6	–30.70
1991–2	–27006.0	8085.6	–18920.4	89158.0	–21.22
1992–3	–42959.3	10335.2	–32624.1	95752.6	–34.07

SOURCE: G.S. Bhalla and G. Singh (1996), p. 57.

private sector investment in agriculture,[9] and hence on the overall growth of Indian agriculture? Looking at the terms of trade, as compiled by the Commission for Agricultural Costs and Prices with the triennium ending 1971–2 = 100, we find that there is a perceptible movement in favour of agriculture. The terms of trade having dipped to the lowest level of 81 in 1980–1, recovered gradually to 92 in 1991–2 and stood at 98.7 in 1994–5 (GOI, 1996). Private sector investment in agriculture, after having stagnated until 1986–7, has shown a clear departure from the behaviour of public sector investments in agriculture. How much impact it had/will have on the growth of agriculture is difficult to say because of the influence of other factors, especially rainfall, and public sector investment. Also, it takes time for the 'price factor' to work its way through to agricultural production. The exact magnitude of this impact depends upon several other bottlenecks in the production system. Studies on Indian agriculture indicate that the aggregate supply response is quite low, at least in the short run. It increases to over double in the long run, which in supply response equations is just 2 to 3 years. But a better method of estimating the impact of liberalization is through a Computable General Equilibrium Model (CGEM) or through a multimarket model, rather than through a single equation approach.

Parikh et al. (1996) have tried to capture the impact of trade liberalization on agriculture through an applied GEM. The results are on expected lines: liberalization triggers growth in agriculture, the impact is more from industrial liberalization than from agricultural liberalization per se. The poor are in the short run adversely affected by the liberalization of agriculture, necessitating a 'safety net'.

[9] Patnaik (1996), however, remarks that the terms of trade have no bearing on private sector investment in agriculture. Once the minimum profitability in agriculture is established, what happens to the terms of trade has no influence on private sector investment, and thereby on growth in agriculture. Private sector investment in agriculture, according to Patnaik, depends basically on public sector investment in agriculture (see Patnaik, 1996: 24–8). But the empirical evidence does not appear to support Patnaik's theoretical postulate. Mishra and Hazell (1996), for example, demonstrate that the terms of trade between agriculture and industry do have a strong bearing on private investment in agriculture for the period 1960–1 to 1989–90. Along with the terms of trade, other factors that influenced private sector investment in agriculture were technology and public sector investment (see Mishra and Hazell, 1996: A9).

Subramanian (1993, 1994) also tried to capture the impact of trade liberalization on different variables through a CGEM combined with a multimarket approach and Social Accounting Matrix. The broad results are in line with those of Parikh et al. (1996) that agricultural liberalization per se has little impact on growth of agriculture, and thereby on the overall growth of the economy, but when this liberalization is combined with liberalization of the manufacturing sector, growth in agriculture is accelerated. Indeed, about two-thirds of the impact of liberalization on agriculture comes from the liberalization of the manufacturing sector. Opening up agriculture runs another danger of raising poverty levels in the short run. This happens especially when agricultural prices rise without commensurate increases in production. On the other hand, reduction in the tariffs on manufacturing helps in reducing poverty levels. From that perspective, opening up the industrial sector first seems a logical choice.

To date what has been the impact of either opening up the industrial sector or agricultural sector, or both, on Indian agriculture? The *Economic Survey*, 1995–6, observes, 'The robust agricultural performance in the last four years is not just the result of normal monsoons, but also due to improved incentives for the agricultural sector as a whole. Comprehensive reforms of tariff rates, trade policy, and the exchange rate system have greatly reduced the earlier bias in favour of manufacturing arising from high levels of protection and has improved the relative profitability of agriculture' (GOI, 1996: 5). I feel this is premature. The growth in agricultural GDP during 1995–6 has been less than 1 per cent, despite a reasonably good monsoon. While the import weighted average tariff has come down from 87 per cent in the pre-reform period to 27 per cent by 1995–6, the growth in agriculture has remained moderate (an average of less than 3 per cent for 1991–2 to 1995–6).

What can be the reasons behind this lack of response from agriculture to this sharply declining anti-agriculture bias? Structural bottlenecks in Indian agriculture appear to provide an answer. These may range from the pattern of landholdings to problems of irrigation development and water management. It may well also be due to the problems in institutional credit for the rural sector. Thus, to get full mileage from the reforms already carried out, it is important to address the supply bottlenecks in agriculture — especially water and credit. Without taking the reforms to these areas, the dream of policy-makers to trigger growth in agriculture through globalization of the economy may not materialize. Eradication of the anti-agriculture bias seems to be an important condition for higher growth in agriculture under the new set of policies, but may not be a sufficient condition.

III.2 At Crop-specific Level

To get an idea of the crop-specific impact of liberalization, we may look at the wedge between their domestic and international prices (as revealed by their protection coefficients) and also examine their resource cost ratios.[10] These may be combined with the domestic profitability in these crops *vis-à-vis* competing crops. This may give an idea of the distortions that lie in the existing cropping patterns and, with the opening up of the economy, how these will change. The ones that have low resource cost ratios, or lower protection coefficients, are likely to flourish more in an open economy environment than those that are high on the resource cost ratio or the protection coefficient front. The greater the divergence from unity, the greater the chances of realizing large efficiency gains from changes in cropping patterns. If we examine these RCRs, or effective protection coefficients, against the domestic incentives (measured domestic profitability as Rs/ha. or in terms of rates of profit over paid out costs), we see the inconsistency between domestic policies and what is indicated by potential efficiency gains from the globalization of agriculture.

We now explore this dimension of crop-specific implications

[10] Resource cost ratio is a variant of the widely used concept of domestic resource cost (DRC). DRC is expressed as the cost of domestic resources that go to save or earn a unit of foreign exchange. DRC is defined as a ratio of the value of non-traded inputs valued at their shadow prices (opportunity costs) that go to produce one unit of output to the difference in the price of output at the world reference price and sum of all traded inputs (valued at world reference prices) that go to produce one unit of output. If the denominator is also expressed in domestic currency, the ratio becomes a pure number, which is termed the resource cost ratio (RCR). The higher this ratio from unity, the greater its allocative inefficiency in the production of that commodity. If the RCR is less than one, it is indicative of efficiency in resource use, and indicative that the production of that commodity (in that region) should be encouraged in an open economy environment. For greater details on the estimation of RCRs, or EPCs, or domestic profitability of different crops in different regions, see Gulati and Sharma (1997).

in somewhat greater detail. Here we look at the resource cost ratios of different crops, their levels of effective protection, and domestic profitability to get an idea of the likely changes in cropping patterns with the opening up of agriculture. The lower the RCRs, the more efficient (allocatively) the production of that commodity, and vice versa. This will also give us an idea of the extent of efficiency gains that can be achieved with the opening up of agriculture. Table 6.4 (Fig. 1) presents these estimates of RCRs, effective protection, and domestic profitability.

Looking at Table 6.4 (Fig. 1), we observe that under the importable scenario for the period 1987–8 to 1992–3, the RCR of wheat is the lowest (0.49).[11] It indicates that the production of wheat as an import substitute takes Re 0.49 of domestic resources to save one rupee worth of foreign exchange. This indicates high allocative efficiency in the production of wheat, which should therefore be encouraged. Wheat is followed by gram (0.49), rice (0.54), cotton (0.66), and coarse cereals like jowar (0.76), maize (0.78) and bajra (0.86) in RCR.[12] The two major oilseeds, groundnut and rapeseed–mustard, also seem to have very high RCRs (1.47 and 1.66 respectively). Thus, in a relative ranking, oilseeds do not appear good on the allocative efficiency test. Wheat, gram, rice and cotton, and coarse cereals seem the most promising crops for efficiency in resource use. This essentially implies two things: one, that there is a need to usher in a technological breakthrough in dry land crops like oilseeds to make them internationally competitive and efficient in resource use; and two, that there is a possibility of gaining from trade, by exporting resource efficient crops like wheat, rice, and cotton, and importing oilseeds. Similar implications for policy emerge if we examine the protection coefficients–nominal, effective and effective subsidy. The indices of domestic profitability (DPI) or rate of profit (RPI) of different crops do not

[11] In an importable scenario, the country is treated as a net importer of commodities under consideration. Accordingly, domestic prices are compared with import parity prices (say cost, insurance, and freight (cif) prices) of similar products. Under the exportable hypothesis, the relevant price is the export parity price, say free on board (fob) price.

[12] In case of *bajra*, there is a bit of problem in correctly estimating the RCR in the absence of any reliable international price series for edible grade of *bajra* (pearl millet). We have used sorghum prices (0.86 times) as a proxy for *bajra* prices in the world market. If oat prices are used as a proxy, the RCR comes down drastically.

TABLE 6.4
EFFICIENCY, EFFECTIVE INCENTIVES, AND DOMESTIC INCENTIVE INDICATORS

Crops	RCR	NPC	EPC	ESC	DP	RP	DPI (sum = 1)	RPI (sum = 1)
Rice	0.54	0.50	0.48	0.54	5445.21	116.61	1.21	0.74
Wheat	0.49	0.58	0.52	0.56	6174.50	106.12	1.37	0.67
Maize	0.78	0.85	0.85	0.91	3576.15	149.83	0.79	0.95
Jowar	0.76	0.91	0.92	0.98	2162.56	102.41	0.48	0.65
Bajra	0.86	0.92	0.93	1.17	1672.10	118.20	0.37	0.75
Gram	0.49	0.84	0.81	0.85	5400.62	183.08	1.20	1.16
Arhar	0.92	1.09	1.09	1.14	6904.43	244.24	1.53	1.55
Groundnut	1.47	1.27	1.23	1.36	5010.14	84.10	1.11	0.53
Rapeseed-Mu	1.66.	1.64	1.69	1.75	7866.39	349.83	1.74	2.22
Soyabean	0.89	1.05	1.06	1.16	4820.29	131.07	1.07	0.83
Sunflower	1.33	1.25	1.30	1.46	4510.40	157.47	1.00	1.00
Cotton	0.66	0.63	0.62	0.81	5236.64	131.82	1.16	0.84
Sugar cane	0.85	0.70	0.69	0.74	12510.46	209.34	2.77	1.33

NOTE: RCR = Resource Cost Ratio; NPC = Nominal Protection Coefficient; EPC = Effective Protection Coefficient; ESC = Effective Subsidy Coefficient; DP = Domestic Profit; RP = Rate of Profit; DPI = Domestic Profit Index with Sunflower = 1; RPI = Rate of Profit Index with Sunflower = 1.

SOURCE: Computed.

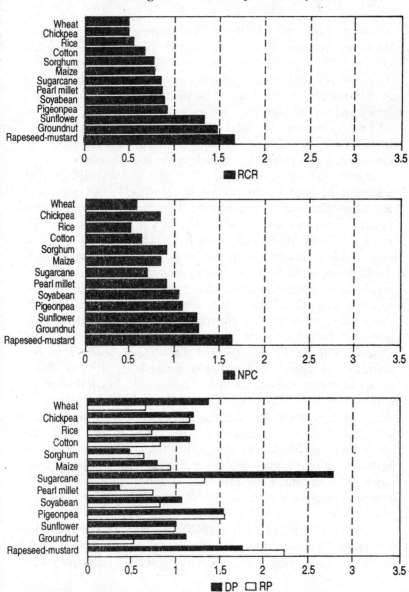

DP = Domestic profitability
RP = Rate of Profit. Domestic profitablity and rates of profit are in relation to sunflower.

Fig. 1: *Efficiency, Effective and Domestic Incentive Indicators*
(1987–88 to 1993–94).

however show any alignment with resource use efficiency. Rapeseed–mustard, for example, is at the bottom of resource use efficiency (RCR) but highest on the profitability index (Fig. 1).[13] This means that domestic policies have worked in such a way as to dissuade farmers from opting for wheat and rice during the late 1980s and early 1990s. This has an important message for those who talk of endangering food security under a liberalized agriculture. Under an insulated agriculture, Indian policy-making has encouraged cash crops like oilseeds at the cost of cereals.

It is worth recalling here the policy pursuits of 1980s that had a significant impact on cropping patterns, self sufficiency, and allocative efficiency of certain crops. There were conscious policy decisions taken to promote self-sufficiency in edible oils through the Technology Mission on Oilseeds, launched in 1986. The first step in this direction was to insulate the domestic market from world prices by cutting down heavily on imports, canalizing them, and letting domestic prices of edible oils/oilseeds rise in relation to competing crops. There were also attempts to introduce new seeds (like sunflower) and undertake measures to augment productivity. In consequence there was a rapid shift in favour of oilseeds. During TE 1986–7 and TE 1992–3, about 7 m. ha. shifted from cereals and pulses to oilseeds. In 1992–3, India achieved almost self-sufficiency in edible oils, but fell short of cereals and had to import about 3 m. tonnes of wheat at an import parity price of about Rs 5000 per tonne, while the procurement price for the domestic farmer was Rs 2250 per tonne. On the other hand, edible oils in the domestic market were priced at least 50 per cent higher than their corresponding import parity price. This indicated the existence of allocative inefficiency in cropping patterns, when viewed in an open economy environment (Gulati, Sharma and Kohli, 1996).

Sharma, Gulati and Pursell (1996) have sought to estimate the impact of agricultural trade liberalization (as against total liberalization encompassing the manufacturing sector) on major crops

[13] Although sugar cane has highest domestic profitability index (DPI), it needs to be interpreted with caution. Sugar cane is a two season crop, and sometimes even three in certain pockets of the country. Accordingly, its profit index (on a per hectare basis) needs to be adjusted for time. If this is done, and say one sugar-cane crop is equated to wheat and rice combined, the relative profitability of sugar-cane falls drastically.

of Indian agriculture. By using a multi-market model, the study indicates that opening up of agriculture alone can raise the price of rice by 6.6 per cent, of wheat by 6.4 per cent, of cotton by 6.4 per cent, and sugar/sugar-cane by about 4.5 per cent, from their base levels. The prices of coarse cereals would however fall by about 10 per cent, of pulses by about 9 per cent, and of oilseeds/ edible oils by 38 per cent. India could be exporting 3.8 m.t. of rice, 5.1 m.t. of wheat, 0.55 m.t. of cotton, and 0.34 m.t. of sugar. Besides these, there are gains in income, employment, wage rate, and tax revenue. A combined index of all these gains, called the efficiency index, goes up by about 4 per cent over the base period. These are reasonable gains, which are somewhat reduced in the event of reduction of subsidies on fertilizers and water. (See Sharma, Gulati and Pursell, 1996).

The above parameters and results of econometric exercises present us with a reasonable degree of confidence that liberalization of the economy will help agriculture. It has the potential of raising output, wages, and employment, thereby triggering growth in other sectors too. The larger part of this impact is likely to come from the liberalization of the non-agricultural sector than from the agricultural sector per se. A pre-condition of the realization of this potential is that the supply side factors in agriculture are in place. If there are severe supply bottlenecks, especially of water (including electricity) and rural credit, then the likely beneficial impact of liberalization in the economy (non-agricultural and agricultural) may be subdued. In that case, what might result from this liberalization is a rising spiral of prices and increasing poverty. To guard against this threat, it is important to carry out reforms in supply side factors, ensuring a high supply response of agriculture, on the one hand, and to provide a 'protective cover' to the poor, on the other. Any complacency in these two areas by the reformers will prove costly to the nation, and its neglect entail the potential of jeopardizing reforms in other sectors too.

IV. THREATS AND COVERS

There are two sets of threats that can constrain agriculture from fully realizing the potential gains from liberalization. The first set consists of bottlenecks in the supply side factors: irrigation, credit, research and development, institutional factors governing patterns of landholdings, and so on. The second set of threats consists of issues relating to food security. This contribution does not focus on these issues in great detail, I have discussed them elsewhere (see Rao and Gulati, 1994; Pursell and Gulati, 1995; Montek Ahluwalia, 1996; Gulati, 1996), but shall nevertheless try to list here the most critical ones, and present a compressed policy package for these.

So far as supply bottlenecks are concerned, the most critical seems to be irrigation. It is well known that public investment in irrigation (basically canals) fell drastically during the 1980s and early 1990s. This trend needs to be reversed, preferably by cutting down on input subsidies, which lately have exceeded even the plan expenditure on agriculture (Gulati and Sharma, 1995). Allocation of greater resources to irrigation alone may not solve the problem. Research in that area reveals that the irrigation sector is in acute need for institutional and price reforms, enabling the farmers to participate in the management of these irrigation projects. In this, the distribution of water and the maintenance of canals below the distributory level is handed over to farmers, who also collect charges for water amongst themselves. This Participatory Irrigation Management (PIM) approach has the potential of revitalizing Indian canal irrigation (GOI, 1992; Gulati, Svendsen, and Roy Choudhury, 1995), and thereby raising the aggregate supply response of agriculture by improving relative incentive structures as a consequence of globalization. Private sector investment in irrigation, primarily through tubewells/wells is becoming costly due to non-availability of adequate electricity. This also calls for price and institutional reforms pertaining to electricity supplies to the farm sector. At present, it is more a 'political will' problem rather than techno–economic or administrative.

On the question of food security, two issues are often flagged. One, that opening up agriculture would lead to diversification of cropping patterns away from cereals and thereby pose a threat to food security at the national level (U. Patnaik, 1996). Two, that food prices will increase with the opening up of exports of agriculture, and the poor would suffer, at least in the short run. While there is weight in the second argument, the first does not seem to be very sound. Unlike the African case, which Patnaik cites in her work, India has a comparative advantage in superior cereals such as rice and wheat. If exports of these are not opened, while exports of other agro-products remain open, or non-cereal crops are protected unduly, it runs the danger of farmers switching away from cereals. This happened in India when oilseeds/edible oils were unduly protected in the name of self-sufficiency, and the country had to import cereals at much higher prices than were being paid to their own farmers. I believe that in order to achieve national food security in a new economic environment, the country should allow the import and export of cereals as an element of trade policy. What is likely to happen is that coarse cereals/ or coarser varieties of superior cereals will be imported and superior cereals/ superior varieties would be exported. Strategically, instead of decanalizing everything at once, pre-determined quotas may be announced, say 5 per cent of the rolling production of the last two years. This should be combined with the introduction of futures markets so that importers/exporters can hedge themselves while playing on international markets. Eventually external trade will have to be freed from quota restrictions.

As regards the second argument that food prices will rise and therefore the poor would be hurt, one strategic choice is to decanalize the import of coarse cereals. Also, the existing Public Distribution System (PDS), which does not target the poor, and suffers from large leakages, must be restructured. In order to do this, coarse cereals or coarser varieties of superior cereals (wheat and rice) may be given to targeted groups of poor people through the restructured PDS. The targeted group may be given a higher subsidy per unit of grain. To plug the leakages, the fair-price shops may be brought under the supervision of local bodies such as the *panchayats*. This we would hope would make the food subsidies more effective in providing a safety net to the poor. The other option is to launch/strengthen major efforts in the countryside to generate employment for the construction and maintenance of rural infrastructure, ranging from roads, canals, watersheds, to community toilets, housing for the poor, Primary Health Centres, etc. But again, unless this is accompanied by institutional reforms where local people have a say in decision-making and supervision of these works, mere allocation of greater resources would not be very productive.

Thus, in conclusion, globalization of the economy, including agriculture, offers an opportunity to correct for the 'anti-agriculture' bias in Indian trade policies that have been in existence since the 1950s. With this, the hidden 'implicit taxation' on agriculture would go down, and the agricultural sector would get an opportunity to respond favourably to these signals. Agriculture can move on to a higher growth trajectory if supply side bottlenecks are freed, and a protective cover is accorded to the poor, at least for some time. If this happens, agriculture can propel growth in other sectors too on a sustainable basis, while promoting intersectoral and interpersonal equity. If, however, reformers busy themselves with globalization exercises and are complacent about supply side problems, or in restructuring the PDS, globalization can prove to be a threat and stall the process of reforms in other sectors too. The degree of success depends upon the vision of reformers, and the priority they accord to going beyond markets and ushering in institutional and price reforms on the supply side.

References

Ahluwalia, Isher Judge (1996): 'India's Opening up to Trade and Investment', in *Policy Reform in India* by Isher Judge Ahluwalia, Rakesh Mohan and Omkar Goswami, and edited by Charles Oman (Paris: Development Centre Seminars, OECD).

Ahluwalia, Montek Singh (1996): 'New Economic Policy and Agriculture: Some Reflections', Inaugural address delivered at the 55th Annual Conference of the Indian Society of Agricultural Economics held at Institute of Rural Management, Anand (Gujarat) on 23 November 1995, published in *Indian Journal of Agricultural Economics*, vol. 51, no. 3, July–September.

Bhalla, G.S. and Gurmail Singh (1996): *Impact of GATT on Punjab Agriculture* (Chandigarh: Institute for Development and Communication Monograph Series – II).

Government of India (1996): *Economic Survey, 1995–6* (New Delhi: Ministry of Finance).

—— (1996): 'Report of the CACP on Price Policy for Kharif Crops, Commission for Agricultural Costs and Prices', GOI, 1996.

—— (1992–3): *Tax Reform Committee*, Final Report, Part I (1992); Part II (1993), (Chairman: Raja J. Chelliah) (New Delhi: Ministry of Finance).

—— (1991): *Tax Reform Committee*, Interim Report (Chairman: Raja J. Chelliah) (New Delhi: Ministry of Finance).

—— (1992): 'Report of the Committee on Pricing of Irrigation Water' (Chairman: A. Vaidyanathan).

Gulati, Ashok (1996): 'Reforms and Policies for Agriculture', in Vijay

L. Kelkar and V.V. Bhanoji Rao (eds), *India: Development Policy Imperatives* (New Delhi: Tata McGraw-Hill).

Gulati, Ashok and S. Mahendra Dev (1996): 'India's Integration into the Global Economy: Medium and Long Term Implications for Indian Agriculture and Linkages to OECD Countries', Paper written for OECD, Paris.

Gulati, Ashok and Anil Sharma (1995): 'Subsidy Syndrome in Indian Agriculture', *Economic and Political Weekly*, Review of Agriculture, xxx (39), 30 September.

—— (1997): 'Resource Use Efficiency, Effective Incentives and Changing Cropping Patterns in Indian Agriculture', mimeo, NCAER (part of NCAER–ICRISAT Collaborative study).

—— (1997a): 'Subsidies and Investments in Indian Agriculture', Paper presented at a workshop on 'Subsidies and Investment in Agriculture' organized by the Rajiv Gandhi Foundation on 17 April, New Delhi.

Gulati, Ashok, Anil Sharma and Deepali S. Kohli (1996): 'Self- sufficiency and Allocative Efficiency: Case of Edible Oils', *Economic and Political Weekly*, Review of Agriculture, xxxi (13), 30 March.

Gulati, Ashok and Garry Pursell (1996): *Trade Policies, Incentives and Resource Allocation in Indian Agriculture*, mimeo, The World Bank, Washington, DC.

Gulati, Ashok, Mark Svendsen and Nandini Roy Choudhury (1995): 'Institutional Reforms in the Irrigation Sector in India', in Mark Svendsen and Ashok Gulati (eds), *Strategic Change in Indian Irrigation* (Delhi: MacMillan).

Ingco, Merlinda (1995): 'Agricultural Trade Liberalization in the Uruguay Round: One Step Forward, One Step Back?', mimeo, The World Bank, Washington, DC.

Krishna, Raj and G.S. Raychaudhuri (1980): *Some Aspects of Wheat and Rice Price Policy in India*, World Bank Staff Working Paper No. 381, April (Washington, DC: The World Bank).

Manmohan Singh (1995): Inaugural Address delivered at the 54th Annual Conference of the Indian Society of agricultural Economics held at Shivaji University, Kolhapur (Maharashtra) on 26 November 1994, and published in *Indian Journal of Agricultural Economics*, vol. 50, no. 1, January–March.

Martin, Will and Alan Winters (1995): 'The Uruguay Round and the Developing Economies', Discussion Paper No. 307, The World Bank, Washington, D.C.

Mishra, V.N. and Peter B.R. Hazell (1996): 'Terms of Trade, Rural Poverty, Technology and Investment — The Indian Experience,

1952–3 to 1990–1', *Economic and Political Weekly*, Review of Agriculture, vol. XXXI, no. 13, 30 March.

Parikh, Kirit S., N.S.S. Narayana, Manoj K. Panda and A. Ganesh Kumar (1996): 'Strategies for Agricultural Liberalization: Consequences for Growth, Welfare and Distribution', mimeo, Indira Gandhi Institute of Development Research, New Delhi.

Patnaik, Prabhat (1996): 'Should Domestic Prices be Equated to World Prices?', *Economic and Political Weekly*, Special Number, vol. XXXI, nos 35–7.

Patnaik, Utsa (1996): 'Export-Oriented Agriculture and Food Security in Developing Countries and India', *Economic and Political Weekly*, Special Number, vol. XXXI, nos 35–7.

Pursell, Garry and Ashok Gulati (1995): 'Liberalizing Indian Agriculture — An Agenda for Reform', in Robert Cassen and Vijay Joshi (eds), *India: Future of Economic Reform* (Delhi: Oxford University Press).

Rao, C.H. Hanumantha and Ashok Gulati (1994): 'Indian Agriculture: Emerging Perspectives and Policy Issues', *Economic and Political Weekly*, Review of Agriculture, XXIX (53), 31 December.

Roy, Jayanta (1996): 'Trade Liberalization: The Road Ahead', in Vijay L. Kelkar and V.V. Bhanoji Rao (eds), *India: Development Policy Imperatives* (New Delhi: Tata McGraw-Hill).

Schiff, Maurice and Alberto Valdes (1992): *The Plundering of Agriculture in Developing Countries* (Washington, DC: The World Bank).

Subramanian, Shankar (1993): *Agricultural Trade Liberalization and India* (Paris: Development Centre Studies, Organization for Economic Co-operation and Development).

Sharma, Anil, Ashok Gulati and Garry Pursell (1996): 'Measuring the Impact of Trade Liberalization on ICRISAT Mandate and their Competing Crops', NCAER, mimeo (part of an NCAER–ICRISAT collaborative study).

Subramanian, Shankar (1993): *Agricultural Trade Liberalization and India* (Paris: Development Centre Studies, OECD).

——. (1994): 'Modelling Agricultural Policy Reform in India', in Ian Goldin, Odin Knudsen and Antonio S. Brandao (eds), *Modelling Economy-Wide Reforms* (Paris: Development Centre Studies, OECD).

7

Fiscal Stabilization and Economic Reform in India

Vijay Joshi

Manmohan Singh will go down in history as the main instigator of the long-overdue liberalization of the Indian economy. But history will also record that his enthusiasm for liberalization was tempered by a conviction that it can only succeed in the context of macroeconomic stability. Manmohan embodies the great Indian tradition of fiscal prudence, now regrettably under severe threat. If fiscal adjustment was less than adequate during his Finance Ministership, it is clear that it was less than he himself would have wished, despite his considerable efforts.

I. INTRODUCTION

The prime objective of macroeconomic policy is to deliver macroeconomic stability, a public good whose provision ranks with law and order as a necessary condition for the maximization of social welfare.

What is macroeconomic stability? Low inflation is almost universally agreed to be one of its defining features.[1] Another feature is internal balance, meaning the correspondence of actual and potential output. The mainstream view is that not all fluctuations in output are pareto-efficient. Government has a role to play in offsetting shocks to the economy or minimizing their adverse consequences for output, consumption, and investment. (Shocks

[1] When inflation rises, it becomes more variable and less predictable; and the resulting increase in uncertainty impairs macroeconomic performance. In India, given the lack of indexation, inflation also increases poverty and is rightly regarded as a social evil.

may be of the traditional Keynesian variety or supply-side shocks such as droughts or changes in the terms of trade.) As important as such short-run stabilization, however, is the achievement of 'long-run stability', which requires that the behaviour of the government and the economy as a whole be compatible with intertemporal solvency and liquidity constraints. In the absence of good policy in this regard, the country would be led towards high inflation or an internal or external debt crisis even if inflation and output performance are satisfactory in a short-run sense.

Can macroeconomic policy contribute to more than mere stability? What about growth and development? The following points are important in this connection. First, macroeconomic policy influences growth through certain crucial relative prices such as the interest rate and the exchange rate. Secondly, stability itself is important for growth, a proposition which now has strong empirical support. Thirdly, many of the interventions that are advocated on growth-promoting grounds, such as the subsidization of education and training, need not compete with macroeconomic stability. The same goes for distributional interventions. In other words, macroeconomic policies can and should be chosen in a way that is sensitive to the claims of growth and poverty alleviation.

In this contribution, I consider briefly some critical issues in the design of future macroeconomic policy in India. I ignore short-term stabilization and concentrate largely on the promotion of long-run stability, bearing in mind that policy has to be conducted in the context of the ongoing structural adjustment/liberalization/economic reform programme. In achieving long-run stability, fiscal policy is obviously of prime importance. Hence, my focus is on long run fiscal stabilization; monetary and balance of payments policies are discussed only as they relate to the central theme.[2]

II. Fiscal Stabilization

The principal challenge for macroeconomic policy in India is to reduce the fiscal deficit of the government and, more broadly, the deficit of the non-financial public sector (NFPS) in a way

---

[2] For an analytical history of India's macroeconomic policies see Joshi and Little (1994). Recent macroeconomic policy and its interconnections with economic reform are extensively discussed in Joshi and Little (1996). See also Bajpai and Sachs (1996).

that is supportive of the efficiency and equity aspects of the reform programme.[3, 4]

I begin by drawing attention to the dangers of excessive fiscal deficits. Firstly, there is the issue of sustainability. Fiscal deficits can be financed by printing money or by borrowing from domestic and foreign sources. Each of these methods, if carried to excess, can lead to a crisis. Printing money over and above the demand for it arising from the growth of real national income amounts to levying an inflation tax on the populace. But the revenue from this tax is subject to a technical maximum and, more importantly, to a political and prudential maximum set by the rate of inflation considered to be 'safe' or 'acceptable'. Financing fiscal deficits by borrowing is unsustainable if the interest rate exceeds the growth rate of GDP. In such a case, any primary deficit net of the inflation tax leads to a debt trap, in other words, to an explosive debt/GDP ratio that must eventually lead to the government reneging on the debt explicitly or implicitly (through monetization and inflation).[5] Secondly, even if high fiscal deficits are sustainable, they may not be optimal because they crowd out investment and therefore reduce growth.[6] If private investment is crowded out by unproductive public consumption, the growth rate of GDP is directly reduced. Even if it is crowded out by public investment, there is a loss in terms of growth if, as is often the case, private investment is more productive than public investment.[7] Thirdly, high fiscal deficits significantly reduce the

[3] I define the non-financial public sector (NFPS) as the aggregation of central and state governments, non-financial public enterprises, and the Reserve Bank of India (RBI). Public sector financial institutions, such as the nationalized commercial banks, are excluded from the purview of the NFPS.

[4] There has been some fiscal adjustment in India since 1991 but it has been inadequate in both quantity and quality. For details, see Joshi and Little (1996).

[5] For a large country like India, the sustainability condition for foreign borrowing is more appropriately stated in terms of the relationship between the interest rate and the growth rate of exports.

[6] This implicitly (but realistically) assumes that Ricardian equivalence does not hold. Note that investment can be maintained if net exports are crowded out by fiscal deficits. But this process rapidly runs up against an external debt constraint, so in practice investment is adversely affected.

[7] Note that the debt sustainability issue and the crowding out issue are connected. A primary deficit over and above the inflation tax is in theory sustainable if the interest rate is less than the growth rate of GDP. But this

flexibility of policy, for example (a) they reduce the government's leeway in responding to exogenous shocks such as droughts or adverse terms of trade changes; (b) they constrain the government's ability to spend for desirable purposes (such as infrastructure or social welfare schemes) since interest payments constitute a growing share of government expenditure; and (c) since deficits have eventually to be corrected, they lead to a high-tax regime that is bad for incentives.

I have set out above the general case for fiscal prudence. But the transition from a high to a low deficit is obviously a task of some delicacy. Two points are particularly worth bearing in mind: (i) the pace of adjustment has to pay attention to the state of the cycle. It is important to speed up fiscal adjustment during periods of boom and recovery when there is a natural tendency for the budget to improve; (ii) the quality of fiscal adjustment is as important as its amount. The deficit should be cut by raising public savings, not by reducing public investment; and public savings should be raised consistently with the protection of social expenditures and improvement in the efficiency of the tax structure.

II.1 Magnitude of Fiscal Adjustment

How much fiscal adjustment is called for? Both 'sustainability' and 'crowding out' considerations are relevant. This topic is the subject of a highly sophisticated literature. Here I take a rough and ready view.

The critical relationship for fiscal sustainability is that between the growth rate of GDP and the interest rate on public borrowing. A significant simplification can be achieved if we can assume that the interest rate is equal to the growth rate. In that case, it would be appropriate on grounds of sustainability to aim for a primary deficit of the NFPS approximately equal to the inflation tax corresponding to an acceptable level of inflation.

---

notion of sustainability is based on assuming constant values of the interest and growth rates. If the primary deficit stays high, the growing volume of public borrowing would drive up interest rates and reduce GDP growth. Thus, the crowding out process could lead to unsustainable debt. Similar considerations apply in the case of foreign borrowing: even if the debt sustainability condition is initially met, persistently high foreign borrowing can raise the risk-adjusted interest rate (and/or lead to credit rationing).

Consider first what constitutes a prudent target for GDP growth. Real GDP grew at about 5.5 per cent per annum in the 1980s, but this rate turned out to be manifestly unsustainable. It would not be prudent to assume a growth rate higher than 6 per cent even assuming a successful reform programme. What can be said about the interest rate? Three points are relevant. Firstly, interest rates on government securities and small savings have followed a rising trend in recent years, following financial liberalization. In 1994–5 and 1995–6, two years of 7 per cent growth raised the marginal real rate on public borrowing to 7–8 per cent (and on company borrowing to 10–15 per cent). This may have been the result partly of the monetary tightening undertaken to contain inflation below the 10 per cent rate prevalent in 1994–5. High real interest rates may fall to some extent if and when an enduring reduction in inflation brings down nominal interest rates. But it may be some considerable time before that happens if the inflation target is 5 per cent. Secondly, financial liberalization is as yet far from complete, so further reduction in reserve ratios and upward pressure on real interest rates is to be expected. Thirdly, real interest rates are high partly for reasons unconnected with inflation control. They are surely also a reflection of the divergence between investment demand associated with growth of 6 per cent or above, and the available supply of domestic saving. Given India's high projected investment requirements, it would be foolhardy to expect this divergence to ease. I conclude that it would not be prudent to assume a real interest rate below 6 per cent.

If the real interest rate on government borrowing is 6 per cent or above, then the upper bound to a prudent fiscal deficit is set by the 'safe' level of the inflation tax. The latter can be roughly estimated as follows. A prudent target for nominal GDP growth is 11 per cent (6 per cent real growth plus 5 per cent inflation). The ratio of base money to GDP since 1980 appears to be fairly stable at around 12 per cent. (Base money is taken to be currency plus the non-interest bearing component of the required cash reserves of banks.) This implies that 11 per cent × 0.12 = 1.3 per cent of GDP is the safe limit for public revenue from the inflation tax and hence also for the primary public deficit. If the real interest rate were assumed to be 1 per cent higher than the growth rate, the safe limit for the primary public deficit would be lower than the safe level of the inflation tax, namely 0.6 per cent of GDP.[8] I conclude that it would be prudent to reduce the primary deficit of the NFPS on sustainability grounds to no more than 1 per cent of GDP.[9] A 'consensus estimate' of the primary deficit of the NFPS in 1995–6 is about 4 per cent of GDP.[10] Thus, the above argument implies that the primary deficit of the NFPS should be cut by about 3 per cent of GDP below the 1995–6 level.

This does not, however, fully describe the dimensions of the required fiscal adjustment. Firstly, note that the overall deficit of the NFPS is about 10 per cent of GDP. A reduction of 3 percentage points of GDP in the primary deficit would still leave the overall deficit of the NFPS in the region of 7 per cent of GDP. Even if sustainable in the long run, this is much too high if the objective is to bring down real interest rates sufficiently to encourage private investment. This implies that on 'crowding out' grounds, the primary deficit should be reduced even more than indicated above. If that is not feasible, then some method must be found of cutting the overall deficit by reducing the interest burden of the public sector. Privatization is the obvious answer, as discussed below. Secondly, attention must be paid to the quality of the fiscal adjustment in terms of protecting public investment and social expenditures (though in both these areas, efficiency improvements would obviously also be desirable).

Thus, the fiscal task could be summed up as follows: (i) cut the primary revenue deficit of the NFPS by 3 per cent of GDP;

[8] This calculation is based on a more general debt sustainability condition that allows for a divergence between the interest rate and the growth rate. See Joshi and Little (1996), Ch. 2.

[9] I do not distinguish above between domestic and foreign public borrowing. This does not matter if interest rates do not differ between markets. As a long run assumption, it would be prudent to assume that the real rate on foreign borrowing is 6 per cent. In the nineteenth century, the world rate of interest on safe bonds was about 3 per cent. The world rate of growth has however risen, which would tend to raise the rate. On top of that in India's case, allowance has to be made for a risk premium and for likely future depreciation of the real exchange rate. See Joshi and Little (1996) for a somewhat more complex treatment of domestic and foreign borrowing.

[10] India does not have a satisfactory set of public accounts, so there is no agreed figure for the primary deficit of the NFPS. My estimate of the primary deficit is a compromise between the estimates of the World Bank (1996, Table I.10) and the Government of India (*Economic Survey*, 1995–6 App. Table 2.2).

(ii) in addition, reduce the interest burden of the NFPS substantially. It should be possible to reduce interest payments by 1.5 per cent of GDP by privatization (see below). The overall revenue deficit of the Centre and state governments combined happens to be about 4.5 per cent of GDP. A reasonable target would therefore be to eliminate the revenue deficit of the consolidated government of which 3 percentage points would be achieved by reduction of its non-interest component and the rest by reduction of interest payments through privatization. I must also add the proviso that in reducing the revenue deficit, efficiency and equity considerations must be respected.

We shall see below that fiscal consolidation along these lines would also help to achieve low inflation and a sustainable current account deficit, which is important given the need to increase investment substantially.

In case the above adjustment is thought to be excessive, it is instructive to compare India with the fast-growing East Asian economies. In India, overall public sector saving is 1–2 per cent of GDP (and the government dis-saves 3–4 per cent of GDP). In many East Asian economies the public sector (mostly accounted for by the government) saves 5–10 per cent of GDP. The contrast could hardly be more dramatic. More generally, private savings and public investment in India are comparable with those of East Asia, but public savings and private investment are markedly lower. The difference in public savings reflects the fact that government consumption expenditure as a proportion of GDP is much higher in India than in East Asia, though the government's tax take is broadly similar. The high rate of private investment in East Asia is substantially the result of better trade policies but a smaller share of government in national income is surely an important enabling condition.[11]

II.2 Modalities of Fiscal Adjustment

I now turn to the options for achievement of the fiscal targets outlined above. On this topic, there is often widespread pessimism

[11] International cross-country regressions confirm that GDP growth is positively related to public savings and/or fiscal surpluses. Other important influences on growth are human capital accumulation and efficient trade policies. See Fischer (1993), Easterly and Rebello (1993), and Chopra et al. (1995).

arising from the fact that apparently most government expenditure is committed. For example, in the case of the central government, the combined expenditure on interest payments, explicit subsidies, and defence was 105 per cent of tax revenue, 77 per cent of total revenue, and 60 per cent of current expenditure in 1995–6. The alleged lack of flexibility in deficit reduction is also apparently borne out by the fact that such fiscal adjustment as there has been since 1990–1 has come principally from a decline in governmental capital expenditure. The primary revenue deficit has declined by only about 1 per cent of GDP and the revenue deficit not at all. Nevertheless, the above view is too pessimistic. In a technical sense, there is far greater room for manoeuvre than implied above (and in ways that increase efficiency and improve equity). The problems are primarily political.[12]

II.3 Taxation

It must be said that raising tax revenue cannot be the centerpiece of fiscal stabilization. This is for two reasons: (i) drastic reduction of tariffs is an essential component of liberalization. Though imports will rise as a proportion of GDP, customs revenue (exclusive of countervailing duties) will and should fall in the long run to say 1.5 per cent of GDP from the present 3 per cent;[13] (ii) the highly distortionary excise tax structure is quite rightly being rationalized in favour of a value added tax. While the latter move is essential from an efficiency standpoint, the best that can be hoped for in terms of its revenue effect is neutrality. The loss of revenue on indirect taxes has to be made up by reversing the abysmal performance of direct taxation. From 1960–1 to 1990–1, direct tax revenue fell by about 1 per cent as a proportion of GDP; it is normal to expect the opposite. Since the reforms began, there have been reductions and rationalization in income and corporate taxes, and their yields have correspondingly risen. There is plenty of

[12] I say 'primarily' not 'purely' because there are some genuine economic problems in reducing structural deficits, in particular the need to ensure that the timing of the reduction is compatible with the management of the cycle. It is however clear that in India the window of opportunity opened up by the strong recovery from 1994–5 onwards has been wasted.

[13] This estimate assumes a uniform tariff of 10 per cent and an imports to GDP ratio of 15 per cent in the long run.

scope of widening the base of both these taxes.[14] Even so, it must be borne in mind that in terms of both rates and overall tax take, India is a high-tax country given her per capita income level. So, while tax coverage should certainly increase, there are strong incentive arguments for bringing down rates further. On balance, therefore, fiscal adjustment in India should come mainly from expenditure and non-tax revenue. A prudent estimate of the net increase in tax revenue (after allowing for the reduction in indirect taxes) would be say 1 per cent of GDP.

II.4 Explicit Subsidies

The rupee was devalued at the start of the reform programme in 1991 and export subsidies were abolished at the same time. The most important of the explicit subsidies that remain are food and fertilizer subsidies amounting to 0.5 per cent and 0.6 per cent of GDP, respectively, in 1995–6. The justification for food subsidies is poverty relief, but they are known to be badly targeted; most of them go to the not-so-poor. Universal entitlement to these subsidies must surely be withdrawn and ration cards refused to those with visible signs of affluence, e.g. owners of cars or telephones. It is also well known that a substantial part of the subsidy goes to covering the costs of the inefficient and corrupt Food Corporation of India (FCI). A bold corrective step would be to introduce food stamps. This would not solve the targeting problem but it would enable the FCI to be drastically scaled down so there would be no need for public distribution and government shops. Government buffer stocks could still be operated to moderate fluctuations in food prices, purchases and sales being made through normal commercial channels. Thus, a radical reform could reduce the food subsidy bill to say 0.3 per cent of GDP without hurting the poor.

Fertilizer subsidies also reach the very poor to a negligible

[14] It is a scandal that in a country in which the middle class is estimated to number between 100–200 million, the number of individuals who pay income tax is about 8 million. Presumptive taxation is an obvious solution but the government's attempts in this area have suffered from the fatal flaw of allowing returns on a voluntary basis. As is well known, there is also significant potential for direct taxation of the incomes of medium and large farmers which, in some parts of the country, have increased substantially over time. But the central government cannot tax agriculture and the state governments are unwilling to.

extent. They are partly subsidies to the inefficient parts of the industry (in so far as retention prices exceed the c.i.f. price) and partly to farmers (in so far as they pay less than the c.i.f. price). In the long run, the subsidy has no sound economic or social justification. There is no reason why the fertilizer industry should receive any more protection than afforded by a low general tariff on all imports. Admittedly, if the subsidy was abolished overnight, half the industry would probably collapse. But that is no excuse for not reducing the subsidy by restructuring the industry and closing down high cost plants in a time-bound manner. There is also no good argument for subsidizing fertilizer to the farmer — prices should rise to import parity.[15] Fertilizer subsidies can and should be eliminated by the turn of the century but, as discussed below, this may have to be done as part of a comprehensive package of measures in the agricultural sector.

II.5 Wages and Salaries

Government employees have been a powerful factor in the level and growth of government expenditures. Public employment and wages rose rapidly over the 1980s, aided and abetted by increased indexation. The States were particularly to blame. Arresting the growth of the wage bill will require pay restraint and a freeze on new employment. As is well known, there is a massive amount of surplus staff in government departments. A rough calculation shows the potential savings in this regard to be easily around 0.6 per cent of GDP even without direct retrenchment.[16]

---

[15] The conventional wisdom of the development establishment of the 1950s and 1960s was that agriculture should be encouraged by subsidizing inputs. This was preferred to higher output prices which did nothing to encourage the new methods that were needed to raise yields. Whatever the merits, if any, of this argument at the time, input subsidies are now clearly counter-productive. Subsidized electricity causes over-pumping of tube-wells. Cheap water results in its excessive use and unduly encourages water-demanding crops. Fertilizer subsidies result in a bias in favour of nitrogen relative to phosphates and potash, while also discouraging organic fertilizers. Further, all of these results of input subsidization work in the direction of capital intensity, thereby tending to reduce employment and create poverty.

[16] Figures for employment in central and state government departments, and per capita emoluments are available in the Economic Survey. The attrition rate from death, retirement, etc. is known to be about 3 per cent per year. A simple calculation based on these figures shows that a freeze in

II.6 Implicit or Hidden Subsidies

The explicit subsidies are only the tip of an iceberg. We must also take account of the massive hidden subsidies that permeate the provision of goods and services by the state (leaving aside pure public goods for which free state provision is the appropriate course). In the case of public services or products, we should count as subsidy the difference between the cost and what is actually recovered. Going back to 1987–8, central government subsidies on economic services were about 4.5 per cent of GDP. Of these, explicit subsidies amounted to 1.5 per cent, leaving about 3 per cent going to industry, transport, and communications. In addition, states' subsidies on economic services amounted to about 4 per cent of GDP. These include the notorious subsidies on irrigation and power. Thus, the combined central and state government subsidies on economic services amounted to a massive 7 per cent of GDP.[17] Since then, there has been little improvement. It has been estimated that aligning water and electricity charges with costs would alone easily yield fiscal savings of 2 per cent of GDP.[18] It would also lead to a more rational use of these inputs and help to correct the massive under-investment in these sectors. Nor would it hurt the poor as they do not, by and large, benefit from these hidden subsidies.

II.7 Privatization and Interest Payments

The points outlined so far relate to reducing the primary deficit. But we saw above that strong fiscal adjustment will also require action to reduce interest payments which have been growing rapidly, both as a result of rising debt and rising interest rates following upon financial liberalization.

Direct reduction of the interest rate on public borrowing would not be possible without bringing back financial repression and thus

---

employment and pay for 4 years would produce savings of about 0.9 per cent of GDP. The text takes 0.6 per cent of GDP as a more realistic figure, allowing for some modest growth in employment and pay.

[17] See Mundle and Rao (1987). Indeed, scope for cost recovery exists in the social services too. It should not be imagined that expenditure on these services mainly benefits the poor. For example, less than half of the states' educational expenditure is on primary education.

[18] See World Bank (1996).

would also be undesirable. Interest payments can therefore be reduced only by retiring debt or curbing the growth of new debt. Assuming that there are limits on the latter due to the difficulty of reducing primary deficits (by more than the minimum of 3 per cent advocated above), the only way out is sale of public assets, in particular public enterprises and land.

In the Indian context, privatization would yield substantial efficiency and fiscal benefits. This is of course predicated on the assumption that the enterprises which are sold off are given much greater freedom of operation than hitherto with regard to investment, pricing, and employment.[19] With some assurance in this regard, however, the enterprises could be sold at a price much higher than the present value of their future dividend payments to the government.[20] So far, the government's disinvestment programme has met with little success, but that is because the government has insisted on retaining a majority of the shares for the foreseeable future. It is not surprising that investors have not been enthusiastic about buying small minority stakes in enterprises whose profitability would be determined directly or indirectly by the government. A well-structured privatization programme could easily contribute fiscal savings of about 1.5 per cent GDP.[21]

[19] If such changes can be put in place, why, it may be asked, is change of ownership necessary? Would public enterprises too not become more efficient in such a climate? Experience all over the world indicates however that managerial autonomy, hard budget constraints, and the exit of unprofitable enterprises are impossible to ensure in the public sector. These arguments apply with particular force in India's political culture.

[20] Even loss-making enterprises can be sold for something. They have assets, and therefore better performance is always possible, given appropriate changes including the break-up of assets. We should note, however, that for privatization to yield a national benefit, the improvement in future profitability must not result from exploitation of a monopoly position. Otherwise, the increased profits would be at the expense of other agents in the economy. Privatization must therefore be combined with competition. In the case of tradeables, this can be provided by international trade. In the case of non-tradeable 'natural monopolies', regulation is necessary.

[21] The Government of India's *Economic Survey*, 1995–6 estimates that the book value of the central government's saleable economic assets is approximately 26 per cent of its non-RBI marketable liabilities, i.e. about Rs 130,000 crores. If an equivalent value of debt is retired, then assuming a 10 per cent interest rate, interest payments would be reduced by 1.2 per cent of GDP. The statement in the text is an approximation taking the following factors into account. On the one hand, the government may have legitimate reasons

II.8 Fiscal Adjustment and Reform:
Potentialities and Trade-offs

The above discussion shows that there is a large potential for fiscal adjustment through a rise in public savings. To recapitulate, we have the following possibilities, expressed as a proportion of GDP: increased tax revenue 1 per cent; reduced expenditure on explicit subsidies 0.8 per cent and on governmental wages and salaries 0.6 per cent; increase in non-tax revenues from cost recovery in economic services, say 4 per cent (out of a possible 7 per cent); reduced expenditure on interest payments as a result of privatization 1.5 per cent. This adds up to potential extra public savings of about 8 per cent of GDP, well above the 4.5 per cent that was suggested in section II.1 above. That in turn leaves room, in addition to fiscal consolidation, for much-needed increases in public investment in agriculture and infrastructure, and in redundancy and poverty-related programmes. The latter, as explained below, are an essential component of the reform package.

It is worth noting here that while there are some conflicts between fiscal adjustment and structural reform, they are on balance mutually supportive. Certainly, interest rate deregulation and tariff reduction have adverse budgetary implications (though a change from quotas to tariffs, helps the budget). It is also all too easy to show that crude and arbitrary measures of fiscal retrenchment can impede structural adjustment. But with careful planning, a policy package can be designed which increases efficiency, promotes equity, *and* saves public money.

I shall give only two examples here of policies that take the relevant interdependencies into account. The first example concerns redundancy. Redundancy can offset the positive effects of fiscal adjustment and reform in their initial stages, before the favourable employment effects come through. Unquestionably, this is the principal factor blocking privatization, which as we saw above would have favourable fiscal and efficiency effects. The solution to this daunting problem is, in principle, quite easy. Since

---

for keeping the ownership of a few enterprises with itself. On the other hand, it could sell the enterprises in many cases at much higher than book value. Furthermore, the figure of Rs 130,000 crores does not include the value of state government enterprises or of land owned by the government, both of which could be sold.

the potentially redundant are being paid full wages to produce little or nothing, the public sector can both make generous redundancy payments and cut expenditure.[22] Note also that these 'copper handshakes' would be largely saved, so privatization with generous redundancy payments could be pushed ahead quite rapidly without fear of inflation. The problem of redundancy was recognized with the establishment in 1992 of the National Renewal Fund (NRF) supported by IDA contributions. It has been used for some public sector voluntary retirement schemes, especially for 75,000 workers in the textile sector. But there are up to 2 million redundant workers in the public sector alone, so the NRF is certainly not big enough to cope with the problem.

The industrial employees who would be made redundant are not poor, and a redundancy scheme would be able to deal with such hardship as does arise, especially as many of them would find employment as the demand for labour grew. A more difficult problem concerns the distributional impact of the elimination of agricultural input subsidies. Agriculture would of course have to be compensated for the change, but that can be achieved by combining it with liberalization of agricultural trade generally (i.e. both outputs and inputs), a move that is in any case strongly to be commended on grounds of efficiency. On balance, free trade would more than compensate farmers for the loss of input subsidies. (There would of course be intercrop and interregional differences: for example, the price of cereals would rise and the prices of sugar and edible oils would fall.) But two undesirable by-products would have to be taken care of. Firstly, some input subsidies would have to continue for subsistence farmers since they would not benefit from the rise in output prices. But this is a case where targeting by size of ownership and operational holding may be relatively easy. Secondly, since food prices would rise, poor consumers would have to be protected by strengthening anti-poverty programmes. This has to be addressed by a mixture of better targeting of the public distribution system (or of food stamps); extending, strengthening, and better targeting of public employment programmes; and larger direct transfers to disadvantaged groups such as the old, the widowed, and the incapacitated.

[22] See Joshi and Little (1996) for an outline of a scheme of 'copper handshakes'. It is suggested that when a government sells an enterprise, it should underwrite the redundancy payments for some limited period.

The political problems should not be minimized. The trade unions have to be convinced that shedding surplus staff and freeing labour markets would benefit workers. The farmers have to be persuaded that the agricultural package of free trade and abolition of subsidies would make most of them better off. The poor are not an organized political force but they are potentially so. Indian political parties have been going in the direction of regional mass politics for some time. Ultimately, the reforms will succeed only if regional political leaderships are convinced and if they convince their constituencies that the reform package would liberate resources and lead to increased social expenditures.[23] The political class has to perform the massive task of spreading the message of reform and creating the trust that is a condition of its acceptance.

III. INFLATION AND FISCAL ADJUSTMENT

The inflation record since 1991 has been less than satisfactory. Inflation averaged 10 per cent per annum from 1991–2 to 1994–5, even though there were no adverse exogenous shocks. It fell sharply in 1995–6 but this was the product not only of severe monetary tightening but also of the pre-election freezing of various administered prices, including food and fuel. In 1996–7, monetary policy has become more relaxed and inflation has begun to edge upwards. There is no reason to believe that there has been an enduring move towards low inflation.

A monetary explanation of inflation fits the 1990s' experience reasonably well. One additional consideration is important, however. This is the continuing cost-push tendency, generated by the strength of the farm lobby, to increase procurement prices even when the food supply position is comfortable, with issue prices following suit due to fiscal compulsions. Moderation of the inflationary process in India would seem to require an unwinding of the distortionary interventions of the government in the food market, in addition to responsible fiscal and monetary policies.

How should disinflation be achieved in the medium run? Firm control of money supply growth is obviously necessary. But if the fiscal deficit is high, real interest rates are driven up and private investment is squeezed. Since high rates of private investment are

23 See Varshney (1996).

necessary for rapid growth, this implies that low inflation becomes incompatible with high growth. An inconsistency thus arises between fiscal and monetary policy. This is of course not an entirely new problem in Indian policy-making. Monetary policy in India has for a long time been guided by the need to 'make room' for fiscal deficits without letting the money supply get out of control. In the pre-reform period, this was achieved by compulsory government borrowing at cheap rates. Inflation stayed low, but at the cost of large spreads between deposit and lending rates applicable to private sector activities.

What has happened post-reform is that the inflation/growth trade-off has sharpened as a result of financial sector liberalization, which has involved a reduction in the government's 'captive borrowing' and a significant deregulation of administered interest rates. Ceteris paribus, these changes can be expected to increase both the level of real interest rates and their sensitivity to changes in fiscal deficits for any given rate of monetary expansion.

The tension between fiscal and monetary policy has been clearly in evidence in recent years. In 1993–4 and 1994–5, interest rates were moderate despite high fiscal deficits because the supply of money, driven by foreign capital inflows, grew rapidly. Growth was stimulated but inflation also rose. In 1995–6, monetary policy was tightened in order to control inflation. Given the loose fiscal stance, interest rates rose sharply. Inflation fell but growth prospects were threatened.

The lesson is straightforward: fiscal adjustment is required to soften the trade-off between inflation and growth.

IV. FISCAL ADJUSTMENT AND THE BALANCE OF PAYMENTS

Although balance of payments adjustment since 1991 has been very satisfactory, there are two reasons why the sustainability of the current account is likely to become an important policy issue in future. Firstly, oil imports are expected to increase rapidly as India's oil production levels off in the next year or two. Secondly, and more importantly, a substantial increase in investment is needed to correct the infrastructural deficiencies that are a major constraint on economic growth.

There is a fashionable view that the size of the current account deficit should be a matter of indifference so long as it corresponds to a private rather than a public deficit. The rationale is that the former would be self-correcting since the private sector can be expected to respect its own intertemporal budget constraints. But India's public accounts are not yet in good order; and even if they were, international experience shows that unsound private borrowing and lending followed by crises and crashes can and do occur. Experience also shows that the pool of internationally mobile net long-term funds is limited and that countries which have successfully run current account deficits of 6 per cent of GDP or more are the exception rather than the rule.[24] Past experience would seem to suggest that a deficit of 2.5–3 per cent of GDP (such as prevailed in the second half of the 1980s) is excessive. But this was at a time when capital inflows were of the debt-creating variety. In the new climate in which India is actively seeking direct and portfolio investment, a more relaxed view would suggest that a sustainable current account deficit of up to 4 per cent of GDP would be sustainable, provided exports are growing rapidly.

The proviso is important. Non-debt-creating inflows have better risk-sharing characteristics than bonds but they do require a considerably higher rate of return, taking one year with another. If there are servicing difficulties, new inflows could dry up even if potential capital losses prevent outflows.

A prudent limit on the current account deficit of say 4 per cent of GDP has important implications for domestic saving/investment balances.[25] Large increases in investment of up to 8 per cent

[24] See Feldstein and Horioka (1981). Canada, Australia, and Argentina ran large current account deficits in the nineteenth century but long-term capital was not then constrained by exchange risk. Some East Asian countries are currently running deficits in the region of 6–8 per cent of GDP, but they have considerably higher growth rates of exports than India. Moreover, they are far more open: in their case, a deficit of 6–8 per cent corresponds to 25–30 per cent of exports; in India's case, it would correspond to 60–80 per cent of exports.

[25] It also has a significant bearing on exchange rate policy. Keeping the current account deficit at the appropriate level will require that the real exchange rate be flexible. In India's circumstances, this in turn is best achieved by a managed float of the nominal exchange rate, a regime that India already operates. For further discussion of the optimum exchange rate regime in the Indian context see Joshi and Little (1994; 1996). The latter source also discusses another important question pertinent to the exchange rate policy: how should the exchange rate float be managed when capital flows are volatile?

of GDP are being envisaged in the context of stepping up India's growth rate and the infrastructural requirements thereof. It follows that India cannot safely rely on foreign savings alone to secure this increase in investment, even if the capital inflows were forthcoming initially; an increase in the domestic savings rate will also be necessary. Since private savings in India are already high, relative to her stage of development, the main burden will have to be borne by an increase in public savings.[26] This underscores the conclusions reached earlier regarding the need for and the scale of fiscal consolidation.

V. Two Critical Issues for Fiscal and Monetary Stability

In this section, I shall discuss two other issues that are critical in the context of future fiscal and monetary stability, (a) the implications of expected changes in Centre–State financial relations and, (b) mechanisms for limiting excessive government deficits and central bank financing thereof.

V.1 Centre–State Relations

It seems highly likely that greater devolution of powers and responsibilities to the states will take place in the future. It is thus pertinent to consider the relevance of such a change for macroeconomic policy.

Though the move to devolution is politically driven, there are some grounds for believing that it would be beneficial from a welfare and efficiency point of view. The general economic argument for devolution is that subnational governments will more efficiently deploy public resources in accordance with local tastes than national governments, since they are closer to the people whose wants vary from region to region. It is also possible that local politicians and officials would have stronger incentives for good performance if responsibilities were more clearly vested in them.

These *a priori* arguments may not be realized in practice since

[26] Note that measures to increase public savings may not result in a one-for-one improvement in overall savings as private savings may fall somewhat in consequence. Financial sector liberalization and modernization will have to proceed rapidly if private savings are to grow.

state or local governments may be more corrupt, nepotic, and inefficient than the Centre. However that may be, the point that I wish to emphasize here is that decentralization has the potential to cause macroeconomic problems if its contours are not precisely defined. In a number of countries, excessive borrowing by sub-national governments has been a major cause of national crisis.

The crucial point is that there could be some benefit from increasing the responsibilities of the states and the revenue they derive from the Centre, but only if the latter accrues on an 'objective' basis, that is a basis that does not depend on the states' own expenditure. Otherwise the states will have an incentive to increase spending and shift the cost to the country as a whole. Should the stipulation that states must live within their means extend to limitation of their borrowing powers? One possible interpretation of a hard budget constraint is that States should be allowed to meet deficits by borrowing in the market but without any possibility of bailout by the Centre. In principle this could work. In practice there are two difficulties. Firstly, the capital market can fail to impose timely discipline. (Note also that subnational governments can obtain 'loans' in the short run by raiding pension funds or accumulating arrears on salaries and bills.) Secondly, if subnational governments get into trouble, it is often politically impossible for the Centre to refuse assistance; and the consequent incredibility of a 'no bailout' rule makes it more likely that states will get into trouble. I conclude that it would be wise to retain the power of the Centre to regulate the borrowing of the states from domestic and foreign sources. Finally, it goes without saying that the States should not have more than strictly temporary access to the RBI.

V.2 An Independent Central Bank? A Fiscal Constitution?

The deeper reasons for the erosion of India's fiscal prudence lie in the twin forces of 'political awakening' and 'political decay'.[27] The former, an inevitable and desirable concomitant of democratization, consists of the increasing self-assertion of groups that were not part of the narrow pre-Independence élite structures. This

---

[27] I owe the terms 'political awakening' and 'political decay' to James Manor. See Manor (1983).

process has led to significantly increased demands on the budget. Unfortunately, it has been accompanied by 'political decay', the erosion of institutions, essential in any well-functioning democracy, that stand above and manage conflict. The mediating role of the Congress party was lost along with the atrophy of its grass-roots organizations. The institutions of restraint, such as the Ministry of Finance and the Reserve Bank, have become more subject to political pressures. The Gladstonian traditions of the civil service and the austerity and high-mindedness of the first generation of post-Independence politicians have crumbled and no longer act as effective barriers to inflationary finance. As a result, increasingly, claims on the budget have been managed by handouts; measures that increase government expenditures or reduce tax and non-tax receipts. It is natural to ask whether in this climate new 'anchors' of stability would not have a useful role to play.

Action in India has so far centred round ending the direct access of the government to borrowing from the RBI. This suggestion was first mooted by the Chakravarty Committee in 1985 in the context of improving monetary control. Laudably, when Manmohan Singh was Finance Minister, the government took a concrete step towards ending the automatic monetization of fiscal deficits through the creation of ad hoc treasury bills. In September 1994 there was an agreement between the central government and the RBI that monetization of budget deficits would be reduced by imposing a ceiling on ad hoc treasury bills for any period of ten working days, and for the financial year as a whole, and that this ceiling would be progressively tightened to phase out automatic monetization through treasury bills altogether over a period of three years.

In fact, this agreement was in practice breached several times in 1995–6 in order to ease the pressure on interest rates coming from the fiscal deficit and the economic recovery. Moreover, it would be inaccurate to portray the agreement, even if it were adhered to, as ending the monetization of deficits. Ignoring foreign borrowing, any given fiscal deficit has to be financed by printing money or by domestic borrowing. This choice cannot be avoided by forcing the government to borrow from the market in the first instance. A decision would still have to be made on whether to avoid a rise in interest rates (that is, to print money by the back door through open market operations) or to adhere to a monetary target and allow interest rates to rise. In India, the central bank is not independent, so this decision would be made by the government itself. Direct or indirect monetization of deficits could only be eliminated by granting full independence to the RBI.

More fundamentally, however, one may question whether central bank independence is the right solution when the principal problem is excessive fiscal deficits. For even if the Reserve Bank were independent it is surely too pious to hope that making the government compete for funds would itself make it fiscally prudent unless we are prepared to drive the system as far as a solvency crisis for the government. A more direct and less painful reform would be to place limits on fiscal deficits themselves. It is interesting to note that such a reform would not require a constitutional amendment. Article 292 of the Constitution says: 'The Union shall have unlimited power of borrowing . . . either within India or outside . . . subject only to such limits as may be fixed by Parliament from time to time.' This is not to say that limits on government access to the RBI are not also helpful. Of course any such erection of barriers to government action must confront the problem that occasions can arise when overriding them would be the optimal policy. Devising the appropriate limits on the government's fiscal and monetary discretion (along with override clauses to cover extreme contingencies) deserves to be one of the burning issues for discussion and action in the near future.

VI. Conclusion

Deep fiscal adjustment is critical for the success of India's reforms. We may argue about the precise permissible level of government or public sector deficits, but it is patently clear that recent deficits are excessive. The fiscal agenda should be wider than simply the attainment of 'sustainability'. What is required is a large reduction in public expenditure, sufficient to reduce interest rates and to stimulate private investment, while protecting public investment and social sector spending and supporting structural change. The technical possibilities are enormous. It is obviously only the nature of the political system and its balance of forces that prevents India from achieving these ends. The future of reform will be endangered, indeed brought to nought, unless this deadlock is broken.

REFERENCES

Bajpai, N. and Jeffrey Sachs (1996): 'Fiscal Policy in India's Economic Reforms', Paper presented at the Harvard Conference on India' Reforms, Boston, December 13–14.

Chopra, Ajai, Charles Collyns, Richard Hemming and Karen Parker (1995): *India: Economic Reform and Growth*, Occasional Paper 134 (Washington, DC: International Monetary Fund).

Easterly, W. and S. Rebello (1993): 'Fiscal Policy and Economic Growth', *Journal of Monetary Economics*, vol. 32, pp. 417–57.

Feldstein, M. and C. Horioka (1980): 'Domestic Saving and International Capital Flows', *Economic Journal*, vol. 90, pp. 314–29.

Fischer, Stanley (1993): 'The Role of Macroeconomic Factors in Growth', *Journal of Monetary Economics*, vol. 32, pp. 485–512.

Government of India (1996): *Economic Survey 1995–6* (New Delhi: Ministry of Finance).

Joshi, Vijay and I.M.D. Little (1994): *India: Macroeconomics and Political Economy 1964–1991* (Washington, DC: World Bank and New Delhi: Oxford University Press).

—— (1996): *India's Economic Reforms 1991–2001* (New Delhi: Oxford University Press and Oxford: Clarendon Press).

Manor, James (1983): 'The Electoral Process amid Awakening and Decay', in P. Lyon and J. Manor (eds), *Transfer and Transformation: Political Institutions in the New Commonwealth* (Leicester: University of Leicester Press).

Mundle, S. and M. Govinda Rao (1991): 'Volume and Composition of Government Subsidies in India 1987–8', *Economic and Political Weekly*, vol. 26, pp. 1157–72.

Varshney, A. (1996): 'Mass Politics or Elite Politics?', Paper presented at the Harvard Conference on India's Economic Reforms, Boston, December 13–14.

World Bank (1996): *India: Country Economic Memorandum*, Washington, DC.

8

Liberalization, the Stock Market, and the Market for Corporate Control: A Bridge too Far for the Indian Economy?

Ajit Singh[*]

I. INTRODUCTION

An outstanding development of the 1990s, closely associated with the economic reform programme initiated by Dr Manmohan Singh, has been the very rapid expansion of the stock markets and their growing role in the Indian economy. Both internal and external liberalization measures, undertaken as a part of the financial reform, as well as the more liberal general economic ethos created by the reform, have largely been responsible for this evolution.

The first part of this contribution reviews the stock market reforms and comments on the available evidence on the effects of stock market expansion on corporate growth and on the real economy. The second part focuses on the proposed next stage of the reform process being urged by the financial community. Their

* I had the privilege of being Dr Manmohan Singh's pupil at the Punjab University, Chandigarh in 1958. Ever since Dr Singh has accorded to me a warm personal friendship, and indeed treated me as part of his family. It is therefore with a deep sense of honour and gratitude that I dedicate this essay to him to mark his 65th birthday.

In preparing this essay I have benefited greatly from detailed comments by Professor Ian Little and Dr R. Nagaraj. The usual caveat applies.

specific proposal is to establish a market for corporate control in order to maximize the benefits from stock market development. The government has recently (1997) published a Takeover Code that suggests that it is not opposed to the evolution of such a market.

Takeovers and a corporate control market would have far-reaching effects on the Indian economy, but there has been little informed debate on this subject. This contribution attempts to invite such a debate by advancing analyses and evidence to suggest that such reform is more likely to harm than help the real economy at India's present stage of development. The proposed reform should therefore be resisted.

II. ECONOMIC REFORM AND STOCK MARKET DEVELOPMENT[1]

Although India has long had a stock market, its development after Independence and up until 1980 ebbed and flowed, but in general had been quite slow. In 1980, the total market capitalization on the Indian stock markets as a proportion of GDP was only 5 per cent. By 1990, following the liberalization measures initiated during the 1980s, the ratio rose to 13 per cent. With the accelerated pace of liberalization under Dr Singh's reforms the stock market growth has been explosive. By end-1993, total market capitalization reached 60 per cent of GDP.

Between 1980 and 1993, the number of mutual funds investors rose from 2 to 40 m., a figure second only to the US (51 m.). In terms of listed companies, the Indian stock market (7,985 companies in 1995) is now the largest in the world, larger even than the US (7,671 companies), with the UK (2,078 companies), and Germany (678 companies) far behind.[2]

The daily turnover of shares on the Bombay Stock Exchange rose from Rs 0.13 bn in 1980–1 to Rs 3.7 bn in 1993–4, an almost thirty-fold increase. The average daily trading volume on the Bombay market in the early 1990s was similar to that in London — about 45,000 trades a day. At its peak trading has occurred at double that rate.

---

[1] The sources of data presented in this section are Mayya (1993, 1995); IFC (1996); Singh (1997a).

[2] Nagaraj (1996) suggests, however, that the Indian figures in this paragraph may be somewhat overstated.

Although Indian stock market growth during the 1980s and 90s has been impressive, so has it been in several other leading emerging markets. In Taiwan, market capitalization as a proportion of GDP rose from 11 per cent in 1981 to 74 per cent in 1991. Similarly, between 1983 and 1993, the Chilean ratio rose from 13.2 to 78 per cent and the Thai from 3.8 to 55.8 per cent. To put these figures in an historical perspective, Mullins (1993) notes that it probably took the US stock market 85 years (1810–95) to achieve a broadly similar increase in capitalization ratio, from 7 to 71 per cent.

In Indian stock market reforms, liberalization has occurred simultaneously with fresh regulation (Joshi and Little, 1996). Liberalization measures have included the repeal of the Capital Issues Control Act 1947 by which the government controlled new share issues and determined the issue price. Externally, liberalization has allowed foreign institutional investors to directly purchase Indian corporate shares. Similarly, Indian companies have been permitted to raise funds abroad.[3]

The flagship of the government's new regulations to ensure transparency and above board functioning of stock markets has been the Securities and Exchange Board of India Act which came into force in January 1992. Under this act, the authorities have attempted to regulate the activities of stockbrokers, merchant banks, and other intermediaries on the primary market. Although the Securities and Exchange Board of India (SEBI) has apparently made progress in some areas, it will be a long time before the Indian stock market loses its justly deserved reputation as being a 'snake-pit' to use Joshi and Little's expressive phrase. Mayya (1995) notes the continuing huge malpractices on the secondary markets.[4]

III. The Stock Market, Corporate Growth and the Real Economy

How has this enormous stock market expansion affected the real economy? Has it brought about larger savings and investment or

---

[3] These capital account liberalization measures are subject to restrictions. See also Joshi and Little (1996).

[4] The great stock market scam of 1992 focused much public attention on these issues.

greater productivity of investment as the proponents of the stock market suggest?[5]

III.1 The Financing of Corporate Growth

At first blush, the answer appears highly positive. During the 1980s and the 1990s, Indian corporations have raised large amounts of capital on a very active primary market to finance their growth. In 1980, Rs 929 m. were raised through corporate securities issuance (Balasubramanian, 1993). This figure had risen to Rs 2.5 bn by 1985, to a huge Rs 123 bn by 1990, and by 1993–4, it reached Rs 225 bn, i.e. a 250–fold increase since 1980. By contrast the general price level rose less than fourfold during this period. New corporate securities constituted 12.8 per cent of the country's gross domestic savings in 1993–4 (Mayya, 1995). Another indicator of an extremely active primary market is that in 1994–5 nearly 1700 companies raised equity capital (either through direct offerings to the public or through rights issues); of these, 369 were new companies (RBI, 1995).

Singh (1995a) has examined the financing of corporate growth in ten industrializing economies (including India) during the 1980s at a microeconomic level. His sample for each country normally consisted of the largest one hundred listed manufacturing companies that existed throughout the period 1980–90. Table 8.1, reporting his results for India, indicates that the average Indian corporation, during the 1980s, financed about 40 per cent of its growth of 'net assets' (the long-term capital employed in the firm) from internal sources (i.e. retained profits) and 60 per cent from external sources. Of the latter, nearly a third came from equity issues and two-thirds from long-term debt. The three financing variables obey the basic accounting identity that the total growth of net assets equals the sum of the internal and external sources of finance. The above results pertain to 1980–90, but in view of the enormous stock market activity in the 1990s, the importance of stock market finance would be even greater for the later period.

This large recourse to external and particularly stock market finance by the Indian companies is theoretically surprising as is

---

[5] See, for example, King & Levine (1993).

the great number of stock market listings. An underdeveloped capital market, by its inability to provide the desired external finance, may be expected to oblige corporations to grow largely from internal sources. Moreover, in an imperfect stock market, which operates like a 'snake-pit', firms would be discouraged from raising stock market finance, and indeed from seeking a listing at all. Economic theory suggests that in an emerging stock market, where information gathering and dissemination activity is not adequately developed, and where most firms have not yet built a 'reputation', the pricing of the firms' shares will tend to be arbitrary and volatile (Tirole, 1991). This should discourage risk-averse firms from raising stock market finance. Moreover, developing country firms are likely to be family controlled, which should also inhibit them from issuing new equity for fear of losing control. Further, as Schleifer and Vishny (1996) note, if there is inadequate legal protection for the investments of minority share-holders (as is common in emerging markets), we would expect households, or even prudent institutions, not to buy company shares.

It will be useful in this context to consider the financing of corporate growth in advanced countries. These corporations are widely thought to follow a 'pecking order' according to which firms rely largely, if not entirely, on internal sources to finance their growth. If more finance is needed, they use long-term loans or bank borrowings, and only as a very last resort go to the stock market to raise funds. When there is a separation of ownership and control, and when managers are able to pursue their own goals, it is not difficult to see why firms may shun the stock market. For management-controlled corporations, internal finance is clearly a cheaper and easier source of finance than the stock market where financing is only available subject to wide public scrutiny. However, in a classic contribution, Myers and Majluf (1984) showed that if there was asymmetric information between managers and shareholders, it would be rational even for profit-maximizing managers to follow the above 'pecking order'.

Myers and Majluf's general argument applies equally to developing country corporations. However, although the average Indian firm in Table 8.1 does deviate somewhat from the expected 'pecking order', it is its heavy reliance on external finance and the considerable use of equity finance that are theoretically more

TABLE 8.1
INDIA: TOP 100 LISTED COMPANIES IN
MANUFACTURING, 1980–90
(Quartile Distributions of Indicators of Financing of
Corporate Growth: After Tax Retention Ratio,
Internal and External Financing of Growth[*])

(percentages)

	Retention ratio	Internal finance	External finance (equity)	External finance. (debt)
Lower Quartile (Q1)	55.0	23.9	3.6	24.2
Median (Q2)	68.0	38.1	16.3	38.9
Upper Quartile (Q3)	76.2	62.0	31.5	57.8
Mean	65.7	40.5	19.6	39.9
Std. Deviation	15.0	32.8	21.9	24.4
Skewness	−0.60	−0.80	0.67	0.29
Kurtosis	0.59	3.10	0.57	−0.01

[*] Averaged over the entire period, normally from 1980 to 1990.
SOURCE: Singh (1997a).

anomalous for the reasons outlined earlier. Further, Table 8.2, which provides comparative data for ten industrializing countries, shows that the Indian case is by no means unique. The typical Korean corporation financed over 80 per cent of its growth of net assets from external sources. The corresponding figures for Turkey, Mexico, and Thailand are 84.7, 75.6, and 72.3 per cent respectively. Table 8.2 also shows that corporations in several sample countries resorted to equity finance during the 1980s to an even greater degree than their counterparts in India. The 'pecking order' theory is comprehensively violated for nearly half the sample countries. Singh (1994, 1995a) has provided an explanation for these anomalous phenomena (including that of the large number of listings in markets such as India's) in terms of: (a) the special circumstances of developing country financial markets in the 1980s, (b) the situation in advanced country markets, and (c) the encouragement of stock market growth by developing country governments in order, *inter alia*, to implement privatization.

TABLE 8.2
ALL COUNTRIES: TOP LISTED
COMPANIES IN MANUFACTURING
(Financing Corporate Growth: After Tax Retention Ratio,
Internal and External Finance of Growth[1]: Median Values)

(percentages)

Country	Retention ratio	Internal finance	External finance (equity)	External finance (debt)
Korea	65.7	15.8	46.9	30.4
Pakistan	65.9	67.5	5.2	23.9
Jordan	48.0	54.8	25.5	5.8
Thailand	48.7	14.7	na	na
Mexico	na	23.1	64.7	1.0
India	68.0	38.1	16.3	38.9
Turkey	37.8	13.4	66.6	16.9
Malaysia	51.7	29.7	48.0	12.0
Zimbabwe	61.7	57.0	43.5	0.0
Brazil	98.3	46.0	37.2	5.6
All	62.9	32.0	41.13	6.0
$^1X^2$	155.6*	147.45*	185.3*	121.4*

NOTE: [1] Average values for the relevant period for each country, normally 1980–1990

$^1X^2$ Statistic for comparison of medians across countries.

* implies rejection of the null hypothesis of equality of medians.

SOURCE: Singh (1995a).

III.2 Is the Contribution of Equity Finance to Indian Corporate Growth Overstated?

In a recent paper, Cobham and Subramaniam (1995) (C & S) suggest that the methodology used in Table 8.1 overstates the contribution of equity finance to Indian corporate growth and therefore exaggerates the apparently positive role of the stock market. Using the alternative methodology of Mayer (1990), Corbett and Jenkinson (1994) (MCJ), the C & S estimate of the contribution of new equity to Indian corporate investment is considerably smaller.

The differences in the empirical results are indeed due to the different methodologies used in the two exercises. The respective methods, however, have important implications for economic interpretation of the results. The following points are salient.

First, MCJ include depreciation as a major component of internal finance, whereas in Singh (1995a) (as in Tables 8.1 and 8.2) it is excluded both from the numerator and the denominator in the relevant ratios. As Singh's research is concerned with measuring the sources of finance for corporate *growth* of 'net assets', it necessarily focuses on the *net* increase in corporate assets — the depreciation provision for replacement is normally required to merely maintain the stock of assets (also see Prais, 1975 for a classic discussion).

Secondly, the MCJ method, when used with the flow-of-funds data (as is generally the case), relates to the corporate sector as a whole, rather than to the individual firms. In this approach intracorporate sector transactions are normally 'netted out' and external finance means funds from outside the corporate sector. Therefore, the question being addressed by MCJ with the flow-of-funds data is: how is 'investment' of the corporate sector as a whole financed, by internal sources (within the corporate sector) and by external sources (from outside the sector, eg. the household or the financial sector)? This is a different question from that addressed by Singh, who uses firm-level accounting data to enquire how individual corporations, rather than the corporate sector as a whole, finance the growth of their net assets, net of depreciation.

Thirdly, the differences in the corporate financing patterns between developed and developing countries are greatly reduced when these patterns are estimated by the use of the same methodology — whether MCJ or Singh (also see Singh, 1995a).

In short, the MCJ and Singh methods are addressing different questions: the latter is concerned with the growth of corporate 'net' rather than 'gross assets', and is considering the financing question from the perspective of the individual firm rather than that of the corporate sector as a whole.

However, leaving aside these methodological issues, two things are clear. Firstly, the stock market has made a far greater contribution in the 1980s and the 1990s to Indian corporate growth than it ever did before. Secondly, the observed pattern of corporate financing for India and several other industrializing countries runs contrary to theoretical expectations.

III.3 The Stock Market Financing of Corporate Growth and the Real Economy

An important reason why so much finance was raised from the stock market by the Indian corporate sector in the 1980s and 1990s was the share price boom that occurred during this period. The Bombay Sensitive Index rose from 123.6 in 1980 to 396.4 in 1985, to 1,040.7 in 1990 to 2,222 in 1992, to over 4,000 by the summer of 1994. The market has however slumped over the following two years, as is reflected in the end-year index values: 1994, 3,845; 1995, 3,109; and 1996, 3,104.

Confining attention for analytical purposes to the decade 1980–90, there was a well over eight-fold increase in share prices, while consumer prices rose by less than 10 per cent per annum during this period. Singh (1995a) estimated that between 1980 and 1985, the total (dividend plus capital gains) nominal return to a stock market investment was 33 per cent and the real return was 23 per cent; the corresponding nominal and real returns for the period 1986 to 1990 were 26 and 18 per cent respectively, which gives an average real return of 20 per cent for the decade as a whole.

There is agreement that the stock market boom of the 1980s was largely policy-induced (Balasubramanian (1993); Nagaraj (1996)). By the early 1980s, neither the development finance institutions (DFIs) nor the commercial banks could meet their government-imposed requirements to lend to the priority sectors at concessional rates and also meet the private corporate needs. The Reserve Bank of India therefore advised the mobilization of household savings through capital market expansion to meet the corporate sector's requirements. This led to several fiscal incentives that helped to greatly increase the number of investors on the stock market, mainly through the growth of mutual funds. In that sense the post-1991 reforms can be regarded as a continuation of the process that began in the 1980s.

The stock market boom created by the entry of large numbers of domestic, and subsequently foreign investors (as external liberalization proceeded in the 1990s) into the capital market, lowered the cost of capital for Indian corporations, encouraging them to raise large amounts of stock market finance. A central question is: has this benefited the real economy?

There is scant empirical work on this subject, but an important recent contribution by Nagaraj (1996) provides very useful information for the period 1980–91. His relevant findings are as follows.

1. The huge increase in stock market financing activity is not associated with either a rise in aggregate gross domestic savings, or equally significantly, with an increase in the proportion of financial savings. Gross domestic savings as a proportion of GDP at market prices reached its peak level of 23 per cent in 1978–9. The savings ratio was, however, generally lower throughout the 1980s, and not higher. The financial proportion of gross domestic savings fell from its peak level of 55 per cent in 1984–5 to 42–5 per cent in the second half of the decade. There was however a great change in the composition of financial savings. The share of corporate debentures and equities in total financial savings rose from 3.3 per cent in the 1970s to 6 per cent in the first half of the 1980s, and to 11.8 per cent during the second half of the decade. Over the same periods, the corresponding figures for bank deposits were 45, 39, and 27 per cent, respectively. Thus the enormous stock market activity in the 1980s basically involved portfolio substitution by households and institutions from bank deposits towards stock market instruments.

2. Using both aggregate accounting as well as the flow-of-funds data for the private corporate sector as a whole, Nagaraj reports a considerable fall in the 1980s in the proportion of either gross or net fixed capital formation which was financed through internal sources, i.e. retained earnings or depreciation. This combined with other evidence in his paper suggests that the increase in external finance available to the corporate sector through the capital market, to an appreciable extent, replaced corporations' internal funds during this decade. This could in part be due to a decline in corporate profitability (see below).

3. Importantly, Nagaraj also reports some increase in the corporate sector's gross fixed capital formation as a proportion of, (1) GDP at market prices, (2) aggregate fixed capital formation. However, whether this observed increase can be ascribed to the growth of capital raised on the stock market is more problematical. Nagaraj finds that whereas there was previously a

statistically positive correlation between the annual growth rates of capital raised externally and corporate fixed capital formation, the relationship between the two variables (including that with suitable lags) has become statistically insignificant in the 1980s. It is however still positive, but the value of the coefficient is much smaller (.25 between 1980–1 to 1990–2, as against .45 between 1961–2 to 1979–80)

4. On the question of whether or not stock market activity has led to improved productivity of investment, Nagaraj provides two pieces of evidence. First, he finds that the growth rate of real value added in the corporate manufacturing sector in the 1980s was lower than that of the registered manufacturing sector as a whole. This suggests that the smaller non-corporate firms, which did not have access to stock market funds, were able to grow at a faster rate than the larger corporate firms. Secondly, there was a secular decline in corporate profitability during the 1980s, a result which is similar to Singh's (1997a) for the hundred largest Indian quoted companies. It could of course be argued that the fall in profitability does not indicate a decline in efficiency, that it simply reflects greater product market competition as a result of general liberalization.

The above hypothesis can fortunately be tested on the data available in the IFC databank which permits a decomposition of the rate of return into two components: the profit margin (profits/sales) and output–capital ratio (sales/net assets). The results show that the secular fall in the profitability of the 100 largest firms in the 1980s was entirely due to a decrease in the productivity of capital rather than a reduction in profit margins. The latter event is what would have been expected if the fall in profitability had been caused by greater product market competition.

It could nevertheless still be argued within a neoclassical frame-work that reduced profitability does not necessarily indicate in-efficiency since the real cost of capital had fallen. The latter however was caused by the stock market boom which was by no means permanent. This leads to a related point concerned with the volatility of share prices. Share prices in India in recent years have been highly volatile (El-Erian and Kumar, 1995). Apart from the other drawbacks of volatility, we note in the present context that it reduces the efficiency of stock market pricing signals for the allocation of investment resources. (Tirole, 1991)

In assessing the effects of stock market expansion on the real economy, in addition to its effect on savings, investment, and the productivity of investment, it is also necessary to examine the impact of foreign portfolio capital inflows. As a consequence of the government's external liberalization measures in the post-1991 period, there was a huge increase in such flows. Joshi and Little (1996) report that non-debt creating private capital inflows amounted to $4.1 bn in 1993–4 and $4.9 bn in 1994–5. Nearly three-quarters of these comprised portfolio equity capital, including share issues by Indian companies on overseas stock markets.

At one level, these capital inflows helped the real economy. The flows contributed to resolving the liquidity crisis of 1991 and to assisting the central bank to build up sizeable foreign exchange reserves; the latter reached a high point of nearly $20 bn in 1994–5. Ironically, these foreign exchange reserves helped to reduce the government's dependence on the IMF, giving it greater freedom to pursue a more independent economic policy if it was politically necessary.

The government has however also been keenly aware of the dangers of such inflows. Although they were non-debt creating, they could not be regarded as being permanent. As Singh (1996a; 1997b) points out, a sudden withdrawal of these portfolio flows for totally extraneous reasons could lead to a negative interaction between two inherently unstable markets, the currency and the stock markets, which could do enormous damage to the real economy (as happened in Mexico). The Indian government has generally followed pragmatic policies and has used sterilization and taxation measures to discourage short-term inflows. I would concur with Joshi and Little's (1996) judgement that government policy in this area has been broadly sensible. Although portfolio capital inflows do create serious macroeconomic difficulties, government policy measures have so far stopped them from doing any harm to the real economy.

To sum up, the available evidence suggests that despite the benefits of stock market expansion for the corporate sector, the real economy does not appear to have benefited from either increased savings and investment or a greater productivity of investment. On the other hand, government policy has prevented any harm to the real economy from the huge capital inflow surges of 1993–4 and 1994–5. It should, however, also be recorded that the evidence on savings, investments, and investment productivity outlined above refers to the period 1980–90. The data for the 1990s could in principle lead to a more favourable verdict. Nevertheless, it is worth noting that the real economy, particularly industry, has achieved its fastest growth in the last two years when the stock market has not been doing well. During 1995–6 and 1996–7 the real economy has expanded at a rate of nearly 7 per cent per annum — quite unprecedented for India. In the same period, the Bombay Sensitive Index has fallen from its peak of over 4,000 in the summer of 1994 to 3,104 on 31 December 1996. All this would suggest that the stock market may have so far been a 'sideshow' with relatively little impact, positive or negative, on the aggregate real economy. However, with the advent of the market for corporate control, the stock market will become much less of a sideshow. It is likely to play a much more prominent role in the real economy, arguably to the latter's considerable disadvantage, as will be suggested below.

IV. THE MARKET FOR CORPORATE CONTROL: THEORY AND EVIDENCE

IV.1 Takeovers and the Stock Market: Analytical Considerations

In textbook theory, takeovers provide an important additional mechanism through which the stock market can promote a more efficient utilization of capital resources. There are two distinct ways in which the establishment of a market for corporate control may do this

(1) The *threat* of takeovers may lead inefficient firms to perform better;
(2) Even if all firms were on their efficiency frontier, the amalgamation of some through the *act* of takeovers may lead to a better social allocation of resources via synergy.

Moreover, there are many quoted companies that hardly ever raise stock market finance as they have adequate internal sources for their expansion. Such firms cannot therefore be disciplined by the normal pricing process of the stock market whereby the efficient companies are rewarded with, other things being equal, high share prices and a lower cost of capital, the inefficient firms facing a higher cost of capital. However, even these firms, if they are inefficient, would be subject to the direct sanctions of the market for corporate control.

Nevertheless, more recent economic analysis suggests several reasons why these potential virtues of a market for corporate control may not actually materialize in the real world. To summarize。

1. Real world markets for corporate control, even in advanced economies, are subject to an inherent imperfection: it is far easier for a large firm to take over a small one than the other way around (Singh, 1971, 1975, 1992). Although a small efficient firm can in principle take over a large inefficient corporation (and to some degree this did happen in the US takeover wave of the 1980s through 'junk bonds'), its incidence is very small (Hughes, 1991).

This consideration is particularly important for developing countries like India where there are large, potentially predatory conglomerate groups (Singh, 1995a). These could take over smaller, more efficient firms and thereby reduce potential competition to the detriment of the real economy. In a takeover battle it is the absolute firepower (absolute size) that counts rather than relative efficiency.

2. The efficient operation of the takeover mechanism requires that enormous quantities of information are widely available — specifically, how profitable is each firm under its existing management and what would be its potential under any other management if it were taken over. Such information is not easily available even in advanced countries (Helm, 1989). For reasons discussed earlier, it would be far scarcer in emerging markets.

3. There are in practice huge transactions costs involved in takeovers in countries like the US and the UK which hinder the efficiency of the takeover mechanism. Changing management through takeover proves to be a very expensive way of accomplishing this task (Peacock and Bannock, 1991). This consideration is particularly important for developing countries which can ill afford such high transactions costs.

4. Recent work based on asymmetric information, signalling, and involving the concept of signal jamming, suggests that the market for corporate control may not be just   inefficient but

may in fact generate perverse outcomes. Stein (1989) shows that under plausible assumptions, if the information about a firm's operations is, or is perceived to be, asymmetric, it may pay rational managers even in rational markets to be myopic. This would lead to short term measures and to lower rates of investment than would otherwise be the case — an issue which is particularly significant for developing countries trying to achieve fast economic growth.

5. A similar socially perverse outcome of the takeover process has been suggested by Schleifer and Summers (1988). They point out that the takeover mechanism in the US is often used as a device not to honour the implicit contracts of workers in the acquired firm with the pre-acquisition management. Such abandonment of implicit contracts, according to the authors, is socially harmful because it discourages firm-specific accumulation of human capital by workers.

Takeovers could also in principle reduce previous over-manning. Which outcome actually prevails will depend on the specific circumstances. It may be suggested that in countries like India with strong employment protection laws, the Schleifer and Summers line of reasoning is not relevant. However, if such laws were to be repealed under the economic reform, this argument would become significant.

6. Grossman and Hart (1980) have suggested that because of the 'free-rider' problem, the takeover mechanism may not work efficiently. Any individual shareholder may feel that his or her action is unlikely to affect the outcome of a disciplinary takeover bid. It would therefore be best not to accept a raider's offer and to wait until the share price increases further after the successful bid. Grossman and Hart argue that if all shareholders act in this way, the disciplinary takeover bids would not materialize. Indeed, in these circumstances, raiders will not have adequate incentives to undertake such bids at all.

The Grossman and Hart theory applies however only to disciplinary bids. In practice, it is difficult to distinguish between such raids and those undertaken for other motives, for example empire-building or increasing monopoly power. The latter motives are, however, likely to be very relevant in many emerging markets because of the presence in these countries, as mentioned earlier, of large conglomerate business groups.

IV.2 Evidence on Takeovers

Although there are embryonic markets for corporate control in a few developing countries (e.g. Brazil, and for that matter even in India),[6] most do not yet have hostile takeovers and fully-fledged markets for control. The evidence on the characteristics and operations of such markets can therefore only come from advanced countries such as the UK and the US.

IV.2.a *Selection Process and the Threat of Takeovers*

Singh's (1971, 1975) were among the first studies to systematically examine the nature of the selection process in the market for corporate control. This involved a comparative analysis of the multivariate characteristics of four kinds of populations of firms: the acquired, the acquiring, the non-acquired, and the non-acquiring. Singh's research was based on takeovers in the UK and covered two periods: one of normal takeover activity (1954 to 1960); and the other, the takeover boom of 1967 to 1970. His results have proved to be extremely robust and have been confirmed in most subsequent studies both for the UK and the US.[7]

The central finding of Singh's exercises can be summarized as follows. Contrary to the expectations of neoclassical theory as well as the folklore of capitalism, selection in the market for corporate control does not take place entirely on the basis of efficiency, i.e. profitability or stock market valuation. Although profitability matters, absolute size matters a great deal more. A large relatively unprofitable company has a much better chance of survival than a small profitable one. Moreover, it is almost invariably the large that take over the small. The acquisition process may thus indeed act in a perverse way since a large unprofitable company can increase its immunity to takeovers through the takeovers process itself — by becoming larger through the acquisition of small firms.[8]

---

6 For Brazil see *Acquisitions Monthly* (Nov. 1966); for India see *Business Line* (March 1997).

7 For the UK studies see Meeks (1977); Cosh, Hughes, Lee, and Singh (1989, 1996); for the US see Schwarz (1982); Mueller (1980; Warshawsky (1987); Ravenscraft and Scherer (1989). For recent review articles see Hughes (1991), Singh (1992, 1993a).

8 See also Greer (1986) and Singh (1971).

IV.2.b Effects of Takeovers: Microeconomic Efficiency

Apart from the threat of takeovers and the nature of the selection process, there is a large literature for industrial countries on the effects of actual takeovers on the post-merger efficiency of acquiring firms. Here there is an important divide between industrial organization studies based on accounting data and studies by financial specialists using stock market data. The former invariably show that on an average, controlling for the effects of industry and of the business cycle, the post-merger profitability of the amalgamating merging firms declines in relation to the weighted average of their pre-merger profitability. Since the amalgamated firm is likely to have greater (and certainly no less) monopoly power than the pre-merger firms considered on their own, this empirical finding is interpreted as indicating that mergers lead on average to a decline in microeconomic efficiency.

A radically different view of the efficiency of mergers comes from specialists in finance who use stock market data and the so-called 'event studies' methodology to investigate the effects of mergers. Here the basic empirical finding is that in the period immediately preceding the takeover event there is on average an appreciation of the value of the victim firm by about 20 per cent, while the raider's stock market value either remains the same or appreciates or depreciates by a relatively small amount. Since the overall result of the merger is an increase of about 20 per cent on average in the stock market value of the amalgamating firms, finance specialists conclude that this reflects an increase in net social welfare.

This inference is, however, subject to an extremely important qualification. It is valid only if the real world share prices are always efficient in Tobin's (1984) fundamental valuation sense, i.e. relative share prices of firms reflecting their relative (rationally) expected earnings. There is considerable support for the hypothesis that share prices are, broadly speaking, efficient in what Tobin calls 'the information arbitrage' sense, i.e. that all information percolates quickly in the market and is therefore immediately reflected in the price. Such efficiency does not however necessarily imply efficiency in the fundamental valuation sense. There is a large body of analytical and empirical work to indicate that share prices are often dominated by the whims and fads of speculators and the so-called 'noise traders'.[9]

[9] See also the collection of papers in the 'Symposium on Bubbles', *Journal*

Several investigators have suggested that the observed increase in the aggregate value of the merging firms is more satisfactorily explained in terms of other theories. Charkham (1989) suggests, for example, that there is at any time a normal share price for a company based on its future prospects, reflecting valuation at the margin. However, when this company is put into 'play', or becomes the subject of an actual or rumoured takeover bid, its price goes up. This does not reflect an increase in the social value of the company's assets, but simply the higher price that has to be paid in order to buy out the intramarginal shareholders for the control of the company. This alternative theory is compatible with the more or less universal finding mentioned earlier of industrial organization economists of a post-merger decline in profitability and efficiency of merging firms. It is also compatible with another important result in the literature that shows that some time *after* the merger 'event', the share price of the acquiring company almost invariably declines.[10]

IV.2.c Takeovers and Industrial Structure

In assessing the economic effects of takeovers, it is also essential to take into account their impact on the industrial structure. Here the evidence for the advanced countries is ambiguous. In the 1950s and 1960s mergers are generally thought to have contributed to an increase in industrial concentration both in the US and in the UK. However, in the 1970s and 1980s, despite the large merger wave of the 1980s in both countries, there was little increase in industrial concentration. The reason for this ambiguity is essentially that changes in industrial concentration also depend on a number of other factors (eg. entry of new firms) which can outweigh the normal concentrating effects of mergers.[11]

IV.2.d Takeovers and Short Term Behaviour

An important allegation against the takeover mechanism in the USA and the UK is that it encourages short term behaviour. At the simplest, the argument is that managers of Anglo–Saxon firms are

---

of Economic Perspectives, vol. 4, no. 2, Spring, 1990.

[10] For the US, by as much as 17 per cent two years after the merger. See also Franks, Harris, and Mayer (1988); Ruback (1988); Hughes (1991).

[11] There is a large literature on these issues. It is reviewed in Hughes (1991) and Singh (1992).

obliged to meet the earnings per share target (set by market expectations) every quarter or every half year, depending on the frequency of the stock market's reporting requirements for corporate ' earnings. If these market expectations of short-term earnings are not satisfied, the firm's share price falls, making it vulnerable to takeover. At the same time, on the other side of the market, the investors who are by and large the institutional fund managers, are also obliged to have a short-term outlook. This is because of the highly competitive structure of the fund management industry and the fact that fund managers' own performances are often judged by their principals on the basis of their performances over relatively brief time periods. The net result is a culture dominated by immediate gain and takeover speculation on both sides of the market.[12]

Survey results for the UK indicate that the chief executives of British companies spend an inordinate amount of their time on 'roadshows' in the form of presentations to investors at home and abroad. Similarly, considerable energy is devoted to either avoiding being taken over themselves, or planning acquisitions of other companies (Cosh, Hughes, and Singh, 1990). This distracts from their principal managerial task of creating new products, winning markets, and satisfying customer needs in an increasingly competitive global economy. Similarly, there is survey evidence for the USA which indicates high 'hurdle' rates and short payoff periods for investments by corporations in that country (Porter, 1992).

IV.2.e The Experience of Japan and Germany

In examining the merits of the market for corporate control in industrial countries, it is relevant and instructive not only to consider the experiences of the USA and the UK but also to look at those of Japan and Germany. The latter two countries do not have a free market for corporate control in the Anglo-Saxon sense, enabling raiders to mount hostile takeover bids against the wishes of the incumbent management. The incidence of hostile takeovers is extremely rare in either country. Odagiri (1994) ascribes the Japanese phenomenon to that country's lifetime employment system in large corporations. It is also due to the pattern of shareholdings in Japanese companies whereby 75 per cent of a typical

---

[12] For a fuller discussion of these issues, see also Singh (1995b). For an opposite perspective, see Marsh (1992).

corporation's shares are held in 'friendly hands', i.e. the corporation's suppliers, subcontractors, and other stakeholders. With only about a quarter of the shares with the general public, it is unlikely that there will be hostile takeover activity. The virtual absence of a market for corporate control in West Germany is attributed by students of the subject to many factors, including the country's corporate culture, the 1976 co-determination act, employee representation on the corporate supervisory boards, and the concentration of share ownership.

In the context of this contribution, a central point is that the lack of a market for corporate control has not in any way held back economic development in these countries. Indeed, the extraordinary post-war success of these economies and their ability to dominate world markets is thought by many to be precisely due to the fact that managers in these countries were not subject to a constant threat of takeovers. This enabled them to pursue long-term investments; to seek to expand their share of world markets rather than to be concerned with short-term movements in share prices or profits.[13] Particularly important in this respect has been the ability of corporations in these countries to invest in the training of their workforces. Equally significantly, with a stable corporate environment to which the absence of hostile takeovers makes an important contribution, the workers have the necessary incentives to undertake expensive investments in firm-specific human capital, i.e. unlike the case in the USA and UK, Japanese and German workers may count on their implicit contracts being honoured.

V. Conclusion and Policy Implications

The enormous expansion of stock markets in India since 1980 has been part of a worldwide trend towards deregulation, financial liberalization, and globalization. The Indian corporate sector has benefited considerably and directly from this evolution which has in a large part been induced by the government's internal and external liberalization measures. Contrary to *a priori* expectations

---

[13] For a fuller discussion of these issues and the survey evidence on managerial objectives in the USA, Germany, and Japan see Abegglen and Stalk (1985); Blaine (1993); Kojima (1995), and Singh (1996b).

concerning developing country firms and capital markets, Indian corporations have been willing and able to raise large sums of money (including more recently foreign exchange) at competitive rates from the stock markets. However, despite this largesse for the corporate economy, it is difficult to detect any gains to the aggregate real economy, at least in the 1980s. During that period there was no rise in the overall savings rate; evidently, all that happened was portfolio substitution by households and institutions from bank deposits to corporate securities. It is also problematic to attribute variations in corporate investments to variations in resources raised from the stock markets, essentially because the latter tended to replace corporations' internal resources, i.e. corporate savings. Nor is there evidence of a more productive use of investment resources. Nevertheless, the government's prudent handling of portfolio capital inflows has ensured that the country did not suffer any serious losses from the surges in such flows that occurred. Thus, as far as the progress of the real economy is concerned, despite their extraordinary expansion during the last fifteen years, the stock markets have so far been a sideshow.

This situation may however change with the advent of a market for corporate control, which would appear to be imminent. As *Business Line* (2 March 1997) reported: 'mergers, takeovers, de-mergers, divestments and de-subsidiarization have become fairly commonplace on the Indian scene, especially over the last two years'. Left to itself, with the enormous profits to be made on takeovers by merchant banks and other players, there may be sufficient political momentum to enable a fully-fledged market for corporate control to emerge within a relatively short period.

The important question is whether the evolution of such a market would be conducive to Indian industrialization and faster economic growth. The review of the analysis and evidence on the markets for corporate control in the USA and the UK indicate several drawbacks, particularly from the perspective of economic development. First, takeovers greatly intensify the normal stock market pressures towards speculation and short term returns. Secondly, there is no evidence that the market works in such a way as to always punish the inefficient and unprofitable companies and reward the efficient ones. Empirically, selection in the market for corporate control occurs much more on the dimension of size than that of profitability or the firm's stock market valuation. Thirdly, an active market for corporate control is likely to seriously distort the incentive system facing corporate managers. In Japan and Germany, which do not have markets for corporate control, managers are induced to seek the organic growth of the corporation they work for. In contrast, incentives in the Anglo–Saxon system emphasize financial engineering and growth by merger. Fourthly, in view of the existence of large conglomerate enterprises in India, as in many other developing countries, a freely functioning market for corporate control runs serious dangers of increasing concentration of industry and of stifling the development of efficient small and medium-sized firms. Finally, it is particularly relevant for developing countries to bear in mind the huge transactions costs involved in takeover activity, as well as the very large unfavourable redistributions of wealth it often leads to (Schleifer and Summers, 1988).

There are serious problems with the present Indian system of corporate governance: conflicts of interest and lack of cohesion among many controlling families, the adverse effects of large interlocking, intergroup investments on small shareholders in group companies; the total exclusion of ordinary shareholders from decisions with regard to corporate restructuring, mergers, divestments, etc. It may therefore appear attractive to deal with the whole gamut of such governance problems through the invisible hand of the market by instituting a takeover mechanism. However, the evidence from advanced countries surveyed in this contribution suggests that the end result of this whole process may not necessarily be better and could be considerably worse than the current situation. The government should follow the example of Japan, Germany, and other countries in Europe and attempt to find other ways of solving these problems of governance. A developing country like India simply cannot afford the burden of the extremely expensive, and hit and miss system of management change that takeovers represent.

India today stands at an important juncture with regard to questions of corporate governance and of further capital market development. One alternative — and unfortunately the one most likely to be followed more by default than by design in the absence of a serious debate — will be to continue the present drift towards the establishment of the market for corporate control. Another, and the one proposed here, is that the government should take a leaf from the Japanese book and simply not allow such a market to develop.

If the government were to accept the wisdom of the second course, complementary actions would be required in two important areas. First, steps should be taken to improve the lead bank system which has been in operation in India for the last four decades. This system has not worked as effectively in India as it has in Japan and South Korea. At the theoretical level, there is general recognition of the many advantages of this system in comparison to a stock market based one. The lead bank system has lower transactions costs and is much better able than the stock market to cope with the problems of asymmetric information and agency costs as well as short term behaviour. Bhatt (1994a, 1994b) has recently provided an excellent institutional and empirical analysis of the reasons why the lead bank system has been less successful in India than in Korea and Japan. His observations and conclusions would be a useful starting point for a purposive programme to remedy the shortcomings of the system in the Indian context.

The second group of complementary policies, in the absence of a market for corporate control, would involve stimulating much greater competition in the product markets. In the normal calculus of a capitalist economy, such competition is the principal constraint on inefficient managements. In the current Indian context, this would require *inter alia* a fundamental rethinking of the government policies on 'exit'.

In conclusion, this contribution will be a fitting tribute to Dr Manmohan Singh if it leads to a serious discussion on the desirability of the market for corporate control in India: should its evolution be welcomed or, as argued here, should it be regarded as 'a bridge too far' at the present and foreseeable level of development of the Indian economy?

REFERENCES

Abegglen, J.C. and G.C. Stalk (1985): *The Japanese Corporation* (New York: Basic Books Inc.).

Balasubramanian, N. (1993): *Corporate Financial Policies and Shareholders Returns — The Indian Experience* (Bombay: Himalaya Publishing House).

Baumol, W.J. (1965): *The Stock Market and Economic Efficiency* (New York: Fordham University Press).

Baumol, W.J., P. Heim, B.G. Malkiel and R.E. Quandt (1970): 'Earnings Retention, New Capital and the Growth of the Firm', *Review of Economics and Statistics*, November, no. 52, pp. 345–55.

Bhatt, V.V. (1994a): 'Japan: The Main Bank System and India: Lead Bank System', *International Journal of Development Banking*, vol. 12, no. 1, January.

—— (1994b): 'The Lead Bank System in India', in Aoki, M. and H. Patrick (eds), *The Main Bank System in Japan and its Relevance for Developing and Transforming Economies* (New York: Oxford University Press).

Blaine, M. (1993): 'Profitability and Competitiveness: Lessons from Japanese and American Firms in the 1980s', *California Management Review*, no. 36, pp. 48–74.

Charkham, J. (1989): 'Corporate Governance and the Market for Control of Companies', *Bank of England Panel Paper*, no. 25, March.

Cobham, D. and R. Subramaniam (1995): 'Corporate Finance in Developing Countries: New Evidence for India', CRIEFF Discussion Paper Series, No. 9512, University of St. Andrews, Scotland.

Corbett, J. and T. Jenkinson (1994): 'The Financing of Industry, 1970–89: An International Comparison', Discussion Paper No. 948, Centre for Economic Policy Research, London.

Cosh, A.D., A. Hughes and A. Singh (1980): 'The Causes and Effects of Takeovers in the UK: An Empirical Investigation for the Late 1960s at the Micro-Economic Level', in D.C. Mueller (ed.), *The Determination and Effects of Mergers* (Cambridge, Mass.: Oelschlager, Gunn & Hain).

—— (1990): 'Takeover and Short-Termism: Analytical and Policy Issues in the UK Economy', in Takeovers and Short-Termism in the UK Industrial Policy, Paper No. 3, Institute for Public Policy Research, London.

Cosh, A.D., A. Hughes, K. Lee and A. Singh (1989): 'Institutional Investment, Mergers and the Market for Corporate Control', *International Journal of Industrial Organisation*, March, pp. 73–100.

—— (1996): 'Takeovers, Institutional Investment and the Persistence of Profits', ESRC Working Papers No. 30, March, University of Cambridge.

El-Erian, M.A. and M.S. Kumar (1995): 'Emerging Equity Markets in Middle Eastern Countries', Paper presented at the World Bank

Conference on Stock Markets, Corporate Finance and Economic Growth, Washington, DC, 16–17 February.

Franks, J., R.S. Harris and C. Mayer (1988): 'Means of Payment in Takeover: Results for the United Kingdom and the United States', in Auerbach (ed.), *Corporate Takeovers: Causes and Consequences*, National Bureau of Economic Research (Chicago: University of Chicago Press).

Greer, D.F. (1986): 'Acquiring in Order to Avoid Acquisition', *Antitrust Bulletin*, Spring, pp. 155–85.

Grossman, S.J. and O.D. Hart (1980): 'Takeover Bids, the Free-Rider Problem and the Theory of the Corporation', *Bell Journal of Economics*, 11, pp. 42–64.

Helm, D. (1989): 'Mergers, Takeovers and the Enforcement of Profit Maximisation', in J. Fairburn and J.A. Kay (eds), *Mergers and Merger Policy* (New York: Oxford University Press).

Hughes, A. (1991): 'Mergers and Economic Performance in the UK: A Survey of the Empirical Evidence 1950–1990', in J. Fairburn and J.A. Kay (eds), *Mergers and Merger Policy* (Oxford) (Second edition).

IFC (1996): *Emerging Stock Markets Factbook 1996* (Washington, DC: IFC).

Jensen, M.C. (1988): 'Takeovers: Their Causes and Consequences, *Journal of Economic Perspectives*, vol. 3, no. 2 (winter), pp. 21–48.

Joshi, V. and I.M.D. Little (1996): *India's Economic Reforms 1991–2001* (Oxford: Clarendon Press).

Kojima, K. (1995): 'An International Perspective on Japanese Corporate Finance', RIEB Kobe University Discussion Paper No. 45, March.

King, R.G. and R. Levine (1993): 'Financial Intermediation and Economic Development', in Colin Mayer and Xavier Vives (eds), *Capital Markets and Financial Intermediation* (Cambridge: Cambridge University Press).

Marris, R. and D. Mueller (1980): 'The Corporation, Competition and the Invisible Hand', *Journal of Economic Literature*, no. 18.

Marsh, P. (1992): 'Short-Termism', in J. Eatwell, M. Milgate and P. Newman (eds), *The New Palgrave Dictionary of Money and Finance* (London: Macmillan), pp. 480–6.

Mayer, C.P. (1990): 'Financial Systems, Corporate Finance and Economic Development', in R. Glen Hubbard (ed.), *Asymmetric Information, Corporate Finance and Investment* (Chicago: The University of Chicago Press).

Mayya, M.R. (1993): *Indian Stock Markets: Problems, Prospects and Prescriptions* (Bombay: Bombay Stock Exchange).

Mayya, M.R. (1995): *Reflections on the Changing Scenario of the Indian Stock Markets* (Bombay: A.D. Shroff Memorial Trust).

Meeks, G. (1977): *Disappointing Marriage: A Study of the Gains from Merger* (Cambridge: Cambridge University Press).

Meeks, G. and G. Whittington (1975): 'Giant Companies in the United Kingdom 1948–69', *Economic Journal*, vol. 85, pp. 824–43.

Mueller, D.C. (ed.) (1980): *The Determination and Effects of Mergers* (Cambridge, Mass.: Oelschlager, Gunn and Hain).

—— (1992): 'The Corporation and the Economist', *International Journal of Industrial Organization*, vol. 10, June.

Mullins, J. (1993): 'Emerging Equity Markets in the Global Economy', *FRBNY Quarterly Review*, summer, pp. 54–83.

Myers, S.C. and N.S. Majluf (1984): 'Corporate Financing and Investment Decisions When Firms have Information that Investors Do Not have', *Journal of Financial Economics*, vol. 13, pp. 187–221.

Nagaraj, R. (1996): 'India's Capital Market Growth: Trends, Explanations and Evidence', mimeo (New Delhi: Indira Gandhi Institute of Development Research).

Odagiri, H. (1994): *Growth Through Competition, Competition Through Growth* (Oxford: Clarendon Press).

Peacock, A. and G. Bannock (1991): *Corporate Takeovers and the Public Interest* (Aberdeen: Aberdeen University Press for the David Hume Institute).

Porter, M.E. (1992): 'Capital Disadvantage: America's Failing Capital Investment System', *Harvard Business Review*, September–October, pp. 65–82.

Prais, S.J. (1976): *The Evolution of Giant Firms in Britain* (Cambridge: Cambridge University Press).

Ravenscraft, D.J. and F.M. Scherer (1987): *Mergers, Sell-Offs and Economic Efficiency* (Washington, DC: Brookings Institution).

Reserve Bank of India (1995): *Report on Currency and Finance 1994–1995* (Bombay: RBI).

Ruback, S.R. (1988): 'Comment' on J.R. Franks, R.S. Harris and C. Mayer, 'Means of Payment in Takeovers', in A.J. Auerbach (ed.), *Corporate Takeovers: Causes and Consequences*, National Bureau of Economic Research (Chicago: University of Chicago Press).

Schwarz, S. (1982): 'Factors Affecting the Probability of Being Acquired: Evidence for the United States', *Economic Journal*, vol. 92, June.

Shleifer, A. and L.H. Summers (1988): 'Breach of Trust in Hostile Takeovers', in A.J. Auerbach (ed.), *Corporate Takeovers: Causes and*

Consequences, National Bureau of Economic Research (Chicago: University of Chicago Press).

Shleifer, A. and R.W. Vishny (1996): 'A Survey of Corporate Governance', NBER Working Paper Series, No. 5554.

Singh, A. (1971): *Take-overs, Their Relevance to the Stock Market and the Theory of the Firm* (Cambridge: Cambridge University Press).

—— (1975): 'Take-overs, Economic Natural Selection and the Theory of the Firm', *Economic Journal*, September.

—— (1992): 'Corporate Takeovers', in J. Eatwell, M. Milgate and P. Newman (eds), *The New Palgrave Dictionary of Money and Finance* (London: Macmillan), pp. 480–6.

—— (1993a): 'Regulation of Mergers: A New Agenda', in Roger Sugden (ed.), *Industrial Economic Regulation: A Framework and Exploration* (London: Routledge), pp. 141–58.

—— (1993b): 'The Stock Market and Economic Development: Should Developing Countries Encourage Stock Markets?', *UNCTAD Review*, no. 4, pp. 1–28.

—— (1994): 'How Do Large Corporations in Developing Countries Finance their Growth?', in Richard O'Brien (ed.), *The AMEX Bank Prize Essays: Finance and the International Economy*, 8 (New York: Oxford University Press), pp. 121–35.

—— (1995a): *Corporate Financial Patterns in Industrialising Economies: A Comparative International Study*, IFC Technical Paper No. 2 (Washington, DC: The World Bank).

—— (1995b): 'The Anglo-Saxon Market for Corporate Control, the Financial System and International Competitiveness', University of Cambridge, Department of Applied Economics Working Paper, No. AF16, March.

—— (1996a): 'Liberalisation and Globalisation: An Unhealthy Euphoria', in J. Michie and J. Grieve Smith (eds), *Full Employment without Inflation* (Oxford: Oxford University Press) (forthcoming).

—— (1996b): 'Savings, Investment and the Corporation in the East Asian Miracle', *UNCTAD Discussion Paper on East Asian Development: Lessons for a New Global Environment*, Study No. 9, Geneva.

—— (1997a): 'The Stock Market, the Financing of Corporate Growth and Indian Industrial Development', *Journal of International Finance* (forthcoming).

—— (1997b): 'Financial Liberalisation, Stock Markets and Economic Development', *Economic Journal*, May.

Singh, A. and J. Hamid (1992): *Corporate Financial Structures in Developing Countries*, IFC Technical Paper No. 1 (Washington, DC: The World Bank).

Stein, J.C. (1989): 'Efficient Stockmarkets, Inefficient Firms: A Model of Myopic Corporate Behaviour', *Quarterly Journal of Economics*, vol. 104, November, pp. 665–70.

Tirole, J. (1991): 'Privatisation in Eastern Europe: Incentives and the Economics of Transition', in O.J. Blanchard and S.S. Fischer (eds), *NBER Macroeconomics Annual 1991* (Cambridge, Mass. MIT Press).

Tobin, J. (1984): 'On the Efficiency of the Financial System', *Lloyds Bank Annual Review*, July, pp 1–15.

Warhawsky, M.J. (1987): 'Determinants of Corporate Merger Activity: A Review of the Literature', summarised in *Federal Reserve Bulletin*, April.

World Bank (1989): *World Development Report, 1989* (New York: Oxford University Press).

9

India's Export Performance: A Comparative Analysis

*T.N. Srinivasan**

I. INTRODUCTION

In the preface to his celebrated study *India's Export Trends*, Dr Manmohan Singh (1964) confessed to 'a feeling of dissatisfaction regarding the attitudes towards export promotion prevailing in India until the late fifties', and with obvious exasperation noted that

one often finds far-reaching policy recommendations being made for the strategy of Indian economic development on the assumption of "stagnant" exports — as if the stagnation of exports was an inescapable phenomenon. Therefore an attempt to study the empirical foundations of "export fatalism" should prove of interest to those entrusted with the framing of Indian economic policy, if only to fortify them in their present largely unverified convictions [p. v.]

It was his hope that such a study might help in removing the then prevalent sense of fatalism 'that export earnings could not be increased significantly beyond their existing level' (ibid.: v). While recognizing that 'the ground lost as a result of neglecting

* I thank Anne Krueger and Ian Little for their comments on an earlier draft. Thanks are also due to Chonira Aturapane, Roderick Duncan, Vandana Sipahimalani and Beata Smarzynska for research assistance. This contribution was written while I was a visiting scholar at the Centre for Research on Economic Development and Policy Reform at Stanford University. I thank the Centre's director, Professor Anne Krueger, for the intellectual and financial support provided by the Centre. Thanks are also due to the Ford Foundation for partial support under grant 950–1341 to the Economic Growth Centre, Yale University.

export promotion in the past could [not] be easily recovered in the future,' he was hopeful that the 'discovery that the stagnation of export earnings was partly a consequence of faulty Indian economic policies could at least induce a more constructive shift of emphasis in economic thinking for the future' (ibid.: v).

Dr Singh attributed India's neglect of exports to two basic factors. One was the fatalistic view that raising export earnings was impossible, and the other was the assurance by 'responsible economists . . . that import substitution, whatever it meant, would by itself be able to solve India's balance-of-payments difficulties, so that India would in fact not need a greatly intensified export effort in the long run' (ibid.: 357). At the time Dr Singh completed his study in 1962, models of development, such as those of Ragnar Nurkse (Balanced Growth), Rosenstein–Rodan (Big Push), Feldman–Mahalanobis (capital goods and heavy industry), were dominant, and these explicitly or implicitly minimized the role of international trade as an 'engine of growth' and emphasized import-substituting industrialization. Against the orthodoxy of the era, Dr Singh asserted that 'whatever the development strategy, the function of international trade as a supplier of "material means, indispensable for development" is likely to retain its importance for most underdeveloped countries in their quest for higher rates of growth' (ibid.: 2).

Dr Singh raised three major questions, namely 'First, what explains the stagnation in India's export earnings from 1951 to 1960? Second, given the existing trends, what are India's export prospects for 1970–1? Third, what are the major policy implications suggested by our analysis of the trends and prospects of India exports?' (ibid.: vii). He evaluated India's export prospects in relation to the then avowed objective of self-sustained growth, in the sense of the Indian economy being able to do without external assistance beyond the normal inflow of foreign capital by 1970–1. He was 'forced to end with a gloomy conclusion that India's export performance in 1970–1 is likely greatly to fall short of the export requirements of self-sustained growth' (ibid.: 228).

Dr Singh's analysis continues to be of relevance, although the questions have changed. First, at the end of the nineties, the issue is no longer the *absolute* stagnation of export volumes and earnings as in the 50s, but *relative* stagnation in the sense of India's lack-lustre performance in comparison to other developing countries in Asia. Second, the objective of self-sustained growth is still salient, except that the growth that needs to be sustained over several decades in the future has to be rapid if poverty is to be eradicated and India is not to fall far behind other countries of Asia. Third, the external and domestic factors (e.g. market structure, demand and supply elasticities, policies) that he deemed relevant for India's export prospects have changed significantly since his study. With the conclusion of the Uruguay Round in December 1993, the eighth of several successive rounds of multilateral trade liberalization, the process of tariff reductions is virtually complete with regard to most goods, and the process of global integration of the markets for goods, services, technology, and capital is accelerating. Thus India's problem of achieving rapid and self-sustained growth need not be as daunting as it was in the late sixties. However, domestic factors, which in fact were found by Dr Singh to be largely responsible for the stagnation of India's exports, still operate. In particular, the process of far-reaching economic reforms that Dr Singh initiated in 1991 appears to be stalled, despite the valiant efforts of P. Chidambaram, his successor as Finance Minister. Unless it is accelerated and deepened, the laudable objective of self-sustained and rapid growth may still be beyond India's grasp.

Dr Singh analysed export prospects for 16 commodities, in a number of which India then had a significant share of world exports and which together accounted for over three-quarters of India's export earnings. By the mid-nineties, either India was no longer a major world exporter in many of them, or they contributed only a small share in India's exports, or both.[1] For example over 75 per cent of world exports of jute manufactures came from India. A little over 20 per cent of India's export earnings in 1960–1 came from jute manufactures in comparison to about 0.6 per cent in 1995–6. India's share of world tea exports, which was 42.8 per cent in 1958–60, fell to 13.6 per cent in 1994. India's exports of cotton textiles (fabric and yarn) accounted for 10 per cent of world exports in volume and contributed about 12 per cent to India's total export earnings during 1958–60. In 1994, textiles, inclusive of yarn and fabrics made from other fibres as well as cotton, still

---

[1] The data on export shares that follow are from Singh (1964: Tables II.1, III.1, IV.2) and Ministry of Finance (1997: Table 6.3, Appendix Tables 7.3 and 7.5).

accounted for 12 per cent of India's export earnings but only 3 per cent of world exports. In addition, ready-made garments, of which there were virtually no exports in 1960–1, accounted for nearly 2.4 per cent of world exports and over 10 per cent of India's export earnings in 1994. The falling trend in India's share in total world exports 'from slightly less than two per cent in 1951 to about one per cent in 1960' that Dr Singh was concerned about, continued for another two decades: the share was 0.42 per cent in 1980 and 0.5 per cent in 1990, the year before the reforms. It has since climbed somewhat to 0.6 per cent in 1994.

In a volume in Dr Singh's honour, it is appropriate to review (in sect. 2) the recent literature on the importance of openness to international trade for rapid growth that motivated his study. This section also touches on the role of openness in East Asia's rapid growth. In sect. 4, I place India's recent export performance in a comparative perspective. In keeping with Dr Singh's eminently practical and policy-oriented approach to economics, I will conclude, in sect. 4, with a few remarks on policy issues, particularly relating to the deepening and acceleration of reforms.

II. OPENNESS TO INTERNATIONAL TRADE AND INVESTMENT AND GROWTH: THE DEBATE AND RECENT RESEARCH[2]

II.1 The Debate

The debate on the role of openness to international flows of goods, technology and capital in the development and growth processes is as old as economics.[3] After all, Adam Smith inveighed against the mercantilists and praised the virtues of openness and competition two centuries ago in *The Wealth of Nations*. Whether trading opportunities represent an exogenous 'engine of growth' (Dennis Robertson, 1940) or expansion of trade is simply an endogenous response to growth, i.e. trade is a 'handmaiden' of growth (Irving Kravis, 1970) was also debated early on. In the mid-eighties many developing countries initiated reforms of their policy regimes that

[2] This section draws on Srinivasan (1996).
[3] Although, since Schumpeter (1961), it is known that the process of development is different from that of growth; for the limited purpose of analysing the dynamic effects of openness, it is not essential to distinguish between the two.

had been, for several decades, inward-oriented, anti-export, and anti-private enterprise, by liberalizing their foreign trade and allowing a greater role for the private sector and market forces. Even as the reforms are underway, some argue that liberalizing restrictions on trade or more generally adopting an outward-oriented development strategy cannot influence the long-run growth rate of the economy but can only have *level* effects, at least in consonance with 'traditional or standard' economic theory (Rodrik, 1996: 14, fn 6).

There is a related, but somewhat distinct, debate about what has been called the East Asian Miracle, namely the sustained and rapid growth of the East Asian economies (Hong Kong, Korea, Singapore, and Taiwan) since the mid-1960s, a growth record matched by few other developing countries. Perhaps the dominant view (Bhagwati, 1996; Krueger, 1987, 1990; and Little, 1996) is that the emphasis on international competitiveness through free trade as in Hong Kong, or through an export-oriented strategy as in Korea has a lot to do with their stellar economic performance. A minority view, vigorously expounded by Amsden (1989) and Wade (1990), and endorsed by Rodrik (1995b, 1997), is that Korean success is at any rate largely due to active and consistent industrial policy interventions that 'shaped future comparative advantage'. Also, some recent empirical research (Lau and Kim, 1994; Young, 1995) which showed that in accounting for East Asian growth, total factor productivity (TFP) growth made only a modest contribution and most of the growth was due to high rates of factor accumulation, has led some (Krugman, 1994) to argue that rapid East Asian growth is as unsustainable as in the failed Soviet system in which also high rates of investment led for a time to rapid growth.[4]

I have shown elsewhere (Srinivasan, 1996) that the assertion of Rodrik (1996) that in traditional theory trade liberalization does not have a long run growth effect is wrong, unless he means by 'traditional theory' any theory that yields that result! I did this first by incorporating trade in the popular closed economy models of

---

[4] The *Economist* (1 March 1997: 23–5) has nicely summarized the debate about the East Asian Miracle. Apparently the slowdown of GDP and export growth in East Asia, *in just one year*, *(1996)*, is deemed by some as convincing proof of their assertion of the unsustainability *in the long run* of rapid growth in East Asia!

early development literature (e.g. Harrod–Domar and Feldman–Mahalanobis models). I then showed that the same result holds in appropriate versions of the neoclassical growth model. In both sets of models in which constant returns to scale prevail, trade liberalization has a long run growth effect because the marginal product of capital is either constant as in Harrod–Domar type models or, even though it diminishes as the capital–labour ratio increases, it remains above a positive lower bound. Indeed, the widely held but mistaken belief that in all neoclassical growth models long-run growth in output per worker is *necessarily* zero without exogenous technical progress of a labour augmenting kind, and hence trade liberalization can have only level effects, arises from the failure to recognize that it is driven solely by the assumption that the marginal product inexorably declines to zero as the capital–labour ratio increases without bound. It is true that a production function with a positive lower bound on the marginal product of capital unfortunately implies that labour becomes inessential as a factor of production as the capital–labour ratio increases without bound. But even if the lower bound is zero, and as such trade liberalization has only level effects on the steady-state path of output, it will still raise the growth rate along the path of transition to the steady state. In labour-abundant developing countries in which initial distortions result in differing marginal product of labour across activities, as they remove such distortions and export labour intensive products at terms of trade, the transition can last a long time.

The distinction between production of capital goods and that of consumer goods in the two-sector Feldman–Mahalanobis model enabled me to compare liberalization of trade in capital goods with that in consumer goods. I showed that while both are welfare-enhancing, the former increases the long-run growth rate of the economy and the latter does not. Since very high (if not prohibitive) tariffs on consumer goods are often the first to be imposed and the last to be lowered in developing countries, including India, this comparison is of some interest.

II.2 Trade and Growth: Recent Empirical Research

The relationship between openness to foreign trade in goods and services, technology and investment has recently attracted a good deal of theoretical and empirical attention. This was stimulated by two strands of research. The first strand consisted of theoretical advances in endogenizing the processes of growth and technical change, as well as in modelling international trade in differentiated products under increasing returns and imperfect competition (Grossman and Helpman, 1991; Rivera-Batiz and Romer, 1991a, b). The second strand was empirical research on convergence, which tested variations of the proposition that regardless of initial conditions, all economies with access to the same technology, with the same intertemporal preferences, and experiencing the same rate of growth of labour force will converge to the same steady state. Surveys of earlier empirical literature by Edwards (1993) and recent literature on trade and development by Harrison (1996) are available. Rodrik (1995a) points to severe problems with data, econometric methodology, not to mention conceptual confusions in some of these studies that cast doubt on their findings. It is possible that countries with a policy of openness to trade are also countries in which macroeconomic stability, fiscal and monetary prudence, and other growth promoting factors are present, so that it would be misleading to read a causal relation between openness and growth. Not all these problems are, however, insurmountable, nor is it inevitable that the findings of all the growth–openness studies would be reversed once the problems are addressed. As such, it would be too hasty to dismiss all the studies as worthless, if, despite all their faults, *several* of them reach the *same* qualitative conclusions that are *also* consistent with *a priori reasoning*.

Before turning to some of these studies, let me note that since 1950 the world economy, and in particular the developing economies, have enjoyed a remarkable growth of output, not only in contrast to the disastrous period between the two world wars, but also in comparison to the period prior to the First World War. Growth in the volume of trade outpaced that in the volume of output, which is an indication of increasing global integration. In 1995 world exports grew by 8 per cent and output by 3 per cent (WTO, 1996). It is clear that the signing of the General Agreement on Tariffs and Trade (GATT) in 1947, and above all the successive rounds of trade liberalization negotiated under the auspices of GATT, have contributed significantly to the growth in world trade and output. Now that the World Trade Organization (WTO) has replaced GATT with a membership exceeding

120 countries in comparison to the 23 countries that signed the GATT in 1947, it can be expected that the process of global integration will be further strengthened.

Let me turn to recent empirical studies on trade and growth. Sachs and Warner (1995) make an ambitious attempt, using data from a cross-section of countries, to assess the growth effects of global integration by relating indicators of trade openness, trade liberalization and its timing to growth and avoidance of macroeconomic crisis.

They define an open economy as one with *none* of five characteristics: tariffs exceeding 40 per cent, non-tariff barriers covering more than 40 per cent of trade, a black market premium of over 20 per cent relative to the official exchange rate on an average during the 1970s or 1980s, a socialist economic system as defined by Kornai (1992), and a state monopoly on major exports.[5] By definition a closed economy is one which has at least one of the five characteristics. Three of their many empirical findings are of interest.

First, open developing economies grew at 4.49 per cent per year during 1970–89, while closed economies grew at 0.69 per cent per year. Open developed economies grew at 2.29 per cent per year, while closed economies grew at 0.74 per cent per year.

Second, being open to trade proved to be important for convergence or catch-up of low income economies with the rich economies. The regressions of growth between 1970 and 1989 on initial income in 1970 for 117 countries showed no evidence of convergence in the sense of a significant negative coefficient for the variable logarithm of GDP in 1970. Indeed, the coefficient was *positive* and close to being statistically significant. However, once trade policy and other relevant explanatory variables are introduced, the coefficient becomes not only negative, but also significant, indicating convergence. The variables that proved statistically insignificant were population density, primary and

[5] This definition is unsatisfactory. With the tariff barrier set at 40 per cent no country is classified on the basis of tariffs alone. Alternative, equally plausible, definitions of non-tariff barriers do not often yield mutually consistent results. Also, some non-tariff barriers could be covert and informal as is alleged to be the case in Japan and some East Asian economies. Besides, the black-market premium is a catch-all endogenous variable that reflects both exchange rate and commercial policy distortions.

secondary school enrolment rates, and the political variables, namely average number of revolutions and coups per year and average number of assassinations per million of population, both during 1970–85. While it is comforting that all the statistically significant variables have coefficients with expected signs, since some of the explanatory variables (e.g. investment rate, relative price of investment goods) including the all-important dummy variable OPEN are endogenous, the estimated coefficients are certainly biased, though it is impossible to assess the seriousness of the bias.

Third, being open lowered the probability of occurrence of severe macroeconomic crises (defined as occurrence of any one of rescheduling of debt by official or private donors, arrears of external payments as reported by the IMF and an inflation rate in excess of 100 per cent). There are several plausible reasons (greater dependence on debt, greater orientation of investment towards non-traded goods, and higher level of state involvement in the economy) why closed economies are more likely to experience severe macroeconomic crises. Out of seventeen (resp. seventy-three) economies classified as open (resp. closed) in the 1970s, as few as one (resp. as many as fifty-nine) experienced macroeconomic crises in the 1980s. These results are to be treated as suggestive, and not definitive, since their statistical test of independence between openness and crisis-proneness is not strictly valid because openness to trade and propensity to macroeconomic crisis could both be endogenous.

Ben-David (1996) also finds a tendency for open economies to converge. He analyses 25 countries with per capita incomes above 25 per cent of that of the US in 1960 which were neither primarily oil producers nor formerly communist. These included the following developing countries: Argentina, Bolivia, Chile, Mexico, and Uruguay. For each country, he forms an *export* group consisting of those countries to which it exported more than 4 per cent of its total exports in 1985, and an *import* group consisting of those countries from which it imported over 4 per cent of its total imports. Both groups ranged in size from a minimum of three to a maximum of nine. Within the trade groups, seven countries (Bolivia, Brazil, Congo, Ethiopia, Ghana, Guyana, and South Korea) which did not satisfy the 25 per cent income cut-off point were also included. He finds that in the export-based (resp. import-based) group 24 (resp. 22) showed income-convergence of which 16 (resp. 17) were statistically significant.

Ben-David and Rahman (1996) use the same countries and trade groups as in Ben-David (1996) to examine convergence in income *per worker* (rather than income *per capita*) and capital *per worker*. They find that the evidence for convergence in income per worker is even stronger than for income per capita while there is no evidence at all for convergence in capital per worker. This leads them to conclude that the primary source of trade-related income convergence is convergence in technologies rather than convergence in capital–labour ratios.

Baldwin and Seghezza (1996) estimate two basic relationships: the first, between trade barriers and income and growth, and the second, between trade barriers and investment, a channel through which trade affects growth. Various data samples and various measures of trade barriers, etc. are used to test the robustness of the conclusions.

The results from their preferred sample of 39 countries that exported manufactures in 1989 suggest that the technology catch-up factor is important for convergence. Initial human capital stock (though not subsequent investment in it) is a significant factor too. Of course, investment in physical capital is as expected significant. Turning now to a channel through which trade affects growth, namely investment, their finding that domestic *and* foreign trade barriers significantly depress investment is very interesting. Clearly domestic trade barriers on the one hand raise the domestic rental rate on capital, but on the other raise the cost of capital goods by raising the price of imported inputs used in their production. The latter effect, which makes investment less attractive, dominates the former which makes investment more attractive. Their result on the deleterious effect of foreign barriers is apparently new — though foreign barriers prove to be less deleterious than domestic ones.[6]

Coe and Helpman (1995) test the impact of openness on the transmission of technical knowledge, and hence on growth of

---

[6] Gary Saxonhouse suggested (in correspondence) that once it is recognized that in a multisector world, domestic and foreign barriers are very likely to apply to different sectors, both could be expected to depress aggregate domestic investment.

total factor productivity (TFP). The basic idea is that technical knowledge is acquired both from domestic research and development expenditures, and from imports, which convey information on the state of technological knowledge in the exporting country. A country that has a larger share of its imports originating in more advanced countries with higher technical knowledge will therefore experience faster TFP growth than one which imports more from less technically advanced countries. For their sample of 21 OECD countries and Israel for the period 1971–90, the results indicate a statistically significant, and similar, quantitative impact of domestic and foreign knowledge stocks on TFP growth.

Coe et al. (1997) apply the analysis of Coe and Helpman (1995) to a set of 77 developing countries for the period 1971–90. Since few developing countries undertake R&D, domestic R&D is not relevant for them. In addition to foreign knowledge stock, they include in their regression the secondary school enrollment rate, the share of imports from industrial countries, dummies for time periods 1971–5, 1975–80, 1980–5 and 1985–90, and their interaction with foreign knowledge stock. Simulations from their regression equation suggest that such spillovers from the North to South are substantial and in 1990 'may have boosted output in the developing countries by 25 billion U.S. dollars. To put this figure in perspective, total official development aid from multilateral and bilateral sources in 1990 amounted to 50 billion U.S. dollars' (Coe et al., 1997: 148).

Turning now to the so-called 'East Asian Miracle', it is beyond dispute that East Asia, consisting of Hong Kong, Korea, Singapore and Taiwan, grew rapidly, managed to increase their share of world exports from 1.5 per cent in 1960 (World Bank, 1993) to 10.4 per cent in 1994 (WTO, 1995) and achieved very high savings and investment rates. Frankel et al. (1996) point out that both sides in the debates on inward versus outward orientation, interventionist versus laissez-faire policy framework, and finally, total factor productivity (TFP) growth versus accumulation of physical and human capital in explaining GDP growth have claimed that East Asian performance supports their case.

Econometrically testing which side is right is not simple, since growth can be plausibly argued to both influence and be influenced by almost all of the variables usually deemed to be exogenous determinants of growth, such as factor accumulation, openness to trade and technical progress, etc. Frankel et al. (1996) address the issue of endogeneity of trade by using not actual trade (as a share of GDP), but 'predicted' trade from a gravity model of bilateral trade, as an explanatory variable in addition to variables proxying human and physical capital accumulation over 1960–85 in explaining real GDP per capita in 1985. They find the effect of openness on growth of East Asia is even stronger when they correct for the endogeneity of openness in their regressions for 123 countries. 'For every one per cent increase in trade as a share of GDP, income per capita is higher by an estimated 0.34 per cent' (Frankel et al., 1996: 13). For individual East Asian countries their analysis suggests that 'openness explains a large amount of growth for Hong Kong and Singapore, and positive (though smaller) amounts also for Korea, Malaysia, and Taiwan. In the Philippines, where growth was *lower* than the world average, a low level of openness explains almost half this gap. Low openness detracted from the growth accomplished by China, Indonesia, Japan and Thailand as well.'

Taylor (1995) also addresses the endogeneity issue by adopting what he calls a structural approach to estimating the factors that influence the dynamics of economic growth, the factors being initial conditions, factor accumulation, natural resource endowments, demographic structure, price distortions and openness, financial intermediation and monetary stability. He finds that while relatively high investment rates were the key to high growth rates in the Asia-Pacific region, with human capital accumulation and low population growth also contributing to high growth, but to a lesser extent, the principal causes of high investment rates were human capital complementarities, a low dependency rate, and low distortions. In his view, the role of distortions underscores the importance of openness to growth, but should be broadly construed to include commercial, financial, and monetary policy (Taylor, 1995: 21–2).

To sum up, the empirical evidence from a number of studies points to a strong and significant effect of openness to trade on growth performance, thus confirming the view expressed long ago by Dr Singh, to repeat, that 'the function of international trade . . . is likely to retain its importance for most underdeveloped countries in their quest for higher rates of growth' (Singh, 1964: 2).

III. INDIAN EXPORT PERFORMANCE IN A COMPARATIVE PERSPECTIVE

III.1 Overall Trends Since Independence

Since the early sixties, a number of measures to increase the incentive for exports of manufactures had been adopted, even as controls over several exports (such as agricultural commodities, minerals) and canalization continued. The measures included: duty drawback schemes (including refund of import duties used in exports), exemptions from sale taxes, cash compensation schemes, rail freight concessions, import entitlement certificates (later changed to import replenishment licences). Many of these were no more than compensations for the implicit tax on exports that the restrictive import control regime imposed. Also, the complexity of the schemes meant that small or new exporters found it difficult to avail of them. In addition, bureaucratic delays, for example, in getting duty drawbacks, diminished their value considerably. Gulati and Pursell (1995) estimate the average value of various export incentives as no more than 8 per cent of the f.o.b. value of manufactured exports.

In spite of several devaluations of the rupee (explicit in 1949, 1966, and 1991, and vicarious in the early seventies when the rupee was tied to a depreciating pound), the rupee was overvalued for most of the period prior to recent reforms, thereby adversely affecting exports. Gulati and Pursell (1995) estimate overvaluation of the rupee to have been around 30 per cent in the eighties. The estimate of real effective exchange rates (REER) (Joshi and Little, 1994: Table 11.3) for exports adjusted for export incentives is plotted in Fig. 2. The same figure also shows the estimates of REER (unadjusted for export incentives) published by the Reserve Bank of India (1996: Statement 230). Clearly, except for the first half of the eighties, there has been a steady depreciation of the REER, although not necessarily to the extent of entirely eliminating overvaluation, if Gulati and Pursell (1995) are right.

It is seen from Fig. 1 that the stagnation of exports that concerned Dr Singh in 1962 continued until 1971. Since then exports have risen, interspersed with periods of stagnation, such as the first half of the eighties. Joshi and Little (1994) estimate a structural model in which the demand for India's exports depends (*inter alia*) on world income and the price of India's exports relative to that of

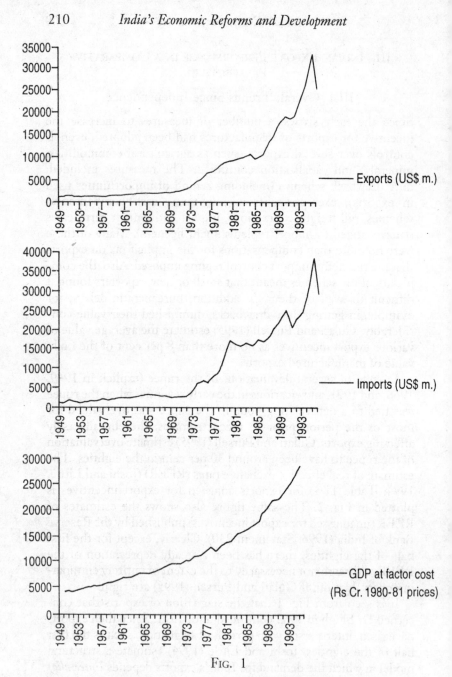

FIG. 1

SOURCE: Ministry of Finance, 1997: Appendix Tables 1.3 and 7.1.

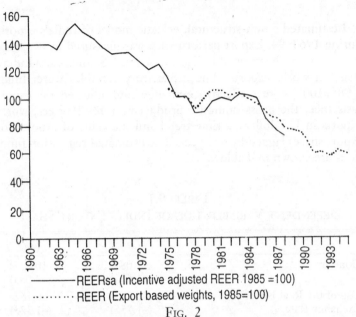

FIG. 2

SOURCE: Joshi and Little, 1994: Table 11.3.
Reserve Bank of India, 1997: Statement 230.

her competitors, and the supply depends on domestic aggregate excess demand and the price of exports relative to domestic wholesale prices. They find that 'the price elasticity of supply of exports is about 0.7 in the short run and 1.1 in the long run, with over 80 per cent of the long run effect coming through within a year. The price elasticity of demand for exports is about 1.1 in the short run and about 3 in the long run, with 80 per cent of the long run effect coming through within two years' (ibid.: 275). These elasticity estimates are not too different from other estimates for India in the literature (Arize, 1990, and references cited therein).

Joshi and Little (1994), while pointing out that 'periods of rapid export growth (for example the 1970s and the late 1980s) were associated with real exchange rate depreciations while periods of slow export growth (for example the 1960s and the early 1980s) were associated with real exchange rate appreciation' (ibid.: 275), also recognize that other factors besides the real exchange rate affect export performance. Indeed, their structural model was motivated by this recognition.

I estimated a non-structural, eclectic model of India's exports during 1963–94. Export performance was measured in two ways for each year: the value of India's exports in US dollars and India's share in world exports. The explanatory variables were: Index (1985=100) of real effective exchange rate adjusted for export assistance, the gross domestic product at 1980–1 prices, world exports in US dollars, a time trend and the value of exports (or export share) lagged by one year. The estimated regression functions are shown in Table 9.1.

TABLE 9.1
DEPENDENT VARIABLE: LOG OF INDIA'S EXPORT SHARE

	(1a)	*(2a)*
Constant	1.082	–10.022
	(1.632)	(–2.085)
Log of the Real Effective Exchange Rate	–0.225	–0.162
	(–1.755)	(–1.323)
Log of Real GDP		0.982
		(2.330)
Time trend	–0.007	–0.052
	(–1.201)	(–2.597)
Log of lagged export share	0.867	0.635
	(8.687)	(4.659)
Adjusted-R^2	0.918	0.929
No. of observations	33	33

Dependent Variable: Log of Total Indian Exports

	(1b)	*(2b)*
Constant	–0.300	–8.465
	(–0.104)	(–1.555)
Log of the Real Effective Exchange Rate	–0.304	–0.278
	(–1.924)	(–2.463)
Log of Real GDP	0.146	0.757
	(0.578)	(1.811)
Log of world exports	0.387	0.448
	(2.789)	(4.454)
Time trend		–0.043
		(–1.954)

	(1b)	*(2b)*
Log of lagged Indian exports	0.383	0.483
	(1.651)	(4.901)
Adjusted-R^2	0.996	0.996
No. of observations	32	33

NOTES: (1)   t-statistics are in parentheses.

(2)   Regression (1b) has been corrected for serial correlation. For regressions (1a), (2a) and (2b) the Durbin's *h* statistic indicated the absence of serial correlation.

(3)   Explanatory variables real effective exchange rate and real GDP are predicted values obtained from the OLS estimation of a regression of each variable on its past two lagged values. Durbin's *h* statistics for these regressions indicated the absence of serial correlation.

(4)   The real effective exchange rate adjusted for export incentives (REERSA) series for 1960–88 in Joshi and Little (1994: Table 11.3) was extended to 1994 by using predicted values of the regression of REERSA on the unadjusted REER in the Reserve Bank of India (1997): Statement 230 for the period 1975–94.

SOURCES: Joshi and Little (1994: Table 11.3).
Ministry of Finance (1997: Appendix Tables 1.3 and 7.1).
Reserve Bank of India (1997: Statement 230).
Yearbook of International Trade Statistics, various issues.

The negative elasticity of both export performance measures with regard to the real exchange rate implies that real appreciation of the rupee adversely affects exports — the elasticity of exports (resp. export share) is in the range (–.304, –.278) (resp. –.225, –.162) in the short run and –.493, –.537 (resp. –.444, 1.690) in the long run. The coefficient of real GDP is positive and highly significant in both equations. On the one hand, higher GDP raises domestic demand and hence would lower exports. On the other, GDP also proxies export supply capacity and, hence, a higher GDP would raise exports. It would seem that the supply effect dominates. The positive coefficient for world exports implies that higher world exports, as is to be expected, also mean higher demand for Indian exports. The time trend is a 'catch-all' variable meant to capture the effect of all other time-varying exogenous factors, and the negative time trend shows that such factors, on balance, have been detrimental to Indian exports.

These findings support the conclusion of Joshi and Little based on their own result

that India is not an exception to the general presumption that the price competitiveness of exports is an important determinant of the volume of exports, and that the relevant elasticities are more than adequate for a real depreciation to improve the current account even with a zero price elasticity of demand for imports [Joshi and Little, 1994: 275.]

III.2 Competitiveness of Indian Exports Since the Mid-Eighties

In the decade 1986–96, the value of India's exports in US dollars grew by over 9 per cent a year in every year but two: the macro-economic crisis of 1991–2 and the following. During 1993–6, growth was nearly 20 per cent per year on average. Although the rate of growth is likely to be considerably slower at about 7 per cent in 1996–7, the growth performance since 1986 has still been impressive in comparison to the previous three and a half decades. Nonetheless, even this performance pales in comparison with what India's competitors have achieved in the same period, indicating in a broad sense India's competitive disadvantage.

It is instructive to compare the trends in market shares of India and her competitors in a few selected commodities in which the developed countries as well as some East Asian economies began to lose their comparative advantage with rising wage costs, and India could have been expected to gain market share. Tables 9.2 and 9.3 provide the data. First, taking market shares in Europe and North America (Table 9.2), China has clearly gained significantly in all the eight commodity groups considered. In commodity group 894 (toys, sporting goods, etc.), China's market share in North America and Europe was very small and similar to India's in 1979–81, but by 1994–5 China's share increased to a whopping 27 per cent in North America and 10 per cent in Europe, while India's share continued to be negligible. The story is the same in commodity group 851 (footwear). India's share increased marginally while China's increased phenomenally. Interestingly, but not surprisingly, the other larger country that stagnated or slowly increased market shares is Brazil, a country whose history of inward orientation was similar to India's.

TABLE 9.2
MARKET SHARES (PERCENTAGE) OF TOTAL
IMPORTS INTO NORTH AMERICA AND EUROPE

Country	Commodity[1]	Partner	1979–81	1988–90	1994–5
Brazil	764	North America (N)	.005	.035	.018
		Europe (E)	.159	.063	.029
	778	N	.411	.103	.115
		E	.096	.134	.169
	842	N	.079	.171	.173
		E	.2	.032	.025
	843	N	.03	.34	.157
		E	.09	.054	.054
	847	N	.014	.025	.007
		E	.019	.006	.004
	851	N	3.975	5.804	4.963
		E	1.032	1.255	.828
	893	N	.051	.141	.089
		E	.029	.05	.035
	894	N	.114	.103	.063
		E	.029	.033	.021
China	764	N	.003	1.126	4.034
		E	.008	.266	1.462
	778	N	.017	.459	2.332
		E	.013	.178	1.970
	842	N	1.259	4.171	4.856
		E	.762	3.014	4.663
	843	N	1.814	5.538	8.387
		E	.235	2.998	4.963
	847	N	2.423	3.827	5.350
		E	1.818	2.864	5.118
	851	N	.348	4.915	23.410
		E	.509	1.349	4.237
	893	N	.050	1.520	6.129
		E	.029	.694	2.917
	894	N	.075	11.682	26.818
		E	.386	5.096	10.118

Table 9.2 (cont.)

Country	Commodity[1]	Partner	1979–81	1988–90	1994–5
Korea	764	N	1.38	2.744	1.989
		E	.548	1.185	1.959
	778	N	.713	1.262	.929
		E	.314	.771	4.874
	842	N	4.340	4.109	2.087
		E	4.051	2.534	.469
	843	N	3.419	3.988	2.013
		E	2.279	1.361	.249
	847	N	.939	2.554	3.003
		E	5.594	3.204	3.142
	851	N	6.526	13.405	2.487
		E	2.295	3.334	1.234
	893	N	.437	1.053	.572
		E	.147	.398	.297
	894	N	3.806	4.363	.917
		E	1.56	2.068	.578
Malaysia	764	N	.68	1.098	2.417
		E	.113	.187	1.073
	778	N	.351	.181	.568
		E	.086	.133	.729
	842	N	.098	.542	.749
		E	.189	.276	.249
	843	N	.152	.710	.569
		E	.213	.276	.320
	847	N	.077	.184	.262
		E	1.503	.716	.675
	851	N	.036	.029	.032
		E	.164	.106	.145
	893	N	.016	.116	.191
		E	.163	.195	.298
	894	N	.040	.625	1.163
		E	.026	.289	.435
Taiwan	764	N	4.8	3.964	2.278
		E	1.255	1.386	1.344
	778	N	1.302	2.551	2.212
		E	.635	1.476	1.547

Country	Commodity[1]	Partner	1979–81	1988–90	1994–5
	842	N	2.873	3.789	1.948
		E	1.269	.635	.261
	843	N	4.254	3.544	1.466
		E	.585	.774	.205
	847	N	1.703	3.078	2.906
		E	2.517	1.715	1.026
	851	N	10.541	11.098	1.645
		E	2.41	2.907	.83
	893	N	3.451	5.802	2.91
		E	.417	1.426	1.009
	894	N	8.931	11.012	5.559
		E	3.757	4.756	1.999
India	764	N	.003	.005	.029
		E	.087	.022	.033
	778	N	.03	.009	.062
		E	.034	.025	.10
	842	N	.074	.167	.332
		E	.44	.537	.611
	843	N	2.497	2.346	3.041
		E	3.673	2.138	2.827
	847	N	.136	1.376	.421
		E	2.385	1.664	2.637
	851	N	.182	.225	.398
		E	.298	.399	.656
	893	N	.015	.009	.040
		E	.008	.017	.059
	894	N	.043	.011	.060
		E	.224	.079	.144
Thailand	764	N	.001	.319	.900
		E	.006	.144	.689
	778	N	.002	.078	.424
		E	.013	.038	.240
	842	N	.131	.541	1.106
		E	.287	1.049	.683
	843	N	.387	.550	1.046
		E	.380	1.069	.672

Table 9.2 (cont.)

Country	Commodity[1]	Partner	1979–81	1988–90	1994–5
	847	N	.111	.215	.558
		E	.486	.633	.526
	851	N	.104	1.069	1.648
		E	.016	.899	1.549
	893	N	.245	.235	.365
		E	.060	.335	.450
	894	N	.014	1.224	1.565
		E	.035	.464	.919

NOTES: [1] 764: Telecom Eqpt, PTS (parts), ACC and ACCES (accessories), NES (Not elsewhere specified)
778: Electrical Machinery NES
842: Men's Outerwear Non-knit
843: Women's Outerwear Non-knit
847: Textile Clothing ACCES NES
851: Footwear
893: Articles of Plastic NES
894: Toys, Sporting Goods, etc.

SOURCE: COMTRADE Data Base 1997 (New York: United Nations: Statistical Office).

TABLE 9.3
MARKET SHARES (PERCENTAGE) IN WORLD EXPORTS

	Market Share	
	1979–81	1992–4
1. Garments		
1.1. Women's outerwear non-knit		
China	3.3	23.5
Hong Kong	16.0	8.0
India	5.7	4.5
Korea	5.5	2.7
1.2. Under garments non-knit		
China	7.7	23.9
Hong Kong	20.0	11.2
Bangladesh	0.0	4.9
India	3.9	4.8
Korea	16.9	4.5
Taiwan	9.3	2.6

	Market Share	
	1979–81	*1992–4*
2. Textiles		
2.1. Cotton fabrics, woven		
China	10.7	15.9
Hong Kong	7.7	9.4
Taiwan	4.1	4.4
Pakistan	2.3	4.2
India	3.1	3.6
2.2. Other woven textile fabric		
China	7.3	15.7
India	6.9	2.5
2.3. Textile articles not elsewhere specified		
China	15.1	24.5
Pakistan	2.3	5.1
India	4.3	4.9
3. Leather and Leather Manufacturers		
3.1. Leather		
Korea	0.1	9.0
Taiwan	1.0	8.1
India	10.0	3.3
3.2. Leather manufacturers		
China	0.3	11.4
Taiwan	5.6	11.0
India	10.0	3.3
4. Headgear, Non-textile Clothing		
China	5.4	25.7
Korea	15.0	11.4
Malaysia	0.7	6.6
India	0.7	5.0
5. Gems		
5.1. Pearls, precious and semi-precious		
Israel	7.9	11.5
India	4.2	10.4

Table 9.3 (cont.)

	Market Share	
	1979–81	*1992–4*
5.2. Gold, silverware, jewellery		
Hong Kong	6.2	9.4
Thailand	1.3	6.8
China	1.2	4.6
India	0.6	3.2

SOURCE: Brahmbhatt et al., 1996.

Between 1980 and 1994, China's share in world exports more than doubled from about 1 to about 2.5 per cent, while India's increased by a half, from 0.4 to 0.6 per cent. This difference is reflected in the market shares of the two countries in world exports of several commodity groups shown in Table 9.3. The commodity groups considered accounted for roughly 40 per cent of India's total exports and about half of her manufactured exports. The picture presented by Table 9.3 is sobering. China gained substantially, while India barely managed to maintain its market share in the two groups of garment and textile exports considered. In the case of non-knit undergarments, Bangladesh achieved a share equal to India's in 1992–4, even though it did not export these in 1979–81. In the case of leather and leather manufactures, Korea and Taiwan gained at the expense of India. India gained significant market share in gems and jewellery, although in the case of the latter, Hong Kong, China, and Thailand did even better.

It is often argued that, China being a non-market economy with the state involved in production as well as foreign trade, Chinese export performance does not necessarily indicate China's competitiveness. Indeed, China's emergence as an export powerhouse has created considerable resistance on the part of the industrialized countries to agree to China's membership of the World Trade Organization (WTO) until China is willing to dismantle layers of protection from competition for its state enterprises and to reveal the full extent of state subsidization of such enterprises. Some, particularly in the United States, seek to leverage China's desire to enter the WTO to alter China's behaviour with regard to Hong Kong, Taiwan, Tibet and extract concessions on a host of other political issues (*New York Times*, 2 March 1992: 1, 8). It is far from clear that India's erstwhile protectionist regime, with its subsidization of state enterprises, export performance, and phased manufacturing requirements placed on foreign enterprises, and a whole host of export assistance schemes, all taken together, was that much different from China's. As such, the argument that China only gained export markets shares relative to India by ignoring comparative cost considerations is not plausible. In any case, as seen from Tables 9.2 and 9.3, other countries besides China also gained market shares compared to India in several commodity groups.

IV. CONCLUSIONS AND POLICY IMPLICATIONS

IV.1 Conclusions

The discussion in the previous sections leads to several conclusions:

1. Recent theoretical and empirical research confirm the importance of openness to foreign trade for rapid growth, as Dr Singh concluded in his study. In particular, such openness has been shown to be a significant factor in the rapid growth of the East Asian economies.

2. The stagnation in Indian exports that so concerned Dr Singh and led to his study continued until the early seventies, followed by some significant growth in the seventies that was not sustained in the early eighties. The relatively rapid growth resumed in the mid-eighties, only to collapse during the macroeconomic crisis year 1991–3. Reforms initiated by Dr Singh contributed to a revival and acceleration of growth during 1993–6. India's share in world exports, which has been steadily declining from about 2 per cent in the late forties to a low of 0.4 per cent in 1980, has increased to 0.6 per cent in 1994. There was, however, a significant slowdown in growth during the first nine months of 1996–7, in part reflecting a slow down in world trade. In part, it might also be a consequence of domestic constraints (see below).

3. Singh hypothesized that 'Domestic policies in India can affect the country's export earnings in so far as the volume of production of export commodities, the domestic demand for them, and also the terms on which they are made available for export' (Singh, 1964: 22–3). A quantitative analysis of India's export performance since 1960 confirms his hypotheses. Both real GDP (a proxy for

the net effect of domestic policies on domestic production of and demand for exportables) and the real effective exchange rate (a proxy for the terms at which commodities are made available for export) were found to be statistically significant in explaining export performance.

4. Dr Singh, while welcoming the belated recognition that 'a greatly intensified effort is a basic condition if the objective of self-sustained growth is to be realized' wondered 'how deep the export consciousness is it is difficult to say', and quoted from the Report of the Import and Export Policy Committee to the effect 'the country had no great export tradition. Nor has one developed so far. Much less have we developed the necessary export apparatus' (ibid.: 338). From a historical perspective, it is incorrect to say that the country had no great export tradition.[7] What is true, however, is that the collapse of free trade and the global trading system between the two world wars, a misidentification of foreign trade with imperialism and of free trade with the failure of colonial authorities to promote industrialization, had led to the adoption since Independence of an inward-oriented development strategy of which exports had not been regarded as an integral part. Even the plethora of schemes for export promotion introduced since the early sixties were neither designed as mutually reinforcing and coherent parts of an export strategy underpinning an overall development strategy nor did they provide quantitatively significant incentives.

5. Although Indian exports grew relatively rapidly since the mid-eighties (barring the crisis years), in comparison with other countries, particularly China, India does not seem competitive in a number of commodities. India should have gained market share as the industrialized countries, old and new, were relinquishing their shares in these commodities with shifts in their comparative advantage. This expected gain did not come about.

IV.2 Policy Implications[8]

I will not attempt to articulate policies to promote exports of specific commodities to particular markets, not only because

---

[7] See Thapar (1966: 24), Kangle (1972: 128, 145, 261, and 262), Digby (1982), Dasgupta (1982: 429–32), and Chaudhuri (1983: pp. 801–7).

[8] By confining myself to policies relating to export performance, I do not

others (Gulati and Pursell, 1995; Pursell, 1996; Brahmbhatt et al., 1996) have done so, but also because most often such policies are far less efficient than those that encourage exports in general. However, some implications for the overall economic policy framework, as it relates to the external sector, do emerge from the discussion in the previous section. First and foremost, in an increasingly integrated world where individuals and businesses have several sources of supply for goods and services, considerations of cost, quality, timeliness, and reliability will determine India's competitiveness. Infrastructural constraints continue to raise the cost of production in India. The latest *Economic Survey* frankly admits 'The visible signs of shortfalls in capacity and inefficiencies include increasingly congested roads, power failures, long waiting lists for installation of telephones and shortages of drinking water. The widening gap between demand and supply of infrastructure also raises questions concerning the sustainability of economic growth in the future' (Ministry of Finance, 1997: 179). The Survey also recognizes that the massive investment needs in infrastructure cannot be met without private sector (domestic and foreign participation). Unless the political differences within the coalition government are resolved and a consensus is built towards tackling the issues of privatization and related labour reforms head on, infrastructural problems will not be resolved.

Second, there is increasing evidence that strong export performance is associated with vertical intraindustry trade which itself is related to foreign direct investment (FDI).[9] According to Chen, Chang and Zang (1995), in China the share of exports from enterprises with foreign investment rose from 0.3 per cent of exports in 1984 to 20.4 per cent in 1992. It is very unlikely that this simply reflects China' requiring, and strictly enforcing, the requirement that such enterprises export specified shares of their output. It is more likely that the cost advantages of producing in China for world markets induced such FDI, rather than the usual

---

intend to minimize the importance of completing and deepening the reforms initiated by Dr Singh. In particular, further liberalization of consumer goods imports, acceleration of privitization, labour market reforms including rewriting labour and bankruptcy laws, and financial sector reforms are vital if India is to achieve sustained rapid growth.

[9] In her comments on this contribution Anne Krueger pointed out that this was not the case in Japan, Hong Kong, and Korea.

inappropriate tariff-jumping type that inward-oriented economies with large domestic markets attract. It is well known that India has attracted far less FDI inflows, not just in comparison to China, but other countries such as Malaysia and Thailand, with India's share in total FDI flows to all developing countries being a minuscule 0.71 per cent in 1994 (Ministry of Finance, 1997: Table 6.13). *The Economist* (22 February 1997: 23) points out, surprisingly 'India's regulations are more welcoming to foreign investors than the rules in most of East Asia', but,

the system simply does not work as it is supposed to. The rules may be liberal in principle, but they oblige the foreigners to deal with middle and lower levels of bureaucracy at the centre and states. Thus, many would-be investors say, the delays, complexities, obfuscations, overlapping jurisdictions and endless requests for more information remain much the same as they always have been.

Third, the infrastructure constraints mentioned earlier also inhibit FDI. According to Wheeler and Mody (1992), not only are infrastructure availability and quality important factors associated with FDI inflows, but they are particularly important for export-oriented FDI concerned with cost competitiveness. It does not help that it takes *5–6 days* for freighters to turn around in Bombay and Calcutta ports in comparison to *6–12 hours* in ports of South-east Asia. A study by the World Bank is reported to have estimated the comparative cost disadvantage to Indian exporters as $80 per container. The capacity and efficiency of functioning of airports, ports, electricity boards, railways, roads and telecommunications are nowhere near where they have to be if India is to compete effectively and aggressively in the world markets for goods, services, and capital.

The empirical research reviewed in sect. 2 has shown that imports from advanced countries convey technological spillovers of research and development expenditures in those countries, and such spillovers are important for the growth of productivity in developing countries. From this perspective as well as from that of cost competitiveness, ease of access to imports of capital goods and intermediates is important. Tariffs on such imports have been considerably reduced, and quantitative restrictions have been abolished. Yet, the fact remains, that even with the reduction announced in the 1997–8 budget, India's maximum tariff at 40 per cent and the likely trade weighted average of about 25 per cent are still high in relation to some of the East and Southeast Asian countries.

Finally, as noted in sect. 2, appreciation of the real effective exchange rate (REER) adversely affects export performance. However, there are no policy instruments that directly influence the trends in the REER. These reflect trends in nominal exchange rates and inflation rates in India and partner countries. The need for fiscal prudence and avoidance of inflationary financing of fiscal deficits can hardly be overemphasized. The Reserve Bank of India, through purchases and sales of foreign exchange in the market, influences the nominal exchange rate. Also, controls on capital account transactions, affect the exchange rate. The rupee is convertible for almost all current account transactions and a committee has been appointed to look into the question of capital account convertibility. The choice of an appropriate exchange rate regime and policy is beset with difficult analytical issues. One thing is however clear: until the domestic financial sector is in sound shape, rushing into capital account convertibility could be disastrous. Financial sector reforms are as yet incomplete. For example, the Finance Minister himself said in his budget speech of 28 February 1997 that he had outlined only 'a very modest opening of one segment of the insurance sector'. Completing financial sector reforms is an urgent task.

REFERENCES

Amsden, A. (1989): *Asia's New Giant: South Korea and Late Industrialization* (New York: Oxford University Press).

Arize, A. (1990): 'An Econometric Investigation of Export Behaviour in Seven Asian Developing Countries, *Applied Economics*, 22, pp. 891–904.

Baldwin, R.E. and E. Seghezza (1996): 'Testing for Trade-Induced Investment Growth', Discussion Paper 1331 (London: Centre for Economic Policy Research).

Ben-David, D. (1995): 'Trade and Convergence Among Countries', *Journal of Development Economics*, 40, pp. 278–98.

Ben-David, D. and A.K.M.A. Rahman (1996): 'Technological Convergence and International Trade', *Journal of Development Economics*, 40, pp. 278–98.

Bhagwati, Jagdish (1996): 'The "Miracle" That Did Happen: Understanding East Asian in Comparative Perspective', Keynote speech
delivered on 3 May 1996 at the Conference on 'Government and
Market: The Relevance of the Taiwanese Performance to Development Theory and Policy' in honour of Professor T.C. Liu
and S.C. Tsiang (Ithaca: Cornell University).

Brahmbhatt, M., T.G. Srinivasan and K. Murell (1996): 'India in
the Global Economy' (World Bank: International Economics
Department) (processed).

Chaudhuri, K.N. (1983): 'Foreign Trade and Balance of Payments
(1757–1847)', in D. Kumar (ed.), *The Cambridge Economic History
of India*, vol. 2 (Cambridge: Cambridge University Press).

Chen, C., L. Chang and Y. Zang (1995): 'The Role of Foreign Direct
Investment in China's Post 1978 Economic Development', *World
Development*, 23 (4), pp. 691–703.

Coe, D.T. and E. Helpman (1995): 'International R&D Spillovers',
European Economic Review, 39, pp. 859–87.

Coe, D.T., E. Helpman and A.W. Hoffmaister (1997): 'North-South
R&D Spillovers', *Economic Journal*, 107 (January), pp. 134–49.

Dasgupta, A. (1982): 'Indian Merchants and Trade in the Indian
Ocean', Ch. XII in *The Cambridge Economic History of India*, vol. 1
(Cambridge: Cambridge University Press), pp. 407–33.

Digby, S. (1982): 'The Maritime Trade of India', Ch. V in T. Raychaudhuri and I. Habib (eds), *The Cambridge Economic History of
India*, vol. 1 (Cambridge: Cambridge University Press), pp. 45–7.

Edwards, S. (1993): 'Openness, Trade Liberalization and Growth in
Developing Countries', *Journal of Economic Literature XXXI*,
pp. 1358–91.

Frankel, J., D. Romer and T. Cyrus (1996): 'Trade and Growth in
East Asian Countries: Cause and Effect?', Working Paper 5732
(Cambridge, Md.: National Bureau of Economic Research).

Grossman, G. and E. Helpman (1991): *Innovation and Growth in the
World Economy* (Cambridge, Massachusetts: MIT Press).

Gulati, A. and G. Pursell (1995): *Trade Policy, Incentives and Resource
Allocation in Indian Agriculture* (Washington, DC: World Bank)
(processed).

Harrison, A. (1996): 'Openness and Growth: A Time Series, Cross-
country Analysis for Developing Countries', *Journal of Development Economics*, 48 (2), pp. 419–47.

Joshi, V. and I.M.D. Little (1994): *India: Macroeconomics and Political
Economy, 1964–1991* (Washington, DC: The World Bank).

Kangle, R.P. (1972): *The Kautiliya Arthasastra, Part II* (Bombay: University of Bombay).

Kornai, J. (1992): *The Socialist System: The Political Economy of Communism* (Princeton: Princeton University Press).

Kravis, I. (1970): 'Trade as a Handmaiden of Growth: Similarities Between the Nineteenth and Twentieth Centuries', *Economic Journal*, 80 (320), pp. 850–72.

Krueger, A. (1990): 'Asian Trade and Growth Lessons', *American Economic Review*, 80 (2), pp. 108–12.

—— (1987): 'The Importance of Economic Policies: Contrasts Between Korea and Turkey', in H. Kierzkowski (ed.), *Protection and Competition in International Trade* (Oxford: Basil Blackwell).

Krugman, P. (1994): 'The Myth of Asia's Miracle', *Foreign Affairs*, 73 (6), pp. 62–78.

Lau, L.J. and J. Kim (1994): 'The Sources of Economic Growth of the East Asian Newly Industrializing Countries', *Journal of Japanese and International Economies*, VIII, pp. 235–71.

Little, I.M.D. (1996): 'Picking Winners: The East Asian Experience, Occasional Paper (London: The Social Market Foundation).

Ministry of Finance, Government of India (1997): *Economic Survey 1996–97* (New Delhi: Government of India Press).

Pursell, G. (1996): 'Indian Trade Policies Since the 1991–92 Reforms' (World Bank: International Trade Division) (processed).

Reserve Bank of India (1996): *Report on Currency and Finance*, vol. II (Bombay: Reserve Bank of India).

Rivera-Batiz, L. and P. Romer (1991a): 'International Integration and Endogenous Growth', *Quarterly Journal of Economics*, 106, pp. 531–55.

—— (1991b): 'International Trade with Endogenous Technological Change', *European Economic Review*, 35, pp. 715–21.

Robertson, D. (1940): *Essays in Monetary Theory* (London: P.S. King & Son).

Rodrik, D. (1995a): 'Trade and Industrial Policy Reform', Ch. 45 in Jere Behrman and T.N. Srinivasan (eds), *Handbook of Development Economics*, vol. 3B (Amsterdam: Elsevier Science Publishers).

—— (1995b): 'Getting Interventions Right: How South Korea and Taiwan Grew Rich', *Economic Policy*, vol. 20, pp. 55–107.

—— (1996): 'Understanding Economic Policy Reform', *Journal of Economic Literature*, XXXIV (1), pp. 9–14.

—— (1997): 'Trade Strategy, Investment and Exports: Another Look at East Asia', *Pacific Economic Review* (1), pp. 1–24.

Sachs, J.D. and A. Warner (1995): 'Economic Reforms and the Process of Global Integration', *Brookings Papers on Economic Activity*, pp. 1–118.

Schumpeter, J. (1961): *The Theory of Economic Development* (New York: Oxford University Press).

Singh, M. (1964): *India's Export Trends* (Oxford: Clarendon Press).

Srinivasan, T.N. (1996): 'Trade Orientation, Trade Liberalization and Economic Growth' (New Haven, Conn.: Yale University) (processed).

Taylor, A.M. (1995): 'Growth and Convergence in the Asia Pacific Region: On the Role of Openness, Trade and Migration', Working Paper 5276 (Cambridge, MA: National Bureau of Economic Research).

Thapar, R. (1966): *A History of India*, vol. 1 (Baltimore, Md.: Penguin Books).

Wade, R. (1990), *Governing the Market: Economic Theory and the Role of the Government in East Asian Industrialization* (Princeton: Princeton University Press).

Wheeler, D. and A. Mody (1992): 'International Investment Location Decisions', *Journal of International Economics*, 33, pp. 57–76.

World Bank (1993): *The East Asian Miracle: Economic Growth and Public Policy* (New York: Oxford University Press).

WTO (1995): *International Trade: Trends and Statistics* (Geneva: World Trade Organization).

—— (1996): Press Release: Press/44 of 22 March 1996 (Geneva: World Trade Organization).

Yearbook of International Trade Statistics (various issues) (New York: United Nations).

Young, A. (1995): 'The Tyranny of Numbers: Confronting the Statistical Realities of the East Asian Growth Experience', *Quarterly Journal of Economics*, vol. 110, pp. 641–80.

III

Poverty and Reform

10

Economic Reforms
and Poverty Alleviation

Deepak Lal

INTRODUCTION

The process of economic liberalization in India, as much as the economic repression that preceded it, has had economists in a leadership position in both the formulation and implementation of the relevant policies. The only one who will however live on as the architect of the Indian reforms is Manmohan Singh, and I am delighted to be able to honour him on this occasion.

Many, though not all the 'government' economists involved in justifying and setting up the dirigiste Nehruvian economic system have now issued some form of *mea culpa*.[1] Manmohan has done much better. As one of the earliest Indian economists to question the export pessimism that underlay the Nehruvian strategy,[2] and particularly after the tragic and untimely death of V.K. Ramaswami, his voice in the government was always geared towards a more liberal economic regime than his other government colleagues and his political masters were willing to stomach. But he bade his time, and most important of all, built up a superb team[3] of young, liberally minded, and technically competent economists under the leadership of another Sikh, Montek Ahluwalia. When as Finance Minister in the Narasimha Rao government he got the opportunity, he

---

[1] For example Dr I.G. Patel in his 1996 address to the Indian Economic Association, and Dr Bimal Jalan in Jalan (1991).

[2] See Singh (1964).

[3] My colleague Al Harberger emphasized the importance of the small teams of technocrats who have overseen the reform process in Latin America in his Ely lecture to the 1994 meetings of the American Economic Association.

boldly began the overdue process of economic liberalization. Despite fears that his departure would lead to a reversal of the reform process, under his successor P. Chidambaram it is still in place, though stalled. But ever since the reform process began, the dirigiste bands have always tried to forestall it by their demands for 'adjustment with a human face'. As this slogan continues to be a thorn in the flesh of reformers in India, the best way in which I can honour Manmohan in this volume is to provide an antidote. A recent comparative study of the political economy of poverty, equity, and growth in 21 developing countries — which did not include India — that Hla Myint and I have recently published provides the means, and much of this contribution is based on our book.[4]

This contribution first briefly identifies the policies that need to be adopted in the next stage of Indian economic reforms. It then notes the continuing philosophical divide between supporters of some form of egalitarianism and those concerned with poverty alleviation. Next, it distinguishes three different types of poverty by their causes, and uses the Lal–Myint findings to show that there need be no conflict between the undoubted need for further and accelerated reform in India and alleviation of all three types of poverty.

I. The Next Stage of Indian Reforms

Even in the areas of past reform there is a great deal of unfinished business: notably to eliminate quotas on consumer goods imports, and to move to full convertibility of the rupee by eliminating exchange controls. There are also whole areas which the reform effort has not yet touched. The common feature of this next phase of reform can be succinctly described as the rescinding of the unviable entitlements to income streams that past dirigisme has created. These have both deleterious macro- and microeconomic effects.

On the macroeconomic front, problems remain in removing the large budgetary subsidies for fertilizers, energy, the public distribution system, and those implicit in carrying loss-making public enterprises and redundant labour in the central and state

---

[4] Lal and Myint (1996).

bureaucracies and parastatals. On the microeconomic side, India's nineteenth century labour laws have hobbled Indian industry for much of this century (see Lal, 1988). They need to be reformed if not repealed. Without the reform of the labour market, the essential privatization of the inefficient and still substantial public sector is well-nigh impossible. Moreover, in the growing global competition for footloose direct foreign investment, these antiquated labour laws pose a serious disincentive for investors in India, when compared to the de facto privatized labour market that now exists in East Asia, most notably in southern China.

These labour market reforms, and the rescinding of other unviable entitlements created by past public interventions is resisted on the grounds that they would worsen either the distribution of income or increase poverty. There is sufficient evidence (see Lal, 1988) that these claims are unfounded. Most of these entitlements have done little to improve income distribution or to alleviate poverty, their most discernible effect being to impair economic efficiency and to corrupt the polity. But precisely for this last reason, politicians will be wary of rescinding them for fear of losing support, thence the politically convenient slogan 'adjustment with a human face'.

II. EGALITARIANISM VS POVERTY ALLEVIATION

To make sense of this slogan it is first important to note an important difference between improving the distribution of income (an aim favoured by egalitarians) and alleviating poverty (one favoured by most other people). A theoretical case for a link between the two was made on the basis of the so-called Kuznets curve, on which more below. But even if valid, this case for improving income distribution would be as an instrument in alleviating poverty and not in promoting equality per se. Hopefully, after the events of 1989, socialists of various hues in India are at least chastened about the feasibility of promoting egalitarianism, even if they think it is still desirable.

Without entering into the sterile debates about the morality of egalitarianism, and attempts to reconcile so-called 'positive' and 'negative' freedom, all we need note is that the egalitarians have now retreated to a position where they claim that the establishment of fully- fledged Western style welfare states in the Third

World is required to alleviate its poverty.[5] This is particularly ironical given that the Western welfare state is everywhere on the defensive if not in retreat. It is this contemporary socialist mutation that is now increasingly identified with the term: blank (fill in any economic policy you like) 'with a human face'.

But is this 'social democratic' case for dirigisme any more valid than the old socialist one for planning, and will an acceleration of India's reforms require the simultaneous creation of a Western type welfare state to alleviate poverty? That is the central question I wish to address.

III. THREE TYPES OF POVERTY

In answering it, there are two distinctions worth noting. The first is between extensive and intensive growth. Extensive growth has occurred for millennia in most parts of the world with aggregate output rising, pari passu, with the expansion of population that has taken place since our ancestors came down from the trees. Per capita income was however relatively low and stagnant during this phase. By contrast the modern era has been marked by intensive growth with a secular rise in per capita incomes as the growth of output outstripped that of population. There has been a two centuries dispute whether such rises in per capita income will alleviate poverty, that is whether the fruits of intensive growth will 'trickle down' and alleviate poverty.

Answering this question is my first task. In doing so it is useful to distinguish between three types of poverty, based on their causes. These are (i) mass structural poverty, (ii) destitution, and (iii) conjunctural poverty. It is worth noting that though this distinction was well known in the past — for instance in discussions in England since the Elizabethan Poor Law — one strategic linguistic move by socialists was to conflate all of them, so that structural poverty, about which nothing could be done until the era of modern growth, was conflated with destitution — for whose relief most societies have adopted remedial measures. A similar confusion for instance surrounds the whole recent discussion by a distinguished NRI theorist of what he calls An Enquiry into Well-Being and Destitution (Dasgupta, 1993). What he is discussing is

---

[5] See the recent *Human Development Reports* put out by the UNDP.

mass structural poverty reflected for instance in malnutrition and ill health, which though ubiquitous in the past — and more widespread than it need be in India today — is different from true destitution.

III.1 Mass Structural Poverty

Mass structural poverty has for most of history been mankind's natural state. Till recently, most economies were agricultural economies, or what the economic historian E.A. Wrigley has called 'organic' economies, whose growth was ultimately bounded by the productivity of land. In such an economy there is a universal dependence on organic raw materials for food, clothing, housing, and fuel. Their supply is in the long run inevitably constrained by the fixed factor — land. This was also true of traditional industry and transportation — depending on animal muscle for mechanical energy, and upon charcoal (a vegetable substance) for smelting and working crude ores and providing heat. Thus in an organic economy once the land frontier has been reached, diminishing returns will take their inexorable toll. With diminishing returns to land, conjoined to the Malthusian principle of population, a long run stationary state where the mass of people languished at a subsistence standard of living seemed inevitable. No wonder the classical economists were so gloomy.

Even in an organic economy there was some hope for intensive growth. The system of market 'capitalism' and free trade outlined and defended by Adam Smith could increase the productivity of an organic economy somewhat from what it was under mercantilism, which together with the lowering of the cost of the consumption bundle, would lead to a rise in per capita income. But if this growth in popular opulence led to excessive breeding, the land constraint would inexorably lead back to subsistence wages. Technical progress could hold the stationary state at bay, but the land constraint would ultimately bite.

The Industrial Revolution led to the substitution of this organic economy by a mineral based energy economy. Intensive growth now became possible, as the land constraint on the raw materials required for raising aggregate output was removed. In particular, coal began to provide most of the heat energy of industry, and the development of the steam engine led to virtually unlimited supplies of mechanical energy. Thus the Industrial Revolution in England was based on two forms of 'capitalism', one institutional, namely that defended by Adam Smith — because of its productivity enhancing effects, even in an organic economy — and the other physical: the capital stock of stored energy represented by the fossil fuels that offered mankind the prospect of eliminating mass structural poverty for the first time in its history. It is possible, as many countries in East Asia for instance have shown, to eradicate mass poverty within a generation, because neither of the twin foundations of the gloomy classical prognostications, diminishing returns, nor the Malthusian principle are any longer secure. A market based liberal economic order that promotes labour intensive growth can cure the age long problem of structural mass poverty.

A crude measure of the extent of mass structural poverty is the so-called 'headcount index' of the proportion of the population below some national but time invariant real poverty line. Using this measure the Lal–Myint country authors found that there was a clear positive effect of per capita income growth on mass poverty redressal in all their countries over the period of study 1950–85. Whilst Gary Fields (1991) — for the same study — found for a larger sample that, in most but not all cases poverty tends to decrease with growth, and that where poverty tends to decrease most the more rapid is economic growth.

For India, Tendulkar and Jain (1995) have recently examined the effects of growth on poverty alleviation — taking account of alternative social welfare orderings — for the period 1970–1 to 1988–9. As they conclude, 'in comparison to the 1970s, the doubling of annual growth rate of per capita GDP in the 1980s was associated with improvement in both the poverty and social welfare situation' (p. 40). In India as elsewhere growth *does* thus alleviate mass structural poverty. In his famous 'tryst with destiny' speech on India's Independence Nehru stated: 'the ambition of the greatest man of our generation has been to wipe every tear from every eye'. The policies he followed however made this impossible because they damaged growth performance. Even the slowly rolling retreat from this past dirigisme has led to higher growth rates and in consonance with all the international evidence, to some sustainable alleviation of India mass poverty. If only India could sustain the spectacular growth rates that East Asia has now shown can be attained even by large economies like China, it is indubitable that mass structural poverty could be eliminated in India within a generation. That is the prize on offer. Nothing stands in the way but political impediments that irrational past *dirigisme* itself has created.

III.2 Destitution

With mass structural poverty ubiquitous till recently, the problem of 'poverty' has historically been confined to destitution. Most of these traditional organic economies were labour scarce and land abundant. The destitute lacked labour power to work the land because they were physically disabled and had no families. This remains a major source of destitution in land-abundant parts of Africa.[6]

With population expansion and the emergence of land scarce economies in Europe and in many parts of Asia, there arose 'the poverty of the able-bodied who lacked land, work, or wages adequate to support the dependents who were partly responsible for their poverty'. (Iliffe, 1987: 5). Their poverty merges with mass structural poverty and growth will, as it has, lead to its amelioration.

No estimates of destitution in India — as far as I am aware — are currently available. Michael Lipton's attempts to find some correlates of destitution, based on village studies, however, show the extremely heterogeneous composition of this group. Thus, for instance, Dasgupta's seemingly reasonable assertion that widows are 'routinely forced into destitution' in India (1993: 323) has been shown to be false by Drèze and Srinivasan (1995) who find 'in terms of standard poverty indices based on household per capita expenditure, there is no evidence of widows being disproportionately concentrated in poor households, or of female-headed households being poorer than male-headed households'.

III.3 Conjunctural Poverty

This leaves conjunctural poverty. In organic agrarian economies, climatic crises or political turmoil are its principal cause. Its most dramatic manifestation is a famine. Since the Indian Famine Code

6 See Iliffe (1987), to whom I owe the threefold classification of poverty.

was devised by the British Raj in the late nineteenth century, it has been known that to deal with what Sen (1982) labels the 'entitlement failures' precipitating a famine, the government should provide income directly (through public works or food for work schemes) to those suffering a temporary loss of income generating employment. This administrative solution has eliminated famines in India.

Finally, the Industrial Revolution has introduced its own source of conjunctural poverty in the form of the trade cycle and the unemployment that ensues in its downturns. But in India's primarily agrarian economy, the seasonal unemployment of landless labour in rural areas is likely to be of greater importance than urban industrial unemployment. Rural public works schemes like the Maharashtra Employment Guarantee scheme (see Ravallion, 1991), have been effective both in preventing famines and in dealing with problems of short-run income variability. Their success however lies in the self-targeting that is made possible by offering a wage that only the truly needy will accept.

III.4 Income Transfers and Poverty Alleviation

Income transfers are the only way of tackling destitution and conjunctural poverty. Traditionally these have been provided by private agencies — the church, private charity, and most important of all, transfers within extended families.

These private transfers were however replaced in most Western societies by public transfers through the welfare state. In assessing the case for Western style welfare states in dealing with the continuing problems of destitution and conjunctural poverty, it is useful first to distinguish between *social safety nets* and *welfare states*.

The distinction between the 'welfare state' and a 'social safety net' essentially turns upon the universality of coverage of transfers under a welfare state as opposed to the restriction of collectively provided benefits under a social safety net to the truly needy. The World Bank's Poverty Reduction Handbook, (PH) noted two essential elements in any design of a social safety net: 'identifying the groups in need of assistance, and the means of targeting assistance to those groups cost-effectively'. It went on to ask: 'Are these questions for public policy, or are they adequately addressed by the traditional family network?' (PH: 2–13)

By contrast, welfare state advocates favour universality as it alone in their view provides a feasible means of achieving the ends sought to be subserved by a social safety net, because of problems concerned with obtaining the requisite information for targeting. Some have argued that, because of the ubiquitousness of imperfect information, markets for risk will be inherently imperfect.[7] Hence, universal welfare states are required as part of an efficient solution to deal with 'market failure'. To deal with this argument would take me too far afield.[8] Suffice it to say that this is a form of 'nirvana economics'[9] — currently fashionable on the Left — but it provides no credible justification for a welfare state.

IV. Two Rival Philosophies

An implicit objective of those who argue against targeting and in favour of universal welfare states is distributivist. To judge its validity it is useful to contrast two rival ethical and political traditions: the *classical liberal* and the *distributivist egalitarian*, which continue to jostle for our attention and colour the various policies offered for alleviating poverty.

IV.1 Classical Liberalism

For the classical liberal it is a contingent fact that there is no universal consensus on what a 'just' or 'fair' income distribution should be, despite the gallons of ink spilt by moral philosophers in trying to justify their particular prejudices as the dictates of Reason. Egalitarianism is therefore to be rejected as the norm for deriving principles of public policy.

This does not mean that classical liberals are immoral! The greatest of them all, Adam Smith, wrote The Moral Sentiments. Both the great moral philosophers of the Scottish Enlightenment — Smith and Hume — recognized benevolence as the primary virtue, but they also noted its scarcity. However, as Smith's other great work *The Wealth of Nations* showed, fortunately, a market economy that promotes 'opulence' does not depend on this virtue

---

[7] See, e.g., Barr (1992).

[8] But see Lal (1993a).

[9] The term is due to Demsetz. For an explication in terms of the recent controversy surrounding the minimum wage, see Lal (1995).

for its functioning. It only requires a vast number of people to deal and live together even if they have no personal relationships, as long as they do not violate the 'laws of justice'. The resulting commercial society promotes some virtues — hard work, prudence, thrift, and self-reliance — which as they benefit the agent rather than others are inferior to altruism. But, by promoting general prosperity, these lower level virtues do unintentionally help others. Hence, the resulting society is neither immoral nor amoral.

A good government, for the classical liberal, is one that promotes opulence through promotion of natural liberty by establishment of laws of justice that guarantee free exchange and peaceful competition. The improvement of morality is left to non-governmental institutions.

From Smith to Friedman and Hayek, however, classical liberals have also recognized that society or the state should seek to alleviate absolute poverty. On the classical liberal view, as my colleague Al Harberger (1986) has noted, there could be an externality, whereby 'the (poor) recipient's consumption of particular goods or services (food, eduction, medical care, housing) or his attainment of certain states (being better nourished, better educated, healthier, better housed) that are closely correlated with an "adequate" consumption of such goods' enters the donor's utility function. As it is the specific consumption of these commodities, not the recipient's 'utility' that enters the donor's utility function, there is no 'utility' handle which can be used, as on the alternative distributivist view to allow distributional considerations to be smuggled into the analysis of poverty alleviation programmes.

Thus the indigent and the disabled are to be helped through targeted benefits. For various merit goods — health, education and possibly housing — these involve in-kind transfers. This is very much the type of social policy package that was implemented in Pinochet's Chile, and which succeeded not only in protecting the poor during Chile's arduous transformation to a liberal market economy, but also led to dramatic long-term improvement in its various social indicators.[10]

[10] See Castaneda (1992) for a detailed account of these social policy reforms and their outcome.

IV.2 Distributivist Egalitarianism

The alternative technocratic approach to poverty alleviation is by contrast necessarily infected with egalitarianism because of its lineage. At its most elaborate it is based on some Bergson–Samuelson type social welfare function, laid down by Platonic Guardians.[11] Given the ubiquitous assumption of diminishing marginal utility underlying the approach, any normative utility weighting of the incomes of different persons or households leads naturally to some form of egalitarianism. But this smuggling in of an ethical norm which is by no means universally accepted leads to a form of 'mathematical politics'. Poverty alleviation becomes just one component of the general problem of maximizing social welfare, where given the distributional weighting schema, all the relevant trade-offs between efficiency and equity, including inter-temporal ones can be derived in terms of the appropriate distribution cum efficiency shadow prices.[12] If the concern is solely with those falling below some normative 'poverty line', this merely implies a different set of weights with the weight of unity say to changes in consumption (income) above the line, and increasing weights to those who fall progressively below the poverty line.[13]

But this is the thin edge of a very big wedge, as far as the defenders of the market economy are concerned. Besides leading to recommendations for all sorts of redistributive schemes, it also leads to a vast increase in dirigisme. To alleviate poverty, an end embraced by classical liberals, they are on this route being led to endorse the creation of a vast Transfer State, which in the long run is incompatible with the preservation of a market economy.

A usual riposte to the classical liberal position of separating questions of alleviating absolute poverty from inequality is that, in theory, a market based growth process could lead to such a worsening of the income distribution, that instead of the poor seeing a rise in their incomes as part of the growth process, they could be further impoverished. This view was strengthened by the so-called Kuznets hypothesis that inequality was likely to

---

[11] See Sugden (1993) for a lucid account of the divergent economic traditions that flow from the technocratic and classical liberal viewpoints.

[12] See Little and Mirrlees (1974) and Lal (1981).

[13] See Ravallion (1992) for a full explication of this approach in the design and evaluation of poverty alleviation programmes in the Third World.

worsen in the early stages of development before it declined, as per capita incomes rose towards current developed country levels. All the empirical evidence, to date, is against the Kuznets hypothesis, and its corollary that growth might not alleviate absolute mass poverty.[14]

V. PUBLIC-VERSUS PRIVATE TRANSFERS

Are public transfers needed, as the welfare state advocates claim, to deal with destitution and conjunctural poverty, and as some assert even to deal with mass structural poverty? We need to briefly examine the relative efficacy of private versus public income transfers.

V.1 Private Transfers

Kin based transfers, reciprocity arrangements, and interlinked factor market contracts have been the major way that traditional societies have dealt with income risk. They have been fairly effective.[15] With the inevitable erosion of village communities it is feared that these private insurance arrangements will break down and that no private alternative will be available to counter destitution and conjunctural poverty in increasingly atomistic industrial economies.

It is in this context that the role of private interhousehold transfers is of great importance. Cox and Jimenez (1990) provide evidence to show that they are of considerable quantitative importance.[16]

---

[14] See Fields (1991), and Squire (1993).

[15] As Platteau (1991) concludes:

Even though empirical evidence is scanty (but not altogether absent), the case can reasonably be made that, barring exceptionally unfavourable circumstances (such as repeated crop failures or crop diseases affecting entire communities), traditional methods for controlling the risk of falling into distress have usually enabled the people to counter natural and other hazards in a rather effective way. [p. 156].

[16] Also see Rempel and Lobdell (1978), Knowles and Anker (1981), Collier and Lal (1986), Oberai et al. (1984), Lucas and Stark (1985), on the significant size and effects of remittances within the rural and between the rural and urban sectors in Ghana, Liberia, Nigeria, Pakistan, Tanzania, Kenya, India, and Botswana.

For example, among a sample of urban poor in El Salvador, 33 per cent reported having received private transfers, and income from private transfers accounted for 39 per cent of total income among recipients. Ninety-three per cent of a rural south Indian sample received transfers from other households. In Malaysia, private transfers accounted for almost half the income of the poorest households. Nearly three quarters of rural households in Java, Indonesia, gave private transfers to other households. About half of a sample of Filipino households received private cash transfers. [p. 206]

Moreover, since the oil price rise of the early 1970s, the poor in South Asia and parts of South-East Asia have found remunerative employment in the newly rich oil states and their remittances to their Third World relatives has helped to alleviate their poverty.[17]

Private transfers have by now been largely 'crowded out' by public transfers in the West. The potential for such 'crowding out' in developing countries has been estimated for Peru and the Philippines by Cox and Jimenez (1992, 1993). There is potentially a large 'crowding out' effect if public transfer systems were to be instituted in these countries. For example, for the Philippines they find that, if a public transfer programme was instituted that gave each household the difference between its actual income and poverty line income, after private transfers adjust, 46 per cent of urban and 94 per cent of rural households below the poverty line before the programme began would remain below the line after it was implemented!

Moreover, the evidence suggests that private transfers are efficient. By relying on locally held information, and on extra economic motivations like trust and altruism, private transfers overcome many of the problems of adverse selection, moral hazard, etc., which have so exercised the 'nirvana' economics 'market-failure' school. For, as Cox and Jimenez, summarizing the empirical evidence, conclude: 'private transfers equalize income; private transfers are directed toward the poor, the young, the old, women, the disabled and the unemployed' (p. 216).

V.2 Public Transfers

Perhaps public transfers can do even better, so that we should not worry if they crowd out private transfers. Public subsidization

[17] See G. Swamy (1981).

of the two merit goods — health and education — are the major public transfers in nearly all developing countries. In addition, social security is important in many Latin American countries.[18]

One question on which there is some empirical evidence is the incidence of the benefits from subsidies for merit goods. This overwhelmingly suggests that their incidence is generally regressive, and that they very imperfect means of helping the poor.[19]

A revealing piece of evidence suggesting that public transfers are not only more inefficient in poverty redressal than private transfers but also crowd them out is provided by a World Bank study. This study

traced public social sector expenditures for nine Latin American countries in the 1980s.. [and] found that real per capita public social spending on health, education, and social security fell during some part of the 1980s in every country in the study. The share of health and education expenditures in total government expenditures also fell, even as that of social security rose. In spite of lower funding, and no apparent increases in equity and efficiency, social indicators generally improved in the 1980s. [PH: Box 3.4]

Apart from obvious statistical and other biases that might explain this anomaly, the most plausible explanation provided is that it might be due to 'the growing role of non-governmental organizations, and the response of the market oriented private sector to enhanced expectations and demand'. Thus there was probably a 'crowding in' of more equitable and more efficient private transfers to replace the decline in public ones.[20]

---

[18] As social security is currently not an important issue in India, we neglect it here. For a discussion of the highly repressive nature of Latin American social security systems see Mesa-Lago.

[19] See Selowsky (1979), Meerman (1979), Jimenez (1989), Deolalikar (1995), Jimenez et al. (1991), Van de Walle (1992).

[20] Another piece of evidence is provided by a simple regression I ran on the state level data on per capita public expenditure on health and education between 1976 and 1986, and the changes in literacy rates and life expectancy and infant mortality rates for India, given in Ravallion and Subbarao (1992). In these cross-sections, I found there was no statistically significant relationship between changes on state level health expenditures and health outcomes, and a statistically significant negative relationship between changes in educational expenditure and literacy!

V.3 Political Economy of Transfer States

The 'middle class capture' of the benefits of social expenditure is not confined to developing countries. It has also been documented for the welfare states of the OECD.[21] A systemic process is clearly at work. It is the political economy of redistribution in majoritarian democracies. In a two party system, politicians will bid for votes by offering transfers of income from some sections of the populace at the expense of others. Models of this political process (which do not need to assume a democracy, but rather the interplay of different pressure/interest groups)[22] show that there will be a tendency for income to be transferred from both the rich and the poor to the middle classes — the so-called 'median voter'. Even if social expenditures are initially intended to benefit only the needy, in democracies such programmes have inevitably been 'universalized' through the political process, leading to what are properly called transfer rather than, welfare states, that primarily benefit the middle classes.

The poverty alleviation that may occur as a by-product of the expansion of the transfer state is moreover bought at a rising dynamic cost. With the universalization of various welfare schemes, political entitlements are created whose fiscal burden is governed more by demography than the conjunctural state of the economy. With the costs of entitlements rising faster than the revenues necessary to finance them, the transfer state, sooner or later, finds itself in a fiscal crisis. This process is discernible both in developing and developed countries.

For developing countries the Lal–Myint study shows how this process is clearly visible in those countries in our sample (Uruguay, Costa Rica, Sri Lanka, and Jamaica) that under the factional pressures of majoritarian democracies have created and expanded welfare states. All four welfare states were financed by taxing the rents from their major primary products. With the expansion of revenues during upturns in the primary product cycle, political pressures led to their commitment to entitlements, that could not be repudiated when revenues fell during the downturn in the price cycle. The ensuing increase in the tax burden on the productive primary sector (to close the fiscal gap) led to a retardation of its growth and

---

21 See Goodin and Le Grand (1987).
22 See Stigler (1970), Meltzer and Richard (1981), Peltzman (1980).

productivity, and in some cases to the 'killing of the goose that laid the golden egg'. Thus, whilst there was undoubtedly some poverty redressal as a result of the expansion of these welfare states, over the long run these entitlements damaged the economic growth on which they were predicated, and hence eventually became unsustainable. Similar processes leading to the fiscal crisis of the state are to be found in many other developing countries.[23] Not surprisingly, many of these countries with over extended welfare states are now seeking to rein them back.

Very similar problems are also visible in the more mature welfare states of the OECD.[24] In some countries that had gone furthest down the public welfare route, the late 1980s and 1990s saw a growing questioning of the welfare state in the West, and in some cases its partial or virtual dismantlement.

VI. Policy Implications

What are the conclusions for policy that follow from this discussion.

The *first* is that nothing should be done to damage the existing private institutions and channels providing private transfer. 'Forbear' should be the watchword for every proposed scheme that seeks to alleviate poverty through public transfers.

The *second* is that, if for whatever reason, public money is sought to be transferred to the 'needy', this is best done through private agencies. Particularly for 'merit goods' — primary health care and primary education — even if there is a case for public financing there is none for public production.

The *third*, is that the very problems of moral hazard, adverse selection, and monitoring cited by 'nirvana economics' as requiring public insurance, in fact argue for fostering the alternative private route that capitalizes on the comparative informational advantage of private agents with local knowledge. These private welfare channels can be promoted by various methods of co-financing them with public funds.

A radical proposal may be worth considering. This would channel all foreign aid and domestic public expenditure on social programmes and on 'safety nets' to alleviate destitution and

---

[23] See Mesa-Lago (1983, 1989) for Latin America.
[24] See Lal and Wolf (1986), and Lindbeck (1990) for the Swedish case.

conjunctural poverty through NGOs (national and international charities). But to avoid the crowding out of private by public transfers, this public funding should only be provided on a matching basis. The only reservation I would have about such a scheme is the continuing economic illiteracy shown by so many NGOs.

Finally, there is the important question of severance payments that will be needed to slim the over-extended and inefficient public sector and the bureaucracies that were set up to manage controlled economies and are redundant with the move from the plan to the market. Such structural adjustment faces political resistance from the public sector workers who face retrenchment and/or cuts in their real wages. Such workers can exert political pressure to prevent the rescinding of their politically determined entitlements to future income streams that are above what they would be able to obtain in the free market. The capitalized value of the difference between their expected public sector earnings (including pension and other benefits), and those they could get in the private sector (adjusted for the probabilities of being hired and fired in the market), represent the rents public sector workers are currently receiving. If their resistance is to be overcome they might need to be compensated for these rents. This is a political rather than an economic argument for severance payments, over and above those that might already exist in the contractual arrangements that may be in force in the respective labour markets.[25]

Given the heterogeneity of the labour force, the rents derived from public sector jobs will differ for different workers, being highest for the 'bad' workers whose market opportunities relative to their entitlements in the public sector are the worst. With imperfect knowledge of each worker's rents, and the difficulty in devising perfectly discriminating severance payment schemes, if the severance compensation is set to persuade the last 'bad' worker to leave the public sector, the intramarginal workers will be receiving more compensation than the capitalized value of their public sector rents. This could mean a very high cost to the fisc. But in some cases (e.g. where the public enterprise is producing negative value added at world prices), shutting down the enterprise even

---

[25] See Rosen (1985) for a survey of the reasons why many labour market contracts will have various forms of severance terms built into them for efficiency reasons.

with this high cost may lead to a gain in net GDP. In others where the enterprise might still be viable after restructuring and privatization, that involves retrenchment, the problem of tailoring a severance package remains.[26]

The most attractive plan that would meet both the objectives of limiting political opposition and reducing the fiscal burden would be one limited to workers not hired by the newly privatized enterprise. This tackles the adverse selection problem whereby the 'good' workers take the severance package and the 'lemons' are left with the new firm. The severance package for those made redundant should be based on the principle of tailoring the benefits to the median redundant worker's public sector rents. This would imply that, if the severance package offered uniform compensation at the level of the rents to the median retrenched worker, all those with lower rents would be better off, and they would provide the political support for the scheme to override those workers whose rents were greater than the median and would be worse off. Little more can be said in principle about the specific terms of these programmes that need to be tailored to local conditions, and in particular the relative bargaining power of public sector workers *vis-à-vis* the state.

Conclusion

My conclusions can be brief. There is no case for attempting to institute a Western style welfare state in India. There are feasible ways of dealing with the inevitable pain that the necessary reform of India's labour market will involve, but it is going to require political courage. Lacking that, only a fiscal crisis — that spills over into an inflationary and balance of payments crisis — of the kind that led to the partial reform of Indian commodity and financial markets, is likely to lead to these desperately needed reforms.[27] Without them the accelerated growth required to banish structural mass poverty from the subcontinent in the near future will not occur.

[26] Papers by Fiszben (1992) and Diwan (1993) provided detailed analyses of the various options, as well as discussions of severance payment schemes in a number of countries.

[27] The role of fiscal crises as precipitating reform is outlined in Lal (1987), and empirically substantiated in Lal and Myint (1996).

REFERENCES

Ahmad, E. (1991): 'Social Security and the Poor: Choices for Developing Countries', *World Bank Research Observer*, vol. 6, no. 1 (Oxford: Clarendon Press), pp. 105–27.

Ahmad, E. et al. (eds) (1991): *Social Security in Developing Countries* (Oxford: Clarendon Press).

Atkinson, A.B. (1987): 'Income Maintenance and Social Insurance, in A.J. Auerbach and M. Feldstein (eds), *Handbook of Public Economics*, vol. 2 (Amsterdam: North Holland), pp. 779–908.

Barr, N. (1992): 'Economic Theory and the Welfare State: A Survey and Interpretation', *Journal of Economic Literature*, vol. XXX, no. 2, June, pp. 741–803.

Castaneda, T. (1992): *Combating Poverty* (International Center for Economic Growth, San Francisco: ICS Press).

Collier, P. and D. Lal (1986): *Labor and Poverty in Kenya 1900–1980* (Oxford: Clarendon Press).

Cox, D. (1987): 'Motives for Private Income Transfers', *Journal of Political Economy*, vol. 95, no. 3, June, pp. 508–46.

Cox, D. and G. Jackson (1989): 'The Connection Between Public Transfers and Private Interfamily Transfers', mimeo (Boston: Boston College).

Cox, D. and E. Jimenez (1990): 'Achieving Social Objectives Through Private Transfers: A Review', *World Bank Research Observer*, vol. 5, no. 2, July, pp. 205–18.

—— (1992): 'Social Security and Private Transfers in Peru', *World Bank Economic Review*, vol. 6, no. 1, January.

—— (1993): 'Private Transfers and the Effectiveness of Public Income Redistribution in the Philippines', mimeo, World Bank Conference on Public Expenditures and the Poor: Incidence and Targeting.

Dasgupta, P. (1993): *An Enquiry into Well-Being and Destitution* (Oxford: Clarendon Press).

Demsetz, H. (1969): 'Information and Efficiency: Another Viewpoint', *Journal of Law and Economics*, vol. 12, pp. 1–22; rpt in his *The Organization of Economic Activity*, vol. 2 (Oxford: Blackwell, 1988).

Deolalikar, A.B. (1993): 'Does the Impact of Government Health Spending on the Utilization of Health Services by Children and on Child Health Outcomes Differ by Household Expenditure: The Case of Indonesia', mimeo, Paper for the World Bank Conference on Public Expenditures and the Poor: Incidence and Targeting.

250   *India's Economic Reforms and Development*

Diwan, I. (1993): 'Efficient Severance Payment Schemes', mimeo May (Washington, DC: World Bank).

Dreze, J. and A. Sen (1989): *Hunger and Public Action* (Oxford: Clarendon Press).

Dreze, J. and P.V. Srinivasan (1995): 'Widowhood and Poverty in India: Some Inferences from Household Survey Data', Development Economics Research Programme, Paper No. 62, London School of Economics (mimeo).

Fields, G., (1991): 'Growth and Income Distribution', in G. Psacharopoulos (ed.) (1993).

Fiszben, A. (1992): 'Labor Retrenchment and Redundancy Compensation in State Owned Enterprises: The Case of Sri Lanka', South Asia Region Internal Discussion Paper', Report No. IDP 121 (Washington, DC: World Bank), December.

Goodin, R.E. and J. Le Grand (1987): *Not Only the Poor* (London: Allen and Unwin).

Harberger, A. (1986): 'Basic Needs versus Distributional Weights in Social Cost–Benefit Analysis', *Economic Development and Cultural Change.*

Harris, R. (1988): *Beyond the Welfare State: An Economic, Political and Moral Critique of Indiscriminate State Welfare and a Review of Alternatives to Dependency* (London: Institute of Economic Affairs, Occasional Paper No. 77).

Iliffe, J. (1987): *The African Poor* (Cambridge: Cambridge University Press).

Jalan, B. (1991): *India's Economic Crisis* (Delhi: Oxford University Press).

Jimenez, E. (1989): 'Social Sector Pricing Revisited: A Survey of Some Recent Contributions', *Proceedings of the World Bank Annual Conference on Development Economics* (Washington, DC: The World Bank), pp. 109–38.

Jimenez, E., M.E. Lockheed and V. Paqueo (1991): 'The Relative Efficiency of Private and Public Schools in Developing Countries', World Bank Research Observer, vol. 6, no. 2, July, pp. 205–18.

Knowles, J.C. and R. Anker (1981): 'An Analysis of Income Transfers in a Developing Country', *Journal of Development Economics*, vol. 8, April, pp. 205–6.

Lal, D. (1987): 'The Political Economy of Economic Liberalization', *World Bank Economic Review*, vol. 1, pp. 273–99, reprinted in Lal (1993).

—— (1988): *The Hindu Equilibrium*, 2 vols (Oxford: Clarendon Press).

—— (1993): *The Repressed Economy*, Economists of the 20th Century Series (Aldershort: Edward Elgar).

Lal, D. (1993a): 'The Role of the Public and Private Sectors in Health Financing', HRO Working Paper No. 33, Human Resources Development and Operations Policy Dept. (Washington, DC: World Bank).

—— (1994): *Against Dirigisme* (San Francisco: ICS Press).

—— (1995): *The Minimum Wage*, Occasional Paper No. 95 (London: Institute of Economic Affairs).

Lal, D. and H. Myint (1996): *The Political Economy of Poverty, Equity and Growth — A Comparative Study* (Oxford: Clarendon Press).

Lal, D. and M. Wolf (eds) (1986): *Stagflation, Savings and the State* (New York: Oxford University Press).

Lindbeck, A. (1990): 'The Swedish Experience', Stockholm: Institute for International Economic Studies, Seminar Paper No. 482.

Little, I.M.D. and J.A. Mirrlees (1974): *Project Appraisal and Planning for Developing Countries* (London: Heinemman Educational).

Lucas, R.E. and O. Stark (1985): 'Motivations to Remit Evidence from Botswana', *Journal of Political Economy*, vol. 93, October, pp. 901–18.

Meltzer, A. and S. Richard (1981): 'A Rational Theory of the Size of Government', *Journal of Political Economy*, vol. 89, pp. 914–27.

Mesa–Lago, C. (1983): 'Social Security and Extreme Poverty in Latin America', *Journal of Development Economics*, vol. 12, pp. 83–110.

—— (1989): *Ascent of Bankruptcy: Financing Social Security in Latin America* (Pittsburgh: University of Pittsburgh Press).

Meerman, J. (1979): *Public Expenditure in Malaysia: Who Benefits and Why* (New York: Oxford University Press).

Mill, J.S. (1948): *Principles of Political Economy*, D. Winch (ed.) (London: Penguin Books, 1970).

Murray, C. (1984): *Losing Ground: American Social Policy 1950–1980* (New York: Basic Books).

Oberai, A.S. and H.K.M. Singh (1980): 'Migration, Remittances and Rural Development', *International Labor Review*, March–April.

—— (1983): *Causes and Consequences of Internal Migration* (Delhi: Oxford University Press).

Peltzman, S. (1980): 'The Growth of Government', *Journal of Law and Economics*, vol. 25, no. 3, pp. 209–87.

Platteau, J.P. (1991): 'Traditional Systems of Social Security and Hunger Insurance: Past Achievements and Modern Challenges', in E. Ahmad et al. (eds).

Psacharopoulos, G. (ed.) (1991): *Essays on Poverty, Equity and Growth* (Oxford: Pergamon).

Ravallion, M. (1992): *Poverty Comparisons — A Guide to Concepts and*

Methods, Living Standards Measurement Study Working Paper No. 88 (Washington, DC: World Bank).

Ravallion, M. and K. Subbarao (1992): 'Adjustment and Human Development in India', *Journal of Indian School of Political Economy*, vol. 4, no. 1, pp. 55–79.

Rempel, H. and R. Lobdell (1978): 'The Role of Urban-to-rural Remittances in Rural Development', *Journal of Development Studies*, vol. 14 (April), pp. 324–41.

Rosen, S. (1985): 'Implicit Contracts — A Survey', *Journal of Economic Literature*, vol. 23, pp. 1144–75.

Selowsky, M. (1978): *Who Benefits from Public Expenditure? A Case Study of Colombia* (New York: Oxford University Press).

Sen, A.K. (1982): *Poverty and Famines* (Oxford: Clarendon Press).

Singh, Manmohan (1964): *India's Export Trends* (Oxford: Clarendon Press).

Squire, L. (1993): 'Fighting Poverty', *American Economic Review*, vol. 83, May, pp. 377–82.

Stigler, G. (1970): 'Director's Law of Public Income Distribution', *Journal of Law and Economics*, vol. 13, no. 1, pp. 1–10.

Sugden, R. (1993): 'A Review of Inequality Re-examined by Amartya Sen', *Journal of Economic Literature*, vol. xxxi, no. 4, December, pp. 1947–86.

Swamy, G. (1981): 'International Migrant Workers' Remittances: Issues and Prospects', World Bank Staff Working Paper No. 481, (Washington, DC: World Bank).

Tendulkar, S.D. and L.R. Jain (1995): 'Economic Growth and Equity: India 1970–1 to 1988–9', *Indian Economic Review*, vol. xxx, no. 1, pp. 19–49.

Van de Walle, D. (1992): 'The Distribution of the Benefits from Social Services in Indonesia, 1978–87', mimeo, Policy Research Working Paper, Country Economics Dept. (Washington, DC: World Bank).

World Bank (1992): *Poverty Reduction Handbook* (PH) (Washington, DC: World Bank).

Wrigley, E.A. (1988): *Continuity, Chance and Change: The Character of the Industrial Revolution in England* (Cambridge: Cambridge University Press).

11

Food Security:
Individual and National

*Kirit S. Parikh**

Manmohan Singh is known around the world as the man who initiated the process of structural reforms in India. Amidst all the accolade he has received from the rich in India and abroad, there is a danger of forgetting that the underlying motivation for structural reforms was to help the poor in India, as the policies we had followed for forty years so steadfastly in the name of the poor failed to deliver much to the poor. As a humanist who deeply cares for the poor in the country, Manmohan Singh has tried to give a human face to the process. For the poor and for a poor nation, there is nothing as important as food security. Thus, we examine the issues and policy options for the provision of food security in India, both at the level of the individual and the nation.

I. FOOD SECURITY IS A PROBLEM OF THE POOR

We are all concerned about food security in some sense or other. A country is food secure when it is able to provide 'adequate' food to all its citizens under all circumstances that can be reasonably expected. Moreover, food should be provided to all as a matter of right without inflicting any humiliation on the poor. How this is accomplished, whether through the market mechanism or through government ration shops, is not fundamental to the notion of food security.

What constitutes 'adequate' food intake is still a matter of

* I gratefully acknowledge extensive help from A. Ganesh Kumar in the preparation of this contribution.

contention among nutritionists. Sukhatme (1978) pointed out the difficulties of defining this, noting that metabolic rates vary across similar (in height, weight, sex) individuals and also across time for a given individual. Also, individuals learn to live with less (or more) calories over time. Srinivasan (1981) provides an overview of these issues. Yet, no matter how one measures hunger and poverty, we find that hundreds of millions of persons suffer from hunger and poverty (FAO, 1986; World Bank, 1986, 1990) across the world and in India (for some recent estimates see Dev et al. (1992), Planning Commission (1985); and Tendulkar and Jain (1995)). The principal reason for hunger is that the hungry have inadequate real income to buy the food they need.

Both persistent hunger and transient hunger, the extreme form of which is famine, have attracted analysts. First, Linneman et al. (1979) with MOIRA, and later Parikh and Tims (1986) and Fischer et al. (1987) with IIASA's BLS (Basic Linked System, Fischer et al., 1988), have underlined that to deal with chronic hunger is to deal with poverty and underdevelopment. The hungry in the world are hungry because they are poor. They are poor because they own too little resources of land, capital, or skills. Hunger is primarily a problem of poverty and not of food production. Thus, if all the poor are given additional income, more food would be demanded *and produced.* But if more food is produced because farmers are given higher prices, the poor whose incomes have not changed, will continue to remain hungry. Thus, food security can be provided to an individual either by increasing her money income or by decreasing the price at which 'adequate' food is made available to her.

Sen (1981) and Drèze and Sen (1989) have extensively examined how to deal with the extreme case of transient hunger, namely famine. It is relatively easy to deal with famines as usually, if the government of the country desires, much international aid is available. Even so, famines have led to large-scale death since the Second World War and the question is why governments do not take effective action in time to prevent deaths due to them. Drèze and Sen stress the role that freedom of the press and media play in mobilizing timely and effective action.

Transient hunger which does not lead to famine but nonetheless aggravates hunger has not received as much attention as persistent hunger and famine. Though there is a vast literature on buffer stocks (e.g. Bigman, 1980; Valdes, 1981; Timmer, 1986; and Pinckney, 1988, 1989), the impact on the poor is, generally, not emphasized.

Temporary loss of income is not infrequent. The poor usually suffer a loss of income when agricultural production is reduced or disrupted due to unusual weather or wars. Apart from such sudden drops in real income, a creeping loss may occur if employment opportunities do not keep pace with the growth in the labour force. The real income of the poor can also fall because food prices rise. If the food prices rise the poor, who are often net buyers of food, get less to eat, and there are many reasons for food prices to increase. When the rains fail, the poor not only lose employment opportunity but food prices also increase. Even when the rains fail in a far off rich country, the price of food for the poor can increase. The rich country would either export less foodgrains or import more and the world market prices of foodgrains would rise. A poor importing country would be unable to import as much as before or receive as much food aid as before and its domestic price would increase. Food prices can also increase when a rich country suddenly changes its policy and decides to import more or export less, as happened in the early seventies when the Soviet Union changed its policy and suddenly imported nearly 20 million tonnes (m.t.) of grains. Even a booming domestic economy can aggravate hunger of some poor people if their incomes do not rise as rapidly as increases in food prices because the incomes of others in the economy rise even faster. When input subsidies, such as the fertilizer subsidy, are reduced, food prices rise and hunger increases. Even when the output prices are increased correspondingly, farmers without a sufficient marketable surplus, and there are many of them in the country, will suffer a loss in real income.

Food security for a country is also a matter of poverty and underdevelopment. If it has enough income, it need not be self-sufficient and can import the food it needs. But if it is poor and deficient in food production, it is vulnerable to transient influences that reduce domestic production or increase world market prices.

Thus, the lack of food security is a problem only for poor people and poor nations. While it is conceivable — for example in some nuclear winter scenarios — that global food production may fall so much below the demand that even the rich nations are short of food, supply shortages are very unlikely. The technological food production potential of the world, even without invoking exotic technologies, is so large (Linneman et al., 1979), FAO/UNFPA, 1980) that inability to produce food at any cost is not likely to threaten the food security of rich nations.

How important are these issues of food security in India? What policy options are available to deal with them? These are the questions addressed in this contribution.

II. FOOD INSECURITY IN INDIA

We have argued above that poverty is the principal cause of hunger. Since our poverty line is derived on the basis of a calorie input norm,[1] we can also take it that an estimate of persons below the poverty line is also an estimate of persons hungry. Fig. 1 plots estimates of the percentage of population below the poverty line

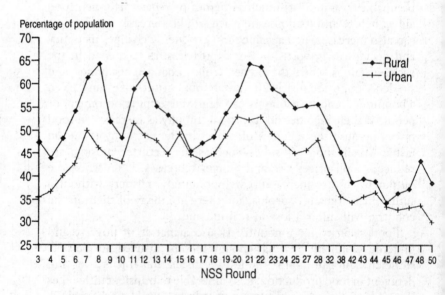

FIG. 1   *Incidence of Hunger — Head Count Ratio (HCR)*

---

[1] The poverty line in India is defined as the total per capita consumption expenditure that will, at 1960–1 prices, provide 2400 Kcal / person / day in rural areas and 2100 Kcal / person / day in urban areas.

(urban and rural). There was no improvement in this head count ratio (HCR) of poverty until the late 1960s. Thereafter, there has been great improvement but many continue to remain poor. Fig. 1 shows that year to year changes in HCR are large, sometimes exceeding 10 percentage points. A change of 5 percentage points is common. Thus large number of persons turn from being non-poor to poor and vice-versa from year to year. The incidence of transient poverty is large.

Ahluwalia (1978) and Dev, et al. (1992) give estimates of various measures of rural poverty by different states in India. The picture is similar to that of poverty trends and extent of transient poverty at the national level.

TABLE 11.1
FOOD SECURITY AT THE NATIONAL LEVEL —
FOODGRAINS (M.T.)

Year	Production	Net imports	Change in stocks	Net availability	Net availability per capita per day (grams)
1982	116.6	1.6	1.3	116.9	454.80
1983	113.3	4.1	2.7	114.7	437.30
1984	133.3	2.4	7.1	128.6	479.70
1985	127.4	−0.4	2.7	124.3	454.00
1986	131.6	0.5	−1.7	133.8	478.10
1987	1·25.5	−0.2	−9.5	134.8	471.80
1988	122.8	3.8	−4.2	130.8	448.50
1989	148.7	1.2	2.7	147.2	494.50
1990	149.7	1.3	6.2	144.8	476.40
1991	154.3	−0.1	−4.4	158.6	510.10
1992	147.3	−0.4	−1.6	148.5	468.80
1993	157.5	3.1	10.8	149.8	464.10
1994	161.2	1.1	7.5	154.8	471.20
1995	167.2	0.4	−1.8	169.4	506.60

SOURCE: *Economic Survey* (various issues).

At the national level a measure of food security would be production, trade, and availability of foodgrains. Table 11.1 shows the variations over time in these measures. It is obvious that production is variable and this variability leads to variability in hunger. Public policy can mitigate this variability in annual availability. Both trade and stock policies have been used by the government for this purpose. Even then, we see that per capita availability has not been wholly smoothened. The standard deviation of net production in million tonnes (m.t.) and net-availability (m.t.) have been 17.46 and 16.11, respectively. The variability in availability has been slightly lower than that in production.

The average per capita availability of foodgrains is an indicator of food security at the national level. With a satisfactory level of availability, other policies should be able to provide adequate food to all citizens and provide food security to individuals. Of course, when average availability is lower, it is the poor whose consumption falls rather than that of the rich. Thus, the variability in the consumption of the poor, i.e. the variability of the number of hungry would be higher than the variability of availability. National level insecurity gets translated into insecurity at the level of individuals.

In principle, the public distribution system was supposed to reduce the variability in the consumption of the poor through provision of subsidized foodgrains through ration shops. By increasing such distribution in years of low availability, the food insecurity of the poor can be reduced.

In calculating availability we have accounted only for changes in public stocks, and believe that private stocks of foodgrains are not carried over from one year to another (barring small amounts to meet short term retail trade inventory requirements). The reason is that the wheat price is always higher in March when the wheat year ends than in April when the wheat harvest starts coming in. It would make no sense for a trader to carry wheat stocks from March to April. Similarly, the price of rice is always higher in September than in October when harvesting begins.

We see that there is considerable food insecurity both at the individual level and at the national level. What are the policy options to provide food security?

III. POLICIES TO PROVIDE FOOD SECURITY TO INDIVIDUALS

III.1 Food Security in the Long Run

The long term solution is of course economic growth that can provide productive employment to all. Once everyone has adequate income, the food system will provide food at a reasonable price to all. Yet economic growth is a necessary but not a sufficient condition for eliminating hunger. Growth creates opportunities for productive employment, but we must create employability and skills among the people to enable them to take up such jobs. This requires that we must invest in education for our people. Even for long-term food security it is important that we now make elementary (primary plus middle school) education compulsory and effective. Certainly, by the year 2000 it should be possible to do so. If this requires that we raise our outlay on education to 6 per cent of GDP from its current level of 3 per cent it would be a worthwhile expenditure. We should note that even at 6 per cent it would be below the level of expenditure, both as a percentage of GDP and in per capita terms, in the East Asian economies.

Apart from creation of skills, there is yet another route along which investment in education brings about long term food security. Studies in many countries, including India, have shown that female literacy results in decline in fertility, infant mortality and better nutritional status for children. A reduction in the growth rate of the population means a quicker increase in per capita income. This is so at least at this stage in India's development where absorption of surplus labour through employment creation is the major challenge facing the country.

While we have not paid adequate attention to education, a critical measure for long term food security, we have taken many measures intended to provide food security in the short term. The most important ones among these are the various schemes of subsidized food distribution, such as the Public Distribution System (PDS), the Rs 2 per kg rice scheme, midday-meal programmes, Rural Works Programmes (RWP) which include the Employment Guarantee Scheme (EGS) of Maharashtra, the Jawahar Rozgar Yojana (JRY), etc. which seek to provide additional income to the poor. We look at these two in turn.

III.2 Food Security Through the PDS

Under the public distribution system, limited quantities per person of selected items of mass consumption, such as wheat, rice, other cereals, sugar, oil, and kerosene are provided at subsidized prices to ration card holders. People are free to buy additional quantities in the open market. The ration cards are now issued to everyone.

The PDS that started out as a rationing scheme during the Second World War was restricted to urban areas alone, and was available to all. During this period, not only was every urban resident entitled to buy from ration shops, but was obliged to as free market sales were not permitted. In a situation of foodgrains shortage this type of PDS made much sense. The PDS restricted urban demand and with urban demand restricted there was adequate food for the rural areas. There was therefore no necessity to extend PDS to rural areas which would have been administratively very difficult. Restricting rationing to urban areas also made sense as the urban population is relatively richer and able to pay more for food, and could have sucked away more than its fair share of foodgrains from the rural areas, which could have led to famines and starvation there. This, as Amartya Sen has pointed out, is what happened during the Bengal famine.

Once, however, free markets were permitted in urban areas, the logic of PDS changed. PDS became an instrument of subsidizing urban consumers and it no longer made sense to extend it to all urban consumers. During the '60s however, the PDS was also a mechanism for selling foodgrains received as aid by the government. Since the cost of obtaining the grain was negligible, the subsidy extended to urban consumers did not burden the government's budget. On the contrary, since the food aid was virtually free, even at the highly subsidized ration prices the government generated surplus from it, which came handy in financing development expenditure. There was thus no compulsion to restrict the PDS only to the poor

Now, however, the PDS is viewed as an important means of providing food security to the poor. The distribution of cereals is supposed to protect the consumption of the poor by ensuring availability of food at a reasonable price. Dantwala (1993) points out that the purpose of introducing PDS was 'to provide food security to the poor, till poverty is eliminated through appropriate macro- and microeconomic policies'. He also argues that the 'PDS should be viewed as an income transfer in favour of the poor'.

In this context I examine the costs and effectiveness of the PDS as a food security measure.

The PDS is not particularly targeted at the poor, yet it is possible to conceive of a situation in which it is perfectly targeted and reaches in the necessary quantities those who need it. How much cereals should be distributed to provide food security? In 1993–4, the poverty gap index for rural India was 9.41 per cent; i.e. the income of the poor needs to be increased by 9.41 per cent to raise their income above the poverty line. It is assumed that this additional income is appropriately distributed among the poor. We can calculate the additional income required as follows:

Necessary	−	*Poverty gap*	×	*No. of*	×	*Poverty*	×	12
additional		*(proportion)*		*poor in*		*line in Rs*		
income				*crores*		*per person*		
(Rs crores)						*per month*		

Since the number of poor in rural India in 1993–4 are estimated to have been 255.6 m., and the rural poverty line was Rs 211.3 / person / month, the additional income necessary amounts to Rs 6098.61 cr. / year. The corresponding figure for urban areas is Rs 1724.33 cr. / year.

The quantity of cereals that should be distributed to the poor through the PDS to provide Rs 7822.94 cr. / year of additional income would depend upon the price subsidy given. With a price subsidy of Rs 3.5/kg the quantity required is 22.35 m.t. / year.

While these amounts look reasonable, it should be emphasized that these are based on assumptions of no leakages and perfect targeting that gives each poor person what s/he needs.

A slightly less stringent targeting requirement is that the PDS reaches only the poor but every poor person gets the same quantity of cereal irrespective of how far below the poverty line s/he is. If we assume that we give enough income support through the PDS to every poor person so that even one in the bottom decile is lifted above the poverty line then we would need a much larger subsidy and much larger quantity of cereals for distribution through the system. For 1993–4, the average expenditure of the bottom decile in rural areas was Rs 100.37 / person / month and the poverty line was Rs 211.30 / person / month. Thus all the 255.6 m. rural poor

TABLE 11.2
IMPLICIT SUBSIDIES FROM CEREALS PURCHASED FROM PDS — RURAL BOTTOM 20 PER CENT OF HOUSEHOLDS

States	Estimated rural population in bottom 20 per cent of households (millions)	No purchase from PDS — Percentage of population	Partial purchase from PDS — Percentage of population	Partial purchase from PDS — Subsidy Rs / capita / 30 days	All purchases from PDS — Percentage of population	All purchases from PDS — Subsidy Rs / capita / 30 days
Punjab	2.90	99.5	0.0	0.00	0.5	0.00
Orissa	5.23	98.8	1.3	1.58	0.0	0.00
Bihar	15.38	98.7	0.7	1.67	0.7	1.72
Uttar Pradesh	26.06	98.6	0.3	1.22	1.1	0.50
Haryana	2.79	96.1	1.5	0.00	2.4	0.00
Manipur	0.21	93.3	2.4	0.60	4.3	1.85
Madhya Pradesh	10.75	88.6	6.7	0.70	4.7	1.90
Rajasthan	7.09	85.5	5.3	2.07	9.1	2.60
West Bengal	9.94	75.3	20.5	1.32	4.2	2.38
Sikkim	0.07	73.9	2.9	0.00	23.2	0.00
Assam	3.53	73.3	24.1	4.72	2.6	8.10
Delhi	0.17	69.6	11.1	0.00	19.3	0.00

States	Estimated rural population in bottom 20 per cent of households (millions)	No purchase from PDS — Percentage of population	Partial purchase from PDS — Percentage of population	Partial purchase from PDS — Subsidy Rs / capita / 30 days	All purchases from PDS — Percentage of population	All purchases from PDS — Subsidy Rs / capita / 30 days
Meghalaya	0.24	69.2	15.0	2.07	15.8	2.35
Jammu & Kashmir	1.24	67.4	15.5	3.51	17.1	8.24
Himachal Pradesh	1.20	66.7	18.6	1.29	14.7	5.19
Maharashtra	9.92	47.4	36.3	0.93	16.4	1.53
Gujarat	5.26	44.6	38.4	1.61	16.9	4.38
Tamil Nadu	8.84	38.3	53.0	1.93	8.7	3.06
Karnataka	6.58	35.6	55.4	1.79	9.0	2.29
Andhra Pradesh	11.59	30.3	56.1	3.62	13.6	3.81
Tripura	0.55	23.6	74.8	3.31	1.7	4.87
Goa, Daman, Diu	0.23	8.7	82.1	4.23	9.2	3.60
Mizoram	0.07	8.7	43.5	6.27	47.8	9.58
Kerala	5.11	6.3	80.4	6.20	13.2	7.42

SOURCE: Parikh (1994).

need to be provided with an income support of Rs 110.93 / person / month. This adds up to Rs 34,024.45 cr. / year and the corresponding figure for cereals distribution through the PDS comes to 97.21 m.t. / year. For the urban areas, the average expenditure of the bottom decile in 1993–4 was Rs 132.84. Thus, a per capita income support of Rs 142.05 / month is required which for the 6.86 m. urban poor implies a total income support of Rs 11693.56 cr. / year and 33.41 m.t. / year of cereals.

Even here we have assumed that only the poor will receive the PDS cereals. Experience with the PDS, however, suggests that restricting it only to the poor may be difficult. Parikh (1994) has analysed who gets how much from PDS cereals based on the NSS 42nd round data (1986–7). The results for rural poor are shown in Table 11.2. It is clear that the income support provided to even to the small fraction of the poor who get it, is meagre in most of the states, and nowhere near the amount necessary to lift them above the poverty line. For the north and central Indian states, which include the bulk of the poor in the country, the implicit income subsidy is less than Rs 2.5 / person / month. It is possible to argue that this is not surprising since at present no particular effort has been made to target the PDS to the poor. However, experience of targeting in Andhra Pradesh is not encouraging. The special white cards meant only for the poor were found to be held by 70 per cent or more of the households.

TABLE 11.3
FOOD SECURITY THROUGH PDS —
RESOURCE REQUIREMENTS

Scheme	Annual expenditure (Rs cr.)	Cereals quantity (m.t.)
1) Perfect targeting — no leakages	7822.94	22.35
2) Equal quantity to all poor but only to poor — no leakages	45718.01	130.62
3) Equal quantity to 70 per cent of the population — 1/3 leakages	88712.85	253.47

NOTES:　(1) Estimates refer to the year 1993–4. (2) Subsidy assumed is Rs 3.5 per kg of cereal. (3) No administrative cost.

If the PDS is to be untargeted and all the bottom 70 per cent of the population (rural and urban) is to get the same level of subsidy, the required expenditure would be Rs 88712.85 cr. / year and the quantity of cereals to be distributed 253.47 m.t. / year

The resources required to provide food security through the PDS are summarized in Table 11.3. The resources, both monetary and the quantity of cereals, required to provide food security through the PDS as it currently operates are way beyond all means at the disposal of the government.

III.3 Food Security through Employment Programmes

Among the various employment programmes, Maharashtra's Employment Guarantee Scheme (EGS) has been the best known and longest running. It has also been widely studied and we know a great deal about it. An excellent review is by Dev (1995).

Maharashtra's EGS which became operative from 26 January 1979, guarantees employment to all adults 18 years and above willing to undertake unskilled manual labour on a piece-rate basis. The act bestows a right to work on every adult person in rural Maharashtra.

The advantages of the EGS are many. It is self-targeting as only the needy will offer themselves for work. The supply of employment has to adjust to demand so that fluctuations in need over seasons and over years are automatically catered for. It is also self liquidating. When economic growth provides opportunities for better paying jobs, people will automatically stop coming for work on EGS programmes. Also, EGS programmes can create productive assets that can increase future rural productivity and employment in the rural economy.

EGS employment fluctuates over years and seasons (Dev, 1995). Thus it created 187.6 m. person days (mpd) of employment in 1986–7, 78 mpd in 1989–90, and 148 mpd in 1992–3. Similarly, in 1990–1 employment in October was 84 mpd but in April it was 331 mpd. Thus EGS is flexible and can deal with transient food insecurity. To deal with transient food security through PDS, it is necessary to know the extent of transient stress and then adjust PDS entitlements approximately. Also, to be effective, this has to be done in time. An elaborate information system and an agile administrative set up are needed. Government bureaucracies are not generally known for their ability to take decisions and act quickly.

How effective has the EGS been as an anti-poverty measure? Person days of unemployment in Maharashtra has fallen much more than in the country as a whole. This is seen in Table 11.4 taken from Dev (1995). Virtually the entire difference in unemployment between Maharashtra and the All India figures can be ascribed to the employment generated by the EGS.

TABLE 11.4

INCIDENCE OF PERSON-DAY UNEMPLOYMENT IN RURAL
MAHARASHTRA AND RURAL INDIA

Year	Maharashtra		All India	
	Male	Female	Male	Female
1972–3	7.7	11.7	6.8	11.2
1977–8	5.9	9.3	7.1	9.2
1983	6.3	7.2	7.5	9.0
1987–8	2.9	3.5	4.6	6.7

SOURCE: Dev (1995).

Despite the EGS, rural poverty has not been eliminated in Maharashtra, though there is some evidence of decline in the depth of poverty (see Dev et al., 1992). Two explanations are offered. First, there are the old, the aged, and the infirm who cannot benefit from the EGS. Some level of poverty can be expected to persist. Second, the EGS wage rate is such that a person working for 300 days a year on it would not be able to lift his family above the poverty line. When the EGS wages were revised upward in 1989, the budgetary allocation for the EGS was not correspondingly increased. Thus some rationing of employment was effected and not all who needed it got employment on the EGS.

Micro studies have shown that a sizeable fraction of expenditure reaches the people as wages. Ravallion (1991) shows that the direct gain to the poor is about 40 to 50 per cent of the government disbursement under the scheme. Ravallion deducts some 10 percentage points from this as the opportunity cost of wages forgone.

From a social point of view this need not be deducted as the jobs vacated by EGS workers would have been available to other workers. This is an important point to recognize. A number of studies have examined who the workers on the EGS are and how many of these are poor (see PEO, 1980; Ravallion, 1991; Walker and Ryan, 1990; Deolalikar and Gaiha, 1993; and Datt and Ravallion, 1992). This debate has missed the point that no matter whether the workers are below or above the poverty line, the EGS employment is a net addition to employment in the society, and that even when some EGS workers are above the poverty line, a part of the work they have vacated would be available to the poor. Thus the benefit to the poor is greater than the benefit from direct employment in the EGS.

Another important benefit of the EGS is that it provides an alternative opportunity for employment to rural workers. It increases their bargaining power and increases rural wages. Gaiha (1996) using the monthly data of the ICRISAT survey of two villages in Maharashtra over 1979–84 finds that agricultural wages are affected in the long term by the EGS wages. If the EGS wage rises by a rupee, agricultural wages would rise by about 18 paise. The impact would of course depend on how much pressure the EGS generates on the labour market which depends on the EGS wage rate, and how easy it is to get employed by the EGS. There may be significant non-linearities in this so that a higher EGS wage rate may lead to a much stronger impact on the agricultural wage rate.

What would it require to provide food security to all the poor in India through an EGS. First of all, the wage rate must be raised so that a person working 300 days a year can lift herself and her dependants above the poverty line. Secondly, the scale of the EGS should be such that it generates wage income equal to the poverty gap. Finally, we should also recognize that while the EGS can be very cost effective, it will not reach the old and the infirm.

What would such a programme of food security for all cost? As noted above, the amount of income support that has to be provided as wages under the EGS would be the same as that required under the 'perfectly targeted PDS' scheme, i.e. Rs 6098.6 cr. to rural poor and Rs 1724.3 cr. to urban poor per year. Assuming that 40 per cent of total expenditure on the EGS reaches the poor as wage income, the total expenditure needed on the EGS is obtained as follows:

Toal wage bill   =   Total expenditure on EGS   ×   Share going as wages

Thus, to provide a total income support of Rs 7822.9 cr. per year as wage payments under the EGS, an expenditure of Rs 19557.3 crores per year is required. This is assuming that all the poor people can be employed under the EGS. However, the old and the infirm amongst the poor are not employable and for them a separate mechanism for direct income transfer is required which should be relatively easy and possible to target. Accordingly, the amount of income support provided as wages under the EGS should exclude the direct income transfer to the non-employable amongst the poor. Assuming that the old and the infirm constitute 5 per cent of the poor, and further that they all belong to the lowest decile, the amount of direct income support required per person would then be the difference between the poverty line and the consumption expenditure of the bottom decile. In 1993–4, this was Rs 110.93 (= 211.3 – 100.37) per person per month in the rural areas and Rs 142.05 (= 274.89–132.84) per person per month in the urban areas. For the 5 per cent of the rural (urban) poor, assuming 100 per cent targeting effectiveness, this would imply an expenditure of approximately Rs 1418 cr. (Rs 494 cr.) per year. The annual EGS wage bill for the remaining poor would be Rs 4680 (6098–1418) cr. and Rs 1230 (1724–494) cr. in the rural and urban areas, respectively, which would imply a total expenditure on the EGS of Rs 14775 cr per year. Together, the fund requirement for the EGS and direct income transfer to the old and the infirm amongst the poor would add up to Rs 16687 cr. per year.

The resource requirements of the EGS and direct transfer to the old and the infirm are thus modest in comparison with that for the PDS, and it should therefore be feasible to pursue a vigorous policy of providing food security to all through the EGS so long as there is sufficient foodgrain available in the country to pursue such a policy. This raises the question of food security at the national level.

IV. National Level Food Security

IV.1 Price Stabilization is the Key

In the preceding section, the discussion on individual level food security implicitly assumed that at the national level there is adequate food. This is because our calculation of necessary income support assumed more or less normal market conditions. Thus, if the measures are to work effectively we need to ensure that at the national level there is food security, i.e. adequate availability of food.

In this section, we define a notion of national level food security and estimate how much it would cost to provide it.

We consider that if food prices are stabilized at some reasonable level, then the country is food secure. This is so because at that price everyone's demand would be met. To stabilize the price, we consider buffer stock operations along with trade (import and export) and find a cost minimizing strategy. A stock-trade strategy of price stabilization implies that in some years when stocks are not adequate, trade will be resorted to. The critical decision is what are the maximum stocks of rice and wheat that would ensure stable prices and would minimize the cost of price stabilization. In this section, we attempt to answer this question.

Here we should note that in the context of national level food security, the PDS operations can be separated from buffer stock operations. While the purpose of PDS is one of distribution of the food grain to the needy, buffer stocks are meant to ensure that adequate amounts of grain are available especially during times of production shortages. Indeed, these two operations could even be carried out by two different agencies.

Also, once adequate availability at the national level is ensured, PDS operations can be based on open market purchases. Thus, we consider buffer stock and trade operations only for price stabilization. This simplifies the analysis.

To simplify the analysis further, I restrict myself to wheat and rice, which are the major cereals that are stocked and traded. They also constitute the bulk of foodgrains production in the country. For example, in 1994–5, rice and wheat production (together) was 146.6 m.t. out of a total cereals production of 177 m.t. and total foodgrain production of 191.1 m.t. Similarly, rice and wheat stocks on 30 September 1996 were 20.1 m.t. out of the total cereals stock of 23.3 m.t.

As already pointed out, private traders have no incentives to carry rice or wheat stocks from one year to the next. Price stabilization has to be done by a public programme. Jha and Srinivasan (1996) have examined a combined stock-trade policy for stabilizing prices and operating the PDS in the context of private traders' stock operations. Our analysis is simple in that we have kept PDS operations separate and have not included private traders' operations on a priori grounds. The results are therefore clearer and easier to interpret.

IV.2   Estimation of Variabilities

Price variability arises due to variability of production, demand and world prices. In designing a price stabilization strategy which relies on trade, we must also account for the large country effect of India's trade in wheat and rice on world prices. Ganeshkumar and Parikh (1997) analyse the problem and provide optimum stock-trade policy for price stabilization which accounts for these variabilities. The details of the principal results presented in this section and the methodology are given in their paper. We first characterize the various variabilities.

Production

The principal source of production variability is that in rainfall. Often, production variability is characterized by looking at deviations from the trend line of yields over historical data. Such a procedure misses out on two important effects. One, the expansion of irrigation may have lowered the impact of weather on yield / production variability. Two, the widespread adoption of high-yield varieties (HYVs) may also have altered the variability. In order to get around this problem, we have used a simulation model in which we simulate production of rice and wheat under the irrigation and HYV level corresponding to 1992–3. We used the AGRIM model (Narayana, et al., 1991) which is an empirically estimated and validated applied general equilibrium model. A number of simulations were carried out in which rainfall variability was characterized by letting the rainfall correspond to the historically observed pattern over different years. The resulting

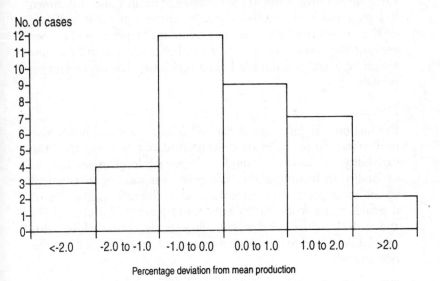

FIG. 2 *Variability in Production — Rice*

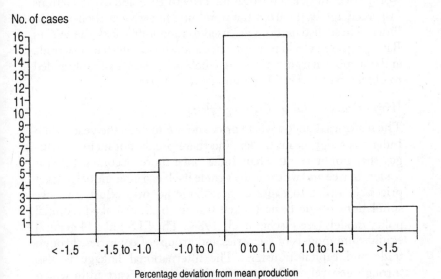

FIG. 3 *Variability in Production — Wheat*

variability in production (in percentage of mean value) are shown in Figs. 2 and 3 for rice and wheat. It may be noted that in 32 out of 37 cases the rice (wheat) output is within ±2.0 per cent (±1.5 per cent) of the average value. The spread of irrigation and the new technology has indeed made Indian agriculture less dependant on rainfall.

Demand

Production variability causes variability in income and hence also in demand. Since the price is maintained at a constant level the variability in demand around its expected level arises due to variability in income alone. We relate variabilities in rice and wheat production to income variability. Income elasticities of demand, taken from Radhakrishna and Ravi (1992) are 0.3979 and 0.3831 for rice and wheat, respectively. These along with variability in income provide estimates of demand variabilities for rice and wheat.

World Prices Variability

World market prices vary from year to year. We take the data on world prices of rice and wheat for 1969 to 1985 and use deviations in percentage terms from the trend line to arrive at their variabilities. These distributions are used to randomly shock the World Bank projected world prices for rice and wheat. International trade and transport margins, assumed to be 5 per cent, are suitably added to obtain export (f.o.b.) and import (c.i.f.) prices.

World Prices — Large Country Effects

The historical data on world prices do not include the years when India was a significant trader, and therefore do not include changes that might result when India once more becomes a major trader. In rice and wheat India's trade itself can alter global market prices. In order to capture these large country effects, we use simulations of the Basic Linked system, BLS, of linked national policy models (see Fischer et al., 1988). The BLS links 34 general equilibrium models of countries and groups of countries through trade and capital transfers. The international linkage is also through general equilibrium. Simulations were carried in which India's trade of rice and wheat were set to different levels. The resulting world market price was compared with the reference run price. In this way we obtained the large country effects of India's trade on world prices. These are shown in Table 11.5. It is seen that wheat prices hardly change as a consequence of India's trade, whereas for both exports and imports the rice price changes substantially. These impacts were added to the randomly perturbed world prices.

TABLE 11.5
PERCENTAGE CHANGES IN WORLD PRICE
DUE TO INDIA'S TRADE OF RICE AND WHEAT

Quantity traded (m.t.)	*Rice*		*Wheat*	
	Imports	*Exports*	*Imports*	*Exports*
0.5	4.02	–3.69	0.57	–0.57
1.0	8.18	–7.11	1.56	–1.14
1.5	12.47	–10.26	2.27	–1.70
2.0	18.31	–11.87	2.98	–2.27
2.5	24.01	–12.94	3.55	–2.70
3.0	32.46	–14.42	4.26	–3.27
3.5	40.24	–16.16	4.97	–3.84
4.0	51.84	–17.64	5.68	–4.40
4.5	59.96	–19.05	6.53	–4.83
5.0	72.10	–20.52	7.24	–5.40

SOURCE: Simulations by us using BLS, a linked system, of national agricultural policy models.

Cost of Stock Operations

The Food Corporation of India (FCI) has a monopoly in operation of food stocks in the country. Its transaction costs and costs of storage are much higher than the comparable costs of private traders. Jha and Srinivasan (1996) estimate that these costs for the private traders are only about 50 per cent of the costs incurred by FCI as reported in the Budget Documents of the Government of India for 1996–7.

We have carried out a sensitivity analysis of FCI's costs, taking it to be 100, 75, 50, and 25 per cent of its present costs in alternative runs.

IV.3 The Target Price

We can select any set of prices as the target prices at which rice and wheat prices are stabilized. The selected prices would have a profound impact on the welfare of the populations. Even the number of persons below the poverty line changes when food prices change. Since India has been in more or less a self sufficient regime over recent years we consider target prices as the prices at which trend level supply will equal demand.

With a set of prices that are higher (lower) the country would be an exporter (importer) in most of the years. The problem of price stabilization becomes a bit trivial in such cases. For example, if the target price is set much above the modal supply clearing market price, we are always a net exporter. The optimal policy in such a case would be to always export the surplus. Of course, if the surplus is unusually large in a given year, we may want to hold the stock for some time and sell it later. On the other hand, if the price is set to a much lower level India becomes a net importer every year and we can conceive of a domestic buffer stock built on imports alone. Yet given the high domestic storage cost of FCI, the optimal strategy in these cases are likely to be to export each year's surplus or import each year's needs. In any case, the approach used here could be easily applied to any other level of target price for stabilization.

IV.4 The Scheme of Analysis

We start with given stocks of wheat and rice; project production on the basis of trend; perturb it by randomly selected weather shock; calculate changes in incomes due to changes in agricultural production and corresponding changes in demand, using income elasticities; calculate domestic supply by adding the initial stocks to production; calculate excess demand; if excess demand is positive import needed grains; if excess demand is negative, i.e. there is excess supply, build up buffer stock up to the maximum storage limit; if the maximum storage limit is reached export the rest; update the level of closing stocks; repeat this for a time horizon of 10 years; and finally compute the total cost of such stock and trade operations. This constitutes one simulation run. We repeat such a run 1000 times and look at the properties of these sets of runs. This is one policy option. We do these for a set of policy options and compare them to find the optimal policy. Details are given in Ganesh Kumar and Parikh (1997).

IV.5 The Results

The results of our simulation exercise show that optimal stock levels depend critically on storage costs. The impact of discount rate is marginal. It is worth noting that even with a stock level of 3.5 m.t. of rice, for most of the years when imports are necessary, rice imports are less than 3.5 m.t. (average + 1 standard deviation). Imports exceed 6.7 m.t. (average + 3 standard deviations) only in 0.27 per cent of the years; i.e. less than 1 year in a hundred. The story is similar for wheat. Even with only 0.5 m.t. of stock, imports exceed 2.2 m.t. (average + 3 standard deviations) in less than 1 year in a hundred and exports exceed 1.7 m.t. in less than 1 year in a hundred years.

These results should not be surprising as we have ensured that the prices of rice and wheat are stabilized at the levels that equate average supply to average demand for each of the two food grains. Implicitly we are following a self-sufficiency policy. If the target price levels were to be raised, demand would have been lowered and much greater exports would have resulted. Similarly, if the prices were lowered, imports would have increased. We must of course recognize that in this simplified partial analysis, there is no guarantee that the price levels are such that they would either induce farmers to produce what is assumed or that they would generate the demand that is assumed. Only a general equilibrium model like AGRIM (Narayana, et al., 1991) can bring about such consistency.

It would however be too unwieldy to do large scale stochastic simulations with a general equilibrium model like AGRIM. Nonetheless, the growth rates of demand and supply are consistent with the growth rates of the Indian economy at 8 to 9 per cent per year over the next 10 years. We have taken these to be on the high side to give the question of national level food security greater interest. At a lower level of growth of demand, the likely output growth may make the country a more or less regular exporter, in which case the national level food security problem becomes trivial.

The optimum maximum stock level is one that minimizes the net present value of the costs of stock and trade operations. The optimal buffer stocks vary from 4.0 m.t. to 8.5 m.t. for rice, depending on the costs of storage operations, whereas for wheat it varies only from 0.5 to 2.5 m.t. With these levels of stock and supplemental trade it is possible to stabilize domestic prices at minimal cost. Table 11.6 summarizes the optimal maximum permissible stock levels.

TABLE 11.6
OPTIMUM MAXIMUM STOCKS LEVELS FOR RICE AND WHEAT
(000 TONNES)

Discount rate (per cent)		Current cost*	75 per cent of current cost	50 per cent of current cost	25 per cent of current cost
Rice	12	4000	5000	6500	8500
	14	4000	5000	6500	8500
	16	4000	5000	6000	8500
Wheat	12	500	500	1500	2500
	14	500	500	1500	2500
	16	500	500	1500	2500

* Refers to cost of stock operations of the Food Corporation of India (FCI).

V. CONCLUSIONS

What should be our policies for food security?

We have argued here that a nationwide EGS with increased wages and easy access to all can provide individual level food security against both chronic and transient hunger to the employable hungry. This can be done at a cost of about Rs 14775 cr. per year. Along with EGS, however, a PDS to reach the old and the infirm who cannot work on EGS would be required. Even counting for that, the EGS with supplementary PDS for 5 per cent of the poor requires around Rs 16700 crores.

We have also shown that even if we are able to restrict PDS only to the poor, it will still cost about Rs 45700 crores to attain similar results. The EGS has the further advantage that the expenditure can generate productive assets. But even if the EGS generates no assets it still remains a more cost effective proposition and is the cheaper of the two solutions.

For the national level food security, a stock-trade policy can ensure availability to stabilize the prices of wheat and rice at modest stock levels.

From our simulations, the message comes out loud and clear. If the buffer stock operations are to be managed at no better efficiency than the FCI's current level, then the optimal stock levels are only 4.0 m.t. and 0.5 m.t. for rice and wheat, respectively.

If the efficiency is to reach the level of private traders (i.e. 50 per cent of the current costs of the FCI) then the optimal stock for rice is 6.0 to 6.5 m.t. and for wheat 1.5 m.t

But if these operations are to be super efficient and costs reduced to only 25 per cent of the present level, even then the stock levels for rice and wheat do not exceed 8.5 m.t. and 2.5 m.t., respectively.

These levels of stocks, combined with a liberal trade policy would stabilize domestic prices of wheat and rice and thus would provide national level food security.

REFERENCES

Ahluwalia, M.S. (1978): 'Rural Poverty and Agricultural Performance in India', *Journal of Development Studies*, 14 (3).

Bigman, D. (1980): 'The Theory of Commodity Price Stabilization and Buffer Stocks Operation', CAER, Israel.

Dantwala, M.L. (1993): 'Agricultural Policy, Prices and Public Distribution System: A Review', *Indian Journal of Agricultural Economics*, 48 (2).

Datt, G. and M. Ravallion (1992): *Behavioural Responses to Work Fares: Evidence for Rural India* (Washington, DC: World Bank).

Deolalikar, A. and R. Gaiha (1993): 'Targeting of Rural Public Works: Are Women Less Likely to Participate?', Discussion Paper Series 93–05, Institute for Economic Research, University of Washington, Seattle.

Dev, S.M. (1995): 'India's (Maharashtra) Employment Guarantee Scheme: Lessons from Long Experience', in Joachim von Braun (ed.), *Employment for Poverty Reduction and Food Security* (Washington, DC: IFPRI).

Dev, S.M., M.H. Suryanarayana and K.S. Parikh (1992): 'Rural Poverty in India: Incidence, Issues and Policies', *Asian Development Review*, 10 (1).

Drèze, J. and A.K. Sen (1989): *Hunger and Public Action* (Oxford: Clarendon Press).

FAO/UNFPA (1980): 'Potential Population Supporting Capacities of Lands in the Developing World', FAO, Rome.

FAO, (1986): 'The Fifth World Food Survey', Rome.

Fischer, G., K. Frohberg, M.A. Keyzer, K.S. Parikh and F. Rabar (1987): *Hunger: Beyond the Reach of the Invisible Hand* (Amsterdam: Martinus Nijhoff).

Fischer, G., K. Frohberg, M.A. Keyzer and K.S. Parikh (1988): *Linked National Models: A Tool for International Food Policy Analysis* (Dordrecht: Kluwer Academic Publishers).

Gaiha, R. (1996): 'Wages, Participation and Targeting — The Case of the Employment Guarantee Scheme in India', *Journal of International Development*, December.

Ganeshkumar, A. and Kirit S. Parikh (1997): 'A Stock Trade Policy for National Level Food Security for India', mimeo, Indira Gandhi Institute of Development Research, Mumbai.

Government of India (1996): *Budget Documents*, Ministry of Finance, New Delhi.

Jha, S. and P.V. Srinivasan (1996): 'Grain Price Stabilization Policies in India', Draft Report Prepared for the World Bank, Indira Gandhi Institute of Development Research, Mumbai.

Linneman, H., J. de Hoogh, M.A. Keyzer and H.D.J. van Heemst (1978): *MOIRA: A Model for International Relations in Agriculture* (Amsterdam: North Holland).

Narayana, N.S.S., K.S. Parikh and T.N. Srinivasan (1991): *Agriculture, Growth and Redistribution of Income: Policy Analysis with a General Equilibrium Model of India* (Delhi: Allied Publishers (India) / North-Holland).

Parikh, K.S. (1994): 'Who Gets How Much From PDS?: How Effectively Does It Reach the Poor?', *Sarvekshana*, January–March.

Parikh, K.S. and W. Tims (1986): 'From Hunger in Abundance to Abundance without Hunger', Executive Report 13, International Institute for Applied Systems Analysis, Luxembourg.

PEO (Programme Evaluation Organization) (1980): 'Joint Evaluation Report on Employment Guarantee Scheme in Maharashtra', New Delhi.

Pinckney, T.C. (1988): 'Storage, Trade and Price Policy Under Production Instability: Maize in Kenya', Research Report 71, IFPRI, Washington, DC.

Pinckney, T.C. (1989): 'The Demand for Public Storage of Wheat in Pakistan', Research Report 77, IFPRI, Washington, DC.

Planning Commission (1985): 'Report of the Working Group for Evolving an Acceptable Methodology for Identification of the Poor', New Delhi.

Radhakrishna, R. and C. Ravi (1992): 'Effects of Growth, Relative Price and Preferences on Food and Nutrition', *Indian Economic Review*, Special Number.

Ravallion, M. (1991): 'Reaching the Rural Poor Through Public Employment: Arguments, Evidence and Lessons from South Asia', *The World Bank Research Observer*, 6 (2).

Sen, A.K., (1981): *Poverty and Famines* (Oxford: Clarendon Press).

Srinivasan, T.N. (1981): 'Malnutrition: Some Measurement and Policy Issues', *Journal of Development Economics*, 8 (1).

Sukhatme, P.V. (1978): 'Assessment of Adequacy of Diets at Different Income Levels', *Economic and Political Weekly*, Special Number, August.

Tendulkar, S.D. and L.R. Jain (1995): 'Economic Reforms and Poverty', *Economic and Political Weekly*, 30 (23).

Timmer, P.C. (1986): *Getting Prices Right: The Scope and Limits of Agricultural Price Policy* (Ithaca, New York and London: Cornell University Press).

Valdes, A. (ed.) (1981): *Food Security for Developing Countries* (Boulder, Colorado: Westview Press).

Walker, T.S. and J.G. Ryan (1990): *Village and Household Economies in India's Semi-Arid Tropics* (Baltimore: Johns Hopkins University Press).

World Bank (1986): *Poverty and Hunger: Issues and Options for Food Security in Developing Countries* (Washington, DC: World Bank).

—— (1990): *Handbook of Trade and Development Statistics, 1985* (Geneva: World Bank).

12

Indian Economic Policy Reforms and Poverty: An Assessment

*Suresh D. Tendulkar**

INTRODUCTION

To Manmohan Singh goes the credit of decisively changing the economic agenda before the nation, namely the necessity of moving to a globally integrated and dynamically efficient market-driven economy by putting in place wide-ranging economic policy reforms aimed at stabilization of the macroeconomy and structural adjustment. Various political parties — both national and regional — may quibble about specific components of the reform process as they adversely affect their immediate individual constituencies. There is however a political consensus about the non-reversibility of the direction of the reform process. Similarly, various discerning observers have been dissatisfied with the quality of fiscal deficit reduction, unhappy about the slowing down of the pace of reforms during the second half of his tenure, and worried over the economic costs of compromises he had to make under political compulsions. Nobody can however deny the

* This contribution could not have been written without the collaboration of my long-time co-author L.R. Jain. I am most grateful to him for permitting its publication under my sole authorship. My grateful thanks are due to Ian Little for his detailed comments. An earlier version of it was presented at the Fourteenth European Conference on Modern Asian Studies at Copenhagen in August 1996. Helpful comments from Ashok Gulati, Vijay Joshi, S. Mahendra Dev, B.S. Minhas, and K. Sundaram are gratefully acknowledged. I accept sole responsibility for the views and opinions expressed and of any shortcomings that may persist.

decisive and correct direction he successfully gave to economic policies and thereby to the economy.

In connection with the reform process initiated since July 1991, legitimate concern has been expressed about the possible adverse impact of reforms on the poor, especially during the transition period from the nearly closed and over-regulated to a globalized, market driven economy. This contribution seeks to explore and assess the relationship between the Indian economic reforms and poverty on the basis of the available empirical evidence on the poverty situation from July 1991 to June 1994 emerging from the four rounds of the National Sample Surveys on household consumer expenditure conducted during this period. With this objective, sect. II provides a very brief background to Indian economic reforms. Sect. III discusses the concept of poverty and the interpretation of the three poverty indicators used here. Certain regularities about the movements in the poverty indicators during the pre-reform period from 1970–1 to 1990–1 and possible underlying factors are indicated in sect. IV. This paves the way for the discussion of the poverty situation during the post-reform period in sect. V. In this context, it is important to note that the observed poverty situation is the outcome of the reform-related policies *as well as* reform-unrelated forces with their autonomous internal dynamics that may reinforce or counteract the impact of reform-related policies. An effort is made in this section to assess how far the observed changes in the poverty situation can be directly or indirectly *attributed to* reform-related policies. Brief concluding observations appear in the final sect. VI.

II. Indian Economic Reforms: The Background

For over three decades of planning since 1950–1, India followed the strategy of import-substitution centred industrialization in an economy that, as a consequence, was virtually insulated from the rest of the world through a variety of rigid restrictions on imports and all transactions involving foreign exchange. Internally too, the large-scale private organized sector was subjected to investment licensing and various other direct discretionary controls involving case by case disposal. These controls constricted the flexibility of the private organized sector in responding to changes in preferences and technology in a functioning market economy.

They also induced directly unproductive rent-seeking activities at the cost of productive investment. The distributional consequences of this policy regime were ambiguous on *a priori* reasoning. In practice, this regime tended to accentuate inequitable urban–rural, or organized–unorganized duality in the Indian economy (Tendulkar and Sundaram, 1995).

The oil shocks of the nineteen-seventies forced the Indian economy into greater participation in international trade because of the dependence on imported oil and the resulting need to pay for rising foreign exchange outlays on petroleum, oil, and lubricants (POL). India easily surmounted these shocks (Mitra and Tendulkar, 1994). The subsequent accumulation of both food and foreign exchange stocks prompted a gradual and halting process of deregulation of the counterproductive aspects of the direct discretionary control regime since the late nineteen-seventies. This phase of deregulation concentrated on removing entry-restrictions through delicensing of selected industries, introducing limited flexibility through broad-banding and other related measures, and made imports easier by relaxing quantitative restrictions mostly on non-competing imports (Pursell and Sharma, 1996) while raising import tariff rates.

Following the foreign exchange liquidity crisis, a wide-ranging process of policy reforms has been initiated since July 1991. It has two components. First, the stabilization of the macroeconomy was aimed at controlling the fiscal and balance of payments deficits and maintaining a low rate of inflation. This was sought to be achieved through an appropriate exchange rate, interest rate, fiscal and monetary policies. The second component of structural adjustment aimed at opening up the economy to international trade and investment through a movement in policies towards a neutral foreign trade regime. A third component was the deregulation of domestic markets. All these components are expected to help the Indian economy on to a higher growth path.

There appears to be a wide consensus that rapid economic growth is a very important instrument for making a lasting impact on reduction in absolute poverty in low-income countries. Barring very few Latin American countries with very extreme and persistent initial economic inequalities (Fishlow, 1995), in most other countries where rapid economic growth has taken place, absolute poverty has been reduced (Fields, 1995; World Bank, 1995). In the Indian context, the avowedly growth-oriented programmes of agricultural transformation — the green revolution — were expected by some critics to accentuate inequalities, result in immiserization and cause a red revolution (see, for example, Frankel, 1974). But those fears proved to be incorrect (see Parthasarathy (1991) for a recent reexamination). Similar apprehensions were also expressed when the rate of growth of Indian per capita GDP in real terms more than doubled during the 1980s. These, too, proved to be misplaced (Tendulkar and Jain, 1995a, 1995b). Given the evidence cited above, the favourable impact of economic reforms on reduction in poverty can be reasonably taken for granted once the economy shifts to a higher growth path. The critical question, therefore, relates to the period of transition before the economy shifts to a sustainable higher growth path.

During the transition period, a number of factors can impact negatively on the poverty situation. Thus, the reduction of the fiscal deficit is expected to bring about a contraction of economic activity, thereby adversely affecting employment and hence poverty. The brunt of fiscal adjustment may (but not necessarily) also fall on public expenditure earmarked for poverty alleviation and the social sectors of health and education. Structural adjustment policies, too, might result in a higher rate of unemployment and/or a decline in real wages.

A word of caution is warranted on at least four counts.

One, a causal connection is *not* necessarily warranted without closer examination just because *a priori* expectations about an adverse impact of reforms on poverty and the observed worsening of the poverty situation during the reform process happen to coincide. This is because the observed poverty situation is caused by at least two broad sets of factors (a) the reform-related policies, and (b) what we may call for want of a better term, 'structural' factors that are usually slow-changing and largely governed by their autonomous internal dynamics. The reform-related policies may either directly impact on the poor or indirectly through their impact on the set of structural factors. The structural factors, including other purely exogenous forces (such as weather-related shocks), influence poverty in ways that may counteract or reinforce the effect of reform-related policies. The observed variations in poverty indicators (examined later in this contribution) reflect the end-result of a complex interaction between the reform-related policies and the structural as well as exogenous causal factors.

Two, as regards public outlays impacting on poverty, it is possible to maintain or even raise their level at the cost of outlays on other items in the budget even during the phase of fiscal contraction. This is a function of political economy and need not be directly related to the underlying rationale of the reform-related policies.

Three, improving the quality and cost effectiveness of public outlays is an integral part of the reforms process, depending on organizational improvements, changes in delivery mechanisms, and so on, so that the same or reduced outlays might be more effective.

Four, in a continental country like India with wide regional variations in administrative and organizational capabilities, the corresponding variations in the effectiveness of utilization of the same amount of public outlays are only to be expected. Inferences about the impact on poverty from the observed variations in budgetary outlays require to be moderated in the light of this and the previous cautionary observation.

Finally, the focal point of reforms being the urban organized industrial sector, and given the closer financial, administrative, and organizational links of the government machinery with the urban than with the rural sector, we expect reform-related policies to have an immediate and greater impact on the urban organized sector with a second order impact on the urban informal sector, and a lagged direct impact on the rural sector. The immediate impact on the rural sector is more likely to be indirect via their effects on the structural factors.

III. POVERTY: CONCEPT AND MEASURES

Poverty defined as socially perceived deprivation with regard to basic needs has several facets. In this contribution we focus entirely on the poverty measures based on exogenously specified normative poverty lines that reflect the socially perceived minimum living standard (MLS for short) with reference to a certain basket of basic needs. The MLS-based poverty indicators need to be clearly distinguished from socially perceived deprivation with regard to individual basic needs such as education, health and nutrition or food. The measurement of poverty in these dimensions requires different databases that are governed by different sets of causal forces and are affected differently by different macroeconomic and structural adjustment policies.

We interpret MLS-based poverty in terms of a lack of purchasing power at the household level to maintain a certain normative basket of basic needs translated into a basket of *privately* purchased goods and services. While the strictly normative concepts of basic needs and public provisioning for their satisfaction go together in public perception, the necessity of permitting market-based private purchases requires justification and arises from a variety of considerations. To begin with, differences in the character of different basic needs require repetitive (e.g. in nutrient intakes), more infrequent (e.g. in clothing), or contingent (e.g. in medical treatment) intakes/purchases of goods and services. In many of these (e.g. in food and clothing habits), heterogeneity in consumer preferences needs to be respected. In others (e.g. in travel and housing) there exist alternative means (or 'technologies') to satisfy the same basic need. It is also necessary to recognize individual-specific discretionary elements in the extent of satisfaction of certain needs such as a need to be mobile or a need for social interaction. In all these cases, market-based purchases rather than public provisioning is clearly a more cost-effective ways of satisfying the concerned basic needs. Equally, rigidly specified quantitative norms that are uniformly applied to the entire population do not make sense in the satisfaction of all basic needs.

In the Indian context, the poverty line reflecting the minimum necessary private purchasing power has been specified in terms of per capita (monthly) total (consumer) expenditure (pcte in short). Both the poverty line as well as the summary indicators of poverty (based on the poverty line) use as database the household consumer expenditure surveys (HCES), which typically collect from each household the information on consumption/purchase of different items over a given reference period of a week/fortnight/month. This contribution is based on the periodically conducted National Sample Surveys (NSS) of household consumer expenditure that use one month as a reference period.

Three brief points need to be emphasized about the poverty line based on HCES. One, MLS being shaped by social perceptions, is never precisely defined but is expected to lie in a narrow range. Two, the uniform nutritional calorie norm of 2100 (urban) or 2400 (rural) used in the Indian context (see Perspective Planning Division, 1979) merely acts as a convenient anchor for estimating the pcte defining the poverty line. In this context, it is important to recognize that a lower than normative calorie intake does not necessarily reflect nutritional or food poverty, nor does the lower than poverty cutoff level of pcte necessarily indicate undernutrition. Measurement of undernutrition requires different yardsticks and survey techniques. Three, even the adopted calorie norms do not possess an objective sanctity (see, Sukhatme (ed.), 1982). In view of these three points, the poverty line is to be treated as an approximate point in a range in which the MLS is expected to lie. As a result, there exists inescapable and inherent elements of arbitrariness in fixing the numerical value of the poverty line. Consequently, it is desirable (as we do subsequently to a limited degree) to experiment with alternative poverty lines.

In this contribution, we propose to present three measures of poverty belonging to the Foster–Greer–Thorebecke class (Foster, Greer, and Thorebecke, 1984). These measures capture three different dimensions of poverty.

The first of these, the headcount ratio (HCR) indicates the proportion of the population below the poverty line. This is the most widely used measure in India.

The poverty-gap index (PGI) is defined by the ratio of the aggregate poverty gap of all poor households to the minimum normative aggregate expenditure for the entire (poor as well as non-poor) population (poverty line multiplied by the total population). This is described as the depth measure of poverty. The reasoning is as follows. If you have two situations with the same population and the same headcount ratio, the one with a higher value of PGI has a larger number of poor who are further away from the poverty line than the other and hence reflects a greater depth of poverty.

The third measure, labelled FGT^*, has as its components, the headcount ratio, the (squared) poverty-gap ratio and the relative inequality amongst the poor as measured by the squared coefficient of variation. Because of its distributional sensitivity and because it incorporates HCR and a variant of PGI, this is regarded as a comprehensive measure capturing the severity of poverty.

As discussed earlier in this section, there are irreducible elements of arbitrariness in specifying the numerical value of the poverty line that is expected to capture the minimum living standard (in terms of per capita total consumer expenditure at the household level) separating the poor from the non-poor. For this reason, we use two alternative poverty lines, namely (a) the official poverty line used by the Planning Commission, and (b) an alternative (lower) poverty line which is lower by about 12 to 15 per cent than the official one. (For specific levels of poverty lines, see notes to Table 1). We refer to measures based on (a) as simply 'poverty' and those based on (b) as reflecting 'lower-end poverty'.

Table 12.1 presents the three poverty measures based on two alternative poverty lines, separately for the rural and the urban population, for the four post-reform rounds (lines 11 to 14) along with comparable measures going back to 1970–1 to provide a perspective.[1]

---

[1] We may mention that the official estimates of poverty in India are solely in terms of the headcount ratio. Our estimates of headcount ratio, given in column (4) of Table 12.1, are based on the official poverty line but differ from the official estimates. The differences can be traced to two sources: (a) differences in the deflators used to adjust the poverty line to prices prevalent during the survey periods of various NSS rounds; and (b) presence or absence of the pro rata adjustment factor given by the ratio of per capita private final consumption expenditure from national accounts statistics to per capita household consumer expenditure (for the rural plus urban population) derived from the corresponding NSS rounds. Quantitatively, the adjustment factor (b) makes a significant difference in (lowering) the level of the headcount ratio in any given year than (a). Headcount ratio based on this adjustment factor, in effect, combines the absolute level of per capita total expenditure from national accounts with the *relative* size distribution from NSS. In our view, the pro rata adjustment is not justified. Our estimates of headcount ratio in Table 12.1 are entirely based on NSS with regard to both the level of per capita total expenditure and the relative size distribution. Till recently, the official estimates had been based on the pro rata adjustment (b). In the Press Note issued on 11 March 1997 by the Planning Commission, the Government of India has also taken a decision to do away with the adjustment factor (b). Differences arising from different deflators persist. However, our estimates of price deflators (for the years from 1970–1 to 1988–9 and 1993–4) are based on more detailed price data and more appropriate procedure than those in the official estimates. We have also experimented with alternative poverty lines and given PGI and FGT* besides headcount ratio in Table 12.1.

TABLE 12.1
POVERTY INDICATORS FOR FOURTEEN TIME POINTS FROM
1970–1 TO 1993–4 BASED ON TWO ALTERNATIVE POVERTY LINES: ALL INDIA RURAL AND URBAN

Sl. No.	NSS survey period	Gini coefficient	Poverty indicators						
			HCR_1	HCR_2	PGI_1	PGI_2	FGT^*_1	FGT^*_2
(1)	(2)	(3)	(4)	(5)	(6)	(7)	(8)	(9)
			Rural					
1.	1970–1	0.28796	57.33	45.29	0.1757	0.1248	0.0731	0.0481
2.	1972–3	0.30514	57.21	45.90	0.1793	0.1281	0.0754	0.0501
3.	1973–4	0.28190	56.17	44.50	0.1675	0.1163	0.0672	0.0430
4.	1977–8	0.31202	54.47	43.06	0.1653	0.1166	0.0685	0.0451
5.	1983	0.30055	49.02	37.54	0.1386	0.0944	0.0545	0.0345
6.	1986–7	0.30191	45.21	34.04	0.1221	0.0810	0.0460	0.0281
7.	1987–8	0.30152	44.88	32.44	0.1126	0.0714	0.0404	0.0238
8.	1988–9	0.29522	42.23	29.97	0.1020	0.0631	0.0354	0.0203
9.	1989–90	0.28239	36.69	24.84	0.0840	0.0500	0.0279	0.0154
10.	1990–1	0.27723	37.48	25.97	0.0911	0.0569	0.0316	0.0180

Sl. No.	NSS survey period	Gini coefficient	Poverty indicators					
			HCR_1	HCR_2	PGI_1	PGI_2	FGT_1^*	FGT_2^*
(1)	(2)	(3)	(4)	(5)	(6)	(7)	(8)	(9)
11.	1991	0.31096	40.07	28.12	0.0933	0.0561	0.0311	0.0171
12.	1992	0.29780	46.12	33.95	0.1181	0.0755	0.0423	0.0247
13.	1993	0.28430	44.19	30.94	0.1046	0.0639	0.0354	0.0197
14.	1993–4	0.28544	39.65	27.65	0.0929	0.0564	0.0314	0.0175
				Urban				
1.	1970–1	0.34560	45.89	37.06	0.1339	0.0961	0.0532	0.0353
2.	1972–3	0.34538	47.00	37.69	0.1357	0.0963	0.0532	0.0349
3.	1973–4	0.31688	49.20	39.33	0.1388	0.0975	0.0531	0.0342
4.	1977–8	0.33679	42.86	33.47	0.1213	0.0860	0.0481	0.0320
5.	1983	0.33360	38.33	28.77	0.0995	0.0674	0.0366	0.0231
6.	1986–7	0.35606	35.39	27.24	0.0949	0.0651	0.0354	0.0225
7.	1987–8	0.35586	36.52	27.23	0.0934	0.0626	0.0338	0.0211
8.	1988–9	0.35625	35.07	26.28	0.0891	0.0596	0.0319	0.0196

Table 12.1 (cont.)

Sl. No.	NSS survey period	Gini coefficient	Poverty indicators					
			HCR_1	HCR_2	PGI_1	PGI_2	FGT^*_1	FGT^*_2
(1)	(2)	(3)	(4)	(5)	(6)	(7)	(8)	(9)
9.	1989–90	0.35601	34.76	26.28	0.0888	0.0597	0.0321	0.0199
10.	1990–1	0.34015	35.04	26.00	0.0896	0.0599	0.0327	0.0206
11.	1991	0.35087	34.79	25.74	0.0883	0.0591	0.0323	0.0203
12.	1992	0.35550	36.37	27.56	0.0937	0.0629	0.0338	0.0210
13.	1993	0.33743	38.86	29.27	0.0997	0.0667	0.0360	0.0223
14.	1993–4	0.34457	30.94	22.63	0.0753	0.0492	0.0264	0.0161

NOTES: (1)   Poverty indicator, marked with subscript 1 refers to its being based on Planning Commission all-India poverty line of monthly per capita total expenditure (MPCTE) of Rs.49.09 (Rural) and Rs 56.64 (Urban) at 1973–4 prices.

(2)   Poverty indicator marked with subscript 2 refers to its being based on Alternative all-India poverty line of MPCTE of Rs 15 (Rural) and Rs 18 (Urban) at 1960–1 prices.

(3)   The poverty lines are adjusted for price changes using the consumer price index (CPI) for the middle range (MR) of the rural and urban population calculated from detailed data for the period from 1970–1 to 1988–9. For later years, the rate of growth (with 1988–9 = 100) in CPI for Agricultural Labourers (Rural) and for Industrial Workers (Urban) has been applied to CPIMR (Rural) and CPIMR (Urban) to work out the price-adjustment factors, respectively.

IV. POVERTY IN THE PRE-REFORM PERIOD

The salient empirical regularities emerging from Table 12.1 are supplemented in this section by findings from our earlier studies[2] for the pre-reform period to provide a convenient perspective.

Rural poverty, in all its dimensions and for both poverty lines, shows a slow decline in the 1970s and a faster decline in the 1980s till 1990–1. A higher and more stable trend rate of agricultural growth in the 1980s than in the 1970s was largely responsible for this outcome. In the 1980s, this was supplemented in years of a dip in agricultural output by the government policy related to drought-relief works, and the use of public stocks to meet the demands of the predominantly urban and universal public distribution system. (See below for an elaboration).

Urban poverty in all its dimensions and for both the poverty lines indicated an increase between 1970–1 and 1973–4 before showing a steady but a much slower (than rural) decline between 1977–8 and 1986–7. It remained virtually unchanged during 1986–7 and 1990–1. In contrast to the rural population, there had been no major target group-oriented direct anti-poverty programmes for the urban population during the entire period. Agricultural harvest conditions had an indirect impact on urban poverty, via their effect on the universally applicable urban public distribution system and the impact of government operations on the open market prices of food-grains.

From our earlier studies, we find that rural poverty in a given year is governed principally by the work opportunities generated by the contemporary and previous year's agricultural harvest situation, on the one hand, and by the supply and the market prices of food-grains, on the other. Both the supply of grains and their retail prices are affected by the government operations in the market for food-grains via procurement and issue prices, and the resulting changes in procurement, in the off-take from the public distribution system and the consequent changes in the public stocks of food-grains, principally rice and wheat. These operations have their impact on the rural retail prices of grains and hence on the rural poor who are net buyers of grains.

[2] Tendulkar and Jain (1995a, 1995b, 1996, forthcoming) and Tendulkar Sundaram, and Jain (1993, 1996)

As regards urban poverty, we take it to be concentrated pre-dominantly in the urban unorganized informal sector charac-terized largely by petty service activities. Of late, however, labour market rigidities in the urban organized commodity producing sector have resulted in an unintended spillover effect on the un-organized commodity producing sector. In a situation of expand-ing demand, the organized sector is said to prefer subcontracting production to the unorganized sector than expanding direct em-ployment. Expansion of demand has taken place as a result of doubling of the growth rate of real per capita GDP in the 1980s in comparison with the 1970s. A rise in the general economic growth rate would have a favourable effect on other unorganized activities too.

We may also mention one interesting rural–urban link that became apparent during the drought year of 1987–8. That year, the public distribution system was served more by depleting public stocks of food-grains than by procurement. This mechanism pre-vented the sucking of grains from the rural to the urban areas that normally occurred in a year of agricultural dip because of the greater concentration of purchasing power in the urban areas. In the absence of this mechanism, rural prices would have been higher than they were and this factor would have neutralized the positive impact of income generation through drought relief works. This, in our view, was the principal reason for the decline in rural poverty in 1987–8 even in a comparison with the normal agricultural year of 1983. Consequently, 1987–8 represents a sharp departure from the regularity noted by M.S. Ahluwalia (1978) for the period from 1956–7 to 1973–4 that rural poverty tended to exacerbate in years of dips in agricultural harvests. The point is that public action in the form of employment generation makes a greater impact on alleviation of poverty when the real value of wage payment in cereal units is not eroded by the increases in rural retail prices of cereals. Expressed in this way, it sounds a truism but it was never explicitly recognized.

V. Poverty in Post-Reform Period

Four rounds of the National Sample Surveys of household con-sumer expenditure conducted during the post-1991 reform period are available to date. The poverty measures based on them are presented in lines 11 to 14 in Table 12.1. The four rounds relate to (July–December) 1991 (line 11), (January–December) 1992 (line 12), (January–June) 1993 (line 13), and (July–June) 1993–4 (line 14).

In the first part of our discussion, we concentrate only on the two full year long rounds for 1992 and 1993–4 because full year long rounds are free from seasonal variations in consumer expenditure and hence in poverty. Also, the impact of stabilization policies and structural adjustment is expected to be reflected with a lag and is unlikely to be felt during the six month (July–December) 1991 round.

After commenting on the possible factors underlying the movements in the poverty indicators in the full year rounds we take an over view of the entire post-reform period, including the two six-month long rounds in the second part of this section.

For comparison with the pre-reform period, we chose two alternative time points, 1987–8 and 1990–1. The year (July–June) 1990–1 has been chosen because it immediately precedes the beginning of the reform process in July 1991. The choice of (July–June) 1987–8 is governed by the following considerations. One, this was meteorologically declared as a severe drought year that triggered off government action to counter its adverse welfare consequences. Two, this was a year of a dip in the food-grains harvest (see Table 12.5 later in this section) and a *reduction* in the poverty indicators in comparison with the agriculturally normal year of (January–December) 1983 — a combination that had not been experienced in the earlier period from 1956–7 to 1973–4 (Ahluwalia, 1978). We have argued elsewhere (Tendulkar and Jain, 1995a, 1995b) that the impact of the stepped up growth rate of the 1980s contributed in a large measure to the greater effectiveness of government action. It would, therefore, be interesting to compare the poverty situation in the post-reform transition period with the pre-reform year that represented a constellation of overall influence of faster growth and government action under favourable circumstances. In commenting on these comparisons, an effort will be made to distinguish the impact of structural factors from that of the reform-related policies discussed in sect. II.

Tables 12.2 (for rural population) and 3 (for urban population) provide percentage changes in the poverty indicators in the post-reform time-points in relation to the selected pre-reform ones.

We have also included a comparison of 1993–4 with 1992 to highlight the changes during the post-reform period.

TABLE 12.2
POST-REFORM POVERTY SITUATION
IN RELATION TO PRE-REFORM PERIOD:
PERCENTAGE CHANGES FOR THE RURAL POPULATION

Sl. No.	Specification	HCR_1	HCR_2	PGI_1	PGI_2	FGT_1^*	FGT_2^*
(1)	(2)	(3)	(4)	(5)	(6)	(7)	(8)
I.	*Percent change in 1992*						
I.1	with 1987–8 = 100	+2.8	+4.7	+4.9	+5.7	+4.7	+3.8
I.2	with 1990–1 = 100	+23.1	+30.7	+29.6	+32.7	+33.9	+37.2
II.	*Percent change in 1993–4*						
II.1	with 1987–8 = 100	−11.7	−14.7	−17.6	−21.0	−22.3	−26.5
II.2	with 1990–1 = 100	+5.8	+6.5	+2.0	−0.9	−0.6	−2.8
II.3	with 1992 = 100	−14.0	−18.6	−21.4	−25.3	−25.8	−22.1

NOTES: HCR : Headcount Ratio
PGI : Poverty Gap Index or depth measure
FGT^* : Distribution sensitive severity measure.
Subscript 1 : refers to measure with higher (official) poverty line.
Subscript 2 : refers to measure with lower poverty line.
See notes to Table 12.1 for details.
SOURCE: Calculated from Table 12.1.

As mentioned in sect. II, on *a priori* grounds, given the very close administrative, financial, and organizational links of public expenditure and policies with the organized sector, we expect the direct impact of the reform-related policies to be immediately felt by the urban organized sector with second order effects on the urban informal sector and still weaker effects on the rural population. The time lag in impact may also be expected to be correspondingly the shortest for the urban organized segment, longest for the rural segment with that for the urban informal sector to lie in between. These *a priori* expectations regarding the impact of reform-related policies are based on our understanding

TABLE 12.3
POST-REFORM POVERTY SITUATION
IN RELATION TO PRE-REFORM PERIOD:
PERCENTAGE CHANGES FOR THE URBAN POPULATION

Sl. No.	Specification	HCR_1	HCR_2	PGI_1	PGI_2	FGT_1^*	FGT_2^*
(1)	(2)	(3)	(4)	(5)	(6)	(7)	(8)
I.	*Percent change in 1992*						
I.1	with 1987–8 = 100	–0.4	+1.2	+0.3	+0.5	0.0	–0.5
I.2	with 1990–1 = 100	+3.8	+6.0	+4.6	+5.1	+3.4	+1.9
II.	*Percent change in 1993–4*						
II.1	with 1987–8 = 100	–15.3	–16.9	–19.4	–21.4	–21.9	–23.7
II.2	with 1990–1 = 100	–11.7	–13.0	–16.0	–17.9	–19.3	–21.8
II.3	with 1992 = 100	–14.9	–17.9	–19.6	–21.8	–21.9	–23.3

NOTES: Same as Table 12.2.
SOURCE: Calculated from Table 12.1.

TABLE 12.4
SELECTED INDICATORS OF STABILIZATION OF
FISCAL AND EXTERNAL SECTOR DEFICITS

Sl. No.	Items	Units	1990–1	1991–2	1992–3	1993–4
1.	Fiscal deficit of Central Government	Percentage of GDP	8.3	5.9	5.7	7.5
2.	Total expenditure of Central Government	Percentage of GDP	19.7	18.1	17.4	17.7
3.	Exports	Percentage of GDP	6.2	7.3	7.8	8.9
4.	Imports	Percentage of GDP	9.4	8.3	9.8	9.4
5.	TradeBalance	Percentage of GDP	–3.2	–1.1	–2.0	–0.5
6.	Current A/c balance	Percentage of GDP	–3.2	–0.4	–1.8	–0.1
7.	Exports (US $)	Percentage change	9.0	–1.1	3.3	20.3
8.	Imports (US $)	Percentage change	14.3	–24.5	10.3	3.2

SOURCE: *Economic Survey*, 1995–6.

of the functioning of the government machinery and backed by the conceptualization of the organizational dualism provided by Myint (1985).

The first two years of reform covering the period of calendar year 1992 (the survey period of consumer expenditure) were marked by severe fiscal contraction and import compression (Table 12.4, lines 1, 2, and 8). The corresponding contraction of economic activity *resulting from* the reform-related measures may be expected to have accentuated urban poverty more than rural poverty in relation to the pre-reform period.

The results in Table 12.2 and 12.3 (lines I.1 and I.2) do not conform to *a priori* expectations for 1992. In relation to 1987–8, urban poverty remained virtually unchanged whereas the increase in rural poverty varied between 3 and 6 per cent for different poverty indicators. In relation to 1990–1, while urban poverty increased only marginally between 2 and 6 per cent, there was a sharp deterioration in rural poverty. There was a sharper worsening of the lower end rural poverty with regard to a lower poverty line than that corresponding to the higher official poverty line. Moreover, the extent of worsening of rural poverty was the highest for the distributionally sensitive severity indicator, somewhat lower for the depth indicator, and the least for the crude headcount ratio indicator. This points to the possibility that the structural and exogenous factors other than the reform-related policies might also have impacted on rural poverty.

In explaining this result, vest art with the major structural factor of agricultural performance and then examine other factors and reform-related policies that might have influenced the rural poverty situation.

Among the structural factors, variations in rural poverty have always been influenced with a lag by the variations in agricultural harvests in general, and those of grain harvests, in particular. A dip in the grain harvest adversely affects rural employment and incomes whose real value gets eroded by a rise in grain prices. This results in a squeeze in the real purchasing power of those at the lower end of the per capita income scale and hence in poverty. This reasoning requires us to assess whether there was a dip in the agricultural harvest in the year immediately preceding the survey year (January–December) 1992. The available weighted index of agricultural production is published on an annual basis

TABLE 12.5
INDICES OF AGRICULTURAL PRODUCTION

(triennium ending 1981-2 = 100)

Sl. No.	Item	1987-8	1988-9	1989-90	1990-1	1991-2	1992-3	1993-4$	1994-5$
1.	All commodities	115.3 (neg)	140.0 (21.4)	143.0 (2.1)	148.4 (3.8)	145.5 (-2.0)	151.5 (4.1)	156.9 (3.6)	164.1 (4.6)
2.	Foodgrains of which	113.5 (-2.8)	138.1 (21.7)	139.1 (0.7)	143.7 (3.3)	137.6 (-4.2)	144.3 (4.9)	150.2 (4.1)	156.3 (4.1)
2.1	Rice	114.3 (-6.2)	141.7 (-7.8)	147.9 (4.4)	149.4 (1.0)	150.2 (0.5)	146.5 (-2.5)	161.5 (10.2)	163.2 (1.1)
2.2	Wheat	131.2 (4.2)	153.7 (17.1)	141.6 (-7.9)	156.6 (10.6)	158.2 (1.0)	162.5 (2.7)	170.0 (4.6)	186.0 (9.4)
2.3	Coarse cereals	91.2 (-1.2)	108.7 (19.2)	120.3 (10.7)	113.1 (-5.5)	89.4 (-21.4)	127.0 (42.0)	106.7 (-16.0)	104.8 (-1.8)
2.4	Pulses	108.3 (-6.0)	136.4 (25.9)	127.1 (-6.8)	148.5 (10.5)	118.6 (-15.6)	126.5 (6.7)	131.0 (3.6)	138.4 (5.6)
3.	Non-foodgrains	118.3 (5.2)	143.2 (21.0)	149.7 (4.5)	156.3 (4.4)	158.8 (1.6)	163.7 (3.1)	168.3 (2.8)	179.1 (6.4)

NOTES:
(1) Figures in brackets indicate percentage change over previous year.
(2) $ refers to provisional.

SOURCES:
(1) Ministry of Agriculture, Directorate of Economics and Statistics: *Area and Production of Principal Crops in India: 1990–3.*
(2) Ministry of Finance: *Economic Survey,* 1995–6.

for the (July–June) agricultural year. Table 12.5 shows that there was a dip in the agricultural harvest in 1991–2 resulting largely from a 4.2 per cent decline in the index for food-grains. Alternatively, the harvest for the immediately preceding (January–December)

TABLE 12.6

PERCENTAGE CHANGE OVER
PREVIOUS YEAR IN THE PRODUCTION OF FOODGRAINS

(in million tonnes)

Sl. No.	Year	Rice	Wheat	Coarse cereals	Total cereals	Pulses	Total foodgrains
(1)	(2)	(3)	(4)	(5)	(6)	(7)	(8)
1.	1987–8	–6.1	4.2	–1.8	–1.8	–6.4	–2.1
2.	1988–9	24.0	17.2	19.4	20.6	26.3	21.1
3.	1989–90	4.4	–7.9	10.4	1.3	–7.2	6.6
4.	1990–1	1.0	12.6	–5.9	2.5	10.9	3.1
5.	1991–2	0.5	–0.8	–20.5	–3.6	–15.8	–4.5
6.	1992–3	–2.8	1.9	42.5	6.4	13.2	6.9
7.	1993–4	10.6	5.4	–16.8	2.7	–2.2	3.9
8.	1994–5	1.1	9.4	–1.5	3.5	6.1	3.7
9.	1991*	0.2	–	–24.9	–7.2	–18.5	–7.8
10.	1992*	–1.1	1.1	38.4	6.2	–0.8	5.4

NOTES: (1) Lines 1 to 8 give percentage changes over agricultural (July–June) years.

(2) We approximate the output of foodgrains for the six months July to December with the *kharif* output of the agricultural year. Line 9 provides the growth rate of *kharif* output in 1991–2 over the corresponding output during 1990–1.

(3) We approximate the output of foodgrain for the calender year by adding the *rabi* output of one agricultural year to the *kharif* output of the next agricultural year. Line 10 provides the growth rate of output for calender year 1992 over the calender year 1991.

SOURCES: (1) Ministry of Agriculture, Directorate of Economics and Statistics: *Area and Production of Principal Crops in India: 1990–3.*

(2) Ministry of Finance: *Economic Survey*, 1995–6.

calendar year 1991 can also be approximated by combining the *rabi* harvest of agricultural year 1990–1 and the *kharif* harvest of agricultural year 1991–2. This can only be done for the food-grains output (measured in million tonnes (m.t.)) that is available during the *rabi* and *kharif* seasons separately. Table 12.6 provides the growth rates of food-grains output (in m.t.) by major crops for the agricultural years as also for two (approximated) calendar years (lines 9 and 10). From this table, it is clear that there was a decline in the output of food-grains by 4.5 per cent in the agricultural year 1991–2 (line 5) or by 7.8 per cent for the calendar year 1991 (line 9).

The impact of the adverse supply-shock was accentuated by the devaluation of the rupee in mid-1991 in order to impart viability to the balance of payments. This widened the gap between export parity prices of rice and wheat and the domestic prices, and made some rise in procurement prices of these grains inevitable. A rise in procurement prices was also necessary to correct the effective disprotection (or taxation) of agriculture during the pre-reform restrictive regime of import controls, export restrictions, and foreign exchange rate policies favouring the industrial sector. The procurement price of wheat was raised by 22 per cent in the marketing year[3] 1992–3. Similarly, the procurement price of the common variety of paddy was raised by 12 per cent in 1991–2 on top of about a 16 per cent rise in 1989–90 and 10 per cent rise in 1992–3 (Table 12.7). We have no basis to judge whether this was adequate or not to offset the effect of devaluation. However, part of the justification for the hike in procurement prices was also derived from the need to compensate the farmers for the withdrawal of the fertilizer subsidy. This has, however been almost totally restored, albeit in a distorted form. The budgetary subsidies on indigenous and imported fertilizers increased gradually from Rs 43.89 bn in 1990–1 to Rs 48.00 bn (1991–2) and Rs 57.96 bn (1992–3).

Farmers, too, held back stock in expectation of a hike in procurement prices. The expectation of rising prices in response

[3] The changes in procurement prices given in Table 12.7 relate to crop year. In the case of wheat, the procurement price for the crop year, say 1991–2, applies to the 1992–3 marketing year. For paddy, the crop year and the marketing year are the same. We are grateful to Ashok Gulati and Mahendra Dev for bringing this to our attention.

Table 12.7
Percentage Chage Over Previous Year in (Annual Avrage) Price Indices

Sl No.	Price Index	87–8	88–9	89–90	90–1	91–2	92–3	93–4	94–5
1.	Wholesale Price Index (1981–2 = 100)	8.2	7.5	7.4	10.3	13.7	10.0	8.4	10.9
	1.1 Foodgrains (cereals and pulses)	9.3	15.9	1.9	8.5	20.7	12.0	7.9	12.3
	1.1.1 Rice	9.0	10.3	5.0	5.3	21.9	14.7	6.8	10.5
	1.1.2 Wheat	6.3	14.1	–3.9	16.2	18.6	11.3	11.5	7.9
	1.1.3 Pulses	19.5	30.7	3.0	10.7	9.2	3.2	19.8	17.9
2.	Consumer Price Index								
	2.1 Agricultural labourers (1960–1 = 100)	10.0	12.6	5.4	7.6	19.3	12.3	3.5	8.1
	2.2 Industrial workers (1982 = 100)	8.8	9.4	6.1	11.6	13.5	9.6	7.5	8.1
3.	Procurement Prices								
	3.1 Paddy, common variety	2.7	6.7	15.6	10.8	12.2	17.4	14.8	9.7
	3.2 Wheat	4.2	5.8	17.5	4.7	22.2	20.0	6.1	2.9
	3.3 Coarse cereals	2.3	7.4	13.8	9.1	13.9	17.1	8.3	7.7

NOTES: (1) Annual average is over financial year.
         (2) Wheat procurement price includes Central bonus since 1991–2.
SOURCE: Ministry of Finance: *Economic Survey*, 1995–6.

to a below-normal harvest as well as devaluation of the currency also led to direct purchases of wheat by traders from farmers and a reduction in market arrivals in wheat-producing states. (*Economic Survey*, 1991–2: 55 and 1992–3: 91.) The wheat procurement declined from 11.07 m.t. in 1990–1 to 7.75 m.t. (or 30 per cent) in 1991–2 and further to 6.38 m.t. (or 18 per cent) in 1992–3. Rice procurement, too, declined from 11.74 m.t. in 1990–1 to 9.24 m.t. (or 21 per cent) in 1991–2. Consequently, throughout 1992, the stocks of wheat and rice with public agencies consistently fell short of the minimum norm. The reported actual stocks of food-grains (with the minimum norm in parentheses) in m.t. as on the first day of the month were 13.9 (15.4) in January 1992, 11.1 (14.5) in April 1992, 13.3 (22.3) in July 1992, 9.4 (16.6) in October 1992, and 11.8 (15.4) in January 1993. (*Economic Survey*, 1994–5: Table 4.9, 79). The wide gap between the actual and the minimum norm of public stocks restricted the manoeuvrability of government action in moderating the adverse impact of the supply-shock and expectational factors on the open market prices of food-grains. Enhancement of public stocks through imports was constrained by the tight foreign exchange situation and the opposition from the farmers to imports of grains.

In order to contain the budgetary incidence of increased procurement prices, the central issue price of rice was raised by 30 per cent and that of wheat by 20 per cent in December 1991. This contributed further to the rise in the open market prices of grains and consistent shortfall in off-take of rice and wheat in relation to allocation varying between 15 and 20 per cent during 1991–2 and 1992–3 (*Economic Survey*, 1994–5: Table 4.8, 78).

The consequence of the foregoing factors was a steep rise in grain prices. The whole sale price index for food-grains increased by 21 per cent in 1991–2 (largely because of rice and wheat) and further by 12 per cent in 1992–3 (Table 12.7, line 1.1). The consumer price index for agricultural labourers (CPIAL) increased at a faster rate than the consumer price index for industrial workers (CPIIW) during 1991–2 (Table 12.7, lines 2.1 and 2.2). Between July 1991 and October 1992 (the major part of the NSS survey period for 1991 and 1992), the annual rates of increase in CPIAL were higher than those for CPIIW and exceeded 20 per cent continuously from October 1991 to August 1992 (*Economic Survey*, 1994–5: Table 4.1, 70). The continuous rise in CPIAL led to a wide spread decline in real daily wages of unskilled agricultural labourers in 1991–2. At the all India level, the decline worked out to a little over 6 per cent (*Economic Survey*, 1995–6: Table 10.6, 172). Combined with a reduction in rural employment arising from the below-normal harvest, this price rise severely affected poor rural households and resulted in sharper increases in the values of all the poverty indicators.

The year 1991–2 was not officially declared as a (meteorologically) drought year so that there were no centrally funded drought relief works. Moreover, the person days of rural employment generated (in financial years) under Jawahar Rozgar Yojna (JRY) declined from 874.6 m. in 1990–1 to 809.2 m. in 1991–2, and further to 782.1 m. in 1992–3 in the face of nominal increases in outlays on JRY. The outlay on the integrated rural development (IRDP) also declined in absolute nominal terms in 1991–2 and 1992–3 compared to 1990–1, with a corresponding reduction in the number of assisted families from 2.9 m. in 1990–1 to 2.5 m. in 1991–2 and 2.1 m. in 1992–3. Although these are direct effects of the fiscal squeeze, the impact of these programmes even in normal years was marginal because of the thin spread in relation to the total number of poor households. Organizational factors and problems with the delivery mechanisms have further limited the effectiveness of these programmes. Finally, drought-relief works have been much more effective in providing immediate and effective relief in years of dip in agricultural harvests than IRDP or JRY. These works did not exist in 1991–2 or 1992–3.

Compared to (January–December) 1992, (July–June) 1993–4 provides an interesting contrast. There was a significant decline in urban poverty in relation to all the three comparison points and in all the poverty indicators (Table 12.3). There was an equally significant decline in rural poverty in relation to 1987–8 and 1992, again in all the poverty indicators. In relation to the immediate pre-reform year 1990–1, however, there was a small increase of about 6 per cent in the crude head count ratio but negligible changes in both the depth and severity of rural poverty (Table 12.2, lines II.1 to II.3).

About 4 per cent annual growth in agricultural harvest as well as in its important component of food-grains during 1992–3 and 1993–4 after the dip in 1991–2 (Table 12.5 and 12.6) appeared to be the major structural factor that reversed in 1993–4 the steep rise in rural poverty during 1992. It moderated the rise in the prices of food-grains (Table 12.7) besides generating additional rural employment. This was supplemented at the margin by a rise in the person days of employment generated under the Jawahar Rozgar Yojana from 782 m. in 1992–3 to 1030 m. during 1993–4. The outlays on rural development were also enhanced over the pre-reform levels. The average all India real wage rate for un-skilled agricultural labour also returned to its 1990–1 level during 1992–3 and increased in 1993–4 by 4.1 per cent over its pre-reform level (*Economic Survey*, 1995–6, based on Table 10.6, 172).

While the above factors should have reduced the rural poverty indicators, the question arises as to why the depth and the severity indicators remained virtually unchanged and the headcount ratio increased, though marginally, in relation to the pre-reform year 1990–1. A possible reason may be the management of public intervention in the market for food-grains. In relation to 1990–1, the support price for the common variety of paddy increased by 51 per cent and that of wheat by 55 per cent. (The annual increase during the marketing year 1993–4 was as high as 20 per cent for wheat and about 15 per cent for paddy (Table 12.7).) As a conse-quence, in comparison with 1990–1, the level of procurement in 1993–4 increased by as much as 16 per cent each for rice and wheat, whereas the level of output of rice and wheat rose by 8 per cent each. The simultaneous increase in the minimum central issue price was of the order of 41 per cent for wheat and 51 per cent for rice between May–June1990 and January 1993, leading to a lower off-take in relation to allocation from the Public Distribu-tion System. The combined consequence was the addition to stocks to the extent of 2.5 m.t. for wheat and 4.2 m.t. for rice. The level of public stocks during 1993–4 consistently exceeded the minimum normative stock requirements (*Economic Survey*, 1995–6: Table 5.8, 86) by a wide margin. Because of additions to public stocks there was a marginal 2 per cent decline in aggregate avail-ability of cereals between 1990–1 and 1993–4 despite about a 6 per cent rise in aggregate output over the same period. The decline in per capita availability was steeper to the extent of 7 per cent for cereals and 8 per cent for food-grains (including cereals and pulses) (*Economic Survey*, 1995–6: Table 1.19, S-24). A more moderated increase in procurement and central issue prices might have re-sulted in a more moderate rise in open market prices and hence a possible decline in rural poverty in 1993–4 in comparison with 1990–1.

Finally, we take an overview in relation to the pre-Reform year 1990–1 of the entire post-Reform period from July 1991 to June 1994, including the two six month rounds. The two six month rounds were omitted so far from discussion in order to delineate possible structural and reform-related factors affecting the full-year rounds of (January–December) 1992 and (July to June) 1993–4. The two six month rounds are included here to detect the patterns in the entire 3-year post-reform period. Table 12.8 presents index numbers of alternative poverty indicators based on the two alternative poverty lines for the four post-reform time points, in relation to the pre-reform year 1990–1, for the rural and the urban population.

Table 12.8 shows, (a) that rural poverty indicators increased significantly and peaked in 1992 before gradually declining and coming close in 1993–4 to their pre-Reform level of 1990–1; (b) that in contrast, urban poverty indicators increased more moderately, peaked during (January–June) 1993 before declining steeply to levels *lower than pre-Reform levels*; and (c) that there was no discernible rural–urban patterns in the values of the pre-Reform levels of the poverty indicators.

Our hypothesis, as stated earlier is that the fiscal contraction of 1991–2 and 1992–3 would have an immediate and adverse impact on the urban poverty as the urban industrial sector was the major focus of reforms. Similarly, the structural adjustment policies of devaluation and changes in the trade policy orientation might also be expected to have a direct and greater adverse impact on the urban organized sector with a second order impact on the urban informal sector. The reform-related policies of devaluation and the reversal of disprotection of the agricultural sector might be expected to affect rural poverty indirectly and adversely with a lag. These hypotheses relating the reform-related policies to rural and urban poverty are not borne out by the regularities noted under points (a) and (b) of the previous paragraph. This again points to the strong possibility that structural factors, that have an internal dynamics independent of the reform-related policies, might have counteracted or reinforced the reform-related impact. We have already discussed these interrelations when commenting on the movement in rural and urban poverty for the two full year rounds

TABLE 12.8

POST-REFORM CHANGES IN POVERTY INDICATORS INDEX WITH 1990–1 = 100

Sl.No.	Description	HCR_1	HCR_2	PGI_1	PGI_2	FGT^*_1	FGT^*_2
(1)	(2)	(3)	(4)	(5)	(6)	(7)	(8)
Rural Population							
I.1	Level of Indicator in 1990–1	37.48	25.97	0.0911	0.0569	0.0316	0.0180
	Index with 1990–1 = 100						
I.2	Jul–Dec 1991	106.9	108.3	102.4	98.6	98.4	95.0
I.3	Jan–Dec 1992	123.1	130.7	129.6	132.7	133.9	137.2
I.4	Jan–Jun 1993	117.9	119.1	114.8	112.3	112.0	109.4
I.5	Jul–Jun 1993–4	105.8	106.5	102.0	99.1	99.4	97.2
Urban Population							
II.1	Level of Indicator in 1990–1	35.04	26.00	0.0896	0.0599	0.0327	0.0206
	Index with 1990–1 = 100						
II.2	Jul–Dec 1991	99.3	99.0	98.5	98.7	98.8	98.5
II.3	Jan–Dec 1992	103.8	106.0	104.6	105.0	103.4	101.9
II.4	Jan–Jun 1993	110.9	112.6	111.3	111.4	110.1	108.3
II.5	Jul–Jun 1993–4	88.3	87.0	84.0	82.1	80.7	78.2

NOTES: See Table 12.2.
SOURCE: Calculated from Table 12.1.

of 1992 and 1993–4. It appears that weather-related factors combined with expectation-induced and political economy factors accentuated the impact of reform-related devaluation of the currency and the reversal of disprotection of agriculture so that rural poverty worsened much more in 1992 than urban poverty. Correspondingly, the adverse impact of fiscal contraction and structural adjustment on urban poverty was possibly counteracted by institutional rigidities in the organized labour market, indexation of urban organized sector incomes (in terms of dearness allowances), and absence of liquidation of inefficient private sector units as also the slow pace of public sector restructuring. The impact of devaluation of the currency softened the adverse effect of tariff reductions on industrial products while tariffication of quantitative restrictions on the consumer goods imports has not even begun with any seriousness. Consequently, the urban organized industrial sector has not been exposed to the external competition to the extent reflected in nominal tariff reductions. The asymmetry in the impact of reform-related policies on rural and urban poverty seems to reflect the interplay of interest group pressures in a pluralistic society where the democratically elected minority government introduced reforms in a situation of crisis with out explicitly articulating and debating their ideological implications.

VI. Concluding Observations

Economic policy reforms involving stabilization and structural adjustments have been undertaken in India since July 1991. In this contribution, we made an effort to explore the causal link between these reforms and the observed changes in the poverty situation during the post-Reform period with the perspective provided by the experience of the pre-Reform period. The poverty situation in any given period was taken to be influenced by the long-term structural factors with autonomous dynamics of their own as well as by the reform-related policies which were expected to have both direct and indirect impact operating through their effects on the long-term structural factors.

On *a priori* grounds, we expected the short-term adverse impact of economic reforms on urban poverty to be more direct and greater in magnitude than that on rural poverty. We observed, however, that urban poverty increased only moderately and declined steeply by 1993–4. In contrast, the rural poverty situation deteriorated sharply in 1992 and reached approximately the pre-Reform level by 1993–4.

We argued that the sharper increase in rural poverty in 1992 was a combined consequence of the weather-related natural forces, constricted manoeuvrability of government action, and certain political economy factors that were influenced by reform-related policies of devaluation of the currency and the intended reversal of disprotection of agriculture. It is important to note that had the agricultural harvest of 1991–2 been favourable, the adverse impact of the reform-related policies could have been counteracted. It is equally important to emphasize that the timing of the reforms was dictated by the economic crisis of mid-1991 which, in turn, was the result of the political instability of the late 1980s, the fiscal profligacy over the previous decade, and the foreign exchange liquidity crunch that triggered reforms so that the devaluation of currency could not have awaited more auspicious timing. We noted, however, that the rural poverty situation in 1993–4 could possibly have been improved with better management of the government interventions in the food economy. In contrast, a more moderate rise in urban poverty followed by a significant decline in 1993–4 was attributable to the slower pace of reforms in the industrial and public sector along with the relaxation of fiscal contraction and a pick up in the general growth rate. Our conclusion is clear, that economic policy reforms can at best be only indirectly responsible for the observed movements in the poverty indicators in the post-reform period.

REFERENCES

Ahluwalia, M.S. (1978): 'Rural Poverty and Agricultural Performance in India', *Journal of Development Studies*, vol. 14, no. 3 (April), pp. 298–323.

Fields, G.S. (1995): 'Income Distribution in Developing Economies: Conceptual, Data and Policy Issues in Broad-based Growth', in M.G. Quibria (ed.), *Critical Issues in Asian Development, Theories, Experiences and Policies* (Hong Kong: Oxford University Press for the Asian Development Bank), pp. 76–97.

Fishlow, A. (1995): 'Inequality, Poverty and Growth: Where Do We

Stand?', in M. Bruno and B. Pleskovic (eds), *Annual World Bank Conference on Development Economics, 1995* (Washington, DC: The World Bank), pp. 25–39.

Foster, J., J. Greer and E. Thorebecke (1984): 'A Class of Decomposable Poverty Measures', *Econometrica*, vol. 52, no. 3 (May), pp. 571–6.

Frankel, F.R. (1974): *India's Green Revolution: Economic Gains and Political Costs* (Bombay: Oxford University Press).

Government of India, Ministry of Finance, Department of Economic Affairs: *Economic Survey*, Annual for various years.

Mitra, P.K. and Suresh D. Tendulkar (1994): 'Adjustment with Growth or Stagnation? India, 1973/74 to 1983/84', Ch. 6, pp. 146–92, in P.K. Mitra (ed.), *Adjustment in Oil Importing Countries: A Comparative Economic Analysis* (Cambridge: Cambridge University Press).

Myint, H. (1985): 'Organisational Dualism and Economic Development', *Asian Development Review*, vol. 3, no. 1, pp. 24–42.

Parthasarathy, G. (1991): 'HYV Technology: The Polarisation and Immiserisation Controversy', *Economic and Political Weekly*, vol. xxx, no. 26, pp. A 69–77.

Perspective Planning Division (1979): *Report of the Task Force on Projections of Minimum Needs and Effective Consumption Demand* (New Delhi: Planning Commission, GOI).

Pursell, G. and A. Sharma (1996): 'Indian Trade Policies Since the 1991–92 Reforms', mimeo, National Council of Applied Economic Research, New Delhi, Revised Draft (Feb.).

Sukhatme, P.V. (ed.) (1982): *Newer Concepts in Nutrition and their Implications for Policy* (Pune: Maharashtra Association for the Cultivation of Science).

Tendulkar, Suresh D. and L.R. Jain (1995a): 'Economic Growth, and Equity: India: 1970–71 to 1988–89', *Indian Economic Review*, vol. xxx, no. 1 (Jan.–June), pp. 14–49.

—— (1995b): 'Economic Growth, Relative Inequality and Equity: The Case of India', *Asian Development Review*, vol. 13, no. 2, pp. 138–68.

—— (1996): 'Growth, Distributional Change and Reduction in Rural Poverty between 1983 and 1987–88: A Decomposition Exercise for Seventeen Major States in India', *Indian Journal of Agricultural Economics*, vol. 51, nos 1 and 2 (Jan.–June), pp. 109–33.

—— (forthcoming): 'Growth, Distributional Change and Poverty Reduction in India: A Decomposition Exercise', in D. Coondoo, R. Mukherjee and S. Chakravarty (eds), *Econometrics: Theory and*

Practice, Essays in Honour of N. Bhattacharya (Delhi: Allied Publishers).

Tendulkar, Suresh D. and K. Sundaram (1995): 'Social Exclusion: Mechanisms, Processes and Labour Market Outcomes: An Indian Case Study', Paper pesented at the Asian Sub-Regional Symposium on Social Exclusion and Extension of Social Protection, 22–5 Nov. 1994 at Pattaya, Thailand organized by the East Asian Multidisciplinary Advisory Team, International Labour Organization, Bangkok (Revised April 1995).

Tendulkar, Suresh D., K. Sundaram and L.R. Jain (1993): *Poverty in India, 1970–71 to 1988–89*, ARTEP Working Paper, Asian Regional Team for Employment Promotion (ARTEP) (New Delhi: International Labour Organization) (Dec.).

—— (1996): 'Macroeconomic Policies and Poverty in India 1966–67 to 1993–94', Report submitted to the South Asia Multidisciplinary Advisory Team (New Delhi: International Labour Organization) (Sept.).

World Bank (1995): 'The Social Impact of Adjustment Operations: An Overview', Report No. 14/76, Operations Evaluation Department, Washington, DC (30 June 1995).

IV

Centre–State Relations

13

Tax Assignment in the Indian Federation: A Critique

Amaresh Bagchi

I. INTRODUCTION

R estructuring the tax system has been central to the economic reforms initiated by Dr Manmohan Singh during his tenure as India's Finance Minister. The objectives were basically twofold: one, to reduce the dependence on foreign trade taxes and orient the tax structure towards an open and competitive economy by removing its inefficiencies and two, to improve the buoyancy of the tax revenues on a sustainable basis so that the current budgets of the government could be balanced and eventually yield some surpluses to finance public investments.

The reforms of 1991–3 brought about extensive changes in the Central government's major taxes — customs, union excises, and income tax. These have yielded some positive results. Income tax revenues have grown at a rate seldom witnessed before and the composition of the Centre's tax structure has undergone a significant shift, with the share of direct taxes in the Centre's gross tax revenue increasing from 18 to 29 per cent in the course of barely five years.

However, the overall buoyancy of the Centre's tax revenue has suffered a set back and, in the absence of compensating improvement in that of the states, the overall buoyancy of government tax revenue in the country has slumped. As regards the efficiency objective, while there has been some notable progress towards a simpler and less distorting tax regime, the system still suffers from many infirmities. This is because there are a number of other taxes, particularly on domestic production and trade imposed at the subnational levels of government — states and local authorities — that garner substantial revenue. The structure and operation of these taxes constitute a source of acute complexity and inefficiency in the entire system. While the reforms have served to a considerable extent to clean up the components of the taxes that fall within the Centre's purview, the taxes in the states' jurisdiction remain virtually unattended. As a result, the centrepiece of tax reforms undertaken in other developing countries in recent years, namely the introduction of the Value Added Tax (VAT) to replace the assortment of levies on commodities and services that typically characterized their tax systems earlier is still missing from the tax reforms in India.

There is reason to believe that a binding constraint on further progress of tax reform in India lies in the division of tax powers between the Centre and the states in the Indian Constitution, and despite several commendable features, there are fundamental flaws in the constitutional scheme that stand in the way of moving towards a structure that can subserve the requirements of a globalizing economy within the framework of a federal polity.

What the appropriate division of tax powers in a federation should be among the different levels of government does not admit of a straightforward answer. The matter has been the subject of intense debate among academicians with divergent views.[1] However, a consensus seems to be emerging from the ongoing debate. This contribution seeks to appraise the scheme of tax assignment in the Indian Constitution in the light of the principles emerging from the debate and the operation of the existing system over the last four and a half decades. An attempt is also made to explore the lines on which the present scheme could be redesigned to help instal a rational and efficient tax structure.

The contribution is divided into four sections, besides the introduction. Sect. II outlines the principal features of the division of taxpowers between the Centre and the states envisaged in the Indian Constitution with a brief appraisal in the light of its operation. Sect. III takes a look at the literature on the subject in an

---

[1] See for instance the essays in McLure (1983), Shah (1994), and Bird, Ebel and Walliah (1995). For a recent overview, see Inman and Rubinfeld (1996).

attempt to draw lessons for India. Sect. IV puts forward some suggestions regarding the lines on which the present tax assignment scheme could be redesigned to orient it to the goals of a dynamic economy. Sect. V concludes.

II. DIVISION OF TAX POWERS IN THE INDIAN CONSTITUTION

II.1 Salient Features

As in most federations, in India the tax powers of the Centre and the constituent units, namely the states, are specified by law.[2] The Union and the state lists in the Seventh Schedule to the Indian Constitution enumerate the powers and functions of the respective levels of government. There is a concurrent list but none of the items figuring in the list except one have any direct bearing on taxation.[3] However, any matter not specified in either the state list or the concurrent list falls within the sphere of the Union. Thus, the Centre can enter tax fields not charted in the Constitution.

Broadly speaking, taxes on foreign trade, income, both personal and corporate, but excluding agricultural income, and duties of excise on goods other than alcoholic liquor and other intoxicants are assigned to the Centre, while powers to levy taxes on land and buildings, agricultural income, sale and purchase of goods (including electricity), and a few specified activities and services like entertainment, advertisement other than in newspapers, and the electronic media fall within the purview of the states. Taxes on mineral rights also fall under the purview of the states, subject however 'to any limitations imposed by Parliament by law relating to mineral development'.

As noted in a companion essay in this volume (Ch. 14), unlike in several other large federations where taxes can be levied concurrently at multiple levels unless specifically forbidden, division of tax powers in the Indian Constitution follows the principle of 'separation', that is, the right to levy a given tax belongs exclusively

---

[2] A notable exception is the USA where the Constitution is silent on the assignment of indirect taxes except tariffs (McLure, 1983).

[3] This relates to 'stamp duties other than duties or fees collected by means of judicial stamps, but not including rates of stamp duty' (entry 44 of List III). Recovery of taxes like other public demands also occurs in the concurrent list (entry 43).

to the tier to which it is assigned. There are a few tax heads mentioned in the Union List which can be levied by the Centre but are to be collected and retained by the states, and some which may be levied and collected by the Union but the revenue is 'assigned to the states' (Arts 268 and 269). Notable among these are stamp duties and excise duties on medicinal and toilet preparations as are mentioned in the Union List, succession and estate duty on property other than agricultural land, terminal taxes on goods or passengers carried by railway, sea, or air, taxes on railway fares and freights, taxes on sale of newspapers and advertisements therein, and on interstate sales and consignments.

Originally, there was no specific mention of local (that is, the third tier) governments' powers in the Constitution. They derived their taxing authority, if any, from the states. Local governments — both urban and rural — were given constitutional status by amendments carried out in 1992, and the functions that can be assigned to them were enumerated separately but leaving it to the state legislatures to decide the specifics.[4] While practices differ from state to state, as a general rule, taxes on real property in urban areas are levied by the municipal governments along with sundry imposts like octroi or entry tax, entertainment tax, licence fees, and the professions tax.

On the face of it, the assignment scheme laid out in the Indian Constitution seems to be in conformity with the established principles of tax assignment in federations. While, as will be seen from the discussion in sect. III, opinions differ on the specifics, it is generally acknowledged that going by the criteria of efficiency and equity, progressive income and expenditure taxes should be with the national government, destination-based product taxes (sales tax) with the middle levels, property taxes with local governments, and all three levels of government should have the powers to realize user charges (McLure, 1983). Division of tax powers in the Indian Constitution fits almost neatly into this pattern. Only in one respect, namely the assignment of the power to tax natural resources such as minerals to the states, would it seem to go against dominant expert opinion (McLure, et al. 1995). However, subsequent developments leading to the assumption of overriding power to levy or regulate the tax on minerals by the Centre appears

---

[4] The 73rd and 74th Constitution Amendment Acts of 1992.

to have corrected the shortcoming in the constitutional provisions in this regard.[5]

The principle of separation, that is, exclusive jurisdiction of each level over the taxes assigned to it that underlies the Indian constitutional scheme would also seem to be a desirable attribute of intergovernmental tax power assignment, in that it makes for simplicity and limits the scope for jurisdictional conflict. The actual working of the scheme has however revealed deficiencies that seriously detract from much of its supposed merits.

II.2 Infirmities

The glaring deficiencies are:

- Sharp imbalance between the taxing powers and spending responsibilities of different governmental levels, necessitating large transfers from higher to lower levels of government, eroding fiscal discipline, and creating a widening vertical fiscal gap;
- dysfunctional allocation of tax bases with lines of demarcation that do not work, creating complexities and adding to costs;
- inadequate safeguards against tax exporting and tax competition leading to jurisdictional conflicts and economic distortions; and
- weaknesses of some of the major taxes because of constitutional limitations of the base, adversely affecting both their revenue buoyancy as well as equity and efficiency.

Accentuating Vertical Imbalance

Although the tax heads enumerated in the state list add up to a substantial number, the assignment of three of the most potent revenue sources to the Centre, namely customs, excise in general, and income tax has implied a high degree of concentration on revenue collection. Taking the taxes collected by local governments into account,[6] the Centre's present share in the total tax revenue works out to about 60 per cent and that of the states and

[5] By virtue of the Mines and Minerals (Regulation and Development) Act of 1957.

[6] Taxes raised by municipalities only. Village level local governments collect very little taxes on their own.

TABLE 13.1
TAX REVENUE COLLECTION BY LEVELS OF GOVERNMENTS (1992–93 AND 1993–94)

| Tax heads | Tax revenue (Rs cr.) | | | | | | | |
| | (1992–3) | | | | (1993–4) | | | |
	Centre (gross)	State (own)	Local	Total	Centre (gross)	State (own)	Local	Total
Direct Taxes								
1. Corporation tax	8899 (100.0)	– (0.0)	– (0.0)	8899 (100.0)	10060 (100.0)	– (0.0)	– (0.0)	10060 (100.0)
2. Taxes on income	7896 (100.0)	– (0.0)	– (0.0)	7896 (100.0)	9123 (100.0)	– (0.0)	– (0.0)	9123 (100.0)
3. Interest tax	716 (100.0)	– (0.0)	– (0.0)	716 (100.0)	727 (100.0)	– (0.0)	– (0.0)	727 (100.0)
4. Wealth tax	468 (100.0)	– (0.0)	– (0.0)	468 (100.0)	154 (100.0)	– (0.0)	– (0.0)	154 (100.0)
5. Gift tax	9 (100.0)	– (0.0)	– (0.0)	9 (100.0)	5 (100.0)	– (0.0)	– (0.0)	5 (100.0)
6. Land revenue	1 (0.2)	614 (99.8)	– (0.0)	615 (100.0)	1 (0.1)	729 (99.9)	– (0.0)	730 (100.0)
7. Agricultural income tax	– (0.0)	111 (100.0)	– (0.0)	111 (100.0)	– (0.0)	107 (100.0)	– (0.0)	107 (100.0)
8. Expenditure tax	151 (100.0)	– (0.0)	– (0.0)	151 (100.0)	229 (100.0)	– (0.0)	– (0.0)	229 (100.0)

Tax revenue (Rs cr.)

Tax heads	(1992–3)				(1993–4)			
	Centre (gross)	State (own)	Local	Total	Centre (gross)	State (own)	Local	Total
9. Property tax	– (0.0)	– (0.0)	1794 (100.0)	1794 (100.0)	– (0.0)	– (0.0)	2012 (100.0)	2012 (100.0)
10. Others*	– (0.0)	521 (100.0)	– (0.0)	521 (100.0)	– (0.0)	577 (100.0)	– (0.0)	577 (100.0)
Total direct taxes	18140 (85.6)	1246 (5.9)	1794 (8.5)	21180 (100.0)	20299 (85.6)	1413 (6.0)	2012 (8.5)	23724 (100.0)
Indirect Taxes								
1. Customs	23776 (100.0)	– (0.0)	– (0.0)	23776 (100.0)	22193 (100.0)	– (0.0)	– (0.0)	22193 (100.0)
2. Union excise duties	30832 (100.0)	– (0.0)	– (0.0)	30832 (100.0)	31697 (100.0)	– (0.0)	– (0.0)	31697 (100.0)
3. State excise duties	327 (4.9)	6287 (95.1)	– (0.0)	6614 (100.0)	239 (3.2)	7120 (96.8)	– (0.0)	7359 (100.0)
4. Sales tax	1026 (4.3)	23005 (95.7)	– (0.0)	24031 (100.0)	843 (3.0)	27297 (97.0)	– (0.0)	28140 (100.0)
5. Tax on purchase of sugar-cane	– (0.0)	115 (100.0)	– (0.0)	115 (100.0)	– (0.0)	227 (100.0)	– (0.0)	227 (100.0)
6. Taxes on vehicles	43 (2.0)	2125 (98.0)	– (0.0)	2168 (100.0)	38 (1.5)	2542 (98.5)	– (0.0)	2580 (100.0)
7. Tax on goods and passengers	34 (2.6)	1274 (97.4)	– (0.0)	1308 (100.0)	2 (0.1)	1445 (99.9)	– (0.0)	1447 (100.0)

Table 13.1 (cont.)

Tax revenue (Rs cr.)

Tax heads	(1992–3)				(1993–4)			
	Centre (gross)	State (own)	Local	Total	Centre (gross)	State (own)	Local	Total
8. Entertainment tax	– (0.0)	488 (100.0)	– (0.0)	488 (100.0)	– (0.0)	560 (100.0)	– (0.0)	560 (100.0)
9. Taxes and duty on electricity	4 (0.2)	1753 (99.8)	– (0.0)	1757 (100.0)	4 (0.2)	1740 (99.8)	– (0.0)	1744 (100.0)
10. Stamps and registration	57 (1.9)	2913 (98.1)	– (0.0)	2970 (100.0)	57 (1.6)	3515 (98.4)	– (0.0)	3572 (100.0)
11. Octroi	– (0.0)	– (0.0)	2568 (100.0)	2568 (100.0)	– (0.0)	– (0.0)	2938 (100.0)	2938 (100.0)
12. Others**	397 (55.5)	318 (44.5)	– (0.0)	715 (100.0)	370 (50.8)	359 (49.2)	– (0.0)	729 (100.0)
Total indirect taxes	56496 (58.0)	38278 (39.3)	2568 (2.6)	97342 (100.0)	55443 (53.7)	44805 (43.4)	2938 (2.8)	103186 (100.0)
Total tax revenue	74636 (63.0)	39524 (33.3)	4362 (3.7)	118522 (100.0)	75742 (59.7)	46218 (36.4)	4950 (3.9)	126910 (100.0)

Figures within parentheses indicate percentage to total.

NOTES: * Includes taxes on professions, trades, callings and employment, non-urban immovable properties, etc.
** In the case of states, includes interstate transit duties, advertisement tax, education cess, tax on raw jute, betting tax.

** In the case of the Centre, includes foreign travel tax, entertainment tax, betting tax.

SOURCE: For Centre and states, *Indian Economic Statistics* (Ministry of Finance).
For Local Governments, NIPFP.

local governments, 40 per cent. Nearly 86 per cent of the direct taxes and 54 per cent of the taxes on commodities are collected by the Centre (Table 13.1). With a much larger share of expenditure responsibilities (around 60 per cent) assigned to the lower level governments, this has implied a marked degree of vertical fiscal imbalance (roughly 20 percentage points). Vertical imbalance of this order is not exceptional (in Canada it is 15 and Australia 20, vide Shah, 1994). The Constituent Assembly records show that India's Constitution-makers were well aware of the imbalance and had accordingly provided for the transfer of Central resources in the form of sharing of revenue from certain taxes and grants-in-aid to redress it (Shiva Rao, 1968).

The arrangements provided in the Constitution for division of tax powers and devolution of revenue from the Centre seemed to be working well for the first twenty-five years. While their total expenditure always exceeded their current receipts, necessitating some borrowing to fund public investment, the combined revenue budgets of the Centre and the states used to produce a surplus, however small, quite regularly, until about the end of the seventies. Fiscal deficits started ballooning from the beginning of the eighties, with even the revenue budgets of both levels of government going into the red (Table 13.2). Corrective measures adopted under the reform programmes since 1991 have contained the fiscal deficits of the Centre but the finances of the states are in a poor shape.[7]

Imbalance in the state budgets is not a new phenomenon, and is inherent in the assignment of tax and expenditure responsibilities in the Constitution. What causes concern is that over the years the imbalance has tended to accentuate. As Table 13.3 shows, the shortfall in the states' own source revenue receipts as a proportion of their current expenditures increased from 36 per cent in 1960–1 to 48 per cent in 1990–1. There has been a reversal of the trend in the past few years but the gap still remains large and unbridged even with devolution.

Revenue receipts as a proportion of expendituers showed a surplus of 5 per cent in 1960–1. However, since 1979–80, revenue deficits have been a recurring phenomenon. Shortfalls in revenue

[7] Of late, even a well administered state like Maharashtra is facing an acute resource crunch and is diverting funds borrowed for development projects to meet current expenditures, *Times of India*, 16 March 1997.

TABLE 13.2
TRENDS IN FISCAL/REVENUE DEFICITS ARE SURPLUSES AS A PERCENTAGE OF GDP
(CENTRE, STATES, AND COMBINED)

	50–1	55–6	60–1	65–6	70–1	75–6	80–1	85–6	90–1	91–2	92–3	93–4	94–5 RE	95–6 RE
Fiscal Deficit (–)														
Centre	–1.27	–4.10	–4.49	–5.21	–3.26	–3.85	–6.53	–8.53	–8.34	–5.89	–5.70	–7.45	–6.10	5.94
States	–1.12	–2.47	–2.64	–3.89	–2.14	–1.43	–3.20	–2.98	–3.39	–2.99	–2.84	–2.91	–3.00	–2.97
Combined	–1.88	–4.00	–5.54	–6.92	–4.59	–4.59	–8.09	–9.32	–9.88	–7.35	–7.19	–8.71	–7.99	–7.15
Revenue deficit(–)/surplus(+)														
Centre	+0.58	+0.40	+0.31	+1.22	+0.38	+1.13	–0.57	–2.12	–3.47	–2.64	–2.63	–4.08	–3.61	–3.00
States	–0.02	–0.44	+0.15	–0.19	–0.04	+1.21	+0.66	+0.21	–0.95	–0.92	–0.72	–0.43	–0.82	–0.87
Combined	+0.56	–0.03	+0.46	+1.03	+0.34	+2.34	+0.09	–1.91	–4.42	–3.55	–3.35	–4.52	–4.43	–3.87

SOURCE: *Indian Economic/Public Finance Statistics*, Ministry of Finance (various issues).

TABLE 13.3

REVENUE SHORTFALL OF THE CENTRE AND THE STATES (1960–61 TO 1995–96 SELECTED YEARS)

(Rs crore)

	1960–1	1970–1	1980–1	1990–1	1992–3	1993–4	1994–5	1995–6
A. Centre								
i. Revenue receipts (net of devolution)	1003	3316	12484	54995	74117	75784	89440	101773
ii. Revenue expenditure	953	3152	13261	73557	92692	108500	123571	137315
iii. Revenue gap (ii–i) as proportion (%) of revenue expenditure	(–) 5.25	(–) 5.20	5.86	25.23	20.04	30.15	27.62	25.88
B. States								
i. Revenue receipts	1041	3422	15036	62754	87091	101965	120248	132994
ii. Less share of Central transfers (current)	392	1367	6588	27828	38465	43196	45365	51229
iii. States' own revenue (i–ii)	649	2055	8448	34926	48626	58769	74883	81765
iv. Revenue expenditure	1016	3440	14136	67860	92150	105440	128017	142380
v. Revenue gap (iv–iii) as proportion (%) of revenue expenditure	36.12	40.26	40.24	48.53	47.23	44.26	41.51	42.57

receipts in relation to expenditure was 30 per cent in 1993–4 and 26 per cent in 1995–6, (Table 13.3).

Finding that large revenue deficits had afflicted all states, and that too at about the same time, the Tenth Finance Commission felt that 'systemic' rather than state-specific factors were at work.[8] What these factors are remains to be fully researched. At one level it would appear that populist politics and the unbridled free rider instinct, 'the tragedy of the commons', are the root cause of the chronic problem. Messages emanating from the New Institutional Economics suggest that the problem may have its origin in the failure of the institutions — of which federal fiscal relations constitute a vital component — to enforce accountability and provide incentive compatibility in the matter of public expenditures and revenue raising (Bagchi, 1996b; Campos and Pradhan, 1996).

That accountability suffers when revenue and expenditure decisions are delinked — as happens with centralization of tax powers and decentralization of expenditure responsibilities — is well recognized. Since it is more efficient to raise taxes at higher levels, some degree of vertical imbalance and so devolution from the higher to lower levels is unavoidable in any form of decentralized governance.[9] But transfers tend to undermine fiscal discipline by reducing the tax price of spending on the part of the recipient government. Hence care must be exercised in designing the transfers to see that accountability is maintained at least at the margin. Many would agree that fiscal laxity in India has been bred to a great extent by faulty design of the transfers (Rao and Chelliah, 1996).

However, if the problem is to be attacked at its roots, the assignment of both taxes and expenditure responsibilities would have to be redesigned with more tax powers to the states so that the need for transfers is minimized. At the same time, the likely

[8] *Report of the Tenth Finance Commission,* para 2.14.

[9] What could be the 'optimal vertical balance' in a given context remains an open question. A recent paper by Boadway and Keen (1995) suggests that because of vertical fiscal externality it may be more efficient to have a system of transfers from the states to the Centre to neutralize the distortions that may arise from state tax decisions. The experience of countries where such upward transfers operated [e.g. in confederate USA, China, India in the 1920s, and more recently in the former Yugoslavia (Mihaljek, 1993), the only exception perhaps being Germany] raises serious doubt about the practicality or even the desirability of such a system.

impact on equity and efficiency would need to be taken into account. For decentralization of tax powers, though conducive to better accountability, unless planned with care, can give rise to inefficiencies and inequities. Moreover, the question of more powers to the states cannot be decided in isolation; the entire scheme of tax and expenditure assignment would have to be reframed together. Budgetary problems of governments have generated rethinking on tax and expenditure allocation among different levels of government even in countries where the federal system has long been operating with remarkable success, such as in the USA and Canada (Rivlin 1992, Banting et al., 1994). It is time a fresh look was taken at the assignment of both taxes and expenditures in the Indian Constitution to bring stability in the government budgets by strengthening accountability.

Dysfunctional Base Allocation

Another basic problem with the Indian tax assignment scheme is that the principle of separation on which it is founded simply has not worked. The bases of several of the Central and states taxes have overlapped while the way in which some of them have been splintered has created severe, though not always obvious, problems.

In the case of direct taxes, it is base splitting rather than overlap that causes trouble. The impact of base overlap that occurs through the operation of profession tax, property tax, and stamp duty on asset transfers along with taxes on income and wealth is contained to some extent by the statutory ceiling on profession tax and the provision of deduction of the other taxes from taxable income, though the combined incidence of the taxes taken together is believed to have been a drag on investment in housing and to have induced evasion (Government of India, 1991). The problems arising from base splitting seem to be more serious. Although under the Constitution, the power to tax incomes is vested exclusively in the Centre, the base of the tax excludes agricultural income. Taxation of agricultural income figures in the state list. What constitutes 'agriculture' in this context has been the subject matter of protracted litigation. The broad principles now seem to be well settled and rules have been framed to determine the 'agricultural' component of incomes derived from composite operations of cultivation and manufacturing, e.g. in the case of the income of tea plantations. Even so, the exclusion of income that still accounts for nearly one-third of the nation's domestic product from the base of the Central income tax, primarily a legacy of the past, continues to be a weak point providing opportunities for abuse, and detracting from both the equity and efficiency of the tax system.[10] To correct the anomaly at least partially and reduce the scope for abuse, the Raj Committee had recommended the inclusion of agricultural incomes in the total income of assessees liable to pay income tax under the central law, for determining the rate of tax applicable to the non-agricultural part of the income which alone can be taxed by the Centre.[11] This recommendation was implemented and has been in operation since 1974, but its impact has been no more than marginal.

The base of excises too is splintered. The power to levy excise duty on goods other than alcoholic liquor and other intoxicants is with the Centre. In the case of Union excises, however, problems arise not so much from the exclusion of intoxicants from the base as from the limitations inherent in taxation of 'manufacturing' on the one hand, and the pitfalls of assessing the 'excisable value' of goods excluding services, on the other. Problems in taxing 'manufacturing' are well known.[12] There are many processes ancillary to manufacturing and it is not easy to draw a line between them for taxation, especially when 'services' do not fall within its purview. Then there are intractable problems of valuation, as manufacturing value can be manipulated by splitting the profit margins through various devices (e.g. by setting up sole selling agencies and so on). Canada struggled with a manufacturers' sales tax for sixty years (Whalley and Fretz, 1990) and finally went in for a federal level value added tax, the Goods and Services Tax (GST) in 1991. The history of excises in India too is replete with unending litigations over definitional and valuation issues. Various artefacts have been devised in the excise law to get over these problems but the difficulties persist. To ease the valuation problem, the Tax Reforms Committee (1991) had recommended extending the net of Union excises to the wholesale stage, allowing the states to

[10] How the 'loophole' is exploited is brought home by a recent advertisement of a 'Good Earth Unit' investment scheme promising '100 per cent tax free agro returns' on fixed deposits, *Times of India*, 31 March 1997.

[11] *Report of the Committee on Taxation of Agricultural Wealth and Income* (1972); Government of India, Chairman K.N. Raj.

[12] See, Mukhopadhyay (1996).

retain the tax pertaining to the margin of wholesalers. For reasons elaborated in NIPFP (1994), the recommendation does not seem to be practicable or legally sustainable. The Union Budget for 1997–8 has proposed the adoption of the 'maximum retail price' (MRP) as the base for Central excise. Given the constitutional limitations on the Centre's powers, it is doubtful that it will stand the test of constitutionality (Mukhopadhyay, 1997).

Then there is the problem of base overlap. Although the Constitution demarcates the area of commodity taxation by assigning the taxes on production, namely the duties of excise in general, to the Centre and the sales taxes (presumably retail sales) to the states, the bases of the two have come to overlap in large measure. Finding it difficult to collect sales tax from retailers, their number being too large to be manageable, the states have moved the point of levy of sales tax mostly to the first sale in the state, which meant manufacturers and importers (into the state). Sales tax is levied on products on the sale price inclusive of excises, and in the absence of adequate arrangement for relieving the tax on inputs, and with the tax falling on both inputs and capital goods, there is a significant degree of pyramiding, resulting in uncertain incidence and distortions in production and consumption. In addition, octroi (or its substitute, the 'entry tax') is levied by local authorities on goods entering their jurisdiction, again without any coordination with the taxes levied at higher levels (except that the rate of octroi tax is controlled by the state governments). In some municipalities octroi is levied at the rate of 4 per cent even on raw materials, and the combined incidence of excise duty, sales tax, turnover tax, and octroi can be so high as to induce manufacturing enterprises to buy their inputs from abroad even when these are produced locally at internationally competitive costs[13]

The overlap between excise and sales taxes would perhaps not matter had the Union excises been confined to their traditionally delimited field. Driven by revenue needs and in order to provide a stable tax base, the government at the Centre has widened the scope of its excises over the years, eventually bringing virtually the entire manufacturing sector under its umbrella with the introduction of

---

[13] For instance, Indian Petrochemicals Ltd. located in Baroda finds it cheaper to buy naphtha, one of its prime inputs, from abroad, while Indian Oil Corporation operating in an adjoining locality exports naphtha produced by it (*Economic Times*, 10 April 1997).

an omnibus head in the excise tariff in 1976, namely 'items not elsewhere specified'. The Constitution-makers could not have anticipated this development while assigning 'the duties of excise' to the Centre.

Overlap has occurred, surprisingly, also between the bases of sales tax levied by the states and the income tax which falls within the purview of the Centre. As an easy way of garnering revenue, many states have levied graduated turnover taxes on dealers with sales exceeding a specified limit, prohibiting their forward shifting. While the courts have upheld the legality of such imposts as falling within the category of sales taxes and so within the competence of the states, from the economic angle the bases of the two taxes in effect overlap to a large extent.

Tax Exportation

In order to delimit the scope of conflicts, India's Constitution-makers, while assigning sales taxation to the states, had hedged their powers with some restrictions. Art. 286 of the Constitution, as it originally stood, debarred the states from taxing, (i) sales or purchases outside the territories of India, that is, international trade; (ii) sales that result in delivery of consumption of goods in another state; and (iii) sales in the course of interstate trade and commerce. An 'Explanation' made it clear that when a sale or purchase takes place outside a state, the state in which the goods are delivered for consumption would have the power to tax it, thus gearing the sales taxes essentially on what has come to be known as the destination principle. Unfortunately, lacking clear operational rules, the principle got sidetracked as the states attempted to realize tax from dealers located in other states selling goods to consumers outside their state of residence, creating acute problems for businesses to operate in more than one state and opening up loopholes for evasion and avoidance through cross-border sales.

To bring some order in the taxation of interstate sales, the Parliament amended the Constitution to include taxation of interstate sales in the Union List and thereafter passed a law, the Central Sales Tax (CST) Act, in 1954, authorizing the levy of tax on interstate sales and delegating the power to administer the tax and retain the revenue to the originating state. The destination principle in sales taxation, which evidently the Constitution-makers had in mind, though not articulated in these terms, while delimiting the scope of the states' powers to tax sales, thus got displaced, somewhat inadvertently by the origin rule, paving the way for tax exportation with all its attendant evils.[14]

The ill-effects of taxation of interstate trade on an origin basis have been documented elsewhere (NIPFP, 1994) and are not discussed here. Suffice it to note that currently one-fifth of the sales tax revenue of the states comes from the CST, net exporters among them gaining at the expense of others. Reflecting the tax exportation occurring through the CST, the share of individual states in the aggregate revenue from ST in the country as a whole diverges significantly from their respective share in total consumption. According to one estimate, the relatively advanced states collect over 40 per cent of their sales tax revenue through tax exportation, while 92 per cent of the tax paid by residents of one of the poorest states (Bihar) accrues to other states (Rao and Sen, 1996).[15] Some states even levy 'export taxes' in the form of purchase tax on export of items like rice (Bagchi, forthcoming).

Taxation of interstate sales is believed to constitute an important factor impeding the growth of the common market in India (Rao, 1993). Yet another impediment has been tax disharmony among the states resulting from intense tax competition.

Tax Competition

While origin based sales taxation provided scope for tax exportation, with little coordination among them,[16] the states have engaged in what is called 'tax war' in the form of lower rates of tax and incentives of various kinds to attract trade and industry to their territories, thereby distorting the location of industries, upsetting equity, and sapping the revenue potential of their chief revenue generator, namely the sales tax.

[14] Theoretical literature on the subject suggests that the origin and destination principle can be equivalent and the origin principle may even be superior under certain assumptions such as flexible exchange rate and wages and so on (see Lockwood, de Meza and Myles, 1995 and Keen, 1993). These conditions do not however seem to hold in the case of states in a federation.

[15] This estimate appears to be on the high side. However, the incidence of tax exportation is undoubtedly significant and is practised by all states in varying degrees.

[16] There are 'Zonal Councils' of the state sales tax Commissioners under the aegies of the Union Finance Ministry to effect some coordination in this regard, but they have been practically inoperative.

Part XIII of the Indian Constitution contains certain provisions that have served to some extent to contain the potential damage to interstate trade from tax competition or otherwise. Art. 301 lays down several restrictions on the legislatures of both the Union and the states in relation to taxation as well as other heads 'in order to make certain that trade, commerce and intercourse throughout the territory of India shall be free'.[17] In the light of these provisions, in a celebrated case, the Indian Supreme Court ruled that variations in sales tax rates that create trade barriers and directly impinge upon trade and commerce are *ultra vires* and thus pronounced a notification issued by one state government reducing the ST rate applicable only to local cement manufacturers to be unconstitutional.[18] Exceptions have however been made by the court in a few subsequent cases whereby certain tax concessions, such as in regard to goods produced by new industrial units in a state have been upheld.[19] The latitude allowed in this, as also in a few other cases, shows that the 'commerce clauses' of the Indian Constitution are scarcely adequate to ensure harmony or prevent tax competition among the states.

Presumably anticipating disharmony, the Constitution-makers sought, somewhat illogically — as the Taxation Enquiry Commission of 1953–4 pointed out — to circumscribe the states' powers of sales taxation with regard of goods declared by Parliament to be of importance to interstate trade and commerce even when these are sold within their own territories. The rate of tax on goods so specified cannot exceed what is laid down as the maximum for the taxation of interstate sales. Through a tax rental agreement — apparently at the behest of the Centre — the states have allowed sales tax on three commodities — textiles, tobacco and sugar — to be substituted by an additional excise duty leviable by the Centre on the understanding that the revenue would be passed on to them. In recent years this arrangement has been resented by the states, and several of them have attempted to circumvent these restrictions in ingenious ways (e.g. by imposing an entry tax or octroi on goods falling within the 'declared'

[17] Supreme Court in Atiabari Tea Company's case (1961), Supreme Court Reporter 809.
[18] India Cement Ltd. *v.* State of Andhra Pradesh (SC) (1968) 69 Sales Tax Cases 305.
[19] Video Electronics *v.* State of Rajasthan (1990) 77 STC 83.

category). Some states have exploited other entries in the state list for instance by imposing a levy on tobacco and high-value textiles in the form of a 'luxury tax'.[20]

Lacking effective border controls and coordination in tax administration among the states, even the origin-based sales taxation has run into problems because of the practice of transporting goods interstate through branch transfer since such transfers not being 'sales' as recognized in law are not liable to sales tax. Pressed by the states to plug the loopholes in the CST Act so exploited by unscrupulous traders, Parliament amended the Constitution in 1982 authorizing the levy of a tax on inter-branch consignments. Consignment tax, if enacted, cannot but compound the inefficiencies and inter-jurisdictional inequities that stem from the operation of the interstate sales tax, and will constitute another roadblock to the growth of a common market in India. It will also heighten the handicap suffered by domestic producers in competing with imports.

Narrow Base

Another drawback of the tax assignment scheme in the Indian Constitution is the exclusion of services from the base of both Union excises and states' sales taxes, the respective entries for both being couched in terms of 'goods' without any reference to services.

Aside from definitional conundrums associated with the taxation of 'manufacturing', implementation of Union excise duties has encountered acute problems because the tax base refers to 'goods manufactured or produced in India', leaving out by implication any service component, and thus creating wide scope for manipulation of the manufacturing value by passing on a substantial part of it as post-manufacturing expense (PME). What constitutes PME has been a fertile ground for disputes. Similar problems have been encountered in sales taxation in so far as the tax is levied on manufacturers. Services now account for over 40 per cent of the GDP and its exclusion from the major product taxes is a drag on the entire tax system and a source of inequity and distortion.

Invoking its powers under the residuary entry in the Union List, the Centre has started taxing services selectively, first by bringing three items under the net and extending it to a few

---

[20] For example the West Bengal Luxury Tax Act 1994.

more. The 1997–8 Union Budget has proposed to add another six to the list. Several of these form business inputs, e.g. clearing agents' fees and transportation of goods by road, while some like the service of outdoor caterers can be regarded essentially as items of final consumption, which in line with the spirit of tax assignment scheme in the Constitution should have been taxable by the states. The Centre has also used its residuary powers to levy a tax on foreign and inland travel, and on the services provided by certain classes of hotels under a so called 'Expenditure Tax'. While the legality of this tax has been upheld by the Supreme Court, clearly there is an overlap with states' jurisdiction as a tax is levied on luxury hotels in some states too.[21]

All in all, the tax scene in India is chaotic. The expectations underlying the demarcation of tax jurisdictions in the Constitution by assigning exclusive powers to the two levels of government with regard to taxes allocated to them has not materialized. On the contrary, there has been de facto co-occupancy of tax bases by both the Centre and the states in several important areas with multiplicity of levies, laws, and procedures. Attempts are being made to bring about a measure of harmony in the states' sales taxes but the process is yet to gain momentum.[22] It is doubtful whether the infirmities of the present structure can be remedied unless the problems are tackled at their root, namely the assignment of tax powers between the Centre and the states.

III. · Tax Assignment in Federalist Economies: Gleanings from Literature

Assignment of tax powers among different layers of government — 'Who should tax, Where and What?', to quote the title of the celebrated Musgrave (1983) paper on the subject — constitutes a

---

[21] As for example, the Tax on Luxuries Act 1987 of Maharashtra.

[22] The reform agenda drawn up by the State Finance Ministers in the wake of the NIPFP (1994) study, contemplated some harmonization of the sales tax rates among the states but put off the consideration of easing out the CST by referring it to a committee of experts. Even the agreement to harmonize the tax rates seems to have been put on hold as several states have gone about changing their ST rates in violation of the understanding even while claiming to introduce VAT for selected commodities. The budget of the West Bengal government for 1997–8 reducing ST on motor-cars to 4 per cent is a case in point.

key component of all multilevel governmental systems. While the matter cannot be decided entirely in isolation from the assignment of functional responsibilities, it is universally recognized that the viability of a federal polity depends critically on how the powers of raising revenue to meet their expenditures are allocated among the respective governmental levels.

The matter would have been simple were it possible for jurisdictions providing public services to apply the market principle and realize the cost of supplying public services from the beneficiaries. Since the beneficiaries of many governmental activities are not identifiable, and nor can the benefits be measured for each person individually, taxes have to be levied by governments to meet their cost. One may argue, that it is still possible to use the benefit principle as a guiding rule on the tax assignment question (McLure, 1993). Thus, it would be in order for a lower level government to levy an income tax on residents within their jurisdiction to recover the cost of a service that caters primarily to their need, e.g. maintaining a park, to cite McLure's example. Unfortunately, there are not many taxes with significant revenue potential, the incidence of which can be confined only to a given geographical area or a clearly definable group of beneficiaries. There are spillovers of various kinds and ramifications that affect everyone, including the jurisdiction levying the tax. Hence tax exporting and tax competition can and do occur in multilevel taxation resulting in inefficiencies.

Distortions and interjurisdictional inequity also result when taxes are assigned on the principle of territorial entitlement in a federation where natural resources are unevenly located and the powers to tax them are assigned to the subnational governments, as illustrated by the experience of Alaska in USA and Alberta in Canada during the oil crisis. At the same time we cannot invoke economic inefficiencies from subnational taxation as the decisive reason to centralize all tax powers as that undermines the principal economic argument for decentralized governance, namely establishing accountability for expenditure decisions by linking them with the obligation to raise the required resources.

Tax competition, it may also be argued, is not all that harmful as it compels governments to 'behave' and perform efficiently as otherwise people vote with their feet in the celebrated Tiebout fashion. The problem is, as in most fields of economic policy, there are trade-offs among the objectives, and in this case, between accountability and autonomy of lower level governments on the one hand and equity and efficiency, on the other.

Keeping in view the trade-offs in relation to specific taxes and the criterion of fair entitlement of the constituent units consistent with economic efficiency, Musgrave propounded three basic principles to guide tax assignment in decentralized economies from which it follows:

- Taxes that help stabilization and redistribution should be central. Hence progressive income and expenditure taxes should be with the Centre;
- Tax bases with low mobility across jurisdictions can be with the states, but those that are locationally concentrated should be with the Centre. Thus, residence based income tax, payroll taxes, destination-based product tax, and property tax should be with the middle level government units. Natural resource tax should be with the Centre allowing some room to the lower level governments to tax businesses and natural resources to recover costs of providing services and neutralize negative externalities from congestion, pollution and so on.
- Governments at all levels should have power to collect benefit taxes and user charges.

(McLure, 1983)

Not everyone agrees with all aspects of the scheme propounded by Musgrave. For instance, McLure (1993), while endorsing the centralization of progressive income taxes, and residence-based taxation of income by subnational governments, disapproves of Musgrave's preference for assigning the corporation income tax and the taxes on natural resources to subnational levels (Musgrave and Musgrave, 1994).

Difference of opinion among experts in the application of the general principles enunciated above to particular taxes is evident also from the debate in Canada over the possible directions for restructuring the division of tax powers between the federal government and the provinces.[23] As a lasting remedy for the budget problems of the federal and provincial governments in Canada in recent years, various suggestions have been put forward for a

---

[23] The summary of the Canadian debate presented here draws liberally on Bird (1993).

radical restructuring of the tax assignment scheme currently operating there whereby the federal government levies, apart from customs tariffs, income taxes and a goods and service tax (essentially a VAT), the provinces exercise concurrent powers of taxation in income tax (both personal and corporate) as well as sales tax and excises, while the local governments levy the property tax. Under a tax collection agreement the personal income tax (PIT) is administered by the federal government for all provinces except Quebec and the corporate income tax in all but three. The provinces set their tax rates as a percentage of the basic federal tax in the case of PIT, and of the taxable income of corporations as assessed by the federal administration.

According to one school, the right way to rebalance the budgets in Canada would be to transfer PIT, the fastest growing revenue source, to the provinces and allocate the corporate, sales, and excise taxes exclusively to the federal government along with such reassignment of expenditure responsibilities as may be necessary (Ruggeri, et al., 1993). In sharp contrast with this proposal, another view favours federal dominance over PIT on equity grounds and corporate taxes on efficiency grounds, and turning over sales taxes entirely to the provincial governments. Imbalance if any in the finances of different levels of government would under this proposal have to be redressed by suitably structured federal–provincial transfers (Boadway, 1992). Yet another proposal suggests assigning, (i) corporate taxes entirely to the federal government; (ii) replacing the GST and federal excises with appropriately increased provincial (retail) sales and excise taxes; and (iii) retaining the present system of PIT collection agreements with more joint federal–provincial collaboration. This, according to the authors of the proposal would meet not only the criteria of equity and efficiency but also have the merit of promoting accountability, simplicity, and flexibility (Ip and Mintz, 1992). Few see any particular merit in 'separation'.

A recent survey of the literature on the subject too notes that the policy advice emanating from theory and practice would seem to be conflicting. However, when taken together, the literature does seem to offer a consistent agenda for the design of a welfare-maximizing tax policy in federalist economies (Inman and Rubinfeld, 1996). Applying the optimal taxation approach to fiscal federalism and building on a model first propounded by Gordon

(1983), the authors of the survey demonstrate why it is irrational to expect a welfare-maximizing tax policy to operate in a decentralized economy when the constituent units are allowed to determine their tax regimes without any constraint. The potential sources of inefficiency and inequity are: tax exportation, politically determined redistribution policies, effects resulting from policies to reduce congestion and pollution in a given state by driving businesses and households to others, competitive spillovers on revenues and costs of public goods, and 'beggar-thy-neighbour' tax competition. Tax exportation encourages overuse of levies of which the incidence falls on outsiders while tax competition may lead to vertical tax inequities and also affect revenue adversely as taxes with mobile bases are likely to be under-utilized. Empirical evidence — cross-border shopping, labour migration, and capital movements in the US — lend ample support for the theoretical reasoning underlying these apprehensions. The brief account of the Indian tax scene given in sect. II would also seem to strengthen the prognostication flowing from theory.

Two possible remedies for the inefficiencies and inequities put forward in the survey are: 'regulation' of state tax bases, and/or institution of grants-in-aid as fiscal incentives that serve to influence state taxes to be resident-oriented, and not source- or origin-based. Where source-based taxation is retained by the states, equalizing grants with larger shares going to 'tax-poor' states and taxing the rich states would be appropriate.

A truly resident-based tax system is not easy to administer at the state level. In the case of income tax it requires information regarding all out-of-state accruals/earnings and for consumption taxes there has to be either full border controls or faithful reporting of out-of-state consumption. Piggybacking a state-chosen tax rate on a centrally laid out tax base provides a good alternative. It is possible also to think of an integrated VAT administered centrally but with a state component, as seems to be under contemplation in Canada (Gendron et al., 1996) and Brazil (Silvani and Santos, 1996).

IV. RETHINKING TAX ASSIGNMENT IN THE INDIAN FEDERATION

As noted in sect. II, the scheme of tax assignment contemplated in the Indian Constitution would, at first sight, seem to conform broadly to the principles flowing from theory. A closer look at the system as it has been operating, however shows that going by the criteria that are now universally considered to be relevant to designing tax assignment in federalist economies, the Indian system performs poorly on most counts. Rather than being conducive to fiscal stability, it has contributed to growing imbalances in the government budgets by weakening the accountability of governments for their expenditure decisions. For better accountability the states must have access to some more tax heads than they have at present, coupled with a hard budget constraint.

Piggybacking on the PIT levied by the Centre (or on a centrally assessed base) can be a step in this direction. With such a system, agricultural incomes can also be brought under the income tax base. This need not interfere with land revenue which can and ought to be assigned to village local bodies. Sharing the tax base is already operative in the case of the income of tea plantations and, barring one or two instances, has been working well.

Deficiencies of the tax assignment scheme in the Indian Constitution are more pronounced in the case of domestic trade taxes. All the potential sources of tax inefficiency or inequity in decentralized federalist economies appear to be at work. Apart from the CST, there are several other taxes that provide scope for tax exportation, e.g. octroi, market fees and cesses on the sale of agricultural commodities. The centralization of the powers of taxing minerals by the Centre has also not helped to keep the tax exporting propensity of states in check, as the high level of cesses on mineral royalties levied in some states shows. On the other hand, tax competition has also emerged as a significant factor creating distortions in business decisions, constraining revenue growth, and fouling up equity. Disharmony is writ large also on the product taxes levied by the Centre and the states, and the attempt to levy Union excise on maximum retail price (MRP). Clearly, the system calls for harmonization or at least some coordination among the states and also between the Centre and the states.

Going by theory and the worldwide trend, it would appear that the approach towards a rational structure of indirect taxation in the country lies in installing a system of destination-type VAT to replace all taxes on domestic production and trade with a comprehensive base covering both goods and services. Since, however, we do not have a clean slate to start from, the key question is how do we go about it?

After considering the pros and cons of various alternatives, such as a national VAT, or an entirely state level VAT replacing both union excises and sales taxes or a concurrently levied central and state VAT, NIPFP (1994) expressed its preference for a value added tax at the state level with selected items of excise at the Centre as the long term goal but moving in the interim to change the state STs into a VAT and the Union excises into a manufacturers' VAT. An earlier study by Burgess, Howes, and Stern (1993) came to a similar conclusion.

It is however increasingly recognized that operating a destination based VAT at the subnational level is not simple. The crux of the problem lies in how to deal with interstate trade in a country where, as in a federation, there are no border controls. Considering the problems insuperable, many are inclined to think that a destination-based VAT can be levied effectively only at the national level (McLure, 1993). It is relevant to note that China centralized its VAT system in 1994 while Mexico had done so earlier, and Switzerland instituted a nationally promulgated VAT in 1995 (Bourne, 1995). The system in operation in the European Union since 1993, under what is called the transitional regime, with zero-rating of intra-Union sales between registered dealers located in different countries within the Union would seem to provide a good model of a decentralized VAT on the destination principle. There is however a growing feeling that the EU system is onerous and administratively not simple (Michie, 1995 and Terra, 1994), and a proposal is now under consideration of the EU to move towards a 'unitary system' (Commission of European Communities, 1996).

Canada's experience with a federal level VAT and provincial sales taxes also shows that independent operation of product taxes at two levels does not provide a satisfactory or lasting solution to the problem of domestic trade taxation. It is in this context that the feasibility of a concurrent VAT, of which a model was put forward in Poddar (1990), deserves attention. The problems of crossborder (i.e. interstate) trade, it is increasingly felt, can be overcome without complete centralization of the levy, if there is an overriding central VAT but allowing room for the states to levy their own VAT or retail sales tax on a common base with some minor variations and under central administration (Mintz et al., 1994).

For a concurrent VAT to be introduced in India — and that seems to hold the best promise for reforming the domestic indirect taxes — it will be necessary to fundamentally change the pattern of tax assignment in the Constitution, moving away from the so called separation principle at least partially and giving concurrent powers to the Centre and the states except with regard to tariffs and corporation tax which should continue to be central and property tax which should remain with local governments. Given the political configuration in the country, can we hope to see any initiative towards such a reform in the foreseeable future?

If Inman and Rubinfeld (1996) are to be believed the chances do not seem to be very bright. In democracies where central decision making is subject to pulls and pressures from individuals and small groups of representatives rather than being framed by a decisive majority, tax failures that arise within a decentralized federalist public economy are unlikely to be handled efficiently. In such a political arrangement, the same economic incentives that lead states to adopt inefficient tax policies like tax exportation will lead their elected representatives to adopt inefficient Central government policies to correct those tax failures and retain source based taxation and overuse Central government grants policy. The current Indian federal fiscal scene seems ominously close to this description.

Whether or not India goes in for the prescriptions that flow from theory and lessons of practice, it is widely acknowledged that for an efficient tax policy to be in place, a federal country requires local and central political institutions to establish such policies and then pursue them with conviction. It is a pity that the institutions for interstate consultation so thoughtfully provided for in our Constitution have not been made much use of, and policy-making in such a vital area as taxation has been going on in virtual disregard of the negative fallout of policies that are pursued by governments at different levels without adequate coordination. A prerequisite for rethinking on tax assignment in the Indian federation is the activation of institutions for Centre–state dialogue and perhaps the creation of some more.

V. Concluding Remarks

Contrary to the impression that has somehow gone round in the country and received support from high powered panels like the

Commission on Centre–State Relations (the Sarkaria Commission), tax assignment in the Indian federal system is flawed in several respects. A fundamental flaw is dysfunctional allocation of tax heads with splintered bases on the one hand, and crippling limitations on some of the major bases, on the other (e.g. that of services from the sales and excise taxes, and agricultural income from the central income tax). Another major flaw has been source-based taxation at the subnational level. The constitutional constraints on the states' powers of source based taxation have not been able to adequately check the inefficiencies, and the system continues to suffer from infirmities stemming from this as also the absence of any effective coordination among different governmental levels. Based essentially on a framework that was devised some sixty years ago (the Government of India Act, 1935) the scheme is outdated and inadequate to meet the requirements of a modern federal economy and seriously needs to be redrawn.

A prerequisite for any move for fundamental reform in an area so sensitive as Centre–State division of tax powers is public recognition of the need for radical change. That in turn calls for a national debate. It is a pity that when rethinking on tax assignment is apace even in well established federal democracies like Canada and the USA, in India the debate has not even begun.

REFERENCES

Bagchi, Amaresh (1995): 'Tax Harmonization in Federations: A Survey of Theory and Practice' (NIPFP Working Paper No. 1).
—— (1996a): 'Harmonizing Sales Taxes in a Federation — Case Studies: India and Canada' (NIPFP Working Paper No. 9).
—— (1996b): 'Fiscal Management — The Federal Dimension', Paper presented at Symposium on Fiscal Policy, Public Policy and Governance, NIPFP, 1996.
—— (forthcoming): 'Taxation of Goods and Services in India: An Overview', in *Public Finance — Policy Issues for India* by Sudipto Mundle (ed.) (New Delhi: Oxford University Press).
Banting, Keith, Douglas Brown and Thomas Courchene (eds) (1994): *The Future of Fiscal Federalism* (Kingston, Ontario: Queen's University).
Bird, Richard M. (1993): 'Federal–Provincial Taxation in the 1990s', in Roy Hogg and Jack Mintz (eds).
Bird, Richard, Richard Ebel and Christine Walliah (eds) (1995):

Decentralisation of the Socialist State (Washington, DC: World Bank).

Boadway, Robin (1993): 'Renewing Fiscal Federalism', in *Policy Options*, Dec. (Montreal: Institute for Research in Public Policy).

Boadway, Robin and Michael Keen (1995): 'Efficiency and the Optimal Direction of Federal–State Transfers' (London: Working Paper, Institute for Fiscal Studies).

Bourne, J.H. (1995): 'The New Swiss VAT', *VAT Monitor*, Jan./Feb.

Burgess, R., S. Howes and N. Stern (1993): *The Reform of Indirect Taxes in India* (STICERD, London School of Economics, EF No. 7).

Campos, Ed and Sanjay Pradhan (1996): *Budgetary Institutions and Expenditure Outcomes* (World Bank Policy Research Working Paper, 1946).

Commission of the European Communities (1996): *Taxation in the European Union* [Sec (96) 487].

Cnossen, Sijbren (ed.) (1987): *Tax Coordination in the European Community, Introduction* (Amsterdam: Kluer).

Government of India (1988): *Report of the Commission on Centre–State Relations* (Chairman: Justice Sarkaria).

—— (1991): *Interim Report of the Tax Reforms Committee* (Chairman: Raja Chelliah) (New Delhi: Ministry of Finance).

—— (1994): *Report of the Tenth Finance Commission* (New Delhi: Ministry of Finance).

Gendron, Pierre-Pascal, Jack Mintz and Thomas Wilson (1996): 'VAT Harmonization in Canada, Recent Developments and the Need for Flexibility', in Perry et al. (eds).

Gillis, M., Carl Shoup and S.G. Sicat (eds) (1990): *Value Added Taxation in Developing Countries* (Washington, DC: World Bank).

Gordon, Roger (1983): 'An Optimal Taxation Approach to Fiscal Federalism', *Quarterly Journal of Economics*, 95.

Hogg, Roy and Jack Mintz (eds) (1993): *Tax Policy in Turbulent Times* (Kingston, Ontario: Queen's University).

Inman, Robert and Daniel Rubinfeld (1996): 'Designing Tax Policy in Federalist Economies: An Overview', in *Journal of Public Economics*, 60.

Ip, Irene and Jack Mintz (1992): *Dividing the Spoils: The Federal–Provincial Allocation of Taxing Powers* (Toronto: C.D. Howe Institute).

Keen, Michael (1993): 'The Welfare Economics of Tax Coordination in the European Community: A Survey', *Fiscal Studies* (London).

Lockwood, Ben, David de Meza and Gareth Myles (1995): 'On the European Union VAT Proposals: The Superiority of Origin over Destination Taxation', *Fiscal Studies* (London), vol. 16, no. 1.

Maslove, Allan (ed.) (1994): *Taxation in a Subnational Jurisdiction* (Toronto: University of Toronto Press).

McLure Jr., Charles, Christine Wallich and Jennie Litvack (1995): 'Special Issues in Russian Federal Finance', in Bird et al. (eds).

—— (1983): *Tax Assignment in Federal Countries* (Canberra: Australian National University).

McLure Jr., Charles (1993): 'The Brazilian Tax Assignment Problem: Ends, Means and Constraints', Paper prepared for International Symposium on Fiscal Reform, Sao Paolo, Sept.

Michie, George (1995): 'Survey on VAT and the Single Market', in *VAT Monitor* (July/Aug. 1990)

Mihaljek (1993): *Fiscal Reform in Yugoslavia*, in Tanzi (ed.).

Mintz, J., T. Wilson and P. Gendron (1994): 'Canada's GST: Sales Tax Harmonization is the Key to Simplification', *Tax Notes International* (March 7).

Mukhopadhyay, S. (1996): *Manufacturing in Central Excise* (Delhi: CENTAX Publications).

—— (1997): 'Maximum Retail Price — A Step Towards Dissastor', *Business Standard* (7 April).

Musgrave, Richard (1983): 'Who Should Tax Where and What', in McLure (ed.).

Musgrave, Richard and Peggy Musgrave (1994): *Tax Equity with Multiple Jurisdictions*, in Maslove (ed.).

National Institute of Public Finance and Policy (NIPFP) (1994): *Reform of Domestic Trade Taxes in India: Issues and Options* (Report of a Study Team led by A. Bagchi) (New Delhi: NIPFP).

Perry, David et al. (eds) (1996): *Essays on Fiscal Federalism and Federal Finance in Canada* (Discussion paper) (Toronto: International Centre for Tax Studies, University of Toronto).

Poddar, Satya (1990): *Value Added Tax at the State Level*, in Gillis et al. (eds).

Rao, M.G. (1993): 'Impediments to Internal Trade and Allocative Distortions in India' (Working Paper 3, NIPFP).

Rao, Govinda and Raja Chelliah (1996): *Fiscal Federalism in India* (New Delhi: Indian Council of Social Science Research).

Rao, M. Govinda and Tapas K. Sen (1996): *Fiscal Federalism in India: Theory and Practice* (Macmillan India).

Rivlin, Alice (1992): *Reviving the American Dream* (Washington, DC: Brookings Institute).

Ruggeri, G.C., D. Van Wart, G.K. Robertson and R. Howard (1993): 'Vertical Fiscal Imbalance and the Reallocation of Tax Fields in Canada', in *Canadian Public Policy*, XIX.

Shah, Anwar (1994): *The Reform of Intergovernmental Fiscal Relations in Developing and Emerging Market Economies* (Washington, DC: World Bank Research Series).

Shiva Rao, B. (1968): *The Framing of India's Constitution* (New Delhi: Indian Institute of Public Administration).

Silvani, Carlos and Paulo dos Santos (1996): 'Administrative Aspects. of Brazil's Consumption Tax Reform', *VAT Monitor*, May/June.

Tanzi, Vito (ed.) (1993): *Transition to Market: Studies in Fiscal Reform* (Washington, DC: IMF).

—— (1995): 'Fiscal Federalism and Decentralization', Paper prepared for World Bank Annual Conference on Development Economics.

Terra, Ben J.M. (1994): 'Report of the Country of Origin Commission', *VAT Monitor*, May/June.

Whalley, John and Deborah Fretz (1990): *The Economics of the Goods and Services Tax* (Toronto: Canadian Tax Foundation).

14

Liberalization, Economic Reforms, and Centre–State Relations

Raja J. Chelliah

I. EMERGING TRENDS IN CENTRE–STATE RELATIONS

It is generally acknowledged that the Indian Constitution is not fully federal, such as those of the United States of America or the Commonwealth of Australia. The founding fathers endowed it with certain pronounced unitary features. The extensive list of concurrent powers stipulated in the Constitution considerably widens the scope of the Central government's jurisdiction. Besides, there are special provisions that place restrictions on the freedom of action of the states. Nevertheless, the Constitution provided the states with a fairly wide area of autonomy in both the economic and social sectors to enable each state to fashion its own level and pattern of services in the key areas of community life.

Many of the provisions that could be considered to restrict the freedom of action by the state governments are in the nature of enabling provisions, to be used only when the fundamental interests of the nation as a whole were affected. For example, Arts. 249, 250, and 356 are in the nature of special provisions that were expected to be rarely used and only when this was absolutely essential. Such a view was expressed by Dr Ambedkar and several other prominent members of the Constituent Assembly at the time the Constitution was framed. Again, the concurrent powers could generally have been used by the Centre to lay down broad policy guidelines and the states could have been left to formulate and implement their own policies within the framework of these guidelines. Regional aspirations would have been more fully satisfied under such a dispensation. In any event, it seems most unlikely that the founding fathers of the Constitution had envisaged that the concurrent powers would either be used to substantially increase the area of effective action of the Centre or that Art. 356 would be repeatedly used for partisan political advantage.

The people inhabiting the territories of the Indian Union are inheritors of a composite culture with many common elements, and also the proud legatees of a worthy historic past. While many traditions and common elements of culture and religion bind them, the people of India are heterogeneous in several important respects: the diversity is not only seen in the different languages spoken by large subnational groups, but also arise from the differences in racial composition, customs, food habits, and several other characteristics of everyday life.

The Indian people are, therefore, ideal candidates for government under a federal Constitution. Thus, in the Indian case, the size of the country and the heterogeneity of its people lend considerable weight to the economic argument for fiscal federalism, that the decentralized provision of public services is more efficient if there are no economies of scale and interjurisdictional spillovers, or that these can be taken care of through an adequate systems of grants (Oates, 1977). The size and heterogeneity also strengthen the case for federalism on political and administrative grounds.

Perhaps because they were concerned about preserving the unity of the country, understandably so in the early years of Independence, the founding fathers settled for a *via media* between a true federal and a unitary Constitution, under which the Central government could intervene decisively when there was a real threat to the national interests. It was probably expected by them that in normal times, the Constitution would be worked on a federal basis.

However, the then ruling Congress Party under the leadership of Pandit Nehru decided that the promotion of rapid growth with social justice was possible only under central planning within a broad socialist framework. The adoption of centralized economic planning with a pronounced socialist bias greatly contributed to the augmentation of the powers of the Central government. Indeed, Central planning covering wide areas of the economy involving as it does centralized decision-making in relation to resource allocation and production activities is the negation of the principle of true federalism. For purposes of planning, the Central government extended its activities and control to most of the important spheres of the economy. For example, by virtue of the power conferred by Entry 52 in the Union List (Industries, the control of which by the Union is declared by Parliament by law to be expedient in the public interest), the Industrial Development and Regulation Act was passed conferring on the Centre control over almost all important industries. Along with the dominant position the Centre had acquired in relation to public sector plans, its relative strength vis-à-vis the states and the private sector increased as a consequence of the introduction of physical controls over economic activities, the most important of them being exchange control, licensing of industry, import control and price control with regard to several important commodities. All these would still not have given the Central government the economic clout it had, but for the vast extension of public ownership, at the Central level, of industrial, financial, and commercial enterprises through nationalization and reservation to the public sector of new starts in key areas. The feeling of helplessness and near subjugation experienced by the states, especially those at the periphery of power, arose from the spectre of overwhelming economic power wielded by the Centre.

To this was added the resentment against what was considered unwarranted federal intervention in the political sphere through the use of Art. 356 and by other means. Such intervention was resorted to almost invariably for the benefit of a political party rather than for the benefit of the Central government as such. Now, under economic liberalization, involving as it does the dismantling of an array of controls and the adoption of a more open, market-oriented economy, the Central government has given up exercising many of its inherent powers in the economic field. Its dominance in several industries has diminished considerably with the entry of the private sector and the termination of price control in several areas. Not only the private sector but also the state governments are now freer to take the initiative and formulate their own policies.

The new sense of freedom engendered by economic liberalization coupled with an end of a single party domination in the political sphere has naturally led to the resurgence of the federal

spirit and the assertion of regional aspirations. Centre–State relations are in a flux now, and there is a demand that these relations
be restructured, including and in particular financial relations.

It is to be hoped that there will be scope for fulfilling the major
aspirations of the states once the process of liberalization is complete and that the development of each state can be autonomously
determined subject to minimum constraints imposed in the overall
national interest. There will be no need to amend the Constitution
to any significant degree. One important constitutional amendment that may be carried out is that suggested by the Sarkaria
Commission: that the residuary powers, except in regard to taxes,
may be given to the states through an amendment of Entry 97 in
the Union List. Apart from that, a convention could be evolved,
through discussions in the Inter-State Council, on the extent to
which the Centre needs to act in the concurrent fields. In some
areas, the Centre may have to legislate and also be active, for
example, in the area of electric power; in many others, it may
merely lay down the broad guidelines, for example, elementary
and secondary education and industrial relations; and in yet others
it may leave the entire matter in the hands of the states.

An agreement on concurrent powers on the lines suggested
above would considerably enhance the area of autonomy of the
states. It would however also be necessary to substantially modify
the processes and procedures adopted by the Planning Commission
in regard to what are called state plans. With a clear shift to a market
oriented economy, the role, structure, and ambit of activity of the
Planning Commission have to be drastically recast. This is a larger
question that cannot be addressed here, but it is seen that already
the responsibilities of the Planning Commission in relation to
resource allocation have been significantly curtailed. In the new
setting, there seems to be no point in going through the same old
motions of plan discussions with the states. The states should be
left to formulate their own plans within the broad guidelines laid
down by the National Development Council (NDC) and the Planning Commission itself. There is no need to call the Chief Ministers
to Delhi; the amount of plan assistance that a state will receive in
accordance with the accepted formulae should be intimated to the
state government concerned.

There should of course be constant interaction between the
states and the Planning Commission through official discussions,

meetings, and conferences. The Planning Commission could also evaluate the plan performance of each state which could be discussed with the state concerned and then be submitted to the NDC for discussion. These changes would once again enhance the states' sense of being in a position to act independently in the important area of economic development.

The Constitutional amendment of Entry 97 in the Union List, the agreement on the extent of use of concurrent powers by the Centre and the changes in procedures in relation to state plan formulation suggested above, taken together with the decentralization brought about by liberalization would do much to satisfy the states' demand for greater freedom of action.[1] In addition, it is vitally important to restructure the financial relations between the Centre and the states and among the states themselves. This is so not only because finance is the lifeblood of government, but also because every step or action taken in the financial field has consequences for the real sector of the economy.

Before discussing the 'burning' topic of intergovernmental financial relations, it is necessary to set down some ground rules that must be observed in formulating or restructuring Centre–State relations in a federation. A federation is much more than a common market, and must not be treated as a mere conglomeration of confederating states. The Central government in a federation must be endowed with sufficient powers necessary

(a)   to safeguard national security;
(b)   to determine the broad outlines of the economic structure;
(c)   to maintain macroeconomic stability;
(d)   to take suitable action to mitigate interregional and inter-state inequalities;
(e)   to take steps for the maintenance of a common market; and
(f)   to ensure that the constitutional rights of the citizens are upheld or enforced in all the federating states.

In addition, of course, it should have the exclusive power to deal with foreign affairs including foreign trade.

[1] In this contribution, I am not discussing purely political questions. However, it may be pointed out that agreement among the major political parties on the provisions to be enacted to ensure that Art. 356 is not used for purely partisan purposes would considerably ease the strain in Centre–State relations.

The present political context created by several regional parties coming together to form the government at the Centre does indeed provide an opportunity of bringing about a more decentralized polity. However, the national elite must explain to the people the need to retain with the Centre certain vital powers, as enumerated above, in order to promote unity, economic strength, and interregional equity. All this would not be possible if we were to agree to the demand put forward in the Anandpur Sahib Resolution of Akali Dal (as reproduced in Government of India, 1984). The demand was that only defence, foreign affairs, currency and communications should be the Centre's responsibilities. A similar demand was also put forward *in a Memorandum on Centre–State Relations* (West Bengal Government, 1977). In this *Memorandum*, it was suggested that the Centre should be assigned only defence, foreign affairs including foreign trade, currency, communications and economic coordination. It stated: 'The role of the Centre should be one of coordination. In areas such as planning, fixing of prices, wages, etc., the Centre may not only coordinate, but also issue general direction.' But the *Memorandum* makes it clear that in regard to economic planning and economic coordination, the Centre will have to be bound by the general guidelines laid down by the National Development Council (NDC) and that the composition of the Planning Commission itself will be determined by the NDC. So, finally, 'nothing beyond foreign relations, defence, communications, currency and related matters should be the exclusive domain of the Centre'. The *Memorandum* really envisages that the Central government will act at the behest of the majority of the Chief Ministers in all economic matters except in regard to currency and communications!

I am constrained to point out that the objectives of maintaining a common market, promoting rapid economic growth, and reducing interregional differences in levels of development and standards of living would be greatly threatened if the Central government's powers and responsibilities were to be restricted to defence, foreign affairs, currency and communications. There is little doubt that this would fragment the economy of the country. It is significant that all economic subjects other than currency, foreign trade, and communications are to be given to the states. If the states are allowed to exercise untrammeled power in relation to interstate trade, industries, prices, energy, interstate rivers, banking, etc., economically India would no longer remain one nation, indeed not even a single customs union.

Most of the state governments or political parties have not asked for such a drastic reduction in the scope, activity, and powers of the Central government as contained in the Anandpur Sahib Resolution or in the West Bengal Government *Memorandum*. It is my contention that the powers granted to the Centre in the Union List should not be pruned beyond granting the residuary powers, barring taxation, to the states. Apart from that, while the area of freedom available to the states should be enhanced in the manner indicated earlier, their powers should be subject to certain constraints needed to safeguard the unity of the country and the common market. Art. 19 (1) of the Constitution provides, *inter alia*, that citizens should have the right to move freely through the territory of India and to reside and settle in any part of it and Art. 301 provides that trade, commerce, and intercourse throughout the territory of India shall be free. These freedoms are, of course, subject to reasonable restrictions, but such restrictions can only be imposed by the President or with his approval. The first mentioned freedom is indeed part of the definition of a nation and both the freedoms are essential to the maintenance of a unified common market. The states in a federation cannot be allowed to impose on their own any barriers to the free interstate movement of goods, labour, and capital.

II. INTERGOVERNMENTAL FINANCIAL RELATIONS

There are three major elements in intergovernmental financial relations in a federation; namely tax assignment, expenditure assignment, and intergovernmental transfers.

As pointed out earlier, it is generally agreed that there are efficiency gains in decentralizing expenditure decisions in all cases where there are no economies of scale and spillovers of costs and benefits are not substantial or can be coped with through Central intervention, e.g. through specific matching grants. Ideally, if sufficient benefit-tax categories of expenditure (within the same geographical area of benefit incidence) can be bunched together, benefit taxes can be recovered from the residents of that area. There would be perfect matching of costs and benefits and expenditure and revenue decisions would be taken by the same group, ensuring fiscal discipline (Breton, 1965; Olson, 1969). This ideal solution is not possible in the real world because of non-availability of tax handles that are productive and at the same time can be confined to the respective regions of benefit incidence. Once we introduce non-benefit taxes of the usual kind, we have to allow for effects on incentives and other economic effects. The areas of incidence of taxes and those of benefit incidence will not coincide, and efficiency in tax collection has also to be taken into account.

In modern federations, while there is considerable decentralization of public expenditure, revenue collection is much more centralized. This is because taxes with mobile bases and those that can (and should) be levied progressively have to be assigned to the Centre — the former because, with mobile bases, people will shift from one jurisdiction to another and the latter because, in order to ensure equitable distribution of taxes among the population, progressive taxes will have to be levied at uniform rates throughout the federation.[2] This asymmetry causes what is familiarly known as vertical fiscal imbalance. Such imbalance necessitates transfers from the Centre to the states (Hunter, 1977).

Since regions and states differ in levels of development and per capita income, horizontal fiscal imbalances also arise in the sense that some states are not able to provide an average standard of services at an average tax price. It is generally agreed that equity considerations require that Central transfers should be effected also to tackle horizontal fiscal imbalance.

A system of federal transfers has to be designed that will place 'enough' resources in the hands of the states in general for them to fulfil their Constitutional expenditure responsibilities and which, at the same time, would make up for deficiency in the fiscal capacity of backward states through special grants distinct from the general transfers to the states.[3] Just as in the case of tax assignment, in designing a system of transfers too, equity and efficiency considerations will have to be kept in view: while deficiency in fiscal capacity

---

[2] Income taxes are of course levied by subnational governments in some federations, but the yield of state income taxes is relatively modest and they cannot be made very progressive. Efficiency in tax collection would also dictate that taxes with broad nationwide bases such as income tax and value added tax are best collected by the Central government.

[3] In this contribution I use the word transfers to mean only transfers on current account, i.e. tax shares and grants on revenue account.

has to be made good, transfers should not be designed in such a way that the recipient states can pass on to the Central government part of their own legitimate burden. That would militate against both efficiency and equity among the states because passing on some burden to the Centre would only mean passing on such burden to the other states.

TABLE 14.1

REVENUE EXPENDITURE OF THE CENTRE AND THE STATES, AND THEIR SHARE IN AGGREGATE REVENUE EXPENDITURE

(Rs crore)

Year	Aggregate revenue expenditure	Revenue expenditure of Centre	Revenue expenditure of states	(3/2) Per-centage	(4/2) Per-centage
(1)	(2)	(3)	(4)	(5)	(6)
1975–6	11847	5325	6522	44.9	55.1
1980–1	23711	9475	14237	40.0	60.0
1985–6	56031	24669	31362	44.0	56.0
1989–90	107704	50873	56831	47.2	52.8
1990–1	122950	55090	67860	44.8	55.2
1991–2	143532	59921	83611	41.7	58.3
1992–3	159056	66906	92150	42.1	57.9
1993–4	183426	77986	105440	42.5	57.5
1994–5 (RE)	219687	91669	128017	41.7	58.3
1995–6 (BE)	244505	102126	142380	41.8	58.2

NOTES: (1) States include Union Territories.
(2) All the basic figures exclude intergovernmental trans-actions Revenue expenditure by the states and Union Territories include interest payments to the Central gov-ernment, which are netted out in the revenue expenditure of the Centre.

SOURCE: *Indian Economic Statistics* (Public Finance).

A review of Centre–State financial relations in India may usefully start with an examination of the trends in the finances of the Centre and the states and their interrelations. Table 14.1 shows the shares of the states and the Centre in aggregate revenue expenditure. It is noticed that the share of the revenue expenditure of the states in the total rose from 55.1 per cent in 1975–6 to 58.3 per cent in 1991–2; it has remained at around that level since then. Correspondingly, the share of the Centre has fallen from 45 per cent in 1975–6 to around 42 per cent in 1995–6. Thus, the major part of expenditure on revenue account is incurred by the states and their share in the 90s is distinctly higher than in the 70s.

TABLE 14.2
REVENUE DEFICIT AND FISCAL DEFICIT OF CENTRE AND
STATES — 1995–6 (AS A PERCENTAGE OF GDP)

Item	1995–6	
	(Rs Crore)	*Percentage of GDP (MP)*
GDP *(Current market prices)*	1078001	
Total Expenditure		
Combined	289658	26.87
Centre (a)	139321 (48.10)	12.92
States (a)	150337 (51.90)	13.95
Revenue deficit		
Combined	42787	3.97
Centre	33331	3.09
States	9385	0.87
Fiscal deficit		
Combined	80203	7.44
Centre	64010	5.94
States (own borrowings)	16193	1.50
Centre (excluding loans to states)	48162	4.47
States (including loans from Centre)	32041	2.97

(a) Figures in parentheses are the percentage to total expenditure.

Table 14.2 shows the shares of the Centre and the states in total public expenditure (Revenue + Capital) in 1995–6 along with their revenue and fiscal deficits. In total expenditure too, the share of the states is larger, at around 52 per cent as against 48 per cent for the Centre. The revenue deficit of the Centre was 3.09 per cent of GDP as against 0.87 per cent in the case of the states. The fiscal deficit of the Centre was 5.94 per cent of GDP in 1995–6 while the combined fiscal deficit of the State governments was 2.97 per cent of GDP. The states' fiscal deficits consist of borrowing from the non-government sector and borrowing from the Centre; borrowing from the Centre amounted to 1.47 per cent of GDP (1995–6). If this amount is subtracted from the fiscal deficit of the Centre, it comes down to 4.47 per cent of GDP. Thus, while the states are responsible for 52 per cent of total expenditure, their share of the deficit comes to 39.9 per cent.

TABLE 14.3
SHARE OF THE CENTRAL GOVERNMENT
IN THE REVENUE RECEIPTS COLLECTED

(percentages)

Year	Gross tax revenue of the Centre/ aggregate tax revenue	Non-tax revenue of the Centre/ aggregate non-tax revenue*	Gross total revenue of the Centre/ aggregate revenue receipts
(1)	(2)	(3)	(4)
1975–6	68.0	58.9	66.5
1980–1	66.4	58.3	64.6
1985–6	66.3	62.1	66.0
1989–90	66.5	64.8	66.0
1990–1	65.6	55.1	64.8
1991–2	65.3	50.4	63.0
1992–3	65.4	57.3	64.1
1993–4	62.1	53.2	60.1
1994–5 (RE)	62.2	43.2	57.9
1995–6 (BE)	62.7	45.5	59.0

NOTE: * Both numerator and denominator exclude interest received by the Centre from the states. The denominator also excludes grants received by the states from the Centre as well.
SOURCE: *Indian Economic Statistics* (Public Finance).

Table 14.3 presents the share of the revenues collected by the Central government in the total revenues collected by the two levels of government. As much as 63 per cent of the total tax revenues is collected by the Centre; this share has fallen over the years. The share of non-tax revenues collected by the Centre has come down even more, from about 65 per cent at the end of the eighties to 45.5 per cent in 1995–6. Taking tax and non-tax revenues together, the Centre collects 59 per cent of the total revenues. Thus, there is a fairly high degree of centralization of revenue collections in the Indian Union, and is particularly marked with regard to tax collections.

Table 14.4 gives the figures of tax revenues accruing to the states, which comprise the taxes levied by them and their shares of Central taxes (tax devolution). The share of taxes accruing to the states in total tax revenues increased from 46 per cent in 1975–6 to 50 per cent in 1989–90 (end of the 80s); it further increased to 55 per cent in 1995–6. The share of the states in total tax revenues, on an accrual basis, has increased during the 90s both because they raise a larger proportion of the total than earlier and also because of a slight increase in devolution as a proportion of tax revenues.

It is interesting that the total tax revenues accruing to the states constituted only 6.6 per cent of GDP in 1975–6; this proportion has been above 8 per cent since 1985–6. In 1995–6 the states had at their disposal tax revenues amounting to 8.3 per cent of GDP.

Lastly, we may look at the share of the states in total revenue accruals (Table 14.5). The total revenues accruing to the states consist of own tax revenues, own non-tax revenues, tax devolution, and grants from the Centre. This total formed 54.6 per cent of the combined revenues of the Centre and the states in 1975–6. The share remained around 61–63 per cent generally in the 80s, and rose in the 90s. It was 66.6 per cent in 1995–6. The Centre which raises 59 per cent of the total combined revenues has, after tax sharing and grants-in-aid, only 33.4 per cent of the total for its own use. It is significant that the total revenues accruing to the states constituted only 9.5 per cent of GDP in 1975–6. It was around 11 to 12 per cent in the 80s, and 12 per cent in 1995–6. Per contra, the revenues at the disposal of the Centre constituted only around half of this percentage of GDP.

TABLE 14.4
The Share of States in the Total
Tax Revenue of the Centre and States

(Rs Crore)

Year (1)	Taxes levied by the states (2)	Devolution of central taxes (3)	Taxes accruing to states (2+3) (4)	Total taxes (Centre and states) (5)	Taxes accruing to states as percentage of total taxes (4/5) (6)	GDP at market prices (7)	Taxes accruing to states as a percentage of GDP (4/7) (8)
1975–6	3573	1599	5172	11182	46.25	78761	6.57
1976–7	4061	1680	5741	12332	46.55	84894	6.76
1977–8	4378	1806	6184	13237	46.72	96067	6.44
1978–9	5003	1953	6956	15528	44.80	104190	6.68
1979–80	5709	3408	9117	17683	51.56	114356	7.97
1980–1	6664	3789	10453	19844	52.68	136013	7.69
1981–2	8295	4258	12553	24142	52.00	159760	7.86
1982–3	9546	4633	14179	27242	52.05	178132	7.96
1983–4	10803	5007	15810	31525	50.15	207589	7.62
1984–5	12343	5853	18196	35813	50.81	231343	7.87

Year	Taxes levied by the states	Devolution of central taxes	Taxes accruing to states (2+3)	Total taxes (Centre and states)	Taxes accruing to states as percentage of total taxes (4/5)	GDP at market prices	Taxes accruing to states as a percentage of GDP (4/7)
(1)	(2)	(3)	(4)	(5)	(6)	(7)	(8)
1985–6	14597	7260	21857	43267	50.52	262243	8.33
1986–7	16701	8360	25061	49539	50.59	292949	8.55
1987–8	19400	9729	29129	56976	51.13	333201	8.74
1988–9	22451	10737	33188	66925	49.59	395782	8.39
1989–90	26056	13097	39153	77692	50.40	456821	8.57
1990–1	30145	14535	44680	87723	50.93	535534	8.34
1991–2	35837	17197	53034	103198	51.39	616799	8.60
1992–3	39530	20522	60052	114165	52.60	705918	8.51
1993–4	46219	22240	68459	121960	56.13	809766	8.45
1994–5(BE)	54547	24843	79390	144372	54.99	953680	8.32
1995–6(BE)	61678	29388	91066	165435	55.05	1098576	8.29

NOTE: States include Union Territories.
SOURCES: 1. Indian Economic Statistics (Public Finance).
            2. Indian Public Finance Statistics 1994–5.
            3. GDP: Economic Survey, 1996–7.

TABLE 14.5
REVENUE ACCRUALS OF THE UNION GOVERNMENT AND THE STATE GOVERNMENTS

Year	Revenue receipts of Centre and states	Revenue accruals of states	Revenue accruals of Centre	Revenue accruals to states as a percentage of total	Revenue accruals to Centre as a percentage of total	GDP at market prices	Revenue accruals of states as a percentage of GDP (2/6)
(1)	(2)	(3)	(4)	(5)	(6)	(7)	(8)
1974–5	11048	6004	5044	54.34	45.66	73235	8.2
1975–6	13687	7475	6212	54.61	45.39	78761	9.5
1976–7	15258	8652	6606	56.70	43.30	84894	10.2
1977–8	16435	9401	7034	57.20	42.80	96067	9.8
1978–9	18775	11008	7767	58.63	41.37	104190	10.6
1979–80	21211	13060	8151	61.57	38.43	114356	11.4
1980–1	23835	15036	8799	63.08	36.92	136013	11.1
1981–2	28881	17504	11377	60.61	39.39	159760	11.0
1982–3	33086	20243	12843	61.18	38.82	178132	11.4
1983–4	36959	22908	14051	61.98	38.02	207589	11.0
1984–5	42993	26220	16713	61.07	38.93	231343	11.3
1985–6	51011	31906	19105	62.55	37.45	262243	12.2

Year	Revenue receipts of Centre and states	Revenue accruals of states	Revenue accruals of Centre	Revenue accruals to states as a percentage of total	Revenue accruals to Centre as a percentage of total	GDP at market prices	Revenue accruals of states as a percentage of GDP (2/6)
(1)	(2)	(3)	(4)	(5)	(6)	(7)	(8)
1986–7	58434	35981	22453	61.58	38.42	292949	12.3
1987–8	66838	42167	24671	63.09	36.91	333201	12.7
1988–9	77512	47767	29745	61.63	38.37	395782	12.1
1989–90	92283	53324	38959	57.78	42.22	456821	11.7
1990–1	99282	62754	36528	63.21	36.79	535534	11.7
1991–2	121619	77959	43660	64.10	35.90	616799	12.6
1992–3	135422	87091	48331	64.31	35.69	705918	12.3
1993–4	147236	101965	45271	69.25	30.75	809766	12.6
1994–5 (RE)	177786	120248	57538	67.64	32.36	953680	12.6
1995–6 (BE)	199578	132994	66584	66.64	33.36	1098576	12.1

NOTE: States include Union Territories.
SOURCES: 1. *Indian Economic Statistics* (Public Finance).
2. *Indian Public Finance Statistics*, 1994–5.
3. GDP: *Economic Survey*, 1996–7.

It cannot be anybody's case that the states are starved of resources, while the Centre is flushed with funds. It is however possible to argue that both the states and the Centre are faced with a resource crunch, and that in this context the Central government's manoeuvrability is much higher.

III.   INTERGOVERNMENTAL FISCAL ARRANGEMENTS

III.1   Tax Assignment

Tax assignment in a federation could follow the principle of concurrency or that of separation. Even if the principle of concurrency is adopted, it has been found that only the Central or Federal government can effectively utilize the more important taxes. In the light of experience with the operation of concurrent powers in the older federations, the principle of separation has been adopted in the newer federations such as Germany, India, and Malaysia (the German system is highly centralized). Under this system, the most important taxes fall to the Central government. The Indian Constitution attempts to embody the principle of separation to the greatest possible degree. However, while *de jure* separation has been achieved *de facto* separation could not be achieved. This is primarily because excise duties were assigned to the Centre, while the sales taxes were assigned to the states and the octroi could be levied by the states' local bodies. This meant, that the domestic trade taxes, that is, internal indirect taxes on commodities, were allowed to be levied by the three levels of government under different guises. Moreover, the states are free to levy any form of sales tax on goods other than those sold in the course of interstate trade, and all the three taxes can be imposed on final goods as well as inputs.

The uncoordinated use of their respective powers to tax goods by the three levels of government led to a complicated, economically irrational, indirect tax system in the country, whose combined incidence could not easily be known. This system obviously led to cascading, escalation of costs, and distortion of producers' choices.

After amending the Constitution, the Central government enacted the Central Sales Tax Act in 1956 empowering it to levy a tax on the sale or purchase of goods other than newspapers, where such sale or purchase takes place in the course of interstate trade or commerce. This tax was introduced on the recommendations of the Taxation Enquiry Commission (1953–4) which argued for a slight or minor departure from the principle of destination in the levy of sales tax. However, the Commission had recommended that the rate of interstate sales tax should not exceed one per cent; but this rate was raised in stages to 4 per cent in the quest for greater resources to finance the successive Plans, disregarding its harmful economic effects. At the rate of 4 per cent, it now acts as an effective barrier to interstate trade and also enables tax exportation by the more industrialized states. Since the tax can be avoided through consignment transfers by a firm located in one state to its own stockyards in the other states before sale in the latter — and this is said to happen on a fairly large scale — there is a clamour to introduce a tax on interstate consignments. It is obvious that if this demand is acceded to, India will cease to be a common market.

The octroi acts as a barrier to trade since it is in the nature of an import duty levied by cities and towns. Besides, it also adds to cascading as it falls on inputs as well as on final goods. The octroi, however, is now being levied only in a few states.

It is also clear that the interstate sales tax, the unremitted sales tax on inputs, and the octroi adversely affect the competitiveness of Indian products in the export markets.

The state governments indulge in tax competition of a welfare decreasing type. Each state tries to attract trade through rate reductions and to attract investment through the offer of more generous sales tax incentives than their neighbours. While there could be some case for limited concessions to make investment in backward areas worthwhile, there has to be broad understanding among the states on capping such incentives and on the circumstances or conditions that would justify them. It is through such consensus, which has been made binding, that the countries in the European Union avoid tax competition amongst their members. The states are themselves beginning to realize that a competitive offer of sales tax incentives is becoming a negative sum game, but it must be pointed out that tax competition among the constituent states in a federation also tends to distort the allocation of resources [for a recent treatment of this problem, see Rao and Sen (1996)].

III.2   Tax Devolution

The Constitution-makers anticipated that the states would need some share in Central taxes to close the vertical fiscal gap that would arise. They therefore stipulated that the yield of individual or personal income tax *should* be shared and that the yield of Union Excise Duties *may* be shared at the discretion of the President. The Finance Commissions, to be appointed every five years, are to make recommendations regarding this and also on the principles that should govern the grants-in-aid of revenues to the states by the Centre. As regards devolution of taxes, the major problem is to determine the quantum of devolution which requires in turn the determination of the size of the likely vertical fiscal gap during any given period.

It is fair to say that the successive Finance Commissions have not succeeded in evolving a consistent theoretical approach to the proper determination of the fiscal gap. One approach would be for the Finance Commission to study the respective Constitutional responsibilities of the two levels of government together with the historical figures and then arrive at a normative measure of vertical fiscal gap. While the greater part of this fiscal gap would have to be closed through devolution, some part could be left to be covered by grants-in-aid to the states with weaker fiscal capacity. It is, of course, not easy to work out the methodology of arriving at a normative size of the gap. The point to note is that the Finance Commissions did not make any conscious attempt to do so. This is partly because a system of centralized economic planning was imposed by the Central government and the growth of the responsibilities of the Centre as well as of the states and their expenditures became crucially dependent on the planning process and on the decisions of the Planning Commission. Consequently, the Finance Commissions (barring the Ninth) tended to accept the growth in expenditures as given by facts and by and large based their recommendations on devolution on the principle of what may be called a modified gap-filling approach. In this approach, the actual base-year level of non-plan revenue expenditures and revenues are accepted as the base, but the projections given by the states are vetted and modified by the application of certain common normative principles. Given this approach, the estimated gaps tended to increase at a fairly rapid rate since, for one thing, the states knew that at the end of every five-year period the estimated actuals for the sixth year would in any case be accepted by the next Finance Commission as the base. Therefore, at least that level of expenditure would be automatically assured.

In the earlier years, particularly during the 60s and 70s, the revenues of the Central government were rising fairly rapidly and faster than their revenue expenditure (because there existed considerable scope for raising taxes from their low base in the 50s). It was therefore possible to keep raising the size of the divisible pool of taxes without too much strain on Central finances. Since the early 80s however, the Central government started running a revenue deficit and its gross tax revenues have been stagnating around 10 to 11 per cent of GDP, and consequently it has not been possible to increase the relative size of the devolution. The size of the devolution had already increased to 85 per cent of personal income tax and 45 per cent of Union Excise Duties by the mid-80s. It would have been much better to have estimated the vertical fiscal gap normatively and to have fixed the proportion of devolution semi-permanently for a period of 15 to 20 years so as to cover a sizeable or a major part of the normative vertical fiscal gap leaving the rest to be covered by grants-in-aid.

The reopening of the question of the relative size of devolution and reconsideration of the principles of distribution of the divisible pool every five years have led to unnecessary pressures and acrimony.

III.3 The Basis of Distribution of Divisible Taxes

The basis of distribution of the shares of taxes among the recipient states has been changing over time. While population (at the 1971 level) has been the major criterion, the Commissions have sought to introduce equalization principles but have tended to attach a relatively minor weight to contribution (the Tenth Finance Commission has totally removed contribution as a factor to be considered even in regard to income tax). Also, equalization has not been attempted in terms of making up any deficiency in fiscal capacity, except indirectly by taking into account the differences in per capita income, or in terms of allowing for cost disadvantages.

Table 14.6 gives the relative proportions of tax devolution,

TABLE 14.6
PER CAPITA TRANSFERS FROM CENTRE ON REVENUE ACCOUNT TO MAJOR STATES (1994–95(RE), 1995–96(BE))

States	Per capita of SDP average 1987–8 to 1989–90	Share in central taxes		Statutory grants		Other non-plan grants		Total non-plan grants	
		1994–5 (RE)	1995–6 (BE)	1994–5 (RE)	1995–6 (BE)	1994–5 (RE)	1995–6 (BE)	1994–5 (RE)	1995–6 (BE)
1. Goa	7364	637.04	544.11	248.29	286.67	5.50	5.49	253.79	292.16
2. Punjab	6996	190.05	213.33	47.59	50.61	0.00	0.00	47.59	50.61
3. Maharashtra	5369	196.86	202.44	4.11	7.69	11.50	6.23	15.62	13.92
4. Haryana	5284	171.83	191.92	1.35	1.73	13.15	9.44	14.51	11.16
5. Gujarat	4602	235.25	248.81	2.04	2.09	17.31	27.85	19.35	29.94
6. Tamil Nadu	4093	292.63	300.12	4.21	11.07	11.94	11.77	16.15	22.84
7. Karnataka	3810	232.61	289.30	1.22	2.80	6.44	11.16	7.66	13.96
8. West Bengal	3750	234.64	262.54	1.47	1.54	9.48	9.71	10.95	11.25
9. Kerala	3532	291.03	330.40	2.04	4.55	8.91	7.10	10.95	11.65
10. Andhra Pradesh	3455	252.39	286.53	22.10	23.66	0.69	0.72	22.79	24.38
11. Madhya Pradesh	3299	249.50	285.28	1.23	1.20	9.08	8.94	10.31	10.14
12. Rajasthan	3092	262.80	295.13	21.62	10.07	20.83	26.57	42.45	36.64
13. Orissa	2945	360.63	372.38	28.93	57.28	12.07	15.38	41.00	72.67
14. Uttar Pradesh	2867	253.28	324.58	4.19	47.07	8.69	7.75	12.88	54.82
15. Bihar	2135	293.15	356.95	42.04	30.59	1.55	7.07	43.58	37.66
Total		253.96	291.46	12.39	20.51	8.86	9.89	21.24	30.40
Percentage of total for all states		58.23	60.31	2.84	4.24	2.03	2.05	4.87	6.29

States	State plan grants		Other plan grants		Total plan grants		Total grants		Total transfers from Centre	
	1994–5 (RE)	1995–6 (BE)	1994–5 (RE)	1995–6 (BE)	1994–5 (RE)	1995–6 (BE)	1994–5 (RE)	1995–6 (BE)	1994–5 (RE)	1995–6 (BE)
1. Goa	134.52	155.60	84.60	52.25	219.11	207.86	472.90	500.01	1109.94	1044.13
2. Punjab	44.86	45.16	88.63	91.70	133.49	136.86	181.08	187.47	371.13	400.80
3. Maharashtra	42.11	68.00	64.98	57.66	107.09	125.66	122.71	139.58	319.57	342.02
4. Haryana	45.42	64.30	99.33	101.08	144.75	165.38	159.25	176.54	331.09	368.47
5. Gujarat	31.95	43.28	80.61	91.74	112.56	135.02	131.91	164.96	367.16	413.78
6. Tamil Nadu	63.26	80.74	30.03	44.35	93.28	125.09	109.43	147.93	402.06	448.05
7. Karnataka	39.86	53.87	137.92	173.73	177.78	227.60	185.44	241.56	418.06	530.86
8. West Bengal	118.50	136.90	30.25	39.37	148.75	176.27	159.70	187.52	394.34	450.06
9. Kerala	99.57	61.74	104.39	122.98	203.96	184.72	214.91	196.37	505.94	526.77
10. Andhra Pradesh	56.72	78.04	89.53	92.63	146.26	170.67	169.05	195.05	421.43	481.58
11. Madhya Pradesh	80.35	87.09	156.49	187.92	236.85	275.01	247.16	285.15	496.66	570.43
12. Rajasthan	104.49	48.90	155.13	163.28	259.62	212.18	302.07	248.82	564.87	543.95
13. Orissa	121.14	77.32	197.77	152.53	318.92	229.85	359.91	302.51	720.55	674.89
14. Uttar Pradesh	105.89	40.86	75.54	83.09	181.42	123.95	194.31	178.77	447.59	503.35
15. Bihar	38.47	41.08	44.01	53.81	82.48	94.89	126.07	132.56	419.22	489.50
Total	73.92	66.00	87.01	95.41	160.94	161.42	182.18	191.81	436.14	483.28
Percentage of total for all states	16.95	13.66	19.95	19.74	36.90	33.40	41.77	39.69	100.00	100.00

NOTE: Excluding special category states. States arranged in the descending order of per capita SDP.

SOURCE: *Reserve Bank of India Bulletin* Dec. 1995 — Finances of State Governments 1995–96 Per capita SDP data as given in the Report of the 10th Finance Commission.

TABLE 14.6A

PERCENTAGE SHARES OF PER CAPITA STATUTORY
TRANSFERS AND TOTAL TRANSFERS FROM CENTRE
TO STATES ON REVENUE ACCOUNT

States	Per capita statutory transfers as a percentage of per capita SDP		Per capita total transfers as a percentage of per capita SDP	
	1994–5 (RE)	1995–6 (BE)	1994–5 (RE)	1995–6 (BE)
1 Punjab	3.40	3.77	5.30	5.73
2 Maharashtra	3.74	3.91	5.95	6.37
3 Haryana	3.28	3.66	6.27	6.97
4 Gujarat	5.16	5.45	7.98	8.99
5 Tamil Nadu	7.25	7.60	9.82	10.95
6 Karnataka	6.14	7.67	10.97	13.93
7 West Bengal	6.30	7.04	10.52	12.00
8 Kerala	8.30	9.48	14.32	14.91
9 Andhra Pradesh	7.94	8.98	12.20	13.94
10 Madhya Pradesh	7.60	8.68	15.05	17.29
11 Rajasthan	9.20	9.87	18.27	17.59
12 Orissa	13.23	14.59	24.47	22.92
13 Uttar Pradesh	8.98	12.96	15.61	17.56
14 Bihar	15.70	18.15	19.64	22.93

NOTE: Excluding special category states and Goa. States arranged
           in descending order of per capita SDP.
SOURCE: *Reserve Bank of India Bulletin*, Dec. 1995 — Finances of State
           Governments 1995–6. Per capita SDP data as given in the
           Report of the 10th Finance Commission.

Finance Commission grants, grants given for plan purposes, and
other grants (for the major states), as also the per capita transfers
to the different states under those heads. From the Table it can be
seen that, taking the figures for 1995–6, statutory or Finance Commission grants form a very small proportion of total transfers (4.24
per cent). Even as a proportion of Finance Commission transfers,
statutory grants amount to only 6.57 per cent. As far as grants are
concerned, Planning Commission grants play a predominant role,

forming 84.1 per cent of total grants (Rs 161 out of Rs 192 in per capita terms). Finance Commission grants being so insignificant, they cannot be expected to play any significant equalizing role. It was pointed out earlier that in making Central transfers, no specific attempt was made to equalize fiscal capacity or to make up for the deficiency in fiscal capacity of the weaker states. However, figures given in Table 14.6A show that statutory transfers as well as total transfers are distributed on a broadly progressive basis in the sense that the trend is for per capita transfers to increase as a percentage of per capita SDP as the latter falls. While it is desirable that per capita transfers should form a larger proportion of per capita SDP in the case of poorer states, it would be more meaningful to link the scheme of transfers to the objective of equalizing fiscal capacity, at the same time ensuring that the poorer states do not slacken in using whatever capacity they have for raising resources.

III.4 Transfers Flowing from the Planning Commission

Plan assistance extended by the Centre to the states consists of loans and current transfers in the form of grants. As far as the major states (that is states other than the special category states to whom special treatment is given because of their small size or hilly character) are concerned, 70 per cent of plan assistance consists of loans and the remaining 30 per cent is in the form of grants. This is presumably on the broad assumption that about 30 per cent of plan expenditure will be on revenue account. Since the Planning Commission gives grants in support of the states' revenue plan expenditure, the Finance Commissions have been led to confine themselves to a consideration of the non-plan revenue expenditure of the states. There is thus a dichotomy in the consideration of the states' expenditure on revenue account. It is interesting to note that the plan assistance distributed to the states is allocated on the basis of the same criteria, whether the assistance is in the form of loans or of grants (see Table 14.7 for the criteria currently adopted). It will be noticed that the criteria adopted by the Planning Commission also do not serve to equalize fiscal capacity. However, since the Planning Commission grants are not related to any anticipated or estimated gaps, they do not affect expenditure decisions by the states at the margin, unlike the Finance Commission transfers.

TABLE 14.7
FORMULA FOR DISTRIBUTING STATE PLAN ASSISTANCE

Criteria	Share in central plan assistance (percentage)	Share of grants and loans	Criteria for distribution to non-special category states
(1)	(2)	(3)	(4)
A. Special Category States (10)	30	90:10	
B. Non-Special Category States (15)	70	30:70	
(i) Population (1971)			60.0
(ii) Per capita income of which			25.0
(a) According to the 'deviation' method covering only the States with per capita income below the national average			20.0
(b) According to the 'distance' method covering all the 15 States			5.0
(iii) Fiscal performance of which			7.5
(a) Tax effort			2.5
(b) Fiscal management			2.5
(c) National objectives			2.5
(iv) Special problems			7.5
Total			100.0

NOTES: (1) The formula as revised in December, 1991.

(2) Fiscal Management is assessed as the difference between states' own total plan resources estimated at the time of finalizing annual plans and their actual performance on the basis of the last five years.

(3) Under the criterion of the performance with regard to certain programmes of national priority, the approved formula covers four objectives, namely (i) population control, (ii) elimination of illiteracy, (iii) completion of externally aided projects on schedule and (iv) success in land reforms.

While the states as a whole are not very happy with the existing system of intergovernmental transfers, the above review shows that there is considerable inefficiency in the system as a whole, and it is not particularly geared to the promotion of fiscal discipline. There is also no serious attempt at the equalization of fiscal capacity. It is important to ensure in a system of federal grants that at the margin expenditure decisions are linked to the raising of own revenues. This consideration has also been lost sight of in the system of federal transfers that has evolved over time.

III.5 Changes in the System of Intergovernmental Transfers

While the relative size of the quantum of transfers on revenue account may be considered adequate since nearly 67 per cent of the combined revenues accrue to the states, the existing fragmented system of transfers should be redesigned. Four important principles must be incorporated into the system, namely (a) stability; (b) inducement to maintenance of fiscal discipline; (c) equalization of fiscal capacity; and (d) autonomy to the states to determine their levels of expenditure without shifting any of the burden to the other states by getting the Central government to pick up the bill.

It is obvious that fiscal discipline cannot be imposed on the States unless the Central government imposes it on itself. From this point of view, the proposal by the Finance Minister in the 1997–8 Union Budget to phase out the system of Central government borrowing from the Reserve Bank of India through ad hoc treasury bills and to replace it by limited, predetermined support by the RBI to Central government borrowing coupled with making available to the Centre an agreed amount of ways and means advance, as in the case of the states, is to be greatly welcomed. Once this new system comes into operation and market borrowing is shared on an agreed basis between the Centre and the states, the states will no longer have any ground to complain that fiscal discipline is being imposed only on them. It would also be necessary for the Centre to consult with the states on important financial matters using the forum of the Inter-State Council. The states should invariably be consulted before the Centre changes any aspect of its financial policy which would have repercussions on state finances, e.g. changing rules regarding the channels of investment of provident funds and revision of the pay scales of Central government staff.

More generally speaking, under the new economic regime and in the new political context, the Central government should act in such a way as to promote cooperative federalism. At the same time it is incumbent on the states to observe rules that are expected to be followed by constituent units in a federation. The most important of them are, (a) they should agree that policies that militate against the common market and against the export efforts of the country must be eschewed; (b) tax exportation must be minimized; (c) there should be competition only of the welfare increasing type; and (d) the better off states should recognize and accept that the Central government must have a surplus in order to perform its equalization function (which should of course be performed without promoting any fiscal indiscipline on the part of the weaker states). The meetings of the Inter-State Council should be used as a forum not only for a dialogue between the Centre and the states but also for dialogue among the states themselves on matters of mutual interest such as tax reform and improvement of interstate communications for freer flow of trade.

IV. Towards Cooperative Federalism

A healthy and smooth functioning of a federation requires that there is a spirit and ambience of cooperation between the Centre and the states, and also amongst the states themselves. In the past, because of the restrictions imposed by centralized planning on initiatives by and the freedom of action of the states, and the unitary bias imposed by the dominance of a single political party, in most discussions on the reform of the system there has been emphasis only on granting more powers and freedom of action to the States. The responsibility of states in a cooperative federation to act in a coordinated and constructive way to promote the common weal and the need for a readiness on their part to accept essential restrictions on their freedom of action in order to preserve the national interest have not been emphasized.

In designing or redesigning intergovernmental relations, an important point to remember is that any change introduced in terms of relations between the Centre and the states almost invariably involves a change in the interrelations between the states and in their relative shares of entitlements and burdens.[4] Thus, increasing the role of devolution of taxes and diminishing that of grants-in-aid would adversely affect the weaker states who could have received larger grants; similarly, reducing the volume of devolution of taxes, distributed largely on the basis of population and substituting it by the devolution of larger taxation powers would adversely affect the states with lower than average taxable capacity;[5] and granting more powers to the Centre in certain areas, say, primary education, might help the poorer states, but that would of course reduce the area of freedom of the states as a whole.

With these preliminary remarks, we may consider the major changes we could recommend in order to move towards a more decentralized polity, keeping in view the need to balance the criteria of national interest, autonomy, and interstate equity.

(a) The Constitution may be amended to grant to the states the residuary powers other than in the field of taxation, subject to the condition that the President would have the power to impose reasonable restrictions in the national interest on the laws to be enacted by the states using the residuary powers.

(b) A consensus should be evolved among the major political parties regarding the conditions under which a legally elected state government could be dismissed by the President under Art. 356.

(c) The Central government should leave some of the concurrent fields to the states; in many others, it should only lay down the broad guidelines in the form of basic laws and leave the state governments free to formulate policies within that framework, and in some important areas the Centre could continue to be active as before. Decisions on this subject could be taken after eliciting the views of the states.

(d) It is desirable that the larger part of grants from the Central government to the states flow through the Finance Commission. To make this possible, first, the distinction between plan and non-plan revenue expenditure should be done away with and second, funds that are now given as grants for plans on the recommendations of the Planning Commission and funds that are given as grants to finance centrally sponsored schemes should become

[4] The relative shares and burdens of the state governments or of the people of the states concerned.

[5] There is thus often a trade-off between the criteria of autonomy and equity.

available to the Finance Commission. That is to say, the Planning Commission's assistance for the state plans should only be in the form of loans to finance capital expenditure,[6] and grants should ordinarily flow through the Finance Commission. If all the Centrally sponsored schemes cannot be given up, they should at least be pruned to the extent of 50 per cent. If this reform is brought about, the Finance Commission will be able to recommend larger grants without increasing the revenue deficit at the Centre and the proportion of grants to devolution could increase in the transfers from the Finance Commission.

(e) It was pointed out earlier that reopening the question of determining the quantum of devolution and the adoption of the modified gap-filling approach led to avoidable acrimony and also tended to encourage expenditure exportation by individual states. Confining the devolution to two Central taxes was all right so long as the proportions shared were relatively small. The existing shares of income tax and excise duties are so high that there is said to be a tendency for the Central government tax policy to be distorted in favour of non-sharable taxes; also, given the high proportion shared, the Centre can benefit very little from the expected buoyancy in the revenue from personal income tax. In the light of these considerations, the recommendation of the Tenth Finance Commission that all the Central taxes may be pooled and that the Central government may share a fixed proportion of its total tax revenue with the states should be accepted. This proportion may be fixed for a fairly long period of 15 to 20 years. A modification that may be suggested to the Tenth Finance Commission's recommendation is that the yield of Additional Excise Duty (AED) now given to the states may be kept separate and, accordingly, the 29 per cent recommended by the Finance Commission minus the proportion of AED (3 per cent), i.e. roughly 26 per cent of total tax revenue minus AED, should be shared.

(f) The distribution of the divisible pool of taxes would be largely based on the criterion of population. It is suggested that the grants given by the Finance Commission should not be aimed at gap-filling but at equalization of fiscal capacity. The fiscal capacity of each major state should be measured through the

---

[6] Except in the case of special category states.

application of average tax rates to potential bases. The difference between average fiscal capacity and the fiscal capacity of a given state should be sought to be matched by an equalization grant if the latter is smaller than the former. Equalization could also be undertaken in the form of specific grants extended to raise standards of key services in those States where the standards of such services are low.

(g) The Centre would, of course, have to continue to give grants to meet extraordinary situations and a limited amount for financing centrally sponsored schemes.

(h) If these changes are brought about, the states would be able to plan their finances better, would have a greater sense of freedom, and would become responsible for maintenance of fiscal discipline.

(i) On capital account, as of now, the states receive Plan assistance and are allocated shares in total market borrowing by the government sector. In addition, they have some other receipts such as shares in small savings and contributions to state provident fund. It is desirable that gradually plan loans be substituted by market borrowings so that after a period of years most of the capital receipts of the states will be derived from the market. The allocation of the plan part of capital receipts could continue to be on the basis of the existing Planning Commission formula. However, the states will deal directly with the market. This would mean a higher interest burden for the states; that could be compensated by payment of an interest subsidy which is now implicitly borne by the Centre. The system of giving plan loans against small saving collections would have to continue.

(j) It would have to be ensured that the proportion of devolution and grants taken together (excluding grants for extraordinary purposes which may become necessary from time to time) to total Central government's gross revenues should not be less than what the states are getting now.

I submit that the system that I have recommended provides a proper blend of the criteria of autonomy, fiscal discipline, and interstate equity. Fiscal discipline and interstate equity are necessary ingredients in cooperative federalism.

REFERENCES

Breton, Albert (1965): 'A Theory of Government Grants', *The Canadian Journal of Economics and Political Science*, vol. 31 (May), no. 2, pp. 175–87.

Government of India, Sarkaria Commission (1987): Report of the Commission on Centre–State Relations (Chairman, Mr Justice R.S. Sarkaria).

Government of India (1953–4): Report of the Taxation Enquiry Commission (Chairman, John Mathai).

Government of India (1984): White Paper on Punjab Situation.

Government of West Bengal (1977): A Memorandum on Centre–State Relations.

Hunter, J.S.H. (1977): *Federalism and Fiscal Balance: A Comparative Study* (Canberra: A.N.U. Press).

Oates, W.E (1977): 'An Economist's Perspective of Fiscal Federalism', in Wallace E. Oates (ed.), *Political Economy of Fiscal Federalism* (Toronto: Lexington Books).

Olson, M. (1969): 'The Principles of Fiscal Equivalence: The Division of Responsibilities Among Different Levels of Governments', *American Economic Review* (Proceedings), vol. 49 (May), pp. 479–87.

Rao, M. Govinda and Tapas K. Sen (1996): *Fiscal Federalism in India: Theory and Practice* (New Delhi: Macmillan India).

15

The Political Economy of Centre–State Relations in India

V.A. Pai Panandiker

I. INTRODUCTION

Federal democracy, demography, and the economy of each state are three factors that determine the political economy of Centre–State relations in India. The interaction between these three central factors operates on the nature and character of Centre–State relations. In consequence, the pattern of relationship varies a great deal, depending upon the specific character of the polity and economy of each state.

No functioning democracy in the world equals India in size and complexity. The sheer size of the Indian electorate of 592 m. in the 1996 general elections is larger than any country in the world barring China. The diversity of Indian society is reflected in the class and caste composition of the Indian electorate. This factor, especially because of the nature of electoral politics, plays an important role in the political economy of Centre–State relations in India.

Over the eleven general elections held for the Indian Parliament since 1952, one of the most important political developments has been the transfer of political power in India from the Western educated urban middle class to a growing number of members of the regionally educated rural and agricultural class. The politics of this newly emerging power élite in India after the 'Mandalization' of Indian polity, which is essentially drawn from the backward and scheduled castes, is qualitatively different from the politics of the urban and basically *forward castes*. The economic priorities of the new political élite are different, and their ability to deal with the complex economic and strategic issues facing the country is limited. The agenda of the new political élite in 'Mandalized' India is dominated by caste and regional considerations. Their skills to deal with a new liberalized and globalizing Indian economy are under strain. Their concern is not with development but what they call 'social justice'. Translated into plain English, it means direct sops to their electoral constituency.

As a result of increasing democratization and the transfer of political power, there is a pronounced demand for greater decentralization of political and economic decision making from the Centre to the states, and from the state to the local level. This has pronounced effects on the political economy of Centre–State relations in India.

The Indian democratic experiment has led to a policy framework that differs from that of the countries of South–East Asia, where either military dictatorships or small elected oligarchies have determined the character of their political economies. In sheer growth rates, these countries have done better than India. However, the strength of India lies in a deep-rooted democratic system, even if it has not resulted in high rates of economic growth and in tales of economic miracles. The miracle of Indian democracy has overshadowed the political economy of the country.

While democracy has propelled one set of forces to work on the political economy of Centre–State relations in India, demography has played its own distinct role. The size of the population and the consequent size of the electorate has its own dynamics. This dynamics has inevitably depended upon the demographic character of the polity. Since ten large states of India account for over 81 per cent of the total population, their demographic weight has a great influence on the political economy of India. In particular, the three mega states, namely UP, Bihar and Maharashtra have considerable influence on the political economy of Centre–State relations. Of these three mega states, UP and Bihar as the two backward states tend to pull in one direction. They want more subsidies, more anti-poverty programmes, more schemes of rural development, and the like. Maharashtra, on the other hand, as a more industrialized and advanced state, creates pressures of a different kind. Maharashtra wants more programmes of industrial development, better infrastructure, better telecom services, etc.

Since the demographic weight of the backward states is greater in the country, at the moment they are better able to dictate the terms of the political economy of Centre–State relations, especially in relation to the national development strategy. This cannot however be taken for granted and as other states join Maharashtra, the demographic equations within the Indian Union are likely to change.

Over time there will be other factors at play, especially the differential fertility growth between the backward and the advanced states. This game will take several decades to unfold, but as India begins to move towards a replacement level of population over the next fifteen to twenty years, the impact of demography may begin to be somewhat different on the political economy of Centre–State relations. The backward states may no longer be able to dictate the developmental priorities of the country.

Demography in India is also confounded by the politics of fertility. In particular, the differential growth rate between Hindus and Muslims, especially in politically sensitive states like UP, has a bearing on their political economy. Programmes of family welfare do not work as well in these states as they do elsewhere. In the social sector, education, especially education of girls, does not have the same political salience as in Kerala or Goa. Hindu–Muslim demography in some of these states has a subterranean influence on the political economy of the Centre–State relations in these areas of the country.

The demographic divide between urban and rural India is yet another factor that has a direct bearing on the political economy of Centre–State relations. The more rapidly urbanizing states like Maharashtra wish to have larger support for urban development schemes. These include power, transport, water supply, sanitation, telecommunications, and the like. These schemes constitute the vitals of their economy and the rural bias reflected in the present political economy of Centre–State relations has often irked the political sensitivities of the more developed states. As the country moves towards a faster pace of urbanization, which will be inevitable, and if India grows at 7 per cent per annum, the pressure of urban demands on the political economy of Centre–State relations is set to rise.

Finally, the discourse of the political economy of Centre–State relations is being dictated by the economy of the states, first of all by the structure of their economies. In those states where agriculture dominates the structure of the state's economy, the nature of political pressures is of a special character. Basically, agriculturally dominated states seek larger subsidies for agriculture, more programmes of rural development, etc., but wherever the states have moved towards a more industrialized economy, such as Maharashtra or Goa, the nature of the demand for changes in the political economy is qualitatively different.

The structural dimension is further accentuated by the growth rates and per capita incomes. In those states where sustained growth rates are higher with consequent higher per capita incomes, the demands on the political economy differ from those of states in the opposite camp. Several states in India have, after the liberalization of the economy in 1991, attempted to attract larger private and foreign investments. Their pressures on the Centre are different from states like Bihar or UP where the growth rates have been stagnant or even negative. The political fallout of low economic growth is visible in the Hindi heartland, especially in UP and Bihar. The Home Minister of India went on record in the Indian Parliament in March 1997 to state that UP is moving towards 'anarchy, chaos and destruction'.

The major consequence of differential growth rates amongst the states of India is on poverty levels. States like Punjab, Haryana, Goa, Kerala, which have relatively lower poverty levels, have different priorities and different demands on Centre–State relations in comparison to states like Bihar, Orissa, or UP. Poverty is one of the most potent political influences on the economic life of the people, profoundly affecting Centre–State relations. Already formulae like the Gadgil–Mukherjee formula for distribution of plan allocations are raising the hackles of the advanced states, and the Centre finds itself in a dilemma whether to help bring down the income differentials in the country or to leave the process to the wider political and market forces. Unfortunately for the Centre, the redistributive justice practiced in the long years of planning through the Finance Commission, the National Development Council, etc. has not worked and income disparities in the country have not narrowed. This raises the important question for Centre–State relations of whether the real action lies at the state level or whether the Centre has any leverage in propelling certain states into action.

Also, India is beginning to feel the impact of a growing middle class. While this is essentially an urban phenomenon, the rural areas are not completely outside the influence of this macro phenomenon. As growth rates in the economy and urbanization accelerate there are bound to be accelerated pressures of the middle class on India's political economy of Centre–State relations.

II. Democracy and its Impact on Centre–state Relations

The size of the Indian population at the beginning of 1997 is estimated at 950 m. and the electorate at 592 m. The size of each state varies a great deal. At one end is a mega state like UP with a population of nearly 140 m. according to the 1991 census and at the other a state like Sikkim with a population of .4 m. in 1991 (Annex., Table 1).

The number of Indian states in 1991 with a population of over 40 m. is 10 out of a total of 25 states besides 7 Union Territories. These large states account for 689 m. or over 81 per cent of the total Indian population and by their sheer numbers dictate public policies and political discourse *vis-à-vis* the rest of the country. Indeed the two mega-states, namely, UP and Bihar account for over a quarter of the Indian population, and along with the two other Hindi-speaking states of M.P. and Rajasthan, they account for 40 per cent of the Indian population. These four states have 204 or over 37 per cent seats in the Lok Sabha out of a total of 543.

The size of these four states and their weight in the Indian political economy is aptly reflected in all political calculations, and indeed in framing national policies. The Approach Paper to the Ninth Five Year Plan (1997–2002) explicitly states:

Large states of the country like Bihar and U.P., which account for a very substantial part of the population have shown negative or constant per capita growth of incomes in real terms. Stagnation or decline of per capita income in these populous states of India accentuates national disparities and has serious consequences for the poverty levels.[1]

---

[1] See, India, Planning Commission, *Approach Paper to the Ninth Five-Year Plan (1997–2002)*, New Delhi, 1997, p. 2

II.1 Complexity of the Democratic Fabric

Indian democracy is indeed a very complex system, both in institutional terms and in terms of processes. Indian democracy is operated by about 788 Members of Parliament, about 4100 members of state legislatures and about 3 m. elected representatives at the *panchayat* and municipal levels from the village to the district. The sheer size and complexity of Indian democracy makes it one of the most massive political enterprises anywhere in the world. Indeed, many foreign observers are often bewildered at how the complex Indian system works at all.

Behind this political complexity lies a diverse social fabric. India has seven major listed religions and 18 official languages excluding English. In addition, the census of 1981 listed 1652 unofficial languages.[2]

The Census of 1991 lists 1091 scheduled castes and 570 scheduled tribes. The Backward Classes Commission of 1980 listed 3743 backward castes in India, although the caste census was discontinued in 1931.[3] The forward castes are themselves divided into many subcastes, giving India a social mosaic of myriad hues. This complexity of the social fabric makes for an intensively difficult electoral scenario where coalitions of castes and subcastes begin to determine the nature of the political economy at the local and state levels.

II.2 Transfer of Political Power

One of the most noticeable features of the Indian democratic evolution affecting the political economy of the country is the dramatic transfer of power that has taken place since the first general elections were held in India in 1952. The total electorate in the 1952 general elections to the Lok Sabha or House of the People was 173 m., whereas in the 1996 general elections the total electorate was estimated at over 592 m. In 1996 over 750,000 polling booths were set up to facilitate access to them by the electorate. The number of persons involved in the administration of the election was over 3.7 m.

[2] India, Registrar General, Census of India 1981, Series I Part IV-B(1): *Population by Language/Mother Tongue* (Table C-7), New Delhi, 1990.
[3] See, India, *Backward Classes Commission*, New Delhi, 1980.

Over the five decades since Independence, there has been a distinct transfer of power taking place in India through the electoral process. This is aptly reflected in the changing composition of the Lok Sabha. In the first Lok Sabha nearly 68 per cent of the members came from legal, educational, industrial, and professional backgrounds. As against this, the percentage of members from an agricultural background was 22.5.

By the ninth Lok Sabha the agricultural classes had over 44 per cent representation while the professional, legal, and educational groups accounted for 29.5 per cent. This change which deeply influences the working of the Indian Parliament is a clear indication of the emergence of a new power élite, and new power equations in Indian politics.

Changes at the state level, from available indicators, are even greater. While full details of the background of state legislators are not available, an overwhelming percentage comes increasingly from agricultural and rural backgrounds. While this is inevitable, given the compositon of the urban–rural population of India, since, according to the 1991 census, nearly 74 per cent live in rural areas, the shift from an urban professional background to a rural agricultural one has had the most dramatic impact on the working not only of Indian democracy but also on the political economy of Centre–State relations.

Apart from transfer of power to a new political class from an agricultural and rural background, there is a marked shift in the transfer of power from the forward castes to the backward and scheduled castes. The backward castes, often referred to as the OBCs or Other Backward Classes, are generally economically and socially deprived sections of the rural community. The 'Mandalization' of Indian politics in 1990 saw a marked shift towards the OBCs. Prominent amongst those who have emerged as the powerful new political élite are the Yadavs or the cattle grazing communities. The Yadavs, especially in UP and Bihar are somewhat more advanced than other OBCs.

The politics of the Yadavs is clearly to claim a larger share of the political and administrative positions at the state level. Their plan is simple. Occupy all the key political and administrative positions, including those in the police, so that the political, economic, and social equations at the state level are transformed for the benefit of their political constituencies.

The transfer of power is, however, not so simple. The backward classes are not a homogeneous group. Many of the other backward classes resent the dominance of a single group like the Yadavs, and continually press their political claims for a share in political and economic power.

Joining the other backward classes are the scheduled castes who constitute, in some states like UP, a significant percentage of the voting electorate. In recent years, the radicalization of the scheduled castes, the traditional untouchable class, has been one of the most profound reflections of the changing character of the Indian polity. These historically depressed classes of Indian society have now been clamouring for a larger share of the Indian political power. In June 1995 Mayawati, a political leader of the Bahujan Samaj Party, became the first scheduled caste woman Chief Minister of the largest Indian state, Uttar Pradesh. This was a development with profound political impact on the emergence of the scheduled castes on the Indian political horizon. While the Mayawati government in 1995 did not last long, the impact of this development on the politics of India has been pronounced. Mayawati returned to political power as Chief Minister of Uttar Pradesh in March 1997. From the point of view of the political economy of India, the transfer of political power to the agricultural, rural, and the backward and scheduled castes has been a major shift since Independence in 1947.

Two factors account for this impact. The first is that the economic priorities of the new political class are significantly different. The power élite of India that ruled in the earlier phase exemplified by Jawaharlal Nehru was essentially preoccupied with India's economic and industrial development. Nehru and his ilk strongly and undoubtedly sincerely believed that India's domestic and global future lay in building a strong industrial and modern technological state. The Nehruvian framework basically set the tone for development policies from about 1950 to 1990.

The new power élite in India generally does not share this macroeconomic vision. The preoccupation of the backward castes and scheduled castes is with agriculture, rural development, and those economic schemes and projects that directly benefit members of their constituency. In consequence, the emphasis for instance is not on greater power generation but on supply of free power to the agricultural and backward communities. There is greater emphasis on the public distribution system, more fertilizers, water, and other subsidies, and generally transfer of incomes from the richer to the poorer, often rural and backward sections of the Indian population.

The second major impact on the political economy is due to the nature of the leadership of the new power élite. The concerns of this leadership are not with the larger issues of the Indian economy. Generally most of the new state level leaders show little understanding and awareness of the macromanagement of the economy of their states. In particular the mega-states of UP and Bihar have seen large budgetary deficits and a distinct decline in their economic growth and near stagnation or even decline in their per capita incomes. The 1990s have seen alarming signs of deceleration of economic growth in these states, and yet their demands affecting the Centre–State relations in economic matters have not been to seek greater investments and socioeconomic development but the transfer of financial resources to non-plan expenditures, often on a highly bloated bureaucracy.

This rise of non-plan or non-development expenditures has eaten into the vitals of the economies of these states, and yet there is little recognition by their leadership of the imperatives of their economic future. The electorate, while showing its frustrations, is unable to find an alternative leadership that will deliver them a better quality of economic and social life.

The transfer of power in India from the forward castes and the urban élite to the backward castes and the rural élite has had considerable effect on the political economy of Centre–State relations. The priorities of the new political élite are different, their focus is different, and their constituencies are different at all levels, national, state, and local.

II.3 Democratic Politics and Decentralization

The democratic politics of India which has now witnessed eleven general elections has undergone a significant transformation. The general elections are by themselves a process of tremendous churnings at the grassroots. These churnings have had a major impact on Centre–State relations.

One of the major impacts has been a demand for increased decentralization of economic power and away from what was termed Congress party federalism. Since the initiation of planning in India in 1951, the role of the Centre under domination by the Congress party, as the principal arbiter of economic policy, had been well accepted. This has had several kinds of influence on Centre–state relations, the most important being centralization of economic decision-making. Decisions on what capital expenditure or investments, or social spending, or for that matter which industries should be set up and where, were taken in Delhi. Central planning and Congress party federalism worked well till about the early 1970s. Ever since, and specially after the 1980s, there has been pronounced pressure from the states to decentralize the economic decision-making powers to themselves. Indeed, one Chief Minister went so far as to say that 'the Centre was behaving like a super power' in economic policy matters which should be within the domain of the state.

This trend towards greater autonomy for the states has been one of the principal factors affecting the Centre–State relationship in India. Whether it is in Jammu & Kashmir or Punjab or Andhra Pradesh or West Bengal, there has been a persistent demand for the Centre to get off the backs of the states and give them greater freedom to make their own economic decisions. The persistent demand for review of Centre–State relations led in the 1980s to the appointment of a Commission on Centre–State relations, commonly known as the Sarkaria Commission. The Commission reported in 1988 and made wide-ranging recommendations on many matters that caused friction between the Centre and the states.

The demand for greater decentralization won another major battle when the Constitution was amended in 1992 through the 72nd and 73rd Amendments to create mandatory elected *panchayati raj* and municipal bodies, essentially institutions of local self-government from the district level down to the village, and in urban areas. At a stroke nearly three million elected representatives were brought into the process of Indian democratic politics.

These three million elected representatives, of whom one-third or one million are women, have been in the forefront of the demand for greater decentralization of political and economic power. Under the amendment of the Constitution in 1992, two new schedules, namely Schedule 11 and 12, were added to demarcate the subjects within the ambit of the institutions of local self-government.

All these developments of democratic institutions in India clearly suggest an emerging politics of greater decentralization. First from the Centre to the states, and second from the states to the bodies of local self-government. It is a long and historical process which has and will profoundly influence the nature of the political economy of Centre–State relations in India in the years to come.

III. DEMOGRAPHY

When India became independent in 1947, India's population was around 350 m. by early 1997 its estimated population was 950 m. The birth rate in 1947 was about 42 live births per thousand population; by 1997 it was estimated at about 28 per thousand. The decadal growth rate between 1951 and 1961 was 21.50, largely as a result of a high death rate. The census of 1991 indicated that the growth rate between 1981 and 1991 was 23.8 or 2.3 per cent,[4] and has perhaps marginally declined to 1.9 per cent in 1997.

By the year 2010, the Indian population is estimated to reach 1200 m.; by 2025, according to World Bank estimates, India's population will be around 1392 m.[5], and that the hypothetical stationary population of India will be 1.88 bn sometime towards the end of the twenty-first century.[6]

III.1 Implications of Population Growth

India is adding nearly 26.7 m. children per year. At the present death rate of about 8.6 m. a year, over 18 m. persons are added to the Indian population every year. They have to be provided with food, clothing, shelter, health care, education, and several other services. Most of these fall within the jurisdiction of the states and are therefore reflected in their demands on the Centre–state relations.

Shelter, health care, and education are fairly capital intensive services. One study estimates that the cost of the basic minimum needs will require about 69 per cent of India's Gross Domestic Product, leaving virtually nothing for the other sectors, including

[4] India, Registrar General, Census of India, 1991, *Final Population Totals*, New Delhi, 1993, p. 98.
[5] World Bank, *World Development Report*, New York, 1993, p. 210
[6] World Bank, *World Development Report*, New York, 1993, p. 288

national defence.[7] While population growth is not responsible for the nation's poverty, it does make the task of poverty eradication that much more difficult.

Thus the food production in the country will have to increase significantly to feed the growing population. If the population of India was to reach replacement level by the year 2000, the demand for food would have been a decreasing load on the national resources. If India's population keeps rising and will only stabilize at around 1.8 bn, India will require 450 to 500 m.t. of foodgrains alone. While it is not impossible for India to produce this level of food-grains, such production levels will place severe strains on India's land, water, and environmental resources, which in turn will have many repercussions on Centre–State relations.

One strong side effect of such large population growth will be on India's urbanization. In 1997, less than 30 per cent of the population lives in urban areas. Even at the present level of urbanization, most of the cities are already unlivable. The population pressure is telling on India's urban life and thus in turn will become a major Centre–State issue. Thus in Maharashtra the urban population, according to the 1991 census, was estimated at 39 per cent; in Goa 41 per cent. The trend is expected to accelerate not only in these states but across the country, including in agriculturally dominated states like UP.

Project this to the year 2025 when the population of India will be around 1400 m., about half of which is expected to live in urban India. How will the Indian states, or for that matter the Government of India as a whole, look after an urban population of 700 m. by the year 2025 or perhaps 1000 m. by the year 2050?

India's estimated birth rate in 1997 is 28 per thousand. By the year 2000 it is unlikely to drop below 26 per thousand — a full five points above the national goal of 21 per thousand. The Government estimates that India will not reach the replacement level of population or birth rate of 21 per thousand before the year 2015.

Interestingly, the growth rate of population amongst the various states of India differs significantly. Goa's birth rate in 1992 was estimated at 14.70 per thousand, the lowest in the country, followed by Kerala at 17.70 per thousand, and Tamil Nadu at

[7] See, Malgavkar P.D. and V.A. Pai Panandiker, *Towards Industrial Policy 2000 A.D.*, New Delhi, Centre for Policy Research, 1977, p. 7.

20.70 per thousand.[8] In contrast, the birth rate in Bihar in 1992 was estimated at 32.30 per thousand, 34.90 in MP, and 36.30 in UP. The Indian average in 1992 was 29.20.[9]

The contrast is similar in terms of the death rate. In 1992, Goa had a death rate of 6.70 per thousand and Kerala 6.00. On the other hand, in Bihar it was 10.60 per thousand, 11.60 in UP, and 12.60 in MP. The Indian average was 9.30 per thousand.[10]

Another factor of great importance in demography is the infant mortality rate (IMR). Here again the contrasts are sharp. The IMR in Goa in 1992 is estimated at 14 per thousand live births; in Kerala 17, while in Bihar it was 73 per thousand live births, 98 in UP, and 104 in MP.[11] IMR has an extremely important influence on the fertility behaviour in the states and the differentials fairly well describe the tale of demographic transition taking place in the Indian states.

III.2   Politics of Fertility Control

India's Centre–State relations are also affected by the politics of fertility control. At the heart of fertility control lies the Hindu–Muslim relationship which brought about the partition of India in 1947. Although Hindus constitute the majority in India, many districts which make up the constituencies for the Lok Sabha have a non-Hindu majority. Twelve districts in India have a Muslim majority, fourteen have a Christian majority, nine have a Sikh majority. Hindus are in a minority in 56 districts in India while at the state level Jammu & Kashmir, Punjab, Meghalaya, Nagaland, Mizoram and Arunachal Pradesh all have non-Hindu majorities.

In many of these states religious and political leaders have had no inhibitions about promoting what is called communal interests to gain political advantage. In general, religious leaders do not support the family planning programme. Some of the political leaders have shown a tendency to use the fertility control programme to provoke their followers and strengthen their political positions. In a newspaper interview in 1989, G.M. Shah, former

[8] Centre for Monitoring Indian Economy, *India's Social   Sectors*, Bombay, 1996, pp. 112–14.
   [9] Ibid.
   [10] Ibid., pp. 115–17.
   [11] Ibid., pp. 118–19.

Muslim Chief Minister of Jammu & Kashmir state underscored the importance of fertility politics in India, especially in the highly polarized non-Hindu state of Jammu & Kashmir. In G.M. Shah's words

The Government has hatched a conspiracy to reduce the Kashmir Muslim population. Farooq Abdullah [then Chief Minister of Jammu & Kashmir] is an instrument of this plot. Our state had an 82 per cent Muslim population in 1947. It is now a mere 54 per cent as the 1991 Census reveals. We should reject the government's family planning programme. This is aimed at further reducing the Muslim population in Kashmir. Every Muslim should have four wives and produce at least one dozen children.[12]

G.M. Shah's provocative arguments are spurious and his statistics erroneous, as the Muslim population of Jammu & Kashmir state in 1947 was 57 per cent and had risen to 64 per cent by the time of the 1981 census. Shah is not the only one to point the finger of discrimination. The Hindu minority in Jammu & Kashmir accuses the Muslim majority of systematic discrimination against the Hindus, as do the Buddhists who are a majority in the Ladakh Division of the state.

After the 1991 census figures on the religious distribution of the population were released, the Bharatiya Janata Party (BJP), which broadly espouses the cause of the Hindus, made a major issue of the differential fertility growth between the Hindus and the Muslims. Writing in a major national daily a senior BJP Member of Parliament, Vijay Kumar Malhotra, stated that 'Hindus comprised 84.99 per cent of the population in 1951, and 82 per cent in 1991. On the other hand, the Muslim population which was 9.9 per cent in 1951 stood at 12.12 per cent in 1991'.[13] The BJP has consistently made a political issue of the differential growth of the Muslim in comparison to the Hindu population — a factor that will influence Centre–State relations in several sensitive areas of the country.

Demographic rivalry dominates politics and the political economy in some states in India, and also influences the overall national scene. Wherever the population issue is sensitive, whether

[12] Shah, G.M. 'Every Kashmir Muslim Should Produce One Dozen Children', *Illustrated Weekly of India*, 2 April 1989, p. 33.

[13] Malhotra, Vijay Kumar, *The Times of India*, 15 January 1996.

in Jammu & Kashmir where the Hindus are in a minority, or in other parts of the country where the population balance between the Hindus and Muslims is delicate, the theme is the same. Electoral groups perceive fertility control as reducing the political status and leverage of the majority community. Given the electoral arithmetic in over 100 Parliamentary constituencies, the family planning programme is an exceedingly touchy political issue and has a major bearing on the political economy of the country.

IV. ECONOMY OF THE STATES

IV.1 Structure of Economy

The structure of the economy of the Indian states varies a great deal. While the emphasis of planning since the 1950s was on industrial development, Indian economic performance as a whole has been less successful than planned. For the country as a whole, in 1994 agriculture accounted for 26 per cent of GDP, industry 28 per cent, and services 42 per cent.[14] In contrast, in South Korea in 1994 agriculture accounted for only 7 per cent of GDP, industry as much as 43 per cent, and the service sector 50 per cent.[15] The share of the industrial sector in China in 1994 was as high as 47 per cent of GDP.[16] Employment in the agricultural sector in 1994 was well above 60 per cent, indicating a preponderant dependence on this sector.

Amongst the Indian states, in 1988–9, only four had a share of industry and mining of over 30 per cent of the net state domestic product. The highest was in Goa with 38.32 per cent followed by Maharashtra with 35.62 per cent, Gujarat with 34.41 per cent, and Tamil Nadu with 30.89 per cent.[17] Despite nearly five decades of planned development, the share of the industrial sector in India was below 30 per cent, indicating that in the political economy of India this sector is yet to become as powerful a sector as agriculture. (Annex. Table II)

[14] See, World Bank, *World Development Report, 1996* (New York: Oxford University Press), 1996, p. 210.

[15] Ibid., p. 211.

[16] Ibid., p. 210.

[17] Centre for Monitoring Indian Economy, *Basic Statistics Relating to States of India*, Bombay, 1994, Table 10.10.

The bigger states like UP and Bihar lagged far behind in this respect. In 1988–9, the share of industry and mining as a percentage of net state domestic product was 20.38 in UP and 23.82 per cent in Bihar. Further down the line were states like AP with 17.73 per cent, Haryana with 19.48 per cent, and Rajasthan with 17.96 per cent. Even in Kerala, which boasts high social development, the percentage was only 20.77, reflecting the political economy of Kerala.[18]

Agriculture still dominates in many of the states. The highest share of agriculture as a percentage of net state domestic product was in Orissa with 50.74 per cent in 1988–9, Rajasthan with 50.26 per cent, Bihar 48.06 per cent, Punjab with 47.09 per cent.[19]

In most of the states, the share of agriculture was over 30 per cent which is the national average. The exceptions were Maharashtra 23.03 per cent, Tamil Nadu 23.49 per cent, and Goa with 17.62 per cent.[20]

The dominance of agriculture in the economy, and also in electoral terms, is a matter which has a profound impact on Centre–State relations, especially in the field of political economy, and merits careful examination. With over 70 per cent of the population residing in the rural areas and 64 per cent still dependent on agriculture, it is no wonder that in the political economy of India, this sector has a major influence on Centre–State relations.

The service sector has grown rapidly in India in recent years. In states such as Maharashtra, Tamil Nadu, Kerala, AP, Goa, Nagaland, and HP, the share of the service sector in NSDP in 1988–9 was above 40 per cent. The rapid growth of this sector in recent years increasingly reflects the changing nature of the political economy of the states,[21] particularly in urban areas, but is also reflective of the changes taking place in the countryside.

Not surprisingly, however, in states like Bihar, the share of the service sector in 1988–9 was only 28.12 per cent, as also in MP where it was slightly higher at 36.63 per cent.[22]

The distinct trend towards industrialization and the growth of the service sector in many parts of the country is reflective of the

[18] Ibid.
[19] Ibid.
[20] Ibid.
[21] Ibid.
[22] Ibid.

global trends, as well as the shifts taking place in the Indian economy. The service sector is dominated by professional classes which suggests a distinct shift in the power equations in the Indian polity. The effects of these shifts are bound to influence the political economy of the states, and in turn the Centre–State relations in the twenty-first century as the shift begins to influence the structural dimensions of both the economy and the polity. Employment in the service sector in India in 1990 was estimated at only 20 per cent, whereas it was 66 per cent in the UK and 68 per cent in Sweden.[23]

IV.2 Poverty Levels

The political economy of Centre–state relations is also influenced by the poverty levels in the states. The percentage of people living below the poverty line varies a great deal in India. People living below the poverty line in 1987–8 according, to one estimate, were as low as 7.2 per cent in Punjab and as high as 44.7 per cent in Orissa.[24] The All India average was 29.9 per cent in 1987–8. Not surprisingly, in the agriculturally dominated states like Bihar or MP or UP, the incidence of poverty was considerably higher. Thus the estimated poverty level in Bihar in 1987–8 was 40.8 per cent, in MP 36.7 per cent, in Orissa 44.7 per cent, and even in Tamil Nadu it was 32.8 per cent.

The political discourse in all these states is greatly influenced by the poverty factor. It is not therefore surprising that in these states where economic development is low and poverty levels high, the political economy is significantly influenced by the poverty issue. In contrast to many developed countries, the voter from the poorer sections in India does not show apathy in electoral politics but plays an active role.

Income disparities between the states is also a factor that has a bearing on Centre–State relations, and these are considerable. At one end of the spectrum, states such as Punjab, Goa, Maharashtra and Haryana have a much higher per capita income. In 1991–2, Punjab with an income of Rs 9643 per capita was the highest in

[23] World Bank, *World Development Report, 1996*, New York pp. 194–5.
[24] Centre for Monitoring Indian Economy, *Basic Statistics Relating to States of India*, Bombay, 1994, Table 10.10.

the country. Haryana too had a higher per capita income at Rs 8690, Goa at Rs 8096, and Maharashtra at 8180.[25]

At the other end of the spectrum, the per capita income in Bihar was Rs 2904 in 1992–3, Rs 4012 in UP, and Rs 4068 in Orissa. The significant factor to be noted is that in states like Bihar the increase in the per capita income over the years has been small or marginal, whereas in states like Punjab or Goa the increase is much larger, reflecting higher growth rate and development.

In consequence, regional imbalances in India have tended to grow creating new problems for managing the political economy of Centre–State relations. As is to be expected, the backward states like UP, Bihar, MP, Rajasthan, and Orissa, which constitute well over 44 per cent of the population and an equally large number of seats in Parliament, demand a greater share of the plan funds. This inevitably is at the cost of the more forward and developed states who feel that the Gadgil–Mukherji Formula the Planning Commission evolved to give additional plan support to the economically backward states places a premium on backwardness. Some of these advanced states argue that instead of helping the country grow faster, the backward states are increasingly becoming a millstone around the neck of the Indian nation.

Maharashtra, Gujarat, Goa, and other faster developing states have always been unhappy at the fact that their performance is not being appreciated and that the Centre is putting a premium on backwardness and is placing the growth rate of the country in fetters. It is indeed a sensitive issue for the management of the political economy of Centre–State relations, and puts the Central Government under tremendous political pressure. So far the more advanced and progressive states have muted their protests, but this can hardly be taken for granted and it is not unlikely that the issue of income disparities leading to discrimination between states in terms of distribution of Central funds will emerge as a major political issue.

IV.3 Size of the Middle Class

Since the 1980s, the emerging middle class in India has begun to make its presence felt. According to World Bank estimates, the

[25] Ibid., Table 10.2.

top 20 per cent of the Indian population accounted for 42.6 per cent of the GDP in 1992.[26] With a GDP of approximately Rs 10 lakh crores in 1995–6, the per capita income of this group amounts to about Rs 25000 which in PPP terms would well be around US $ 5000.

The emerging importance of a growing Indian middle class should not be underestimated. The new middle class in India is essentially an urban phenomenon. But with the growth of the rural economy, an increasing number of professional and other services are also visible in rural India. With the spread of the service sector in rural areas, whether in health services or education or other sectors such as banking and so forth, important changes in this respect have been brought about in the Indian countryside. Over the next few years, this process will accelerate making the impact of the middle class felt even in the rural areas.

The real impact of the urban middle class is already being felt in India. It is estimated that in 1997 the urban population in India is well over 250 m. Even assuming 60 per cent of this population as the urban middle class, the numbers are in excess of 150 m. By the year 2000, the size of the urban population in India is likely to exceed 350 m. and by the year 2025, India could well have an urban population of 700 m.

The growing economic clout of this middle class will be but-tressed by their political clout as the share of the urban electorate as a percentage of the total will rise over the next few years. Under these circumstances, the Indian middle class, which already has a major influence on India's political economy, will play an even more influential role in the political economy of India and in India's Centre–State relations. This is already visible in the Union Territory of Delhi where, according to the 1991 census 89.9 per cent of the 8.4 m. population lives in urban areas.[27] The situation in Maharashtra, though not as pronounced as in Delhi, is also moving in a similar direction.

This directional change will be one of the most significant influences on India's political economy of Centre–State relations because of the enormous impact of the Indian middle class not

[26] World Bank, *World Development Report, 1996*, New York p. 196.

[27] Centre for Monitoring Indian Economy, *Basic Statistics Relating to States of India*, Bombay, 1994 (Table 1.9).

only on the economy but also on key sectors such as banking, communication, and the electronic and print media.

V. CONCLUSION

The political economy of Centre–State relations in India reflects in a significant way the working of the Indian democracy, the demographic changes that have occurred and are still emerging, and the character of the economies of the Indian states. It lies at the heart of the large, complex, and diverse country that is India. It is a rapidly changing scenario with new paradigms replacing the old ones. India is on the path of large-scale change. In the short run up to about fifteen years, Indian political economy will perhaps be greatly influenced by the increasingly vocal and politically powerful backward and scheduled castes. In the long run, say by the year 2015, the Indian middle class, growing at the rate it is, will be the most formidable influence on Indian political economy for the rest of the twenty-first century making India a major political and economic global power.

TABLE 1
POPULATION STATEWISE (1991)

(000's)

States/Union Territories	
INDIA	846,303
States	
Andhra Pradesh	66508
Arunachal Pradesh	865
Assam	2414
Bihar	86374
Goa	1170
Gujarat	41310
Haryana	16464
Himachal Pradesh	5171
Jammu & Kashmir*	7719
Karnataka	44977
Kerala	29099
Madhya Pradesh	66181
Maharashtra	78937
Manipur	1837
Meghalaya	1775
Mizoram	690
Nagaland	1210
Orissa	31660
Punjab	20282
Rajasthan	44006
Sikkim	406
Tamil Nadu	55859
Tripura	2757
Uttar Pradesh	139112
West Bengal	68078
Union Territories	
Andaman & Nicobar Islands	281
Chandigarh	642
Dadra & Nagar Haveli	138
Daman & Diu	102
Delhi	9421
Lakshadweep	52
Pondicherry	808

*   The population figures for Jammu & Kashmir are as projected by
    the Standing Committee of Experts on Population Projections.
SOURCE: 1991 Census Handbook, Registrar General and Census
    Commission, Government of India.

TABLE II
PERCENTAGE SECTORAL SHARE IN STATE INCOME (1988–89)

States	Agriculture and allied activities	Industry and mining	Services
Andhra Pradesh	40.7	17.7	41.5
Assam	42.4	22.4	35.2
Bihar	48.1	23.8	28.1
Gujarat	28.9	34.3	36.8
Haryana	44.9	19.5	35.6
Karnataka	36.3	27.6	36.2
Kerala	37.1	20.8	42.2
Madhya Pradesh	45.6	26.4	28.0
Maharashtra	23.0	35.6	41.3
Orissa	50.7	20.2	29.1
Punjab	47.1	20.3	32.7
Rajasthan	50.3	18.0	31.8
Tamil Nadu	23.5	30.9	45.6
Uttar Pradesh	43.0	20.4	36.6
West Bengal	35.5	27.8	36.7
Arunachal Pradesh	50.0	17.3	32.7
Goa	17.6	38.3	44.1
Himachal Pradesh	36.4	22.0	41.6
Jammu & Kashmir	–	–	–
Manipur	48.1	12.4	39.5
Meghalaya	–	–	–
Mizoram	–	–	–
Nagaland	25.2	24.7	50.1
Sikkim	–	–	–
Tripura	–	–	–
Delhi	–	–	–
Pondicherry	22.3	51.0	26.7
All India	34.4	26.1	39.5

– Data not available

SOURCE: Centre for Monitoring Indian Economy; Basic Statistics Relating to States of India, September, 1984, Economic Intelligence Service, Mumbai.

Name Index

Subject Index